D1552186

Advanced Fly Fishing for Great Lakes Steelhead

Advanced Fly Fishing for Great Lakes Steelhead

Rick Kustich

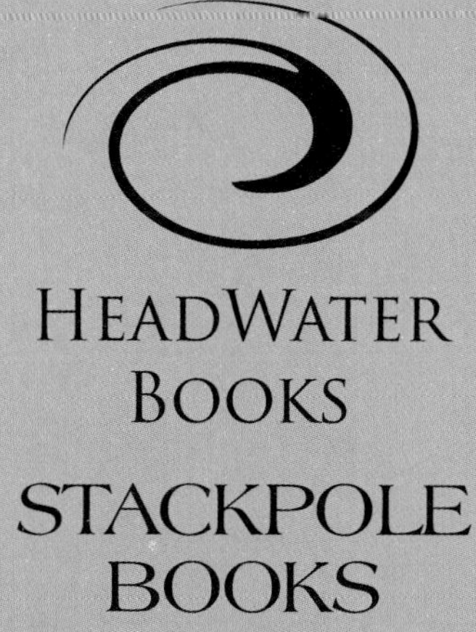

HEADWATER BOOKS
STACKPOLE BOOKS

Published by
STACKPOLE BOOKS
5067 Ritter Road
Mechanicsburg, PA 17055
www.stackpolebooks.com

Printed in China

First edition

10 9 8 7 6 5 4 3 2 1

Library of Congress Cataloging-in-Publication Data

Kustich, Rick.
Advanced fly fishing for Great Lakes steelhead / Rick Kustich. — First edition.
pages cm
Includes index.
ISBN 978-0-8117-0792-3 (hardcover)
1. Steelhead fishing—Lake States. 2. Fly fishing—Lake States. I. Title.
SH687.7.K875 2013
799.1757—dc23

2012026428

To Sarah, always follow your passion . . .

CONTENTS

ACKNOWLEDGMENTS

A book can never be completed by simply working alone. A supporting cast is essential for a comprehensive finished product. Not only have the following individuals made this book possible, but through my interactions we have forged or furthered many important relationships.

I am grateful to my true love and soul mate Karen Ford who has provided her support and caring in many ways during numerous days on the water and hours in front of the computer. My brother Jerry has been a constant source of direction since I began to fish. We have experienced many of the waters of the Great Lakes together, and some of our combined research for other writing projects has provided the source for integral text included in this book. Nick Pionessa and I have fished together for years. His expertise in casting, presentation, and fly design has provided the basis for many thoughtful discussions that have helped in forming the theories and conclusions included in the book. His masterful photography appears throughout, including the creatively prepared fly plates.

Larry Halyk has kept me in the know on Ontario and Great Lakes steelhead management for almost twenty years now both as a professional biologist and avid angler. Biologist Jon George has also provided thoughts relative to his important work with Great Lakes steelhead. Special thanks to fly-fishing industry professional Jerry Darkes, who is always there to help anytime it's needed and to Jim Wilson for his friendship and guidance.

I am very thankful for the efforts of some of the region's top professionals, who provided flies, photography, or knowledge. Kevin Feenstra and Mike Verhoef provided both flies and

Using a boat to cover some hidden steelhead holding water. KEVIN FEENSTRA PHOTO

photography specific to their home regions. Bob Blumreich, Vern Burm, Charlie Dickson, Jeff Liskay, John Nagy, Geoff Schaake, Greg Senyo, Vince Tobia, and Rick Whorwood made special fly pattern contributions along with a handful of other anglers and tiers. John Fehnel, Jon Ray, Matt Sipple, and Scott Earl Smith contributed photography of their home rivers. Also, special thanks to Vince Tobia for the use of his steelhead camp over the years.

Publisher Jay Nichols has been a true pleasure to work with on this project. His comments and suggestions during the process came from an angler's perspective, which has enriched its content. I was able write the book I had in mind, deviating very little from my original outline.

My angling journey has been touched by many others through the years. More than a few have influenced my development as an angler by providing tips or information on tackle and destinations. I am grateful for all the acquaintances and friendships that ensued. Not only has this contributed importantly to my development and in many ways to this work, but has made the journey a rich one.

INTRODUCTION

In historic and geological terms, the Great Lakes are infants. Melting glaciers that began to recede only 12,000 years ago carved the earth's surface, creating a series of deep depressions. Their formation continued slowly and was completed roughly just 2,500 years ago. The result was a chain of freshwater oceans that stretch from western Minnesota to eastern New York State.

In the years after their formation, the Great Lakes successfully evolved into fertile bodies producing and supporting a diverse mixture of life. Their rich bounty and use as a mode of transportation drew European settlers to their banks. Population centers developed and now define many of the lakes' shorelines.

But the proximity to such a large number of inhabitants wasn't good for the Great Lakes from an ecological perspective. As industry and populations exploded along their banks, the lakes became dumping ponds for unmitigated waste disposal. By the 1960s such shortsighted abuse had taken a deadly toll. The contamination negatively impacted the health of fish, birds, and humans. One of the largest threats was caused by excessive amounts of phosphorus entering the lakes. The resulting overabundance of algae and reduction of oxygen reduced the lakes' carrying capacity and threatened to topple the entire ecosystem. The evidence was quite visible as fish kills often lined the lakes' shorelines.

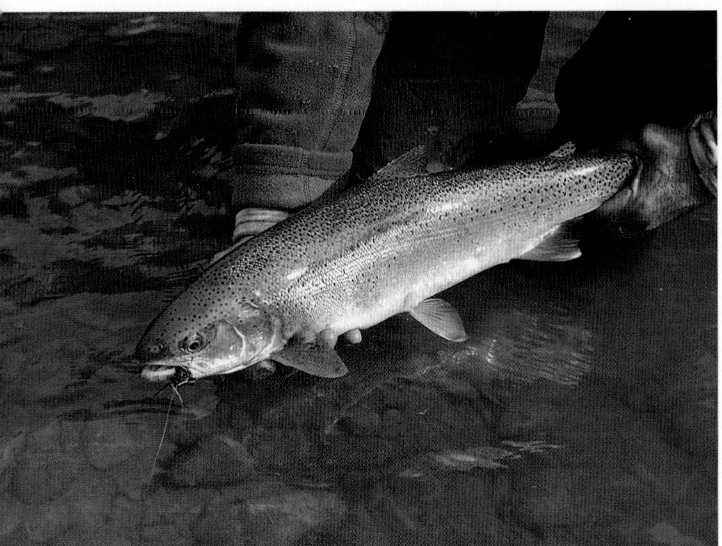

The Great Lakes Water Quality Agreement was instrumental in improving the health of the lakes.

Significant measures were needed to save the lakes and thankfully were realized in the form of the binational Great Lakes Water Quality Agreement in 1972, which was amended in 1978 and nine years later in 1987. The lakes showed incredible resiliency and by the mid-1980s were on their way to a recovery. While continued threats to the future of this expansive freshwater resource lurk around every corner, the rebirth has resulted in healthy fish populations throughout the entire chain.

The steelhead's connection to the Great Lakes region came in two waves. Native to the Pacific coast, steelhead were brought to the Great Lakes region in the 1870s as the United States Fish Commission began to redistribute native species through the use of railroad cars. It is believed that fish from a tributary of the McCloud River in California were the first to arrive in the New York State hatchery at Caledonia, which holds the distinction of being the birthplace of the Great Lakes steelhead fishery. By the end of the 1800s, steelhead had been planted in all five lakes, and small pockets of self-propagating populations had developed. Written historical accounts of Great Lakes steelheading through the early to mid 1900s are sketchy, but anecdotal evidence indicates fairly strong returns of wild populations on a number of rivers.

The next wave of steelhead recruitment to the Great Lakes region hit 100 years later. The problems that had become so painfully apparent in the 1960s had left the balance of life in the lakes wildly askew. An overabundance of baitfish combined with an overall lack of predators threatened to crash the entire system. Help was enlisted from the Pacific coast in the form of chinook and coho salmon and steelhead, which were brought in in an effort to gain a sense of equilibrium. The plantings of steelhead throughout the 1970s established runs in rivers that had little or no reproduction and bolstered the possibilities of greater natural reproduction where proper water quality existed. While the chinook and coho created an incredible fishery on the lakes and chaos on the tributaries, the steelhead eventually emerged as the true king of the rivers of the Great Lakes.

Great Lakes steelhead fishing has slowly gained a reputation as one of the top fisheries in North America. Skeptics of the fishery point out that Great Lakes fish may not be "true"

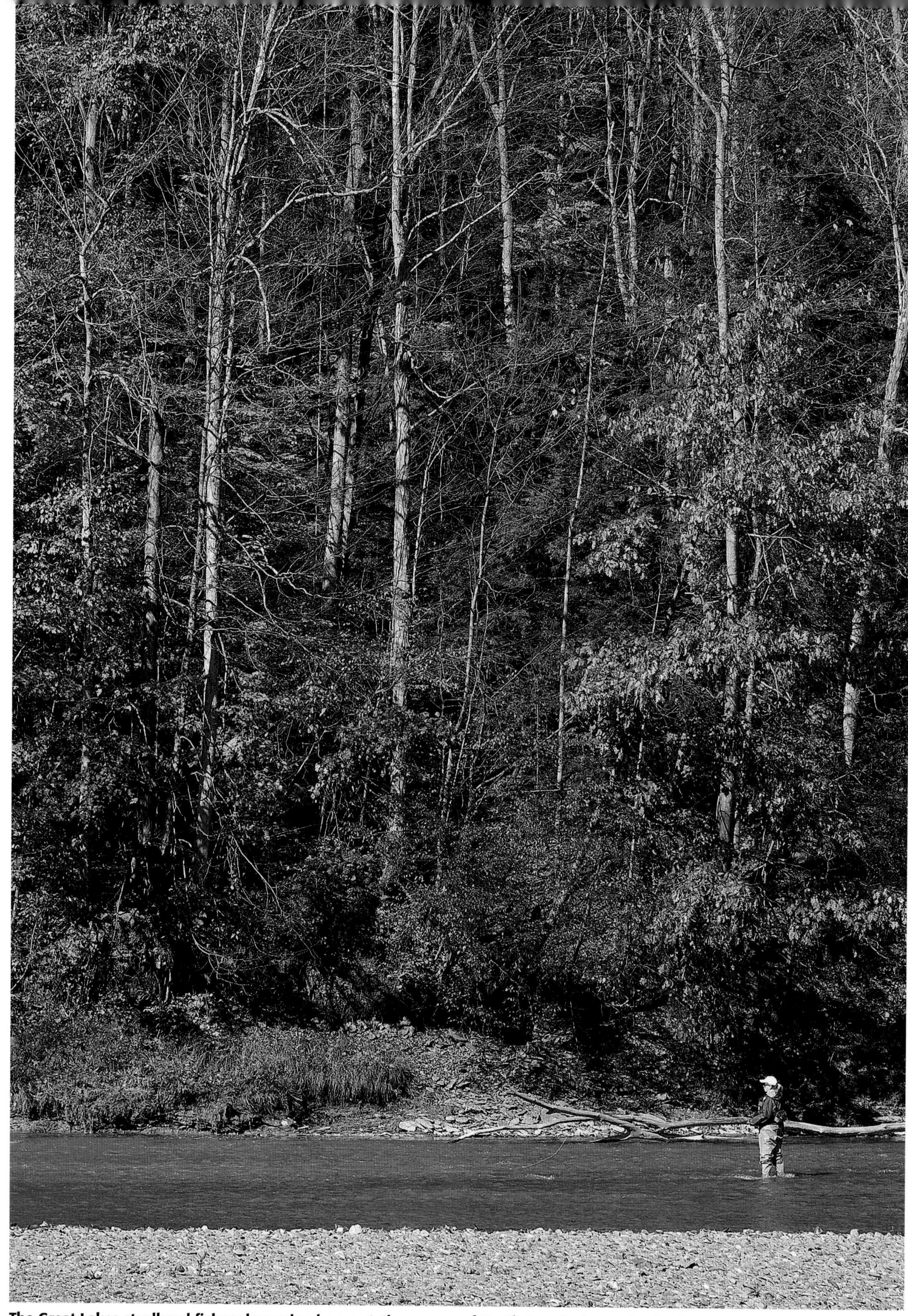

The Great Lakes steelhead fishery has gained a reputation as one of North America's top destinations.

steelhead because they are not anadromous like their native counterparts. The debate has been contested in magazines and web sites for years. Ontario biologist Jon George has a long history studying steelhead on the Pacific coast and in the Great Lakes. His research has allowed him to conclude unequivocally that there is no anatomical difference between Pacific coast and Great Lakes steelhead.

For me it is simple. I fish for steelhead on the Pacific coast as well, and the same equipment, flies, and techniques work in the Great Lakes as well as out west, clearly demonstrating the similarity in behavioral characteristics.

The tremendous steelhead fishery that we know today did not occur by accident; however, to some degree, it started that way. It has taken years for the Great Lakes to shake the reputation of overcrowded rivers and questionable Pacific salmon angling practices—issues that still remain on a few rivers. But most fisheries are now managed to present the best legitimate opportunity for the stream and river angler. Much of this change has occurred because professional managers, fishing clubs, and conservation groups have swayed public opinion. Over the last two decades, dedicated fisheries managers and volunteers have fought to lower kill limits, increase natural reproduction, and educate anglers about catch-and-release. Some argue that there is too much reliance on hatcheries, especially on rivers that have greater potential for natural reproduction. But when managed judiciously, planted fish create or enhance watersheds with insufficient water quality for producing wild fish.

As a kid growing up on the banks of the Niagara River, I dreamed of living in a famous fishing destination. Now entering my fourth decade of fishing the Great Lakes, I feel quite fortunate that such a world-class fishery has been developed at my doorstep. When I began fly fishing the region's streams and rivers in the late '70s, I found very little written on the subject. This prompted my first book, *Fly Fishing the Great Lakes Tributaries*, a primer for fly anglers looking to experience the fishery. By the mid '90s steelhead had moved into the top spot in the minds of most Great Lakes anglers. This was true for me as well, and my fishing effort was focused almost entirely on steelhead. My lifelong fishing partner and brother Jerry and I released *Fly Fishing for Great Lakes Steelhead* in 1999, which focused on the history, fish, techniques, and rivers, and earned praise as a fresh look at the fishery, helping to shape its future.

Advanced Fly Fishing for Great Lakes Steelhead in a sense represents the completion of a trilogy. The last 10 to 15 years have seen significant changes in attitudes, improvements in the fisheries, and technological advancements in equipment that require yet another treatise on the subject. My experiences during that time have opened my eyes to new and exciting approaches to Great Lakes steelhead fishing, approaches that are cataloged here in these pages.

Progressive management in recent years has led to a high-quality fishery.

Steelhead fishing is in many ways an expression—how one approaches the sport and the fishery can speak volumes. My own philosophy has evolved over years spent in pursuit of steelhead. Quantity of the catch has given way to the quality of the experience. In fact, learning to cast and fish a fly properly has become a reward in itself—catching steelhead has become the byproduct of enjoying the mere act of fishing. I strive toward techniques that put me in constant contact with the water and that find a balance and harmony with the flow of the river.

The measure for me has become the experience. The quality is enhanced by beautiful rivers, plenty of room to fish, challenging techniques, and of course, fresh silver steelhead. The experiences found in the Great Lakes region are wide and varied. But with the proper approach, the experience can be on par with that found in the best fisheries in world.

This book isn't intended to be the last word on Great Lakes steelheading but rather an update on how far the fishery has progressed and a look into the future. The objectives of this work are fairly simple—to present many thoughts and observations from over 30 years of experience, to provide insight aimed at increasing the quality of the fishing experience, and to discuss techniques and strategies for the Great Lakes fishery that have not been discussed in depth prior to this book.

My hope is that *Advanced Fly Fishing for Great Lakes Steelhead* will allow anglers to see the fishery in a different light while providing information to increase the angling experience.

CHAPTER 1

Equipment and Rigging

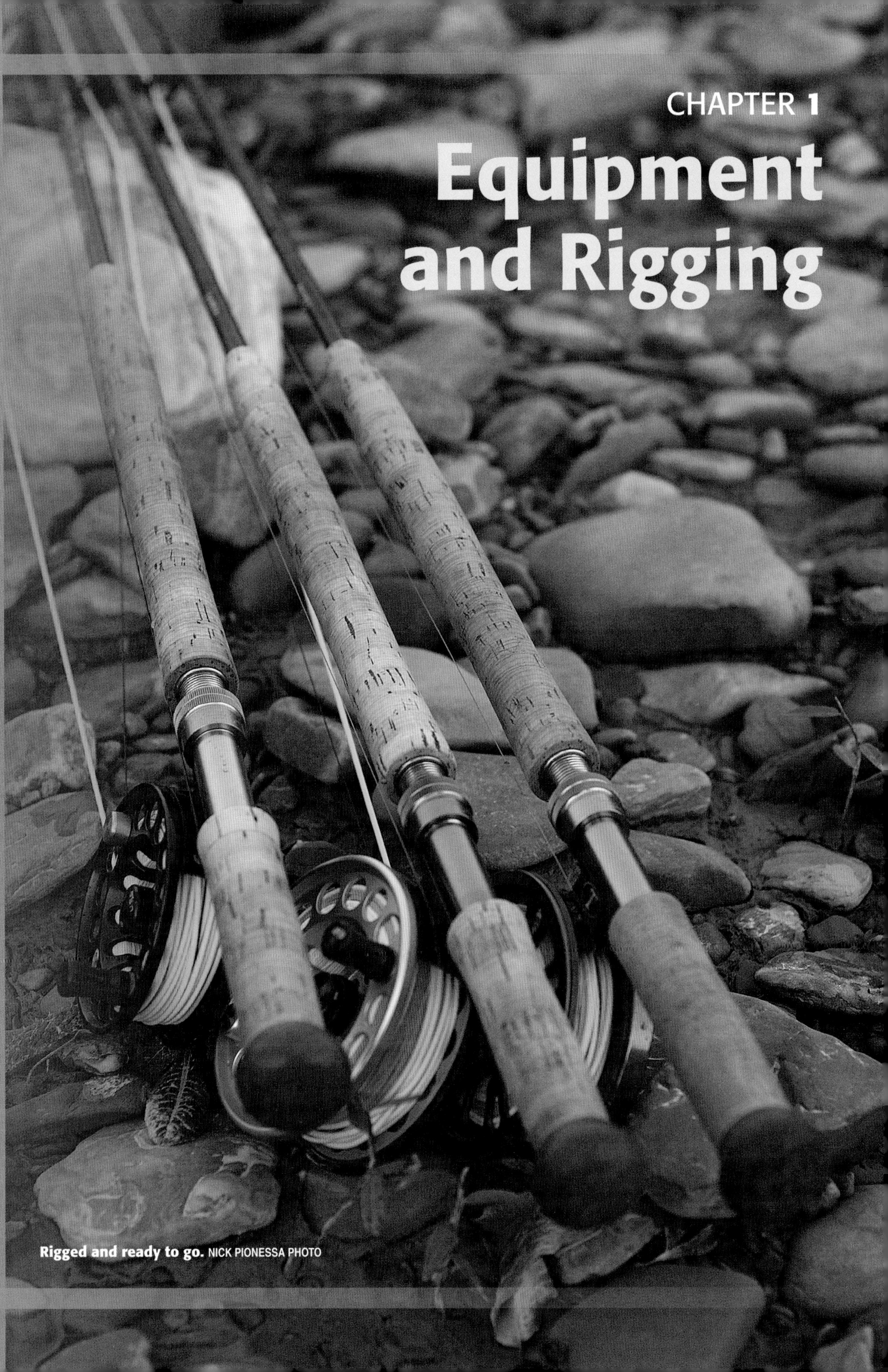

Rigged and ready to go. NICK PIONESSA PHOTO

A discussion of the equipment and rigging used for steelhead fly fishing is a logical starting point for *Advanced Fly Fishing for Great Lakes Steelhead*. Properly rigged equipment is essential for success and enjoyment of the overall experience. Quality equipment doesn't have to be expensive and can be found at a range of prices. The most important aspect of equipment and rigging is that it matches up with the size and volume of the water and the techniques being used.

Technological advancements can be seen in all fly-fishing equipment. Such advancement has influenced the way many anglers approach their favorite waters. The most significant change is that equipment has become lighter. Rods, reels, clothing, and even waders with reduced weight are more versatile to fish with and less fatiguing. Options for rigging have also changed dramatically in just the last few years, resulting in a nearly infinite combination of lines and sinking-tips to meet the challenges of any river.

Rods

When it comes to fishing equipment, technology has had the greatest impact on rods. In just the last 10 to 15 years, rods for steelhead fishing have become lighter and stronger. This has allowed rod designers to produce longer rods that can be fished with one hand and streamlined two-handed rods that are a joy to use on daylong outings. Engineering advancements allow rod designers to more fully understand flex points and recovery rates in order to produce rods that are more powerful and easier to cast. The equipment available today allows anglers of varying abilities to cover the region's largest waters as well as its tightest, brushiest rivers. I only wish that some of these rods were available 35 years ago.

Single-Handed Rods

Many streams and small rivers in the Great Lakes region can be covered comfortably with a single-handed rod. Length, weight, and balance are all keys to selecting the proper rod for steelhead fishing. Longer rods pick up line more efficiently and have greater line control. Longer single-handed rods also better facilitate one-handed Spey casting techniques, which can be a significant benefit on tighter rivers with little backcasting room. I believe that 10 feet is the minimum length for an effective Great Lakes steelhead rod.

Longer single-handed rods are a great advantage when dead-drifting a fly. A key element in attaining a natural drift and reducing the negative impact of drag is to limit the amount of fly line resting on the water's surface. A longer rod reaches farther, resulting in less line on the surface. In instances when the fly is fished far enough away from the casting position that some fly line rests on the surface, the reach of a longer rod will

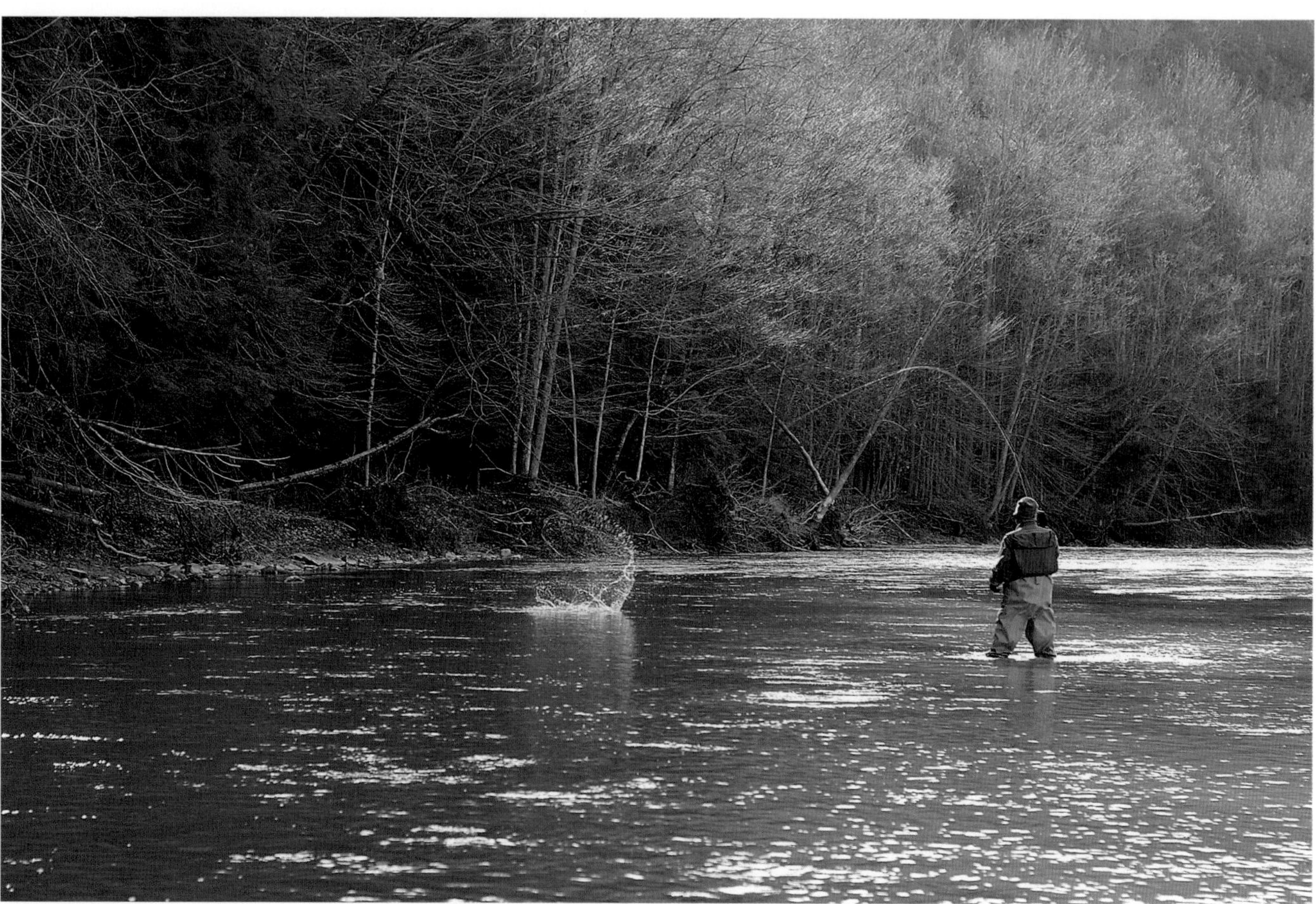

Vince Tobia battles a big steelhead in the tail of a pool. NICK PIONESSA PHOTO

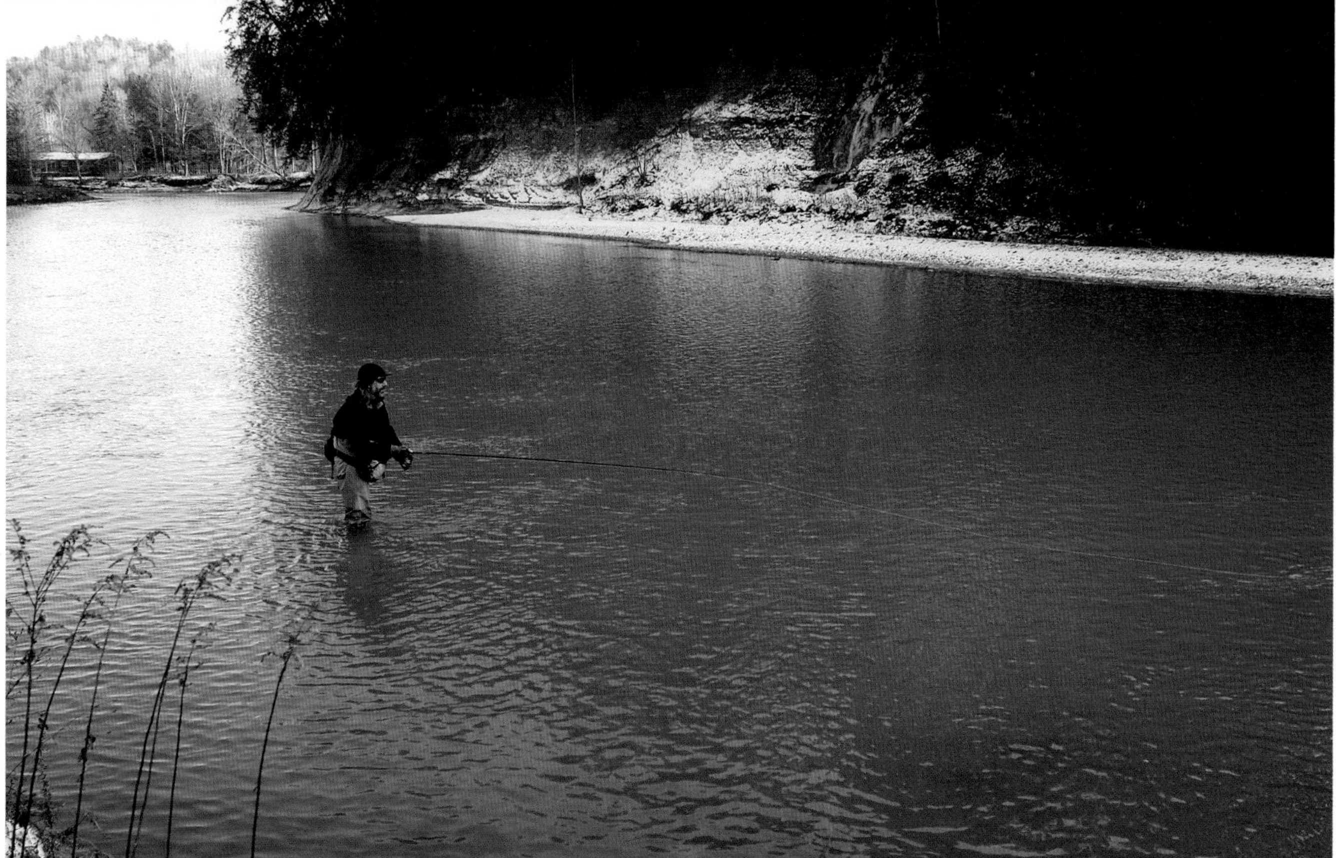

Nick Pionessa uses a switch rod to cover a modest-size pool.

provide easier mending and more acute line control. Today some 10½- or 11-foot rods are designed specifically for one-handed use. The extra 6 to 12 inches exponentially increases the rod's leverage and overall effectiveness.

The advantage of a longer rod's leverage also helps in fighting a steelhead. Longer rods allow an angler to exert more pressure during the fight. This is especially important for adding side pressure when battling a stubborn fish. The only difficulty about landing a steelhead with a longer rod is that the fish will be farther away, reducing the ability to get ahold of its tail or to net it to end the fight. But this is a small disadvantage compared to all the positive aspects of a longer rod.

Single-handed rods built for 7-weight lines are best for Great Lakes steelheading. Six-weight rods can be functional on smaller waters and 8-weights have their place on the region's larger rivers with heavy currents. Personally I feel that a 6-weight can be too light when fighting a sizable steelhead, and an 8-weight can be a bit cumbersome to cast all day.

Faster-action single-handed rods have their advantages in windy conditions, when using a heavy tip or casting weighted flies. A faster-action rod also has an advantage in line pickup and mending. But many anglers prefer a more moderate action where the rod bends deeper into the blank. Along with delivering a smooth line with a greater tolerance for inefficiencies in the casting stroke, a medium action generally loads better in short casting situations. Also, a rod that bends more throughout its length will typically do a better job protecting against break-offs during a battle with a steelhead since the breaking strength of the tippet is cushioned over a longer and softer surface area.

Lightness and balance determine how enjoyable a rod is to fish. One that is heavy in the tip will require extra energy or force while fishing. You'll feel discomfort from a tip-heavy rod in your wrist and forearm. A reel with the proper weight to balance the setup will reduce or eliminate arm fatigue. You can test a rig for balance by resting the midpoint of the handle on your index finger while the line is extended through the guides. A balanced rig will remain level while resting on your index finger.

Switch Rods

A switch or two-hand assist rod is designed to be cast with one or two hands. It is a style of rod that has rapidly gained popularity and has wide application for the Great Lakes steelhead fishery. Most switch rods are 10½ to 11½ feet in length and are constructed with an extended butt for two-handed casting. A good switch rod is light enough to be cast and fished with one hand but also powerful enough to cast 80 feet or longer with two-handed Spey techniques.

Versatility is the main advantage of the switch rod. The added length results in greater line control and pickup, which makes a switch rod a highly effective tool for presenting a dead-drifted fly. But it can be equally effective with change-in-direction Spey casts used in conjunction with the wet-fly swing technique. With a switch rod, you can change from single-handed to two-handed techniques on the water by making simple modifications to the rigging. This makes the switch rod a good tool for an angler who is transitioning from a single-handed rod to a two-hander and Spey techniques.

Switch rods generally range from 5-weights up to 8. I prefer a 7- or an 8-weight for two-handed casting techniques, although the lightness of a 6-weight has its advantages when using it as a single-handed rod for an extended period. A reel that balances the rig is even more important with a switch rod than with a one-hander since the extra length of the switch will make fishing with it more fatiguing if it is tip heavy.

Switch rods match up well with smaller rivers and more intimate water. From a two-handed casting perspective, my preference is to use a switch rod on water where 60- to 70-foot casts can cover most or all of the river's width. I have found the switch rod to be ideal for the wet-fly swing on smaller rivers since it can be rigged to handle short casts as well as long ones. On smaller streams and rivers, a full two-handed rod may be too cumbersome.

Switch rods are generally rigged with a shorter head line for maximum efficiency and versatility. A shorter head creates a smaller D loop when Spey casting and allows for use in tighter areas such as a brushy shoreline behind the casting position.

A disadvantage of the switch rod is that some may be a little too unwieldy to cast with a single hand all day. Also, the casting distance with two-handed Spey techniques will generally not be as great as with a full two-hander, and the casting technique will require more precision with a switch rod.

The switch or two-hand assist rod has totally changed my perspective on smaller rivers. Since taking to Spey fishing almost exclusively for Great Lakes steelhead, I had abandoned some of the smaller rivers that I had so enjoyed with a single-handed rod. Now I have rediscovered some of this water using the switch and Spey casting techniques. A good number of the streams and rivers in the Great Lakes fall into the small to medium-size category and are perfect candidates for switch rods.

Two-Handed Rods

If I were to point to one item that has increased my enjoyment, challenge, and overall experience with respect to the Great Lakes steelhead fishery, it is the two-handed rod. I started using a two-hander about 17 years ago, but only in the last 12 have I changed my approach to Great Lakes steelheading because of the two-handed rod.

Popularity of the two-hander has surged in the region, which is something that my brother and I predicted in *Fly Fishing for Great Lakes Steelhead.* Each year hundreds of participants attend Spey gatherings held on some of the best rivers in the region, and I witness more two-handers on the water every season.

On my first trip to British Columbia in the mid '90s, most steelhead anglers that I saw fished with single-handed rods. In recent years that trend has changed entirely, and almost all now wield two-handers. Because of the smaller average size of

Nick Pionessa forms a D loop for another cast. Switch rods are perfect for fishing smaller streams and rivers.

Two-handed rods from 12 to 14 feet work well on medium-size to larger rivers. NICK PIONESSA PHOTO

Great Lakes rivers, I wouldn't expect two-handers and Spey fishing to reach that same level of popularity, but one day this past season on an Ontario river I ran into six other anglers, all of whom were casting two-handers.

There are two main reasons for my love of fishing with a two-handed rod. First is the tactical advantage. Most of the two-handers that I use in the Great Lakes region are 12 to 14 feet in length—they act as long levers, reducing strain on the body and increasing the ability to control line. The second reason is simply the sheer joy of casting and fishing a two-handed rod. I use a variety of Spey casts to efficiently complete the change of direction required for fishing the wet-fly swing. The cast is an art form in itself, balancing the power of the rod with the timing and delicacy of proper hand movement.

The true captivation of two-handed rods and Spey fishing for me doesn't lie in just the casting but also in the fishing. When Spey fishing, I feel an intimate link to the water. Since the line and leader touching the water's surface assist in loading the rod for the forward stroke, the Spey caster is almost always in connection with the river. With depth and current flow impacting every cast, one develops a keen awareness of the water. But ultimately the Spey approach is about rhythm and systematically covering the water in a near-effortless manner.

Rod technology has created lighter, powerful rods in the 12- to 14-foot range good for Great Lakes fishing. Spey casting itself has gone through a bit of a renaissance with a movement toward lines with shorter heads that carry and shoot running line through the guides as opposed to the more traditional longer belly lines. The shorter heads make it easier to use lighter two-handers under 13 feet. The shorter heads also create a more versatile tool capable of easily handling heavy sinking-tips and weighted flies.

A two-handed rod is designed with a more distinct lower grip and a longer upper grip when compared with a switch rod and is made for full-time use with two-handed casting. For modern Spey casting, the bottom hand controls the cast more than the upper. Most casters place the dominant hand on the top grip, but learning to cast with either hand up is a useful skill for Spey fishing in windy conditions and in tight areas. A two-handed rod may appear cumbersome at first, but with practice it becomes a graceful and very effective tool.

A beautiful sight—a big bend in the rod caused by a heavy steelhead. NICK PIONESSA PHOTO

The length of the two-hander provides the ultimate line control. Mending is replaced by simple manipulation where the movement of the rod tip easily changes the position of the line, resulting in full control over the speed of the fly. Acute presentation can be attained in a wide variety of fishing conditions. Two-handed rods facilitate long, efficient casts that allow for wider coverage of a pool and keep the fly in the water longer. When covering a pool with the wet-fly swing, an angler using a two-handed rod simply has an advantage in presentation and being able to cover more water with less effort.

You can cast efficiently with two-handed rods and effectively cover medium-size to larger rivers. NICK PIONESSA PHOTO

Two-handed rods match up best with the region's medium-size to larger rivers, generally those with a width of approximately 70 feet or greater. A good number of rivers throughout the Great Lakes meet these criteria, and the better ones are developing an increasing following of Spey fishers. Rivers with lower fishing pressure accommodate two-handers best because they provide plenty of room to work a pool. On more crowded rivers, finding Spey fishing water may take more thought and strategy. But another advantage of a two-hander, especially on rivers with heavy fishing pressure, is that you can cover water that other anglers simply can't reach.

A balanced rig is important for each type of fly rod, and this is especially true of a two-hander. The balance point is where your rod hand is positioned while fishing, which is usually halfway to two-thirds up on the upper handle. Test the balance by resting the rod and reel on your index finger with the line running through the guides as if fishing. It is more common for a rod to be tip heavy than butt heavy. It may take a substantial reel to balance some two-handed rods, especially longer models. In some cases additional weight may be added to the butt of the rod. Adjustable reel seats that allow for flexibility in positioning the reel may be the solution in the future. There is a movement in Spey fishing toward shorter, lighter rods, which has made the process of balancing much easier. A tip-heavy rod can be extremely fatiguing to the wrist and forearm and negatively impact the fishing experience.

Reels

The reel is the key to a balanced fishing rig, and the first consideration when selecting a reel is its weight. While advancements in technology allow for the production of lighter reels, one that is too light, especially for a switch or two-handed rod, will be a detriment. Consider the backing, fly line, and line running through the guides too when testing for balance.

The next consideration is capacity. The spool must be able to handle the entire fly line. The thicker diameter of a Spey line can fill a spool quickly. With the variety of Spey line designs, it is difficult for a manufacturer to provide accurate details of line capacity; think carefully about the line capacity for your rig. Most reel manufacturers produce a Spey model that will accommodate a range of lines. You should be able to exchange spools easily to quickly change fly lines for various conditions or techniques.

The most important mechanical aspect of the reel is the drag system. Drag systems have advanced a long way in recent years, and there are a number of high-quality reels available

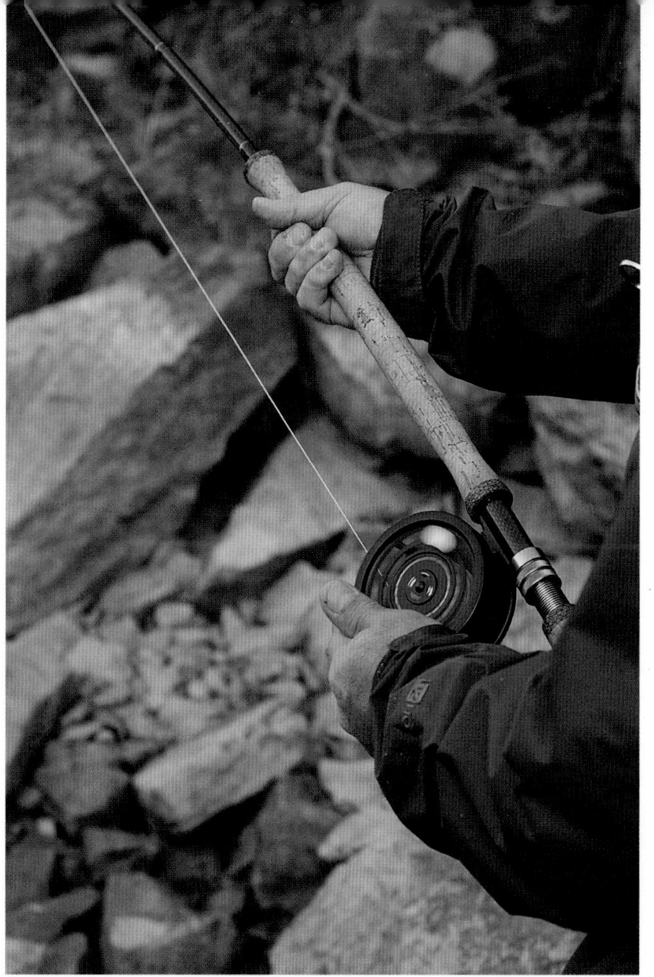

with sealed drags at a wide range of prices. From my perspective, the key is smoothness. There should be little to no startup inertia when a steelhead begins a run and takes line from the reel. Steelhead are known for their quick start to begin a run. Any stickiness in the drag can result in a broken tippet or the hook being pulled from the fish's mouth.

I prefer an adjustable drag system that has a wide range of settings. I generally keep my drag set at light tension so that it is easy for a fish to take line. It seems as though when a steelhead is allowed to run freely, it tires quicker, and the chance for a successful landing is increased. This is especially true when you are using a lighter tippet. A lighter drag setting also allows for a more exciting fight. Some anglers prefer reels without adjustable disk drags that just have a simple light spring tension for steelhead fishing.

Sometimes having the ability to tighten the drag is critical. When the room to fight a steelhead is limited because you can't follow it downriver or there is an obstruction in the water such as a logjam, you can't allow the fish to run too far. Placing the drag at the tightest setting forces the fish to fight for each inch of line that it takes from the reel. This can help tire the fish, even in a confined area. Of course, this approach requires a

***Left:* Balance and capacity are two important characteristics of a proper reel.** NICK PIONESSA PHOTO

A smooth drag with very low startup inertia is essential for fighting a steelhead.

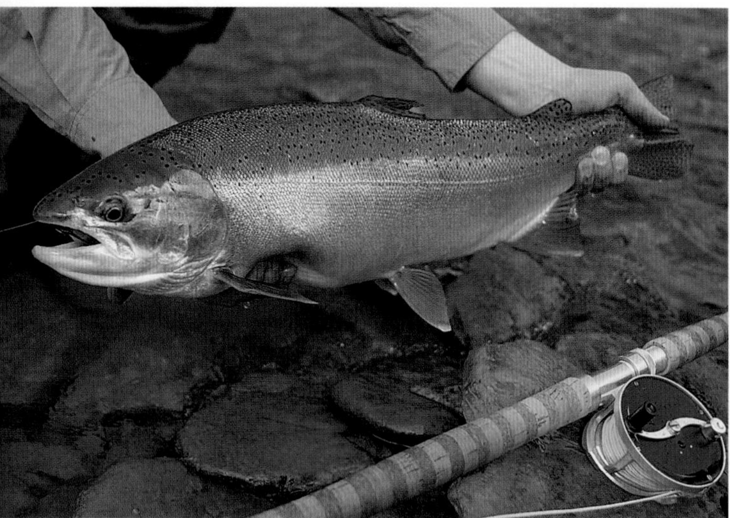

A classic reel was used to land this bright steelhead.
NICK PIONESSA PHOTO

heavy tippet. On one particular tailout that I regularly fish on one of my home rivers, the water directly downstream is so fast and heavy that it is nearly impossible and extremely dangerous to follow a steelhead. But rigged with a strong tippet and tight drag, I can usually keep any fish I hook in the pool.

Lines

An understanding of line tapers and weights is essential for balancing a fly rod and for you to choose a line that works best for the type and size of the water you are fishing. The options of line tapers on the market for both single-handed and two-handed rods can be overwhelming. When choosing a taper, keep in mind the main objective of the line given the rigging and presentation. Also, it is always best to cast a line on the rod you intend to use it with, if possible, since the performance of a line can vary dramatically from rod to rod.

Lines for Single-Handed Rods

Myriad fly lines are available on the market for single-handed rods. For steelhead fishing in the Great Lakes region, two basic designs work well, depending on the water and the technique.

For fishing egg patterns, nymphs, and small wet flies with a dead-drift technique, a line that can easily turn over an indicator, weight on the leader, and possibly a weighted fly works best. A floating line with a short, aggressive front taper will satisfy this requirement, and most are marketed under names such as nymph taper or indicator taper. Dead-drift lines are usually designed with a high-riding tip and typically have a high-visibility color in the front 5 to 10 feet.

Generally, the entire head of the line will range from 40 to 60 feet. While these lines are designed to be fished at a fairly short range, it is helpful to have a longer head and rear taper for mending and line control. The ability to maintain acute control over the line allows for longer dead-drift presentations and easier line pickup. Some of this capability is lost with a shorter head when the running line extends past the tip of the rod. The thin diameter of the running line does not have sufficient mass to maintain control over the rest of the line.

Fishing larger flies with the wet-fly swing or waking dry flies works best with an entirely different line configuration. These lines are generally marketed under the designation of a steelhead taper. This design has a long overall head of over 60 feet and a long back taper for mending and overall line control. Steelhead tapers are designed to make it easier to pick up line at the end of the swing and to hold a significant amount of line in the air for ultimate casting distance. And while the front taper isn't as aggressive as a nymph or indicator line, it is short enough to easily turn over big flies and sinking leaders. New technology that allows lines to ride high on the surface makes it much easier to pick the line up off the water.

Standard 10- to 15-foot sinking-tip lines have a significant application in Great Lakes steelheading. Tips with sink rates of 3 to 8 inches per second are effective at placing the fly in the steelhead strike zone. The style of line designed for interchangeable tips makes perfect sense for anglers swinging flies with a single-handed rod. It eliminates the need to carry a variety of full sinking-tip lines on extra spools or reels. A sinking-tip of 12 to 15 feet is looped to the floating portion of the line. This style of line is versatile: tips of varying sink rates can easily be exchanged to meet the current speed and depth of the water being fished.

When it comes to fishing small to medium-size rivers with a single-handed rod, I have had good success with lines designed to cast heavy or wind-resistant flies. This type of line is extremely versatile as it can be combined with a long leader and weighted fly for swinging as well as a sinking leader and unweighted fly. This style of line will also handle weight on the leader and an indicator. Generally this style of line will have a 40- to 45-foot head with a thick front taper and be capable of shooting considerable line for longer casts.

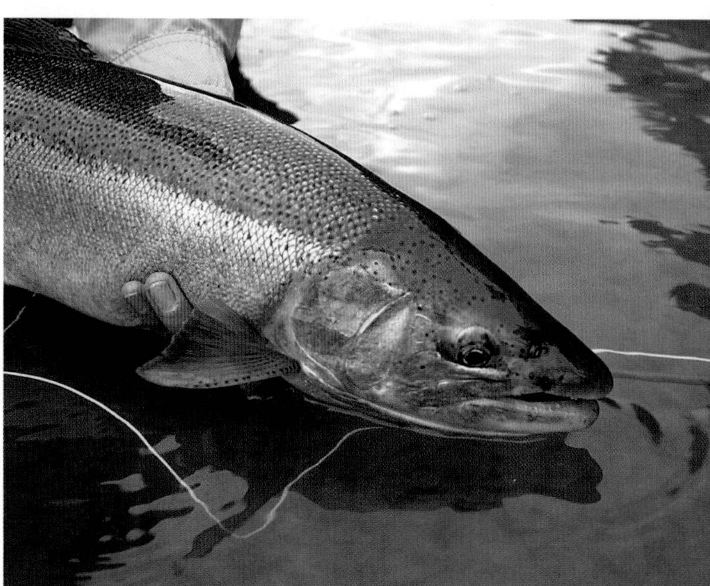

Lines with longer heads are a good match for a single-handed rod and the wet-fly swing.

Fish on! I'm battling an acrobatic early-season steelhead. NICK PIONESSA PHOTO

Lines for Switch and Two-Handed Rods

One of the most complicated aspects of Spey fishing with a switch or two-handed rod is selecting a line. So confusing are the choices that I think it discourages some anglers from using a two-handed rod before they even try to fish with one.

Rod length, the size and speed of the water being fished, casting conditions, and personal casting style all factor into proper line type. The choices are wide and varied and have evolved over the years, but this evolution has accelerated recently due to the growing interest in Spey fishing. Historically, Spey lines were designed much like a double taper and cast with a slow, methodic stroke. Modern lines are designed on the same principles as a weight-forward line and are cast in a manner that shoots the running line for casting distance. The head length, taper, and weight are the key characteristics to consider when selecting a line.

Almost all weight-forward-type lines for switch and two-handed rods are floating lines, but many are designed with a loop for interchangeable tips. For steelhead fishing in the Great Lakes, you will need to loop a sinking-tip or sinking leader onto a floating head.

The length of the head varies widely and generally includes the sinking section looped onto a floating head. You can use head lengths as short as 30 feet on a switch rod and heads as long as 70 to 80 feet on full two-handers.

I prefer longer heads when fishing bigger rivers. A long head requires less stripping of running line at the end of the swing to begin the next cast. This makes a longer head more efficient and a bit less tiring to cast.

The line with a longer head requires better casting mechanics than shorter lines, and most anglers find the longer head more cumbersome when handling heavy tips and weighted flies. Most midlength to longer heads that are useful in the Great Lakes are 50 to 65 feet long and are designed with a smooth progressive taper that promotes line speed and casting distance with the capacity to cover over 100 feet of river.

The line with a longer head is my choice for covering bigger rivers when using a floating line or an interchangeable tip version with sinking-tip rates up to a type 8 and either unweighted or slightly weighted flies. The longer head also influences casting style. Wider, broader movements of the rod are required to set up and make the cast, and your hand positions need to be higher to leverage the rod.

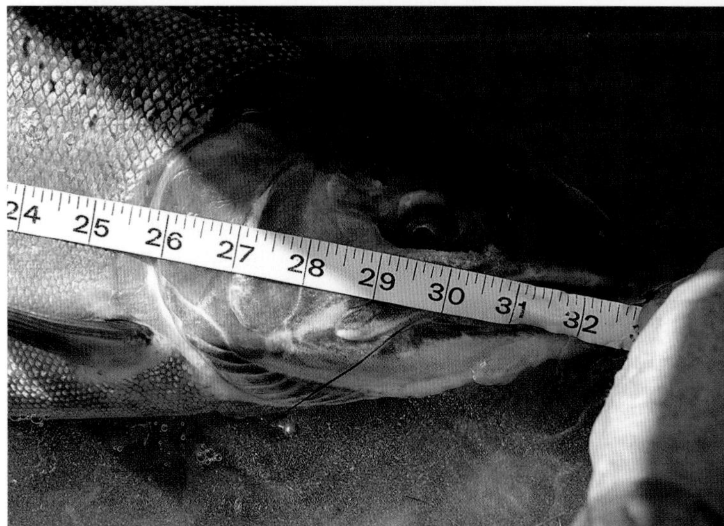

An above-average Great Lakes fish. NICK PIONESSA PHOTO

Lines with shorter heads play a large role in Great Lakes steelhead fishing because of their versatility. A shorter head matches the size of many of the region's rivers. The most popular style of the shorter heads is the Skagit line. The line derives its name from a steelhead river in the state of Washington where the line style was developed. Early in my Spey fishing experience in the Great Lakes, I independently drew a similar conclusion—that a short, aggressive taper worked well for handling heavy tips and weighted flies. Back before Skagit lines were on the market, I used an overlined pike taper to meet the same objectives.

All Skagit lines have a loop on the front end for easily changing sinking-tips. Some Skagit lines are designed with a loop at the end of the rear taper and are looped to the running line section for a relatively easy exchange of heads. Others are seamlessly fused to the running line. The floating portion of the head is generally 20 to 32 feet plus another 8 to 15 feet of tip section. This typically creates a total head in the range of 30 to 45 feet. Each manufacturer's Skagit heads vary in length by grain weight.

Skagit tapers are approximately twice the diameter of a mid to long belly line built for the same rod. This larger diameter creates a significant amount of mass capable of easily handling heavy sinking-tips and heavily weighted flies. Also, the thicker diameter makes it easier to bring the tip and weighted fly to the surface at the end of the swing. These qualities make the Skagit taper a top choice when fishing deep, swift water.

The Skagit setup is also perfect for streams and rivers where the casting position is backed up near brush or steep gorge walls. Since the Skagit is shorter than a mid or long belly line, it creates a smaller D loop, which in turn requires less room behind the casting position. The compact design of Skagit lines for switch or even single-handed rods results in an even smaller D loop and is ideal for the tight casting situations that are common in the Great Lakes region.

Another advantage of the Skagit line is that it is relative easy to cast. The weight and bulk of the taper load the rod quickly, and the shorter head requires less precise casting mechanics than longer heads. Its casting ease often makes the Skagit my choice on windy days since I can handle a wide range of casts with this style of line, especially when casting with my off hand. The short head is also an advantage when fishing water that requires deep wading.

The Skagit setup requires its own modifications to the basic Spey cast. Heavy tips and weighted flies need a nearly continuous motion or sustained anchor point throughout to keep everything at the surface to effectively complete the cast. The

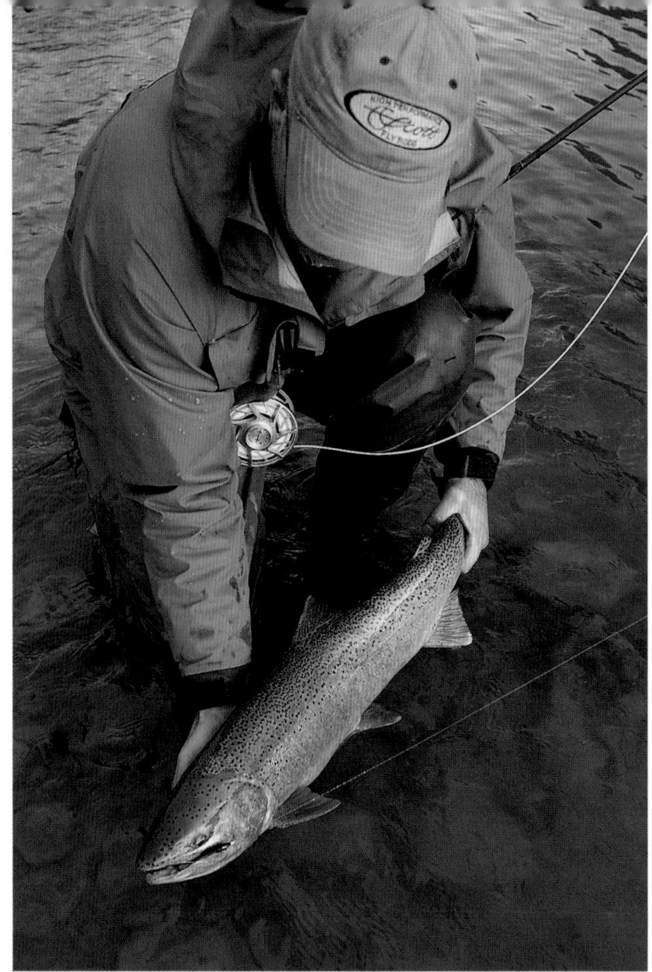

***Right:* I used a Skagit head rig to catch this male steelhead in a fast tailout.** NICK PIONESSA PHOTO

Lines with longer bellies work well with lighter tips and lightly weighted flies. NICK PIONESSA PHOTO

The continuous motion and moving anchor of a Skagit cast. NICK PIONESSA PHOTO

Skagit line is generally matched with shorter rods, and the forward casting stroke is slower and more deliberate than that of other casting styles. With the weight of the head attached to thin running line, the Skagit setup can be cast great distances. But it is its ability to fish well close in and cover a wide range of conditions and situations that makes this taper a very important one for Great Lakes steelheading.

Another style of the short-head Spey line is the Scandinavian or Scandi head. A Scandi head has a much longer and smoother front taper than a Skagit head. This style of line is designed to generate significant line speed and is capable of being cast incredible distances. Most Scandinavian heads are designed with a loop on the front end for an easy exchange of heads and leaders. Some are also designed with a loop on the rear end for changing heads, which eliminates the need to carry extra spools. Still other designs have a sinking portion fused to the floating section. I prefer the versatility of loops on both ends of the head.

Scandi heads are typically 30 to 45 feet in length and require a 12- to 15-foot light tip or leader in order to establish a suitable anchor point. The proper length of the head will depend on such factors as the length of the rod, wading depth, room behind the casting position, and the size of the river. Shorter rods, deep wading, and tight fishing conditions all favor a shorter head. But one of the advantages of the Scandi design is the versatile head length as longer heads can be matched with big rivers and can effectively cover big water.

Generally, shorter rods can be used with both the Skagit and Scandi heads. I feel that a shorter rod is less fatiguing to fish with and that it makes the fight of a steelhead more enjoyable. A good rule of thumb many anglers use to select head length is a 3 or 3½ to 1 ratio of head to rod length. In other words, a 12-foot rod would match with a head of 36 to 42 feet in length. This approach to rod length is a very basic guide, and it generally considers Skagit head length tip and Scandi head length exclusive of the sinking leader and tippet. This reflects the casting style required for each head.

Since the Scandi head design has a long front taper, it won't effectively handle the heavy tips and flies like a Skagit head will. Scandinavian heads are best matched with tapered sinking leaders of 12 to 15 feet.You add 4 to 5 feet of monofilament tippet to the sinking leader to bring the total leader length to about 19 feet. Sinking leaders with fast sink rates are capable of covering significant depths. Long monofilament leaders can also be used to fish on or near the surface. I like Scandi heads for their smooth feel and ability to launch a substantial amount of line. This style of line matches well with many Great Lakes rivers.

Neil Houlding casting a long, tight loop with a Scandi head.

Scandi heads work best with a style of Spey casting referred to as underhand casting, which uses a short, efficient stroke to generate maximum line speed. You place your hands closer together than with other styles of Spey casting. Underhand casting relies on a solid anchor point and acceleration on the setup to form a deep D loop, which loads the rod. The power of the forward cast comes from the bottom hand as the top acts mainly as a guide. At the end of the forward stroke, your bottom hand and the butt of the rod come into your midsection. The rod should stop fairly high to throw the line toward the horizon. This style of casting combined with a Scandi head generates a cast with a tight loop that efficiently cuts through the air.

Scandi heads are capable of shooting long distances.

Recently line manufacturers have introduced heads that are a hybrid of the Skagit and Scandi style. The objective is to create a line with the key advantages of each type. The result is a line with a more progressive taper than a standard Skagit, making it smoother to cast but still with enough mass to handle heavier tips and flies.

If the length of the head and taper isn't complicated enough when considering lines for two-handed and switch rods, then add in the concept of head weight. It takes substantially more weight in the line to load a 7-weight two-handed rod than a 7-weight single-handed rod. The line weight designation of a Spey line considers the entire head, but only the first 30 feet determine the line weight of a single-handed line. Actually, determining the weight of a Spey line uses a sliding weight point so that there are varying weight recommendations depending on the length of the line.

The America Fishing Tackle Manufacturers Association (AFTMA), which first established a fly line table for single-handed rods a number of years ago, has more recently produced a chart on Spey line weight determination. While the table for single-handed rods has one weight recommendation in grains with an allowable tolerance for each line designation, the Spey line chart has four columns based on head length.

In the chart, H represents shooting head and is measured at 40 feet; S represents short belly and is measured at 55 feet; M is for midlength belly and is measured at 65 feet; and L is for long belly and is measured at 75 feet. The chart below combines the AFTMA single-handed and double-handed line weight recommendations in grains. Note that Spey lines have a tolerance of plus or minus 30 grains from the number in the chart. Tolerance on single-handed rods varies from plus or minus 8 for a 6-weight and plus or minus 10 for a 9-weight.

Although Skagit and Scandi heads fall within the length range of a shooting head, the AFTMA chart does not really address these tapers directly. The head column in the chart mainly refers to shooting heads for overhead casting. In my experience, the recommended grain weight of a Skagit or Scandi head lines up closely with that of the short belly line. The short, mid, and long belly lines list the recommended line weight on the packaging, and most have a two or even three line range, such as 7/8. I normally match my rod with the lower number, in other words, placing a 7/8 line on a 7-weight rod.

Skagit and Scandinavian heads are often packaged with a grain weight designation. When considering the proper weight, do not include the weight of the tip or leader that will be added when casting. Since my Skagit or Scandi heads are similar in grain weight, the short belly recommendation for each line weight, I generally use a 510 to 570 Skagit head on an 8-weight. My selection in grain weight for a Scandi head would be less. There is a nearly infinite number of line and rod combinations, and selecting the right line has much to do with the action of the rod and personal casting style. Finding the right one can take a lot of trial and error. Spey gatherings are a perfect place to discover the feel of various rod and line combinations.

Spey Line Weight Determination

Line weight	Single-handed	Two-handed			
		Head	Short	Mid	Long
6	160	250	420	460	600
7	185	300	470	510	650
8	210	360	530	570	710
9	240	430	600	640	780

Leaders and Tips

The terminal end of the fly-fishing rig directly impacts the presentation of the fly. The properties of the leader or sinking-tip help determine the depth of the fly and how naturally it fishes. Match the leader or sinking-tip to the technique you are using, the size of the water, and the overall conditions. The wide variety of leaders and tips can be overwhelming, but an understanding of leader diameter and sink rate will go a long way toward selecting the proper rig. In many cases leader or sinking-tip selection is a matter of trial and error and will vary by river or pool. Keeping notes on successful rigging for a certain river or set of conditions can be very useful for future outings.

Leaders for Dead Drifting

The main objective of the dead-drift technique is to present the fly so that it appears to be moving naturally with the flow of the current. While proper mending and line control will enhance a dead drift, leader design for this type of fishing is a key starting point. The larger the diameter or surface of the leader material, the more negative impact varying currents will have on attempts for a natural drift. While many manufactured leaders are sufficient for dead-drifting flies for steelhead, custom designed leaders with a low-diameter midsection and tippet will perform best. A basic low-diameter leader consists of a 20 percent butt section of .021- to .019-inch material. This fairly thick butt section helps turn over the fly. The middle section steps down significantly to .013- to .011-inch material and makes up 50 to 60 percent of the leader. The remaining 20 to 30 percent consists of 1X to 3X tippet. The longer tippet aids in attaining a natural drift.

Success with the dead-drift approach. NICK PIONESSA PHOTO

Another style of leader for dead drifting is a right-angle leader. This takes the concept of low-diameter material to the next level and creates what many steelhead anglers believe is the most effective way to dead-drift a fly. The leader starts with a 3- to 4-foot butt section of .019- to .017-inch stiff leader material. The butt section is then attached to an indicator. Yarn indicators are often used with this setup. The simplest approach is to use an indicator that has a loop, as the butt section can easily be attached to the indicator with an improved clinch knot. A tippet of 5 to 8 feet is then attached directly to the butt section to complete the leader. You can do this by forming a loop in the butt section and tying an improved clinch knot with the 1X to 3X tippet. When the knot is complete, slide the tippet down to the knot between the butt and the indicator, forming a right angle in the leader.

The right-angle setup has a few tactical advantages. The angle of the long tippet maintains a more positive connection to the fly, reduces the bow that the current creates in conventional leaders, and increases sensitivity. Because of the long, low-diameter tippet, the fly will sink faster and maintain a truer drift throughout the presentation. Less weight will have to be added to the leader to sink the fly, so it is also a stealthier approach. Casting with this rig requires a slower stroke and a more open loop on the delivery.

Leaders for Tight-Line Presentations

When presenting the fly on a tight line, as required in the wet-fly swing or when waking a dry fly, a tapered leader that efficiently transfers energy to the fly is essential. Manufactured knotless

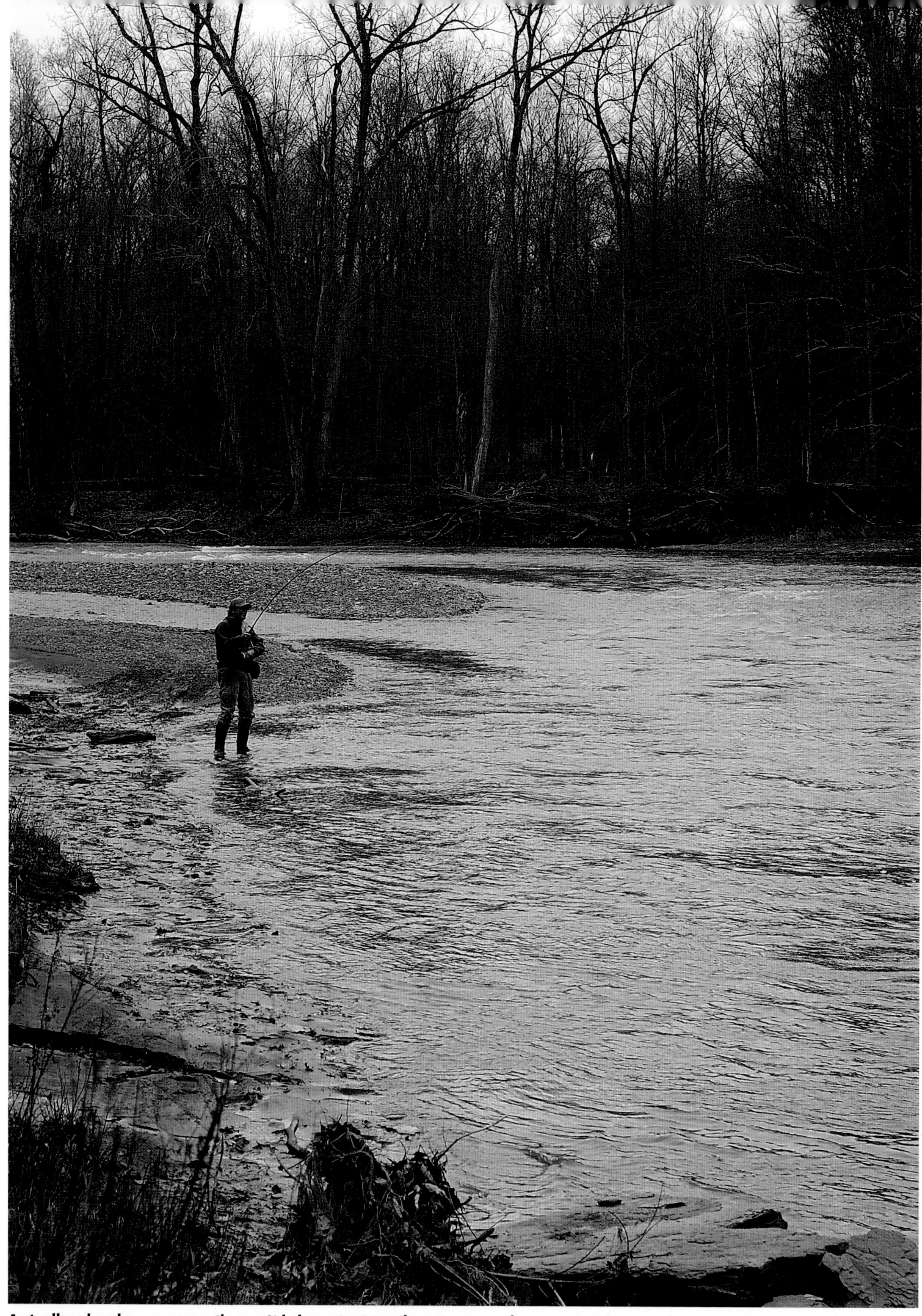

A steelhead makes an energetic run. It is important to take extra care when constructing your knots to make sure they are as strong as they can be. NICK PIONESSA PHOTO

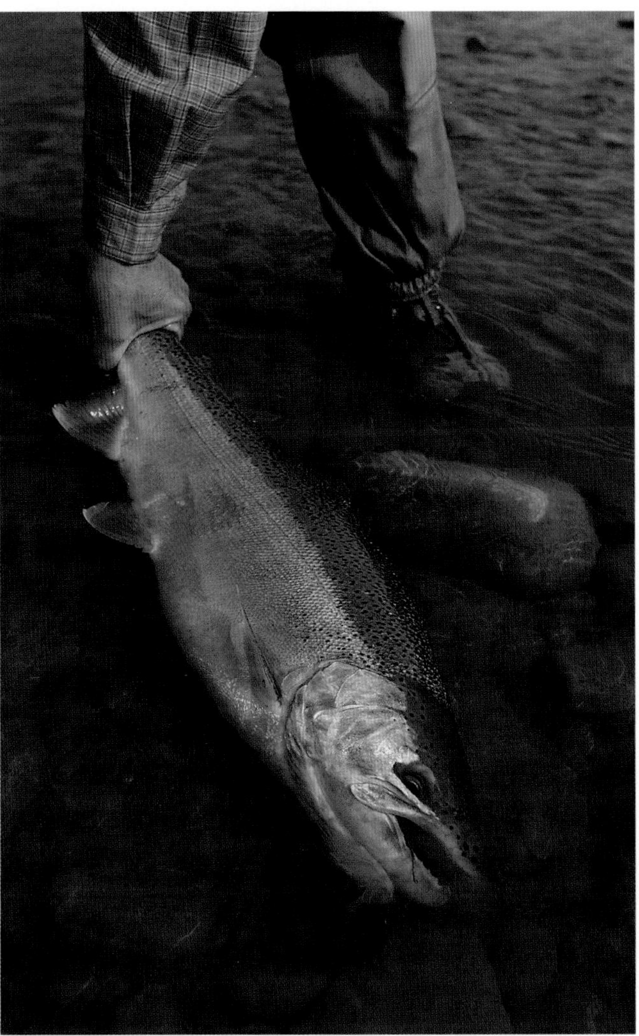

A large male steelhead that was fooled by a purple Spey fly.
NICK PIONESSA PHOTO

leaders marketed as steelhead or salmon leaders perform well under most conditions. However, when using weighted flies I prefer a hand-tied leader with a heavy butt section that can easily lay out a straight leader even with weight at the end. A basic leader for a tight-line presentation consists of 50 percent butt section of .023 to .019 material, 30 percent middle section of .019 to .013 material, and 20 percent tippet section.

The tippet of a tight-line leader should be fairly stout. I normally use a tippet of 12- or 10-pound-test, and occasionally when fishing tight areas I even use 15-pound. When a steelhead takes a fly on a tight line and turns downcurrent, there can be a significant shock to the tippet. The tippet strength has to be sufficient to withstand this force. I hate breaking off fish, so I always fish with sufficient strength tippet.

Anglers who are accustomed to dead-drifting flies for steelhead are often intimidated by using heavy tippet as it goes against the stealth mindset. But the main reason that light tippets are used in dead drifting is to attain a natural drift. When you swing a fly on a tight line, you want to swim the fly, which can be accomplished just as effectively on a stout tippet as on a light one. Also, when you use this technique, a steelhead will generally see the fly from the side or the rear and will be attracted by the movement so that the diameter of the tippet will not likely be a deterrent to a strike.

A leader for tight-line presentations will vary between 9 and 14 feet in length, depending on the length of the rod. Shorter leaders will be used with single-handed rods and longer lengths with two-handed rods. This type of leader is used for fishing wet flies near the surface or riffle hitching a dry to fish on top. Using a weighted fly makes it a stealthy rig to fish near the bottom in low, clear water on small to medium-size rivers.

With any leader, proper knot construction is critical to its effectiveness. I place a loop at the butt end of all my monofilament leaders. I prefer a perfection loop for its lower profile. A blood knot creates a straight line connection for when you tie your own leaders. A double surgeon's knot is a great alternative, and while stronger than the blood knot, it does not create a straight connection. It is a good knot for onstream leader repair, especially in difficult weather conditions. It is critical to carefully tie all knots and to sufficiently lubricate them before tightening. Make sure all knots are tight and properly seated as the friction caused by a loose knot will significantly weaken the strength of the leader material.

Take extra care with fluorocarbon material. For a stealthy approach in very clear water, the low light refractive properties of fluorocarbon seem to make a difference. When constructing a knot with fluorocarbon, you need to thoroughly lubricate the loose knot and tighten it slowly. The heat generated from quickly tightening an unlubricated fluorocarbon knot will weaken the knot.

Sinking-Tips and Sinking Leaders

Sinking-tips and sinking leaders are both designed to perform the same task—to take the fly below the surface of the water. The main difference between the two is that a sinking-tip is integrated into the fly line and a sinking leader is generally added to the front end of a tapered fly line. Sinking-tips can be integrated seamlessly as part of the fly line, or they can be added to and removed from interchangeable style lines using a loop-to-loop connection. The interchangeable tip arrangement gives a much greater degree of versatility, which can be very important in steelhead fishing. Sinking leaders are looped onto the front end of a floating fly line.

Generally a sinking-tip is a more significant piece of fly line that factors into the length and weight of the line for purposes of loading the rod for casting. Some tips are tapered and others simply a level piece of line. Sinking leaders are generally a lower diameter than a sinking-tip and cast in the same manner on the front end of a tapered floating line as a monofilament leader. Both tips and leaders can be used with lines for single-handed and two-handed rods.

At the front end of the sinking-tip or sinking leader is a short length of monofilament leader or tippet. For sinking-tips I usually loop on a two-section leader. When using an unweighted or slightly weighted fly, use a tippet with a breaking strength of 10- to 15-pound-test and a length of 1 to 3 feet. The butt section is approximately a foot of a slightly higher breaking strength material than the tippet. You can reach greater depths when using a heavily weighted fly and a Skagit system by using a longer monofilament section. Both the butt and tippet are lengthened to attain a total leader of 6 to 10 feet. Loop the butt section to the sinking-tip. The extra breaking strength of the butt protects somewhat against the abrasion that can occur at the loop-to-loop connection. You can also construct the monofilament section of the sinking leader in two pieces or loop the tippet directly to the sinking leader for a lower profile.

While integrated sinking-tips have a place mainly with single-handed rods, interchangeable tips make the most sense for meeting the variable conditions of Great Lakes rivers and streams. Most interchangeable tips can be grouped into two categories: those with a front taper that are designed to sink from 3 to 8 inches a second, and those constructed of level line with sink rates up to 12 inches per second. The latter are constructed from materials such as T-14, LC-13, and CT 200 or 330. Tapered tips of 10 to 15 feet are used with exchangeable tip weight-forward lines for single-handed rods and for mid belly Spey. The heavier level tips are generally used with Skagit lines for two-handed, switch, or even single-handed rods.

Sinking leaders are also available in a range of lengths and sink rates. Most range from 7 to 14 feet with sink rates of 3 to 7 inches per second. While sinking leaders work well on the front end of a weight-forward line, I have found that cutting back the floating taper by a few feet will help turn over a sinking leader. But this isn't the case with a Scandi head, where the sinking leader will complete the length needed to cast the head.

Nick Pionessa happily displays a broad, bright steelhead caught on a sinking-tip. NICK PIONESSA PHOTO

Selecting the proper tip for each fishing situation can be a bit of a process. Water depth, speed, and even temperature can affect tip selection. You can catch Great Lakes steelhead at any depth in the water column, especially when water temperatures are above 40 degrees F, but fishing the fly near the bottom will generally result in more takes. Selecting a sinking-tip that consistently places the fly in the preferred zone given the characteristics of the river being fished will increase the chances of a hookup.

Tapered sinking-tips of 10 to 15 feet match up well with Spey lines that are midlength or longer and with interchangeable tip single-handed lines. With a two-handed rod, type 3, 6, and 8 sinking-tips can be used to cover medium-size to large rivers with slower to moderate currents. (The type denotes the sink rate of the tip—type 3 equals 3 inches per second.) Type 3 tips work best in shallow water or when attempting to fish the fly well off the bottom for aggressive fish. Types 6 and 8 are practical for fishing the fly closer to the bottom.

Level tips provide a good solution for delivering big, weighted flies to significant depths and when fishing heavy currents. The level materials such as T-14, LC-13, and CT 330 have sink rates greater than type 8. And while an argument can be made that the lower diameter of a tapered type 8 tip will slice through the current better than the thicker diameter of the level material, its ability to easily handle heavy flies gives the

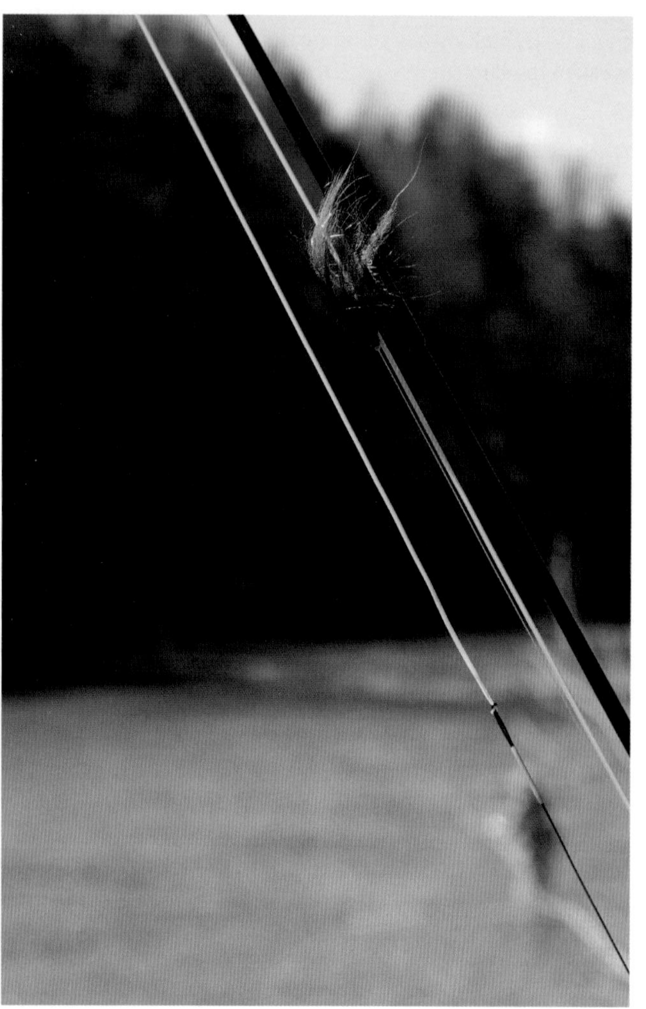

Loop-to-loop connections allow for an easy change in sinking-tip length or sink rate. NICK PIONESSA PHOTO

level tip the clear advantage for reaching the greatest depths. These level materials can be purchased in long lengths and custom cut with loops placed at both ends to create a series of tips for a variety of depths. Tips of 6 to 15 feet are typically used with Skagit style lines.

One way to build a series of level tips of varying lengths is to maintain a consistent length of the entire tip. By splicing lengths of intermediate line of a like diameter to the level tip, you can establish a constant length of the entire tip. For instance, one tip could be 14 feet of level sinking-tip, another could be 9 feet of sinking-tip and 5 of intermediate, and a third could be 7 feet of each. Each tip would reach different depths but would allow you to maintain a similar casting stroke because of the equal length. Commercially manufactured tip systems such as these are available on the market.

Sinking leaders generally have sink rates up to 7 inches per second, and those from 3 to 7 inches per second are best for Great Lakes steelhead fishing. Sinking leaders of 7 to 10 feet in length are perfect for single-handed rods and for covering small to medium-size streams and rivers. Those 10 to 14 feet in length match up well with longer belly and Scandi heads.

I tend to select my tips by feel and trial. My starting point is a rule of thumb that I've developed after years of experience. A type 6 tip of 12 to 15 feet seems to effectively cover water with a speed of 2 to 3 miles per hour and a depth of approximately 3 to 4 feet. Water speed can be judged by walking speed. The average speed for walking is between 2 and 3 miles per hour. A brisk pace for most people is 3 miles per hour. Depth is more of a judgment call, but analyzing depth by the color changes in the water can be fairly reliable. A slower sink rate will be required in slower or shallower water and a faster sink rate in quicker or deeper water.

Maintaining notes on sinking-tips and other rigging gives you a useful tool for future outings. NICK PIONESSA PHOTO

Part of my system for selecting a tip requires maintaining detailed notes on which tips work best on which pools. It is important to note how tip requirements change for various river levels. Of course, notes will be most relevant on streams and rivers that maintain their character from year to year. But even for those rivers that shift and change with high-water events, notes on sinking-tips will still provide a general guide.

The length of the sinking-tip factors into the depth that it will obtain. For instance, a 6-foot piece of T-14 will sink throughout the presentation to the same approximate depth as a 15-foot type 3 tip. When using a midlength head, many anglers maintain the same tip length but change the sink rate of the tip to vary the fly depth. When using a Skagit head, many anglers vary the length of a level sinking-tip to change the fly depth. The same length-to-depth relationship also applies to sinking leaders.

It is also possible to take a more scientific approach to sinking-tip selection. Pacific Northwest steelheaders Tom Keelin and Bob Pauli have developed a sinking-tip system based on hours of controlled research. Under this system, the building block for determining the proper tip is to establish what length of a particular tip material is required to sink an unweighted fly to a depth of 1 foot at the end of the swing or at the hangdown with a current speed of 3 miles per hour.

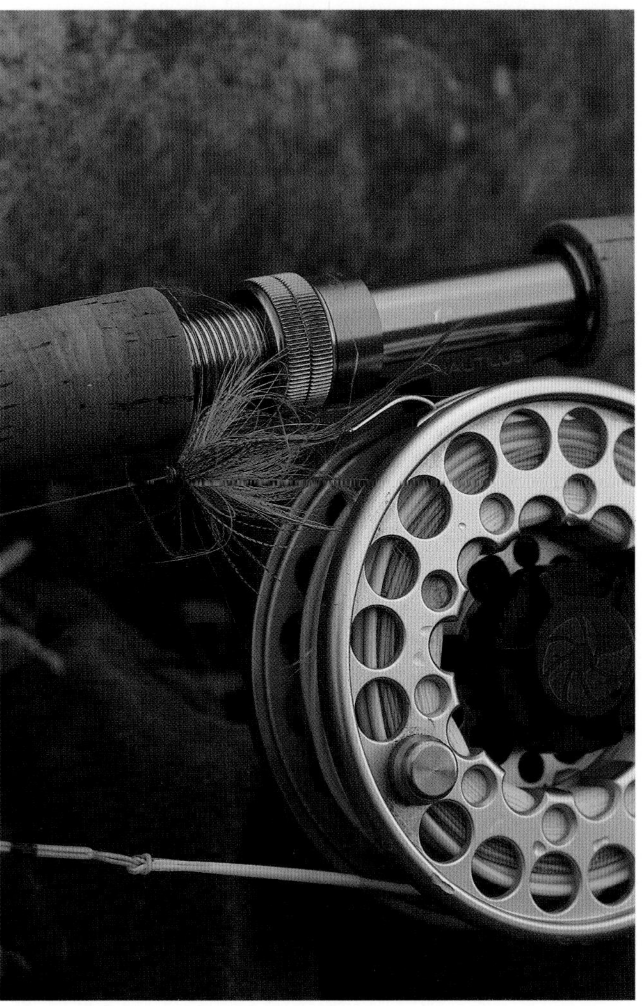

Interchangeable tips provide the most versatility for steelhead fishing in the Great Lakes. NICK PIONESSA PHOTO

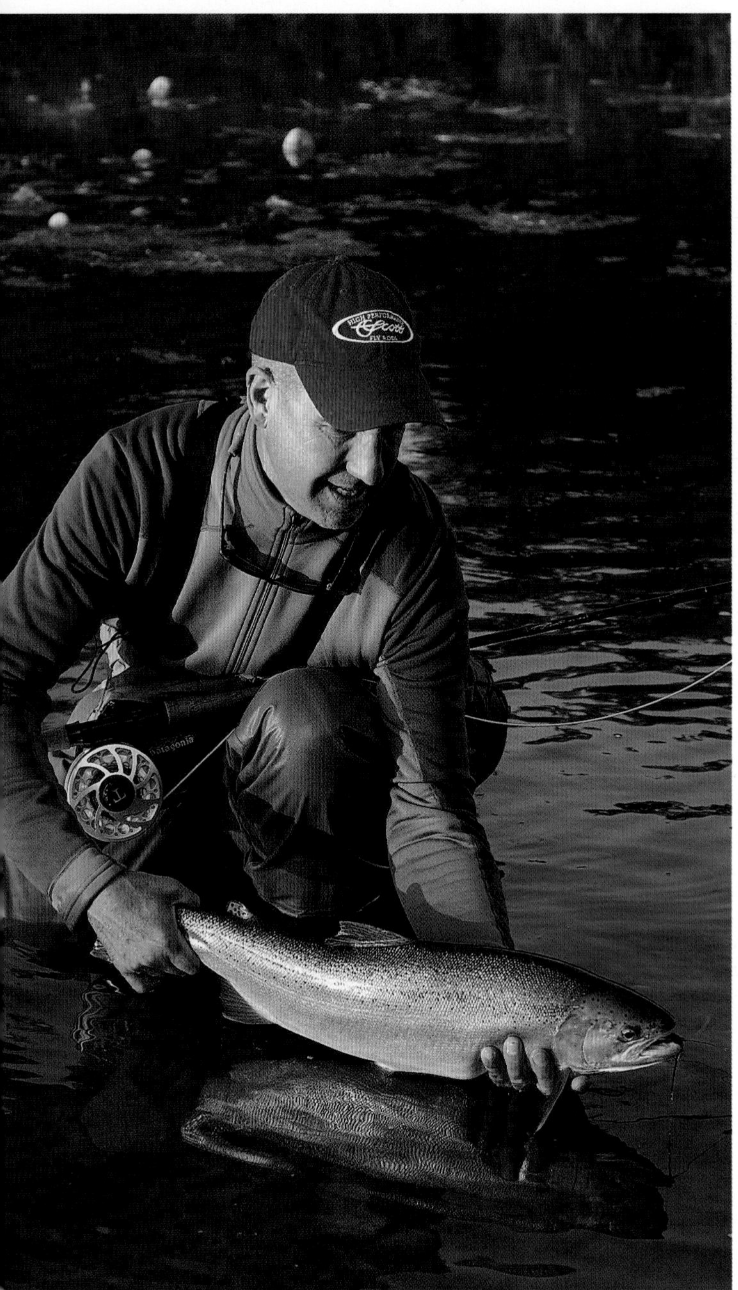

Proper clothing and wading gear are critical to enjoyment and success. NICK PIONESSA PHOTO

This system provides valuable information on comparing one tip with another. It also provides a calculation for determining the proper tip for a given situation. Details of this research and online calculation models are available on Tom and Bob's website at www.flyfishingresearch.net.

While interchangeable tips are generally easy to put on and take off, for purposes of establishing a fishing rhythm I usually attempt to fish an entire run with one tip. I prefer my tip to be slightly too light rather than too heavy. A tip that is heavy for the water may place the fly too close to the bottom where it will hang up often and disrupt the enticing movement of the swing. I make slight adjustments to the sink rate and fly depth by changing the angle of the cast. An angle across-river or even slightly up will allow the tip and fly to gain more depth than a cast that angles downriver. An upstream mend just after the tip hits the water will also allow for great depth.

Clothing

Since the best steelhead fishing occurs in the fall, winter, and early spring, proper clothing is essential to enjoying the experience. Anyone who has spent time in the Great Lakes region knows the weather can be nasty and can change without warning. In many situations an angler's clothing may be his or her most important piece of fishing equipment. The principles of dressing properly apply to days with air temperature in the 20s as well as the 60s. Anytime there is even cool air, especially combined with wind, you can become uncomfortable if you are not properly prepared. I remember a number of days when being able to meet difficult conditions head-on resulted in a high-quality day of steelhead fishing. The satisfaction of having defeated the elements puts an exclamation point on a great day.

Proper layering is the key to staying comfortable in the outdoors. The objective of dressing for cool or cold is simply to prevent heat loss. When you are out fishing your body can lose heat in two basic ways: conductive and convective heat loss. Conductive heat loss is caused by direct contact. Wet conductive heat loss occurs almost 25 times faster than dry conductive heat loss, which greatly emphasizes the need to stay dry. This includes both moisture from the outside, like rain or snow, and moisture from the inside caused by perspiration trapped within clothing.

Convective heat loss is caused by the movement of air. The "windchill" concept is the best example of this type of heat transfer. This is when the impact of cold temperatures is increased by the cooling effect of wind.

The key then to staying warm in cool or cold temperatures is effectively managing moisture while blocking the impact of the wind. A three-layered clothing system of the proper materials will accomplish this. The three basic layers are a wicking layer, an insulating layer, and an outside protection layer.

The main purpose of the wicking layer is to transport moisture away from the body. An effective wicking layer is made from a nonabsorbent synthetic fiber that insulates as well as wicks moisture, such as Capilene. Wicking layers are available in various weights or thicknesses to meet a range of weather conditions. Since cotton absorbs and holds moisture, it should never be worn next to the skin if you are trying to keep warm.

The insulating layer can consist of synthetic fibers such as fleece or natural fibers including wool. However, synthetic fleece is preferred for a number of reasons. The synthetic fibers of fleece can wick away moisture and are less absorbent than natural fibers. Fleece maintains its insulating value even when wet, has the ability to dry faster than natural fibers, and weighs less. Loft is also important in a quality insulating layer. In other words, fibers that do not compress will do a much better job maintaining their insulating value. A 200-weight fleece top and pants make a good insulating layer under most conditions.

Keeping moisture away from your body is key to remaining comfortable in a range of weather conditions. NICK PIONESSA PHOTO

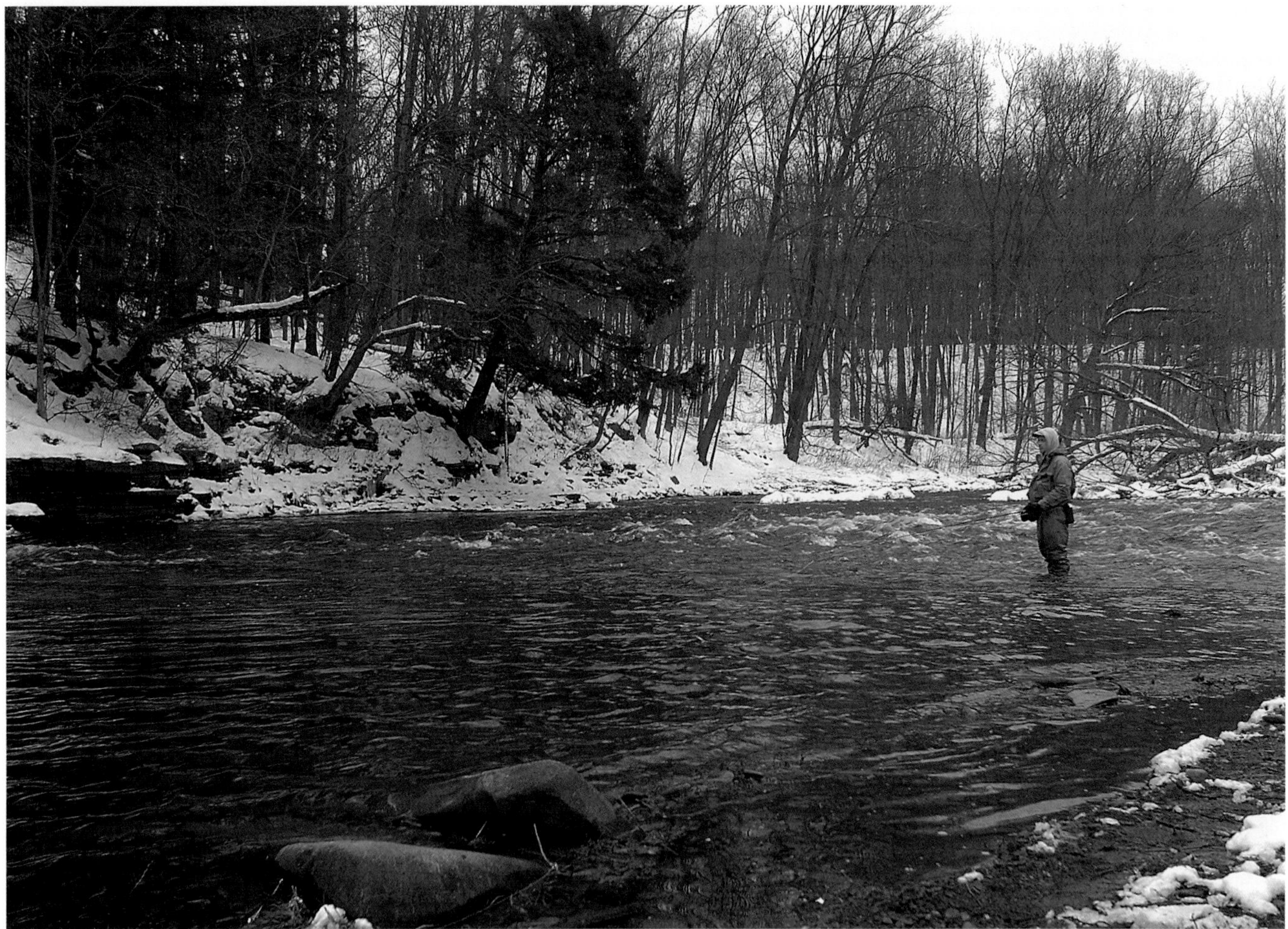

Staying dry and keeping your extremities warm are the keys to enjoying a day of winter steelheading. NICK PIONESSA PHOTO

The outer layer plays a dual role. It must keep the insulating layers dry by protecting you from the accumulation of moisture generated by the body and by moisture from outside sources like rain or snow. It is vital that the outer layer be breathable. Breathability relates to the transfer of moisture vapor and should not be confused with wicking. A breathable garment allows moisture to escape in the form of gas, completing the process of keeping moisture away from the skin. Not all breathable materials are created equal. Some develop leaks easily, and others do not breathe effectively. Outer layers with Gore-Tex have historically been considered the top performers in the area.

In cold weather, you cannot stay fully comfortable without taking care of your extremities. A hat with a combination of wool and fleece is essential as significant heat loss can occur through your head. Gloves can also be extremely important in cold weather. I prefer gloves with either WindStopper or Windbloc to prevent the effects of the wind from further stealing heat from my hands. A fingerless style provides warmth on cooler days, but for extreme cold I prefer a style with a mitt that folds back to form a fingerless glove.

Socks are also important, and layering keeps the feet as dry as possible. Wear a synthetic wicking sock next to your skin and an insulating sock over the wicking sock to absorb moisture and maintain warmth. The inherent problem with the feet is that the boot area of a wader, whether stocking-foot or bootfoot, will not allow moisture to escape to the outside. This further emphasizes the need for the insulating sock to maintain warmth even when damp.

The proper wader is also extremely important in keeping warm and comfortable. Breathable waders have revolutionized stream and river fishing. Some of the same principles that make a breathable wader comfortable in the summer also make it effective in cold weather. Breathable waders allow moisture to evaporate, keeping the skin dry and warm. However, when the water temperatures dip below 40 degrees F, it is difficult to keep your feet warm in stocking-foot waders. Insulated bootfoot breathable waders are better for such conditions.

It is important to find the right combination of clothing and wading wear for each situation. Clothing that one person finds comfortable under certain circumstances may differ significantly from what another prefers. With today's technologically advanced clothing and outerwear, you rarely have an excuse for being uncomfortable. This is extremely important if you have limited hours to spend on the water. There is no sense in being miserable while steelhead fishing.

CHAPTER **2**

Casting

Charlie Dickson prepares to make another cast. NICK PIONESSA PHOTO

In previous books and articles on the Great Lakes fishery, I spent little effort on casting. To me casting has always been the means to being a proficient angler. Only recently have I started viewing casting as a separate act.

Learning the intricacies of Spey casting has changed my perspective. Spey casting is not difficult to learn but takes possibly a lifetime to master. The process forces a deeper understanding of mechanics, which improves all aspects of casting and fly line control and maintenance.

Since proper casting is an important building block for most of the techniques and strategies described in this book, proper coverage of the basics and some thoughts on adapting casts to actual fishing situations seem essential. This chapter will not only focus on Spey casting techniques, but also cover ideas on adding some variations that will assist in using a single-handed rod.

Spey Casting

Spey casting was first developed on the River Spey in Scotland in the mid-1800s at least partially because of the high cliff walls found along some of the river's popular pools. In order to effectively fish these pools, an angler had to be positioned so close to the wall that a backcast with a conventional rod and line was impossible. With ingenuity and the development of long two-handed rods, a new style of casting was born. Spey casting not only allowed for lengthy casts with a minimum of line passing behind the angler, but also provided for an efficient change-of-direction cast, which is an important component of the wet-fly swing technique.

Spey casting has changed and matured over the last 150 years. Much of that change can be attributed to technological changes in rods and lines. Rods are much shorter and lighter than those first used on the River Spey. Some of those rods exceeded 20 feet in length! With shorter rods came shorter lines, and modern Spey casting techniques developed as anglers aimed to meet the specific challenges of various rivers. The evolution of Spey casting has accelerated greatly in the past 10 to 20 years.

While the basic concept of Spey casting was developed with two-handed rods, the casts have been adapted to much shorter switch rods and even single-handed rods. Ideas on how to incorporate Spey techniques into single-handed presentations will be covered later in the chapter. This section will focus on double-handed casting with two-handed and switch rods.

As part of the evolution of Spey casting, various styles have developed. The advent of shorter heads and the concept of shooting line have really changed the game. Traditional long rods and long belly lines controlled with wide sweeping movements were able to cast a significant distance without shooting line. But this style required heavier equipment and had limited

Spey casting has evolved rapidly in recent years.

Hand position and grip are important components of a proper Spey cast. NICK PIONESSA PHOTO

application when it came to casting sinking-tips. Lines with shorter heads provide greater versatility when casting heavy tips and flies. But more importantly those lines provide for a compact movement when setting up the cast and a tight, efficient casting stroke when delivering the fly. Shorter heads define the modern Spey casting movement and make learning this style of casting much easier.

This chapter covers the basics of Spey casting as it pertains to the Great Lakes steelhead fishery. It will discuss some of the nuances of the popular styles, especially as they impact fly delivery and presentation. This chapter should be considered a primer on the subject, as there are volumes of books and dozens of videos dedicated to the details of this growing subset of fly casting.

Getting Started

For anglers who are experienced with a single-handed rod but new to two-handers, it may take some time to become comfortable casting with both hands. While it may be cumbersome at first, certain elements of single-handed casting apply to Spey casting with a double-hander. Anglers proficient with a single-handed rod usually pick up Spey casting quite easily.

Getting started includes proper hand and body positioning. Most anglers begin casting with the dominant hand on the upper grip and the other hand on the lower grip. In time it will be important to be conditioned to cast with either hand on top to meet various fishing and weather conditions. Since most of the power of a proper Spey cast is generated with the lower hand pulling into the body, casting with the off hand on top is less difficult than it may seem.

Hand positioning and grip play a very important role in making a good cast. In modern Spey casting, you generally position your hands closer together than with more traditional styles. A good starting point for a standard length two-handed rod is to allow both arms to hang straight down and grab the top and bottom grip so that the hands are apart by the approximate width of the hips. The hands will generally be closer together on very short two-handers and switch rods. Over the years, my casting style has developed and changed dramatically, which includes a nearly complete repositioning of my hands. I have moved my top hand from close to the top end of the grip to near the bottom. I have found this position creates a more compact stroke, generating a tighter loop and more line speed.

The grip of the top hand should be fairly firm with the thumb wrapped around the cork. The index and middle fingers of the top hand control the loose line and running line when you are both fishing and casting. The bottom hand should have a loose grip that allows the butt of the rod to rotate slightly. I generally keep the rod positioned so that my index and middle fingers are in contact with the cork along with my thumb. This simple, quick movement of bringing the bottom hand into the body during the forward stroke can generate significant power.

The position of your body is also very important. I generally place one foot ahead of the other. By moving the foot that is opposite to the top hand forward, I can move my body more freely. In other words, when I am casting with the right hand up or off the right shoulder, I move my left foot 12 to 18 inches closer to the target. This position allows my hips and shoulders to rotate during a cast, resulting in greater power, efficiency, and even accuracy.

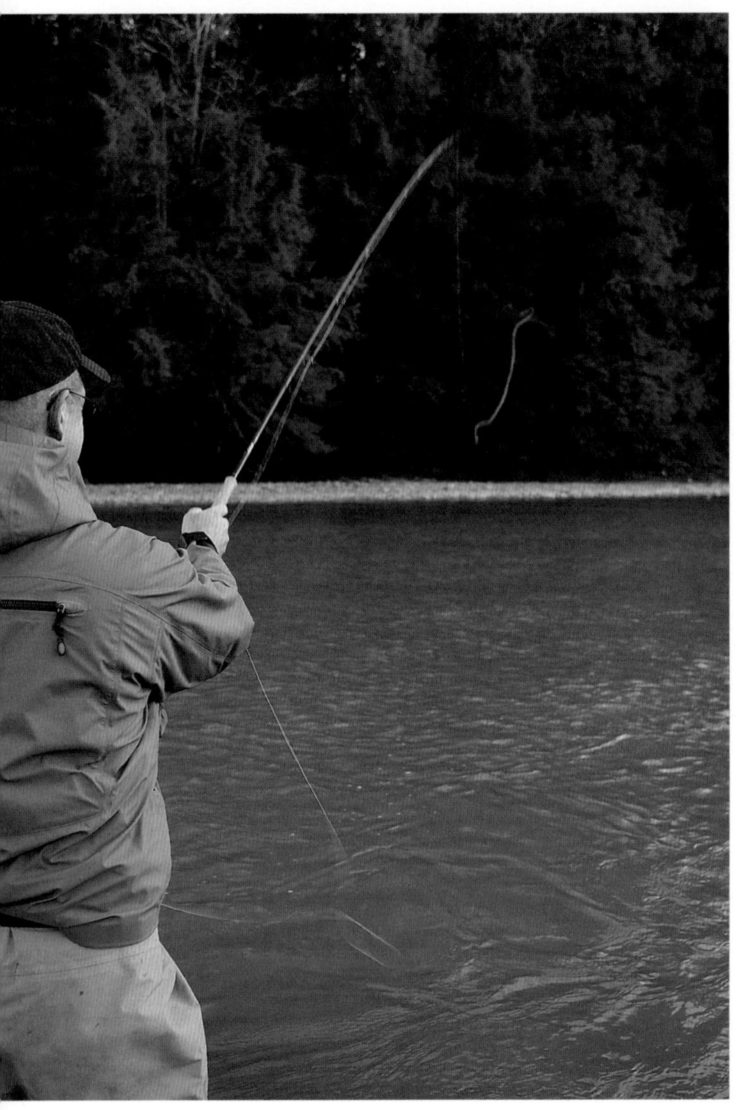

Pounding out another cast: proper body positioning is important for efficient, powerful Spey casts. NICK PIONESSA PHOTO

Forward Spey

You need to learn Spey casting on the water. While Spey casting is meant to be practiced specifically on moving water, the first building block in learning the various types of casts is the forward Spey, which can be learned and practiced on stillwater. The main difference between a Spey cast and a conventional fly cast is that Spey casting doesn't use a conventional backcast with the line straightening behind the casting position to load the rod for the forward cast. The backstroke motion or setup of the Spey cast throws the line to the rear, but the tip of the line and leader remain in contact with the water. Only a minimal amount of line passes behind the casting position, forming a loop from the rod tip to the surface. The momentum of the line moving to the rear combined with the drape of the line from its tip load the rod for the forward delivery. While in a normal Spey cast some line passes behind the casting position, adjustments can be made so that virtually no line goes past that point. (See the photo sequence on pages 26 and 27.)

Although there are some similarities to a roll cast, a Spey cast generally has less line in contact with the water and greater line speed generated by using two hands. Always practice without a hook and wear glasses to protect your eyes. Since a Spey cast can generate high line speed, make sure the line is moving in a direction that is not on a collision course with your body. This is especially a concern in live fishing situations. Pinch down the barb just in case the worst happens.

One of the most difficult aspects of learning to Spey cast is getting the feel for the acceleration and proper rod movement to form the D loop. If you leave slack in the line at the start of the forward Spey, a portion of your casting movement will simply be used to pick up the slack, which wastes energy and reduces the power of the casting motion. If you raise the rod upright when forming the D loop, the line moves in a plane that is too close to your casting position. Raising the rod also frees up too much line, creating slack and making it difficult to establish a proper anchor point.

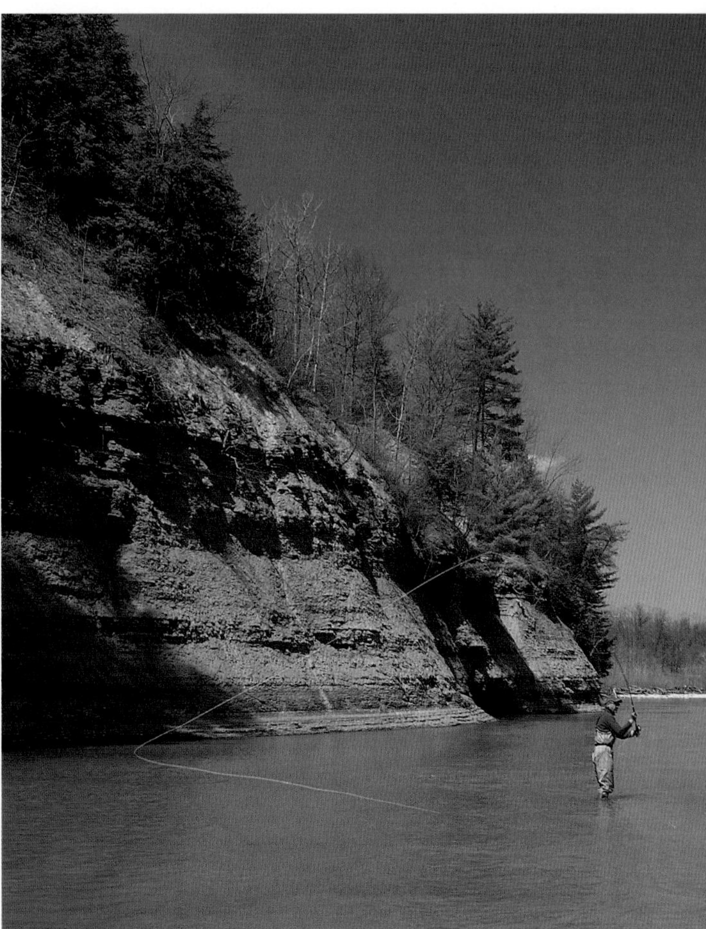

When looking at a Spey cast from the side, the rod forms the straight line of the capital letter D, and the drape of the line to the water completes the formation of the letter. The most energy-efficient D loop forms more of a point in the line as opposed to a smooth curve. A D loop that forms an angle has more energy, which loads the rod deeper and makes casting easier. NICK PIONESSA PHOTO

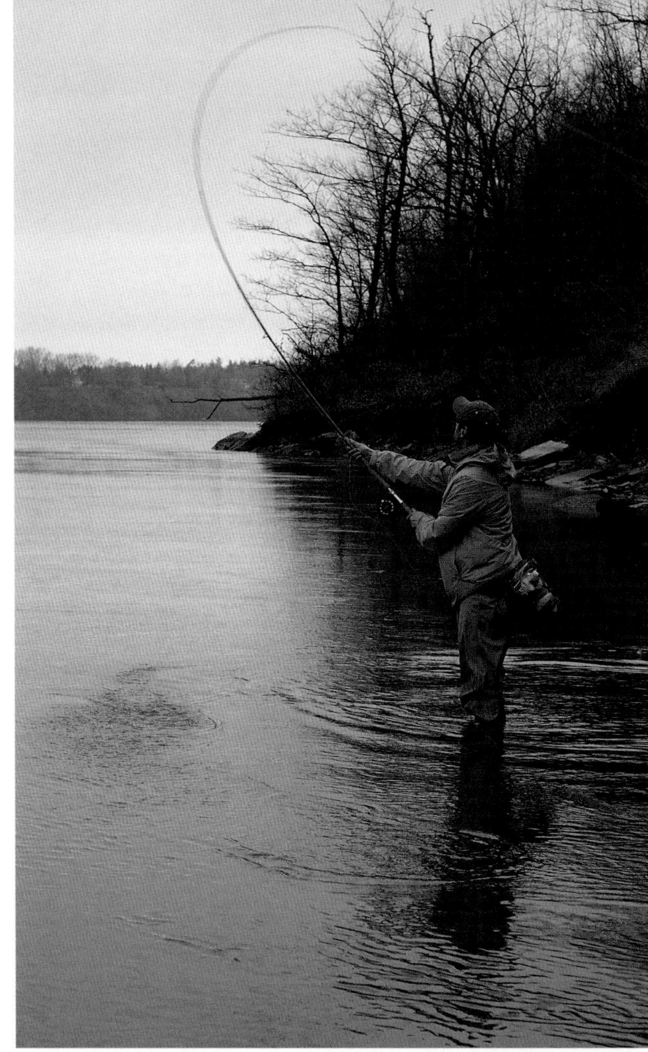

A good D loop allows a two-handed rod to load deep into the butt section, which creates power in the cast. NICK PIONESSA PHOTO

The anchor point is the point where the line and leader meet and remain on the water to form the D loop and create resistance for the forward stroke. The anchor point should be approximately a rod's length away at a 45-degree angle from the casting position. It is extremely important to keep the anchor point well to the side of your body. In other words, when you cast with your right hand up or off the right shoulder, the anchor point should be a good rod's length off to the right. When casting, I always keep a close eye on my anchor point position. Before I start a forward stroke I want to make absolutely sure that the line is not set up to collide with my rod or body. If it is, abort the cast and start over.

If you do not lift the rod to begin the rearward stroke or if you keep the rod flat throughout, too much line will rest on the water's surface. The anchor point will extend well out in front of the intended target zone, and the resistance caused by the line on the water will make it impossible for an efficient forward stroke.

Focus on freeing the line to start the D-loop stroke and set it up with an accelerated sweeping movement with the rod ending up at eleven o'clock. Analyze each cast to ensure that the anchor has set in the proper spot and there is sufficient energy in the D loop. Make adjustments as necessary. Forming a proper D loop is the foundation for each and every Spey cast.

When the rod stops and the D loop is formed, the momentum is used to power the forward stroke. You might want to pause slightly prior to moving the rod forward or you might want a continuous movement, first sweeping back and then rolling right into the forward cast. Casting style and rigging determine whether to pause. Using weighted flies and heavy sinking-tips will require a more continuous movement to prevent the fly and tip from sinking. If the fly or line sinks too much below the surface, excess resistance is created and it becomes impossible to complete the cast.

Before beginning the forward stroke, make sure that the anchor point is properly positioned and all of the fly line is pointing in the direction of the cast. Make the forward Spey by pushing forward with your top hand and pulling in with your bottom hand. Accelerate the rod through the stroke, stopping abruptly at one or two o'clock. Greater acceleration can be gained by being heavy on the lower hand. It is fairly difficult for casters with years of experience casting a single-handed rod to grasp this idea initially. More reliance on the top hand will generally result in slow line speed and a more open casting loop. Efficient use of the bottom hand can result in a much more compact casting loop that flies farther and is more effective in the wind.

Training your mind and body to consistently perform the forward Spey, in my opinion, is the most important step to becoming a proficient Spey caster. Practice this motion until you have committed it to muscle memory, and all the various Spey casts will be much easier to learn and use in fishing situations.

Shooting Line

Learn the forward Spey simply by casting the head of the line. Once you can do that proficiently, you'll have enough line speed and momentum to propel the head a significant distance as it pulls loose running line through the guides. To shoot line, pull 20 to 30 feet or more from the reel and rest it on the water's surface near your legs. Position the head past the tip of the rod and pinch the running line with the index and middle finger of your upper hand.

As you make the forward stroke and stop the rod at the one to two o'clock position, lift the index and middle fingers of your upper hand off the cork to free the running line to travel through the guides. Greater line speed and a more compact casting loop allow you to cast farther. Shooting line is critical when fishing since it allows you to cover big water. The running line can lie on the water's surface during most fishing situations. However, if you are standing in heavy current, the tension caused by the downriver movement of the water can act as resistance to the running line, hindering the ability to shoot through the guides. This occurs even in moderate current when casting long distances with great lengths of running line. One way to offset this problem is to form a couple loose coils with the running line and hold them in your lower hand. Pinch the running line against the lower cork and release it as the line pulls through the guides. This takes some timing and coordination but is useful in certain situations.

Forward Spey

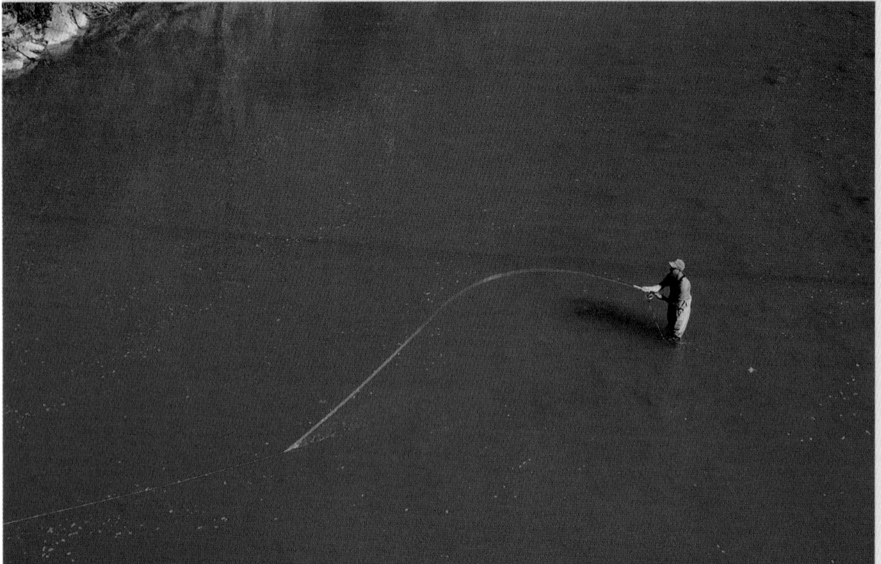

Start the forward Spey by getting the head of the fly line beyond the tip. Allow the fly line that is beyond the tip of the rod to rest on the water, and move the rod back and forth parallel to the water's surface while taking line from the reel to work the full head of the line beyond the tip. Roll cast to straighten the line.

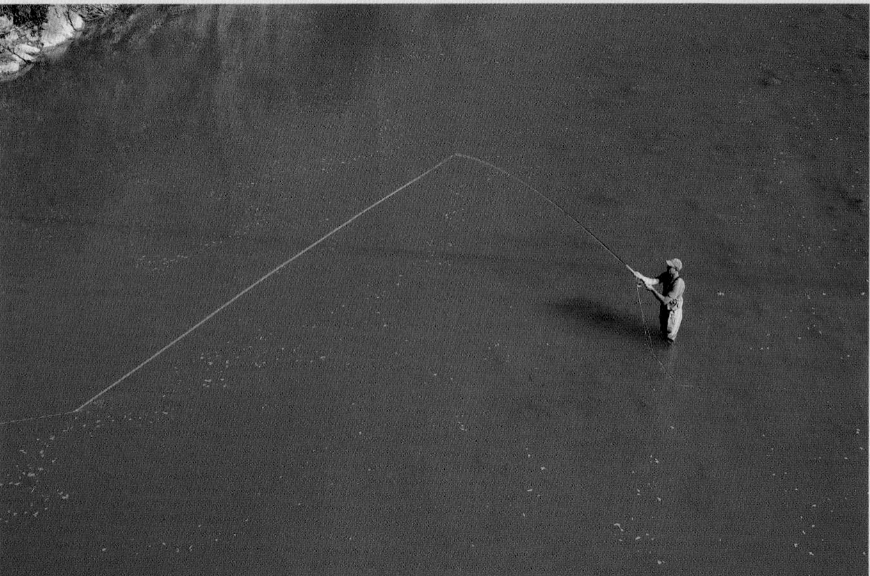

Position the rod tip low to the water with little or no slack, and putting your weight on your front foot, slowly lift the rod to free the line from the water's surface.

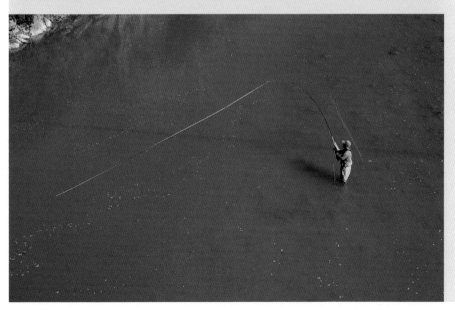

Sweep the rod off to the side using a fairly flat movement. This angle will help place the anchor point—the point where the line and leader meet and remain on the water to form the D loop—away from the body. The rod should never dip during the stroke.

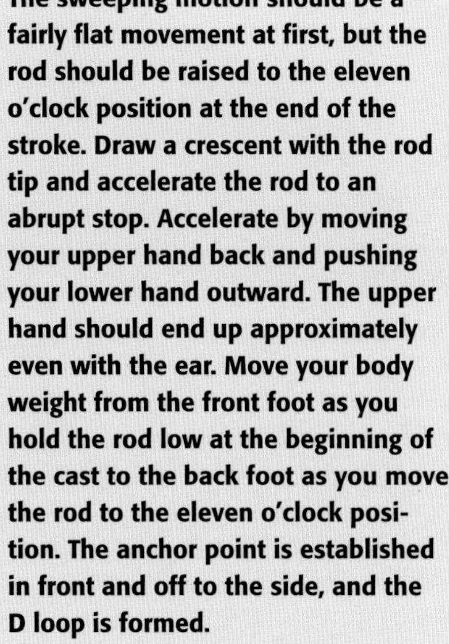

The sweeping motion should be a fairly flat movement at first, but the rod should be raised to the eleven o'clock position at the end of the stroke. Draw a crescent with the rod tip and accelerate the rod to an abrupt stop. Accelerate by moving your upper hand back and pushing your lower hand outward. The upper hand should end up approximately even with the ear. Move your body weight from the front foot as you hold the rod low at the beginning of the cast to the back foot as you move the rod to the eleven o'clock position. The anchor point is established in front and off to the side, and the D loop is formed.

Accelerate through the forward stroke, pulling the bottom hand in toward the body to help create a tight casting loop. Shift your body weight to the front foot during the forward stroke.

NICK PIONESSA PHOTOS

Single Spey

While the forward Spey is an integral part of every version of a Spey cast, it doesn't address one of the main objectives of this form of casting—change of direction. The single Spey does provide for a change in direction. It is fairly simple and very efficient. When performed properly it is also quite powerful. However, its efficiency requires more acute timing than other Spey casts, and beginners may find it slightly more difficult to learn. (See the photo sequence on pages 29 and 30.)

Use the single Spey with your right hand up when fishing river left (while looking downriver), or when the current is moving from right to left. Use it on river right with your left hand up. Proficient anglers use this cast from either bank to maximize fishing time.

Each Spey cast begins after the fly has swung out and is hanging down. The key is placing the rod in the eleven o'clock position while at the same time putting enough energy in the line to create a D loop that will adequately load the rod. A good anchor point and D loop are essential. As the forward stroke begins, line, rod tip, and fly should be lined up in the same plane in the direction of the cast.

Always set up the fly and anchor a rod's length upriver from your casting position before beginning the forward stroke. When you raise the rod at the beginning of the cast, continue with the cast immediately. A pause at this point allows the line to sag back to the water's surface and creates too much line resistance to set up the cast. Use a fairly flat rod movement to create the smooth curve of the trough, dipping the rod and raising it to the eleven o'clock position. Stop the rod near the eleven o'clock position—allowing it to drift too far back will steal energy from the D loop. The movement to set up the D loop and anchor point takes timing and practice.

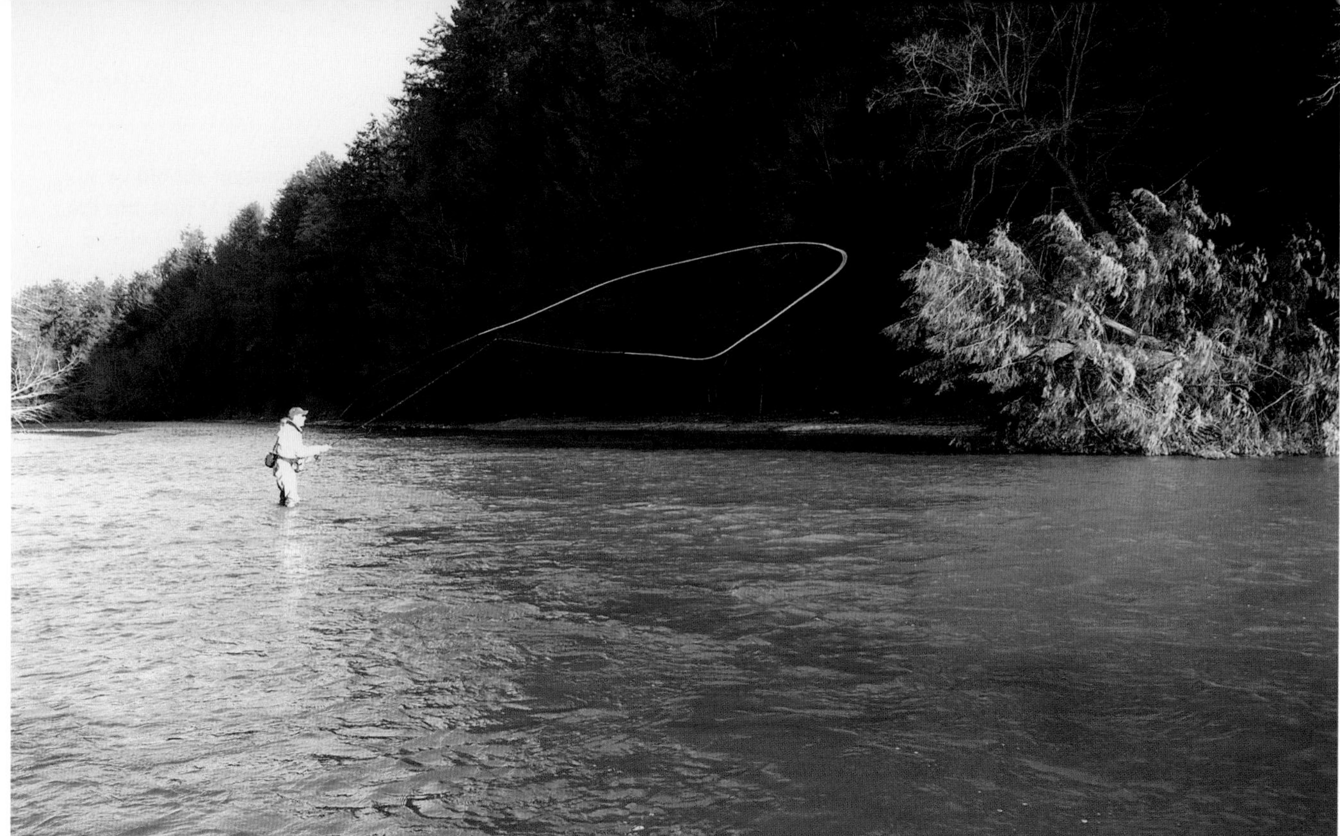

With a well-timed forward stroke, the momentum of the head of the fly line will shoot the loose running line to create a long cast.

When learning a new cast, the key is concentrating on the setup. Pay close attention to the mechanics of the setup on the change-of-direction Spey casts. Turn your body slightly to take a look at the D loop to see if it is forming properly. A poor cast is often the result of a poor D loop.

Double Spey

The double Spey (pages 31 to 33) may sound like more work than the single Spey, but it is actually an easier cast to learn. The extra movement of the rod reduces the acute timing you need in the single Spey. You use the double Spey with your right hand up when fishing river right, or when the current is moving from left to right. When fishing river left, your left hand is up.

Be sure that the rod tip stays high and draws a straight line as your upper hand starts to move across your body for the forward stroke. If the rod tip is too low or it dips, the line will stick and the fly will remain too far below the anchor point position. An acceleration that's too aggressive will put the fly dangerously above your casting position. Never attempt to finish a cast when the fly is even with or upriver from your casting position. Start the rod low when you begin to draw the crescent and accelerate into the D loop. If the tip starts too high, you won't have sufficient energy for the D loop.

Snap T

An alternative to the single Spey for fishing with your right hand up on river left is the snap T. The snap T requires an extra move, but the timing isn't as critical, so the snap T is a good option for novice casters. It is also a good cast for handling heavy sinking-tips. (See pages 35 to 37.)

This cast requires a bit of patience in the setup. The cast generally works best with a slight pause between the end of the setup and the beginning of the forward stroke as it takes extra time for the D loop to fully form.

The first phase of the cast is critical. At the beginning of the cast, as you lift the rod to one o'clock, draw the tip in a straight line. Then as the rod pushes out toward the opposite bank, the tip should move upstream until it is approximately even with your upstream shoulder. Next, with an exaggerated acceleration, move the rod tip down and back upriver, drawing a line underneath where the tip was after the initial rise of the rod. After you lift the rod just past vertical, visualize drawing a backward C with your right hand up for the proper travel path for the rod tip (or a forward C with your left hand up).

This C-shaped movement will control how far the line and fly land upstream of your casting position. Too wide a C—taking the rod tip beyond the upstream side of your body—will place the line well upstream of your casting position, making it difficult to line up the fly line on the setup. Too shallow a C and the fly will not travel above your casting position. Anytime this happens, start over. I like to draw a slightly wider C to place the fly just above the anchor point area since the current will bring the fly downriver to the desired position. Always keep an eye on the fly and know where it is before beginning the forward stroke.

The cadence of this cast is key: The first phase requires a quick, aggressive movement and then a brief stop. The setup then requires a strong acceleration to form a deep D loop. Then, allow the D loop to fully form before pounding out the forward stroke.

Single Spey

Start the single Spey with the tip low and rod, line, and fly lined up in the same plane. Strip the running line back so that just the head of the line extends past the rod tip.

Lift the rod to free the line from the water's surface.

With the line freed, the rod points to the sky.

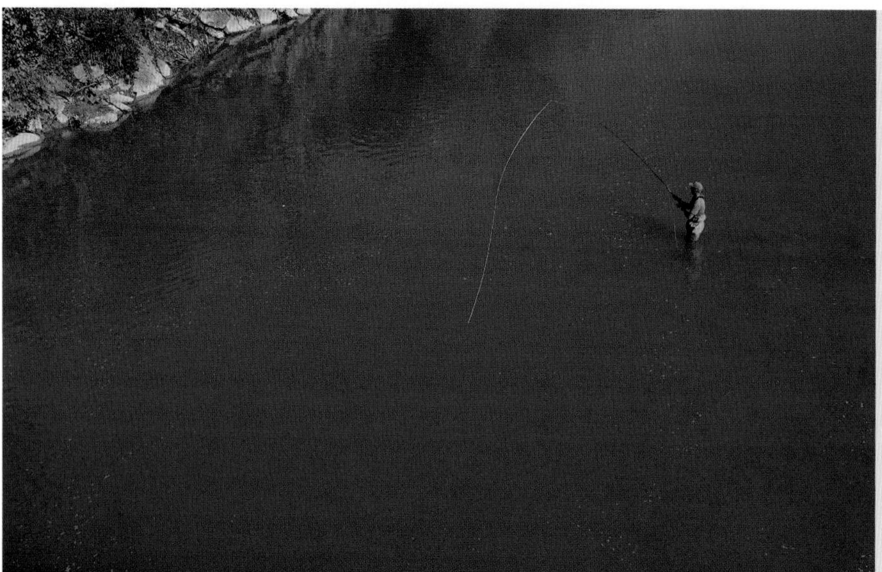

Dip the rod tip while moving across and in front of the casting position. Move the rod in an accelerating and sweeping fashion, reaching a trough in the dip when it is directly in front of you, and then sweeping it faster, up into the eleven o'clock position.

This movement should free all the line from the water, splashing it down and forming the D loop. As the line splashes on the water's surface, it should be pointing in the direction of the target.

Begin the forward stroke immediately. Complete the forward cast using a heavy bottom hand.

NICK PIONESSA PHOTOS

Double Spey

Start the double Spey with the rod tip low. Strip in running line so that only the head of the line extends past the tip.

Lift the rod tip so that it points to the sky, freeing the line.

With the rod pointing away from your casting position, draw a straight line across the horizon, moving your upper hand across your body in an accelerated movement.

When your upper arm is fully extended across your body, drop the rod parallel to the water, pointing upriver. At this point the fly line lies on the water lined up with the direction of the current, and the fly is positioned at or near the anchor point.

Bring the rod back across your body with a flat movement.

Accelerate throughout the movement.

Draw a crescent with the rod tip as it accelerates into the eleven o'clock position. The rod should never dip as it moves into position, and the acceleration should rip the line that lies in front of your casting position into a powerful D loop.

With the line pointing toward the target and the D loop formed, begin the forward cast.

Finish using an accelerated forward stroke.

NICK PIONESSA PHOTOS

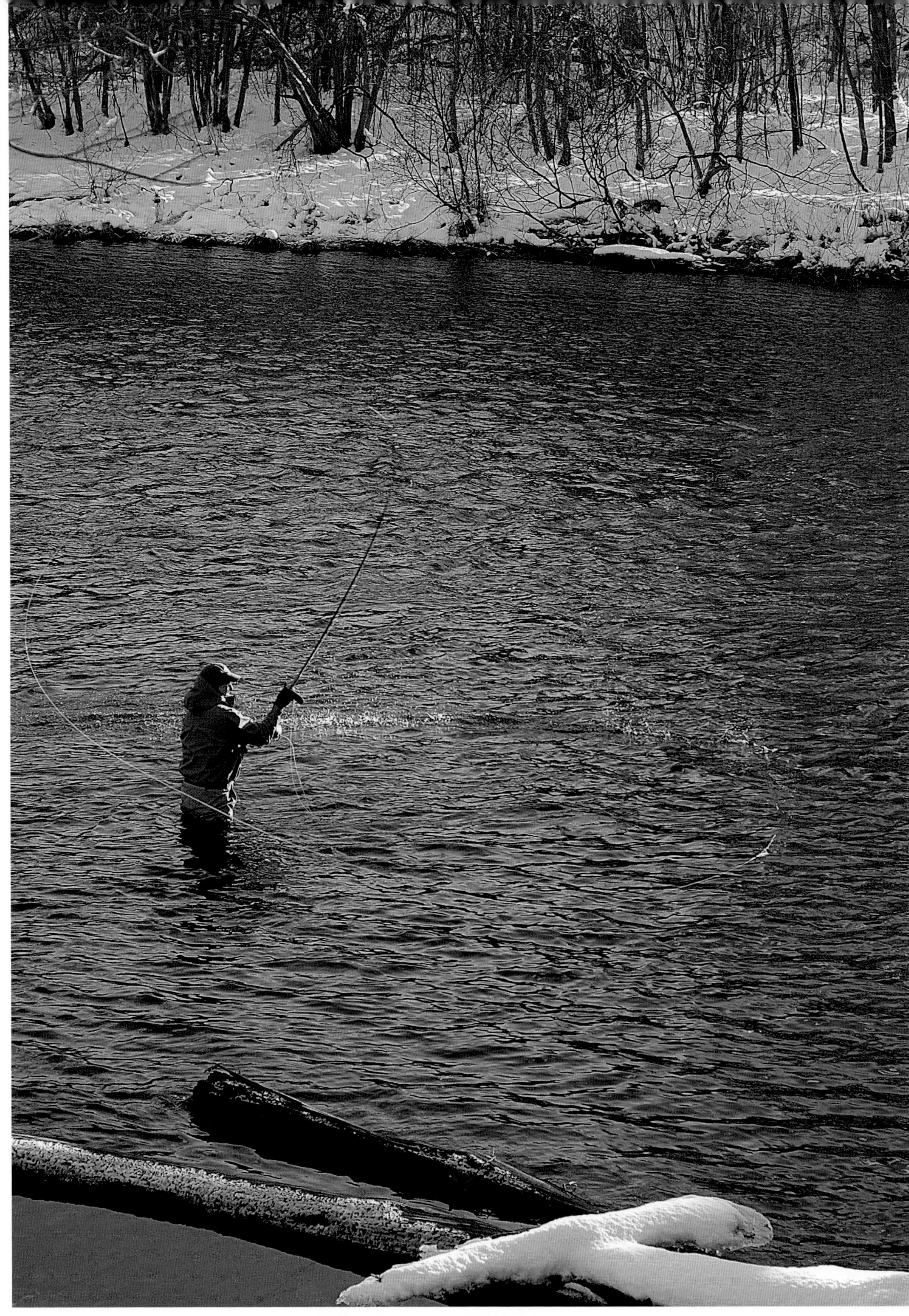

I rip the line across the surface to finish a double Spey cast. NICK PIONESSA PHOTO

Snap T

Start the snap T with the rod low, the line tight, and the tip pointing downstream.

Slowly lift the rod until the tip is angled toward the sky but remaining in a downstream direction.

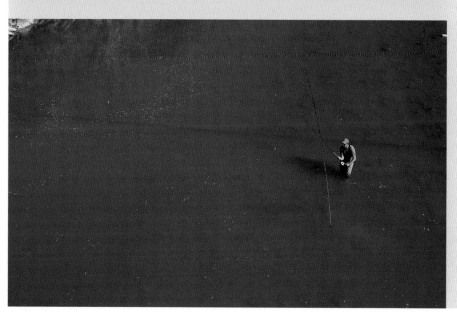

When the rod is nearly vertical, push the tip out toward the opposite bank while accelerating slightly past vertical. Then push the rod down with a quick, accelerated motion or snap in a downstream direction angled toward the near bank.

The movement ends with the rod low and parallel to the water with the fly upstream of the casting position, placing the fly near the anchor point.

After the fly has hit the water, draw the tip of the rod across your body in a flat, low movement, never allowing the rod to dip. The rod tip should ride low across your body. If the rod tip is too high as it moves across, it will lift line from the water and the D loop will lose energy.

Once the rod tip clears your body on the upstream side, raise the rod to the eleven o'clock position. This movement should be a strong acceleration that rips the line off the water and generates a D loop with sufficient energy.

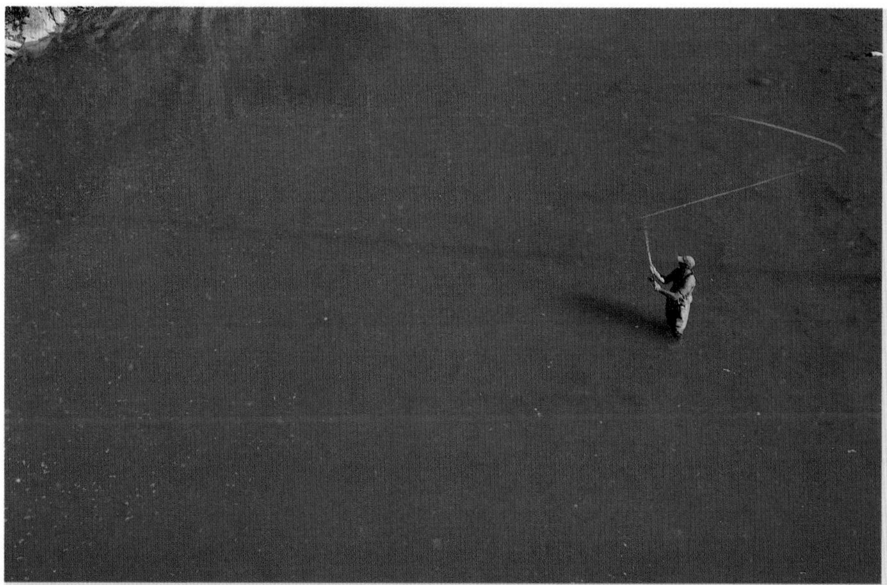

With the line pointing toward the target and the D loop formed, begin the forward stroke after pausing slightly.

Complete the cast by accelerating and using the bottom hand.

NICK PIONESSA PHOTOS

Snake Roll

The snake roll (pages 39 and 40) is an alternative to the double Spey when fishing with your right hand up on river right or with your left hand up on river left. It is a more efficient cast than the double Spey, placing the fly back in the water in much less time than the double Spey. It is also a stealthier cast that creates less disturbance on the water. But the snake roll is bit more difficult to perform when using a heavy sinking-tip and a weighted fly.

The efficiency of the snake roll is born from its simplicity. To start the cast, angle the rod with the tip pointing downriver. Too steep of an angle with the rod and there will be no power in the D loop, but if the angle is too low, the fly and anchor point will end up well downstream of the desired area. Some trial and error will be required to get a feel for the proper circumference of the round portion of the "e" that you draw with your rod tip. Too small an "e" and too much line will remain on the water to form a proper D loop. If the "e" is too large, the line and anchor will end up behind your casting position.

I like the simplicity of the snake roll and use it often when fishing a lighter tip. I also use this versatile cast to change directions with a single-handed rod when dead-drifting a fly.

Perry Poke

There are more Spey casts and variations of these casts than those discussed above. However, these basic casts allow you to meet almost any fishing situation found in the Great Lakes. One additional movement that can be quite helpful in successfully completing the above casts is the Perry poke. The Perry poke isn't actually a cast itself but is an add-on to a standard cast. I use this movement when a cast doesn't set up properly or when fishing confined areas.

Setting up a snap T.

When using the Perry poke with one of the above casts, the setup is the same except that you use less power to set up the initial D loop. Instead of making a full forward stroke, you drop the rod weakly in the same direction as if making a full stroke. This should form a long, narrow section of slack line on the surface. At this point you form a full D loop with a flat, accelerating movement, raising the rod to eleven o'clock just as you do in the forward Spey. A full forward stroke that begins just as the D loop is completing its formation will send the line out with power.

The Perry poke works well when you have made a mistake in the mechanics of the setup—instead of aborting the cast and starting over, this move can safely keep a cast alive. You can even do it two or three times in succession until the fly line and anchor point line up for a proper cast.

I commonly use the Perry poke when fishing with a gorge wall or trees right up against my back. To fish one of my favorite rivers requires making 50- to 60-foot casts with very little fly line passing behind my casting position because of a steep rock wall and no wading room. To use the Perry poke in this situation, I start with a single or double Spey that forms a soft D loop where the line passes just slightly behind my casting position. The soft D loop is formed by holding back on the acceleration during the setup. With the single Spey, however, it is still critical to free enough line to place the fly above the casting position. Once the D-loop is formed I make a subdued forward stroke. This stroke has more energy than simply laying the rod forward as described in the paragraph above, as it sends the line out far enough to set up the anchor point about 20 feet or so beyond the casting position and off to the side. Now I can set up a full D loop from this new anchor point back to the casting position without any line passing behind me. A full forward stroke completes the cast.

No matter where you fish, you'll find circumstances that prevent a full D loop. Using the Perry poke makes your casting more versatile, and you'll usually be able to cast in even the tightest areas.

Roll Cast

As a fly completes the swing in moderate to heavy currents, the flow pushing against a tight line brings a sinking-tip and fly to the surface. However, when the line swings into a soft, slow current, the fly may sink deeper, and without the push of current, it can be very difficult to raise a sinking-tip and fly out of the water on the initial part of the cast without the assistance of the current.

You can use a simple roll cast to bring the fly to the surface, and then begin any standard Spey cast. The roll cast used in this context is not a complete and separate cast but rather, like the Perry poke, an additional movement in the setup.

Perform the roll cast by lifting the rod up to the one o'clock position, accelerating back to eleven o'clock, and driving the rod forward with your bottom hand, stopping the rod at ten o'clock. This movement will not form a D loop like a forward Spey, as the line will barely move behind your casting position. But by raising the rod, you should free enough line from the water's surface that it doesn't create too much tension. The rod tip should move in a straight line during the forward stroke to generate enough power to lift the line off the water so that

Snake Roll

Start the snake roll with the rod angled low and pointed downstream.

Angle the rod slightly toward the near bank. Raise the rod slowly but continue to accelerate throughout the setup of the cast.

Draw a lowercase e with the rod tip (or a backward "e" if your left hand is up) to pull the fly to the anchor point.

Finish the "e" by continuing with a tail that brings the rod to the eleven o'clock position. A continued acceleration throughout the setup will create a deep D loop and sufficiently load the rod.

With the snake roll there is nearly no pause between the setup and forward stroke. The line should hit the water to set the anchor as you lift the rod to eleven o'clock.

The forward stroke should be made instantaneously.

NICK PIONESSA PHOTOS

the line extends itself all the way out to the fly. With the rod tip moving in a straight line, a tight loop is formed, which will stretch the line so that it will be tight to begin the Spey cast.

The roll cast should be made downstream without any attempt to change directions. Stop the forward cast at ten o'clock to form the casting loop, but then drop the rod low to begin the Spey cast. Begin the cast as soon as the line hits the water after completing the roll, before the tip and fly begin to sink. The roll cast will work best with lines that have shorter heads, and it is extremely useful for preparing the line to begin a Spey cast or to reposition the line if a cast has to be abandoned because it was set up improperly.

Practice

All these movements and casts require practice in order to become proficient enough to take them live with a fly on a steelhead river. Prior to learning to Spey cast I wasn't one to practice my casting to any large degree. But repetition and developing muscle memory are essential for learning to Spey cast.

These casts are best practiced on moving water. A perfect practice area allows you to easily move from one side of the river to the other so that you can practice all the casts.

You can practice effectively on stillwater. You can perfect the rhythm of the forward Spey with either hand up on a lake or pond. I practice on stillwater by making a series of 90-degree Spey casts using the casts described above and alternating which hand is up. It is best to practice this way with a floating line since there is no current to assist in keeping a sinking-tip at the surface. You can also practice on grass using a long leader developed for this purpose. This type of leader is knotted with long tag ends on the knot to create resistance on grass and simulate loading the rod in the same manner as line loads on the water. This isn't nearly as good as practicing on water, but it is a reasonable substitute when it's the only option. Always practice with yarn or a fly with the hook point cut off.

Adjusting to Fishing Conditions

Learning to Spey cast under fairly controlled conditions doesn't always prepare you for the variables you'll encounter on a steelhead river. We all typically select days to practice when the winds are light to moderate, and we find areas where we can wade knee deep or less. While these conditions are ideal for learning, actual fishing situations can be frustrating. By paying close attention to the conditions, you can make adjustments that will result in more productive presentations and reduce the possibility of physical injury.

The depth of the water has a noticeable impact on casting. While it is easiest to Spey cast in water that is calf deep, I often fish in water that is up to my thighs. This position can allow for covering more water and allows the fly to swing into deeper flows and remain there on the hang down. This increases the amount of holding water that the fly is fishing through. But wading in deeper water reduces the two-handed rod's leverage advantage.

When my casting begins to fall apart, it is almost always because of water depth. I raise my arms slightly when setting up the cast to gain back some of the lost length. But the most important step to take to combat wading depth is to make very precise, flat movements to set up the D loop. I have to be careful not to make any sloppy casting movements. Since the reduced leverage allows more line to rest on the surface, I need to make slightly stronger, more accelerated movements to set up the cast. Lines with shorter heads also make it a bit easier to fish in deeper water. When I know I will be wading deep most of the day, I may also opt for a longer two-hander to gain back some of the leverage.

Another factor that creates a casting challenge is wind. The essential rule when Spey casting in windy conditions is to keep the anchor point off the downwind shoulder. When the wind is blowing against your dominant shoulder, for safety's sake the choices are to cast with your opposite hand up or to cast with the rod finishing the setup across your body. In other

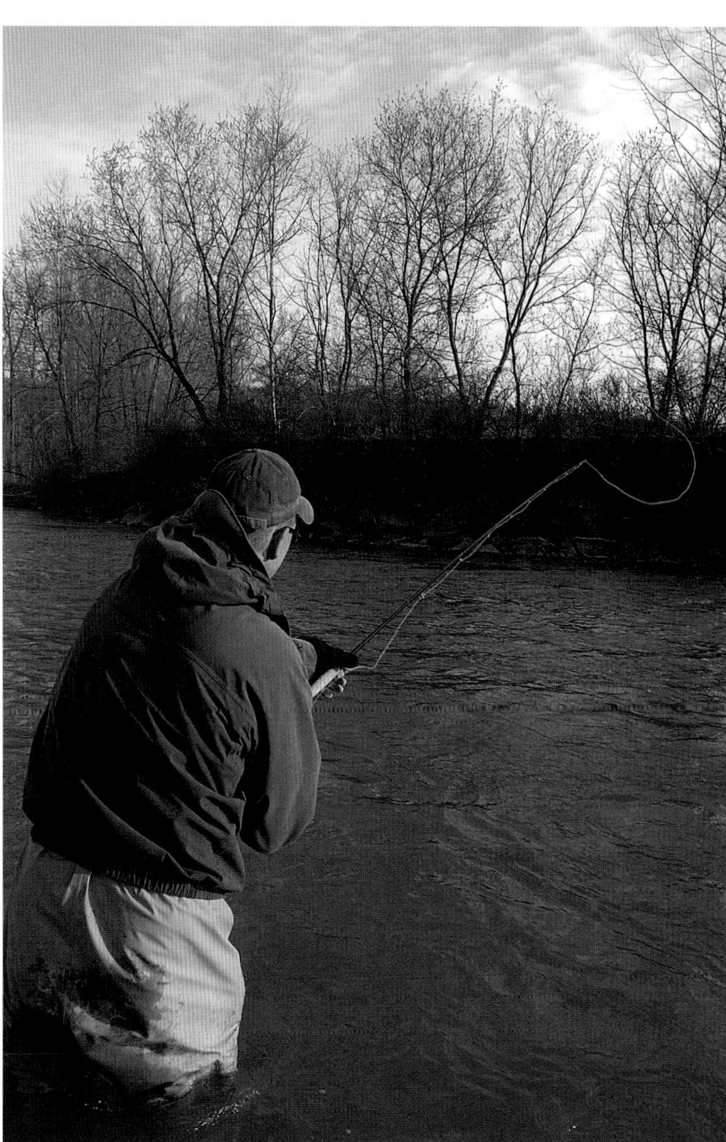

With a stiff breeze blowing on my dominant shoulder, I deliver the cast with my off hand up. NICK PIONESSA PHOTO

Nick Pionessa makes a backhanded cast on a windy spring day.

words, form the D loop off your left shoulder with your right hand up and vice versa. Some casters can do a cross-body or backhanded cast quite effectively. But using the opposite hand up seems to generate more power and distance and is my preference for dealing with the wind, especially when fishing bigger water.

Learning to cast with the nondominant hand up takes some practice. It is a bit like learning to Spey cast all over again. But the dominant hand plays such an important role in the lower position that relying on a strong bottom hand to move inward can greatly control the cast and the upper nondominant hand can act more as a guide. Also, the rhythm you learned with the dominant hand up on the basic cast carries over to having the opposite hand up and greatly shortens the learning curve.

But backhanded casting does have its place and is probably the simplest solution to dealing with an on-shoulder wind for a beginning caster. Since the forward stroke is the same, but just angled across the body, most casters can quickly adjust to this approach, especially when using shorter heads. The key is understanding the setup so that the anchor point ends up downwind of the body. With the right hand up, the cast setup will be made in the same manner as if with the left hand up. In other words, from river right you use a snap T and from river left a double Spey to set up the cast. This is opposite for backhanded casting with the left hand up. I tend to use backhanded casting when fishing smaller waters with a switch rod or light two-handed rod.

Current speed impacts the initial movement to begin the setup. A stronger current will help lift the line and fly to the surface as you raise the rod to start the cast. Current speed is an especially important factor when using a heavy tip or a heavy fly. In slower water speed, where the fly often ends up, it will take additional effort to get a heavy tip or fly moving into the setup. The roll cast is effective, but since it is an added movement it takes more time to make the cast. The other option is to start with the rod tip nearly touching the water, raise the rod, and use a little extra force and acceleration during the first movement of the cast. It will take a sense of feel to find the right amount of force.

One of the most challenging aspects of Spey casting is the constantly changing factors that impact the cast. These factors force a Spey caster to be in tune with the river and to create a greater connection than when fishing with a single-hander.

Single-Handed Rod Tips

Presenting the fly with either the dead-drift approach or the wet-fly swing requires at least some change in direction because of the movement of the current. There are few simple tricks you can use when fishing with a single-handed rod to make the cast more efficient and effective.

Dead Drift

The dead-drift approach typically requires short-range casts with additional weight and an indicator attached to the leader. When making an overhead cast with this type of rig, a longer pause on the backcast allows the leader to fully straighten out and positions the rod for a successful forward cast. Lifting the rod slightly before beginning the backcast will free the line, lift the leader, and allow you to make the backcast without expending so much energy. Make the forward cast with a larger arc and a slower acceleration at the beginning, slightly overpowering at the end to create a tuck cast.

When fishing in confined areas or to more efficiently cover the water, use a roll cast for presenting a dead-drifted fly. Longer rods will assist in making a roll cast since they help remove a greater amount of line from the surface of the water. As with Spey casting, too much line on the surface will create excessive tension and make the cast less efficient. When working with a fairly short line, say 20 to 30 feet, which is common when dead-drifting a fly, a slight change in direction can be made with a roll cast. The more the cast is angled upstream, the less change in direction will be required to make the next cast.

The key to an efficient roll cast is in the forward stroke. The roll cast has typically been taught to conclude with a big, open arc in order to remove all the line from the water. It is much more efficient to raise the rod, bring it back to eleven o'clock, and without a pause begin the forward stroke before too much fly line settles back to the surface. The forward stroke should be more compact; you should smoothly accelerate and stop the rod abruptly at one or two o'clock. Make the change of direction by bringing the rod to the eleven o'clock position and sweeping the fly line so that it lines it up with the target. Complete any modifications you need to make during the forward stroke to guide the cast in the intended direction.

Wet-Fly Swing

The 90-degree change of direction the wet-fly swing requires is a bit more labor-intensive with a single-handed rod than with a two-hander. This is especially true when using a longer line. But there are a few tricks that can make the task easier. Using a line with a longer belly, like those marketed as steelhead or salmon tapers, aids in picking up line off the surface after the swing is complete. The longer belly will also make it easier to carry more line in the air.

The key to the cast is line pickup. Line should be stripped back only to a point where the entire head of the line is still past the rod tip. For shorter casts where the head of the line is inside the tip, do not strip any line at all. The rod tip should start low, almost touching the water's surface. The backcast starts with a steady acceleration to an abrupt stop at eleven o'clock. The tension of the line on the water helps load the rod but also poses a problem if enough power isn't generated to free it from the surface. To overcome this obstacle, haul on the line by moving your line hand straight down to greatly increase the power and velocity of the backcast. This allows the rod to stop at eleven o'clock with the line remaining parallel to the water.

Swinging a fly on a New York tributary to Lake Erie.
NICK PIONESSA PHOTO

The roll cast is effective when working with a short line.
NICK PIONESSA PHOTO

In order to complete the 90-degree change, you'll need to make one or two false casts. Each backcast and forward cast should change the angle by 20 to 30 degrees. On the initial backcast, you should begin to pick up line as though the line will stay on a straight plane, but complete the movement by sweeping the rod slightly so that the final movement throws the line on a slight angle. One of the principles of casting is that the line will follow the direction of the rod tip when it comes to a stop. Each back and forward stroke changes the direction of the cast slightly, completing the 90-degree angle with the final forward cast. A haul on both the back and forward casts keeps the line speed high and delivers the fly with a straight line and leader.

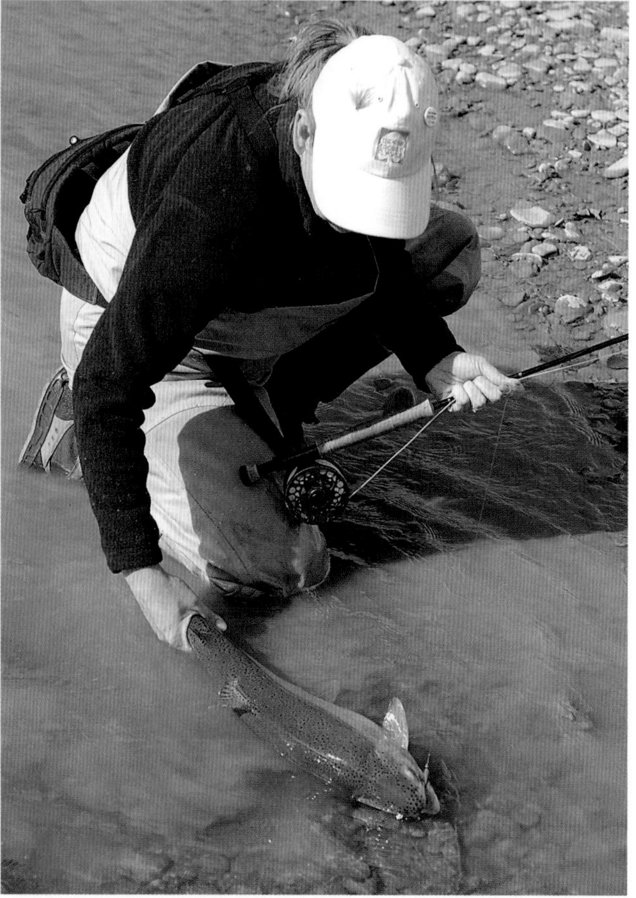

Above: **Using one-handed Spey techniques to cover the tail-out of a pool.** ***Left:*** **Suzanne Pionessa tails a nice steelhead.**
NICK PIONESSA PHOTO

Single-Handed Spey Techniques

While fly presentation can be managed with the techniques above, learning Spey casting movements will prove extremely beneficial when fishing with a single-handed rod. Almost every Spey cast can be made with a single-handed rod, which not only creates a more efficient delivery, but also is a significant advantage on smaller streams and rivers with no backcasting room. Even if you don't need to cast a long distance, you can use Spey techniques to maneuver around almost any obstacle.

I find myself using bits and pieces of Spey casts almost every time I use a single-handed rod, no matter what species I am pursuing. For example, I may use the first part of a snake roll to get the line in the air for an overhead cast or use the single Spey instead of a roll cast to deliver a dead-drift presentation.

It is nearly impossible to Spey cast as far with a single-handed rod as with a two-hander because of the leverage of the longer rod and the efficient use of both hands. But you can create line speed and significant distance by forming a good D loop and hauling on the line during the forward stroke. Lines with short heads and aggressive front tapers work best with one-handed Spey casting. There are a few lines on the market designed for single-handed Spey casting. A good option is a Skagit line that balances with the single-handed rod.

CHAPTER 3

Techniques

An angler selects his technique for fishing small, intimate steelhead pools. NICK PIONESSA PHOTO

The fly-fishing techniques that are successful for steelhead in the Great Lakes region are quite varied. Most of the techniques used in the region originated on inland trout streams or Atlantic salmon rivers. Adaptations to these techniques have been made to meet the demands of the region's rivers and streams. And advancements in the technology of rods and lines have allowed new twists or greater refinement of existing technique.

The techniques used for steelhead can roughly be divided into two categories—those that attempt to present a fly with the natural drift of the current and those that present a fly that moves and swings in the current. Some techniques tend to be more effective under certain conditions purely from a hookup standpoint. In my opinion, certain techniques are more enjoyable to fish and master and create a more complete experience even if they result in fewer fish brought to hand. This chapter looks at all aspects of presenting a fly for Great Lakes steelhead.

Dead Drift

Many food sources for fish inhabiting rivers and streams are simply swept along with the current. Eggs, nymphs, and other forms of aquatic life that are injured, dead, or can't control their movement in the water are carried along with the current. The dead-drift technique replicates this natural movement by drifting a fly in a manner that moves freely with the current. But attaining a dead drift at the proper depth can be more difficult than it sounds. Rigging, casting, and line manipulation are all important elements for the dead-drift approach.

The dead-drift approach works well when fishing smaller streams, for pocketwater and short runs, and for colder water temperatures. A dead-drift fly is accessible to a fish—a fish does not have to move far to feed. For this reason, the dead-drift approach can be quite effective and can result in a high number of hookups when good numbers of fish are present. It is also a good way to get started fly fishing for steelhead.

Standard Dead-Drift Approach

The basic approach to dead-drifting a fly requires a long single-handed rod, preferably 10 feet in length, and a floating line with an exaggerated front taper that will easily turn over a weighted fly and weight on the leader. You'll commonly use a strike indicator when dead-drifting, which not only helps you detect a strike, but also aids in gauging the quality of the drift. The tip of a high-floating fly line can also act as an indicator. A low-diameter leader, as discussed in the equipment chapter, helps to slice through the current and encourage a more natural presentation.

The standard dead-drift approach covers water to 40 feet or so in front of the casting position. Beyond that length it becomes difficult to control the drift with a single-handed rod as too much line will rest on the water's surface. The surface currents pulling and pushing the fly line will inhibit the fly from drifting naturally with the current. Working with a shorter line is often preferred when dead-drift fishing because you'll have better line control. Stealthy wading can go a long way toward getting into proper position.

When using an indicator, place it on the upper end of the leader. An adjustable indicator that is easily moved up and down the leader provides the most versatility. The general rule of thumb is to place the indicator up the leader by approximately one and a half to two times the water depth. Most anglers prefer an indicator that rides high in the current and is easy to see in any type of water.

Weight added to the leader in the form of twist-on or split shot in combination with any weight on the fly allows the fly to efficiently reach the bottom zone of the current without hanging on the bottom. While there are a number of more complicated and cumbersome dropper systems for adding weight to the leader, placing the weight directly on the leader approximately 20 to 24 inches above the fly is the simplest. Always check the local regulations regarding adding weight to the leader because some rivers and states restrict the type of materials or placement.

Indicators come in the form of lightweight air-filled plastic, foam, cork, and yarn. Because of the light weight and resulting ease in casting, the plastic style has rapidly gained popularity. An eye on the indicator allows for an easy connection—thread a loop in the leader through the eye and over the indicator.

Begin the standard dead-drift approach by taking a position across from a suspected holding area. Cast up and across at about a 45-degree angle. The best cast for dead-drifting allows the fly and weight to contact the water before the fly line. This can be accomplished with a tuck cast, which is performed by overpowering the forward stroke. The extra energy transmitted to the end of the rod forces the tip downward at the end of the stroke, which in turn forces the end of the leader to point downward as well. Keep an upstream belly and some slack in the line as it rests on the water's surface by concluding the cast with an upstream reach or by making an upstream mend immediately when the line hits the water. The tuck and reach allow the fly to quickly attain the desired depth.

On smaller, brushier waters where backcasting room is limited or to make water coverage more efficient, a roll cast can be quite beneficial. With some practice, you'll be able to make the tuck and reach cast at the end of a roll cast. However, you can improve efficiency by using a single-handed Spey cast, which is also more powerful and more versatile than the roll cast. The strength of the Spey cast is the ability to easily change directions. And quick change of direction is a key element to covering water when using the standard dead-drift approach. After the cast is completed, manage the line to maintain some slack, which aids in retaining a dead drift. Start with the rod low and raise it as the fly drifts directly in front of your casting position. At this point, the fly should have attained the desired depth. With the rod at an angle to the water and your arm extended, anywhere from a foot or two up to 10 or 12 feet of fly line should rest on the water's surface. The drift continues to a point quartering downstream and is prolonged by lowering the rod tip and following the drift downstream.

During the drift, watch the indicator or tip section of the fly line closely to ensure that it moves at the same rate as the

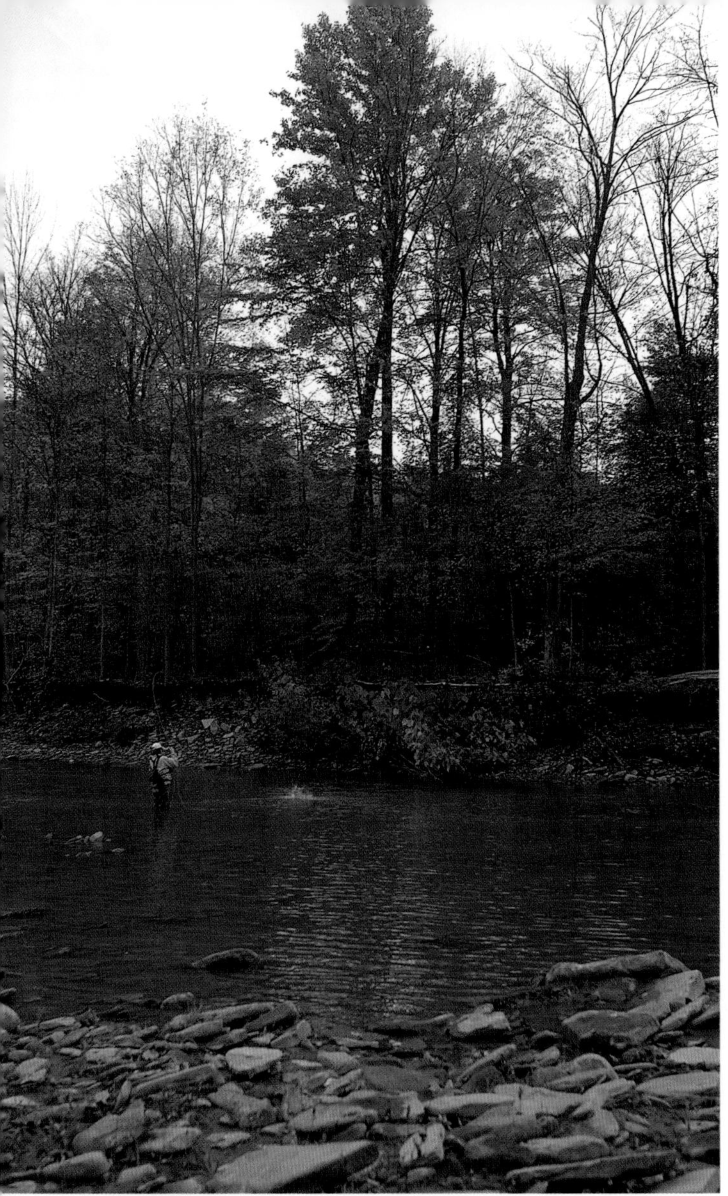

Proper line control is a key element to successful dead-drift presentations. NICK PIONESSA PHOTO

current. Mending and manipulating line are critical to maintain slack in the line and to avoid a downstream belly. This is the part of dead-drift fishing that is interactive and a bit challenging. Every drift is different. I prefer to limit mending unless necessary to reduce the possibility of disturbing the natural drift of the fly. An effective mend should reposition the line or add slack, all without moving the fly. Visualize the drift of the fly near the bottom of the river or stream. Keep in mind that the current at the surface will be faster than that along the bottom. Occasionally when fishing a plunge pool or pocket where the surface current is dramatically stronger than that below, a significant mend may be required to reposition the indicator.

A style of mending that can be used to add slack is referred to as stack mending. This type of mending will allow the fly to reach greater depths without adding more weight. It can also be used to extend the dead drift. Stack mending involves making a series of upstream mends while feeding additional line. Roll your wrist upstream while moving the tip of the rod upward to push slack line out. The effect is that slack fly line

A wild steelhead that fell for a dead-drifted fly.
NICK PIONESSA PHOTO

piles or stacks in a way that releases all tension from the leader and fly. You can use stack mending in most dead-drift situations—it is an approach that creates an efficient, long presentation as it allows the fly to attain natural drifts well below the casting position.

In direct contrast to a slack-line approach is the concept of maintaining direct control over the indicator. This approach assumes that even if the indicator or tip of the fly line is drifting free, the faster surface currents are pulling the fly at a greater rate than the current below. This approach uses a shorter line with little resting on the water's surface. A series of upstream mends slow or check the drift of the indicator and in turn slow the presentation of the fly. The mends should be fairly subtle so that the indicator doesn't actually move upstream. When you do this properly, the fly will present itself at the rate of the bottom current or slightly slower.

While the indicator or tip of the line provides the key information on the drift of the fly, its main function is to demonstrate when a fish has eaten the fly. The indicator stops or jumps as the result of a take or when the fly has become lodged on the bottom. Proper weighting of the fly and leader minimizes the number of times you connect with the bottom. If the indicator stops drifting, firmly set the hook in an up- and downstream direction. Being decisive with the hook set is important as a fish can pick up a fly and then drop or spit it out quickly. With the smaller flies used with dead drifting along with more subtle takes, the hookup-to-land ratio is often lower than it is with some other techniques.

Right Angle

Right-angle nymphing is an effective variation of the dead-drift approach that uses low-diameter leader material to slice through the current more efficiently than thicker material and create a much more natural drift. The key to this approach is in the rigging and leader construction. Construction of the right-angle leader is described in the equipment chapter.

The right-angle approach can be used in a range of water types and works especially well in slower currents. It can also be used a little more efficiently in situations requiring 40- or 50-foot casts. As with the standard approach, you will normally make the cast up and across. Maintaining slack in the line enables the rig to drift naturally with the current. Stack mending can be important when right-angle nymphing too.

Since the low-diameter tippet is the only leader material below the top of the water, there is less surface area for the varying currents to act upon. The result is a highly effective drift that can cover more water than the standard dead-drift approach.

Tight Line

Tight lining or high sticking is another version of dead-drifting a fly below the water's surface. This approach requires close positioning near the suspected lie of the fish. Careful wading is critical. Generally, only 10 to 15 feet of line extends past the tip of the rod. The leader is similar to the standard dead-drift leader described in the equipment chapter except that a fluorescent butt section is often used to aid in the detection of a take, since a strike indicator isn't used with the tight-line method. Some anglers prefer to run a very long piece of tippet off the butt section so that the fly will sink fast. Since long casts are not required, lobbing out a longer piece of tippet isn't too difficult. The leader should normally be approximately the length of the rod.

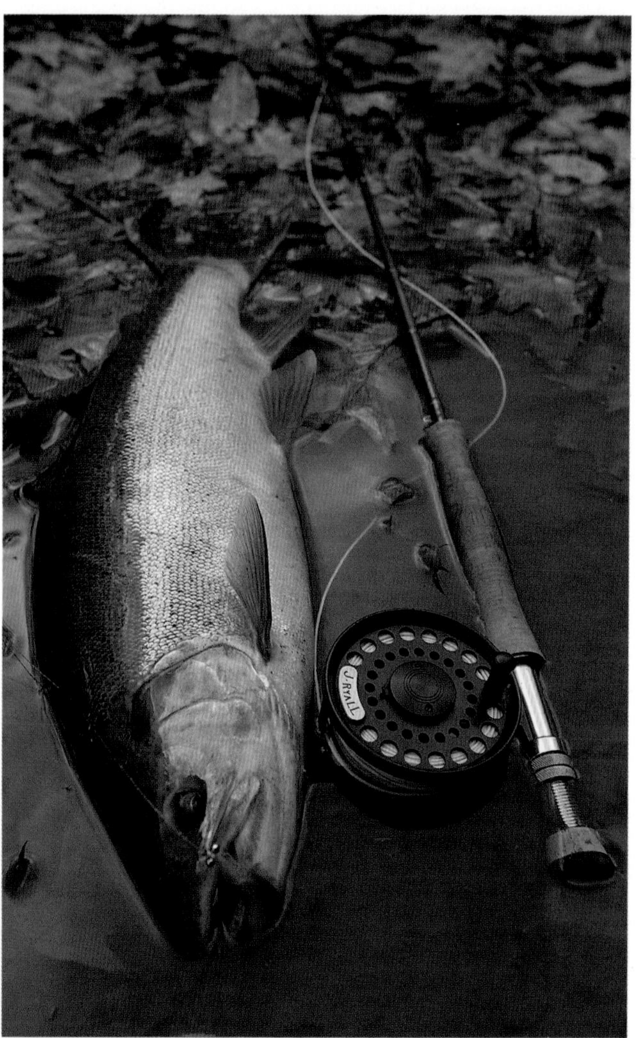

This fish was caught on a small Lake Erie tributary using a long leader, weighted fly, and single-handed rod.
NICK PIONESSA PHOTO

The tight-line approach works well on smaller streams and on fast runs and pocketwater. On bigger rivers this approach requires strong wading abilities to get in position and stay there. Careful wading will allow you to get closer to a steelhead's lie without alerting the fish.

Cast up and across. The weight of the fly combined with any weight added to the leader should cut through the surface tension and sink the fly to the bottom quickly. Hold the rod up high at a 45-degree angle throughout the presentation and allow the fly to drift down from the casting position until the fly begins to swing.

Very little if any fly line rests on the water, resulting in a tight connection to the fly. Takes may be determined by feel because the fly comes to an abrupt stop when grabbed by a steelhead. Of course, snagging on the bottom generates a similar sensation. If the rig hangs up too often, adjust the weight of the fly or weight on the leader. The fluorescent butt section of the leader may also indicate the subtle take of a fish, especially in slower water. If the butt section stops or darts upstream, set the hook.

Because of the weighted fly, weight added to the leader, and a short section of fly line past the tip of the rod, a slow open loop works best with the tight-line approach. The cast can be made using a roll cast or standard backcast. When you use a standard cast, make sure the leader straightens out entirely on the backcast before moving forward.

The tight-line method lends itself to using two flies in tandem, but I have never been an advocate of this approach. On a number of occasions I have seen the second fly become lodged somewhere in a fish's body, including the eye, during the fight. However, it is a very popular rig, and for good reason. It allows an angler to present two entirely different patterns at one time, increasing the odds for selective fish.

A typical way to rig the tandem setup is to use a heavily weighted nymph as the main fly and a small egg pattern for the trailer. Attach the trailer to the main fly by first attaching the drop tippet to the eye or the bend of the hook of the main fly with an improved clinch knot and then tying the other end to the eye of the trailer fly. The distance between the two flies should be approximately 20 inches. A tandem rig also works well with the standard dead-drift approach. Use extra care when removing a hook from a fish when you are using tandems. It is very easy for the second hook to become lodged where it shouldn't, including human flesh. It is a good idea to use barbless hooks when fishing tandem rigs.

A type of short tight-line presentation popular in Europe is called Czech nymphing. While it is similar to the approach discussed above, it incorporates an entire system. Czech nymphs are heavily weighted, low-profile patterns tied to represent scuds and caddis larvae. The patterns can be tied in a wide range of colors from natural browns and olives to fluorescent pinks and oranges. The standard Czech nymphing rig uses

Switch rods, because of their length and versatility, can be used for dead drifting as well as more traditional steelhead techniques that use Spey casting.

three flies approximately 20 inches apart with the heaviest of the three positioned in the middle. This approach may appeal to anglers who prefer not to add weight directly to the leader.

Switch and Two-Handed Rods

One key to effective mending and line control is rod length. The length of a switch or full two-handed rod is essential for efficient Spey casts, but the benefits of these rods also extend to the line control necessary for maintaining a dead drift. While using a switch or two-handed rod to dead-drift a fly would be sacrilege to many, the concept does make a lot of sense. The extra length lends itself to more acute line management and easier pickup.

While it may seem cumbersome to use a switch or two-handed rod in this manner, short Spey casts to reposition the fly are nearly effortless. The switch rod may make more sense than a full two-hander as it provides the benefits of being able to cast double-handed as well as the ability to fish the rod with a single hand. The switch, as its name implies, also provides for an easy on-river change from dead drift to more traditional steelhead techniques using full Spey casts. The switch or two-handed rod can be used with any of the dead-drifting techniques discussed above.

This approach to dead drifting is beginning to gain some momentum, and there are lines on the market designed to make short Spey casts with an indicator. These lines allow extra weight on the fly and leader to easily turn over and ride high on the surface during the presentation.

Wet-Fly Swing

When it comes to fly fishing for steelhead, I am definitely biased. Fishing a taut line and presenting the fly as it swings across the current is, in my opinion, the most satisfying way to fish for and hook a Great Lakes steelhead. The wet-fly swing is an interactive method that keeps me in constant control and in contact with the fly. And the take of a steelhead on a tight line angled downstream is exciting and often explosive.

While the wet-fly swing can be readily employed with a single-handed rod, especially on streams and smaller rivers, the 90-degree change of direction required for this technique is the reason Spey casting was developed. For this reason I always use a switch or two-handed rod for the wet-fly swing, and the rhythm I develop using the flow of the water while Spey casting enhances the overall experience. However, short Spey casts with a single-handed rod can also be very useful when swinging a fly. Advantages of longer rods in both casting and line control add to the technique's effectiveness on larger waters.

I greatly enjoy fishing a switch or two-handed rod. First there is the tactical advantage of an 11- to 14-foot rod—an efficient

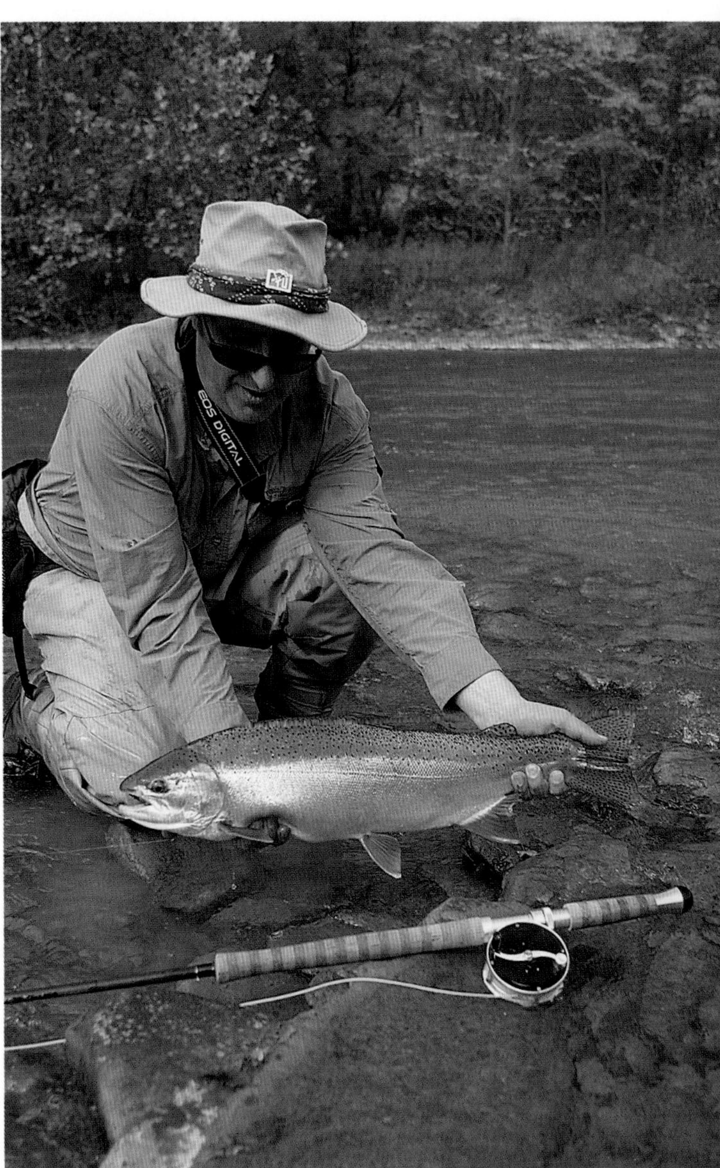

Charlie Dickson admires a beautiful steelhead.
NICK PIONESSA PHOTO

lever that reduces strain on the body and significantly increases line control capabilities. But my true interest lies in the sheer pleasure gained by fishing a switch or two-handed rod. The Spey cast done right is in itself a work of art. It is mechanical poetry in motion, combing brute power with the delicate accuracy of timing. But the true joy doesn't lie in the casting; it lies in the fishing. In no other form of fly fishing do I experience such a complete and intimate link to the water than when I am Spey fishing.

Since the line on the water's surface loads the rod for the forward stroke, wading depth and current speed impact each and every cast. The connection of line to the water while generating the cast requires a constant awareness of flow and depth. Except for those few seconds when the fly streams through the air, there is always a connection to the water.

Ultimately it is the overall rhythm that this approach creates that makes it so captivating. Minutes fade into hours and hours into a day on the river. When all goes right I am able to completely cover the water with a smooth, effortless style. This provides a confidence that the fly has been seen by any and every steelhead in the pool, and even if a fish doesn't take, I have the satisfaction of fishing the water well.

Sinking-Tip or Sinking Leader

A sinking-tip or sinking leader is my preferred way to deliver a fly when using the wet-fly swing. For sinking-tips I always choose the exchangeable types for range and versatility. The leader/tippet for a sinking-tip or sinking leader will typically be 3 to 4 feet in length. The concept of a short leader seems to go against the grain for anglers who are accustomed to the stealth of a long monofilament leader. However, a short leader keeps the fly close enough to the sink source to consistently attain a certain depth.

Generally the sinking-tip and short leader will not cause a steelhead to shy away. The fly is generally presented on the broadside or as it swings away, and the fish reacts to the movement of the fly without paying attention to the sinking-tip or sinking leader.

In faster water I use a weighted fly to pierce the surface tension and allow the fly to sink at the same rate as the tip or sinking leader or faster. This is also my preferred rig when covering a deep slot, especially up against the far bank. While a weighted fly can be a little more difficult to Spey cast, using a Skagit setup minimizes its impact on casting. I have found that using a longer monofilament leader/tippet section of 6 to 10

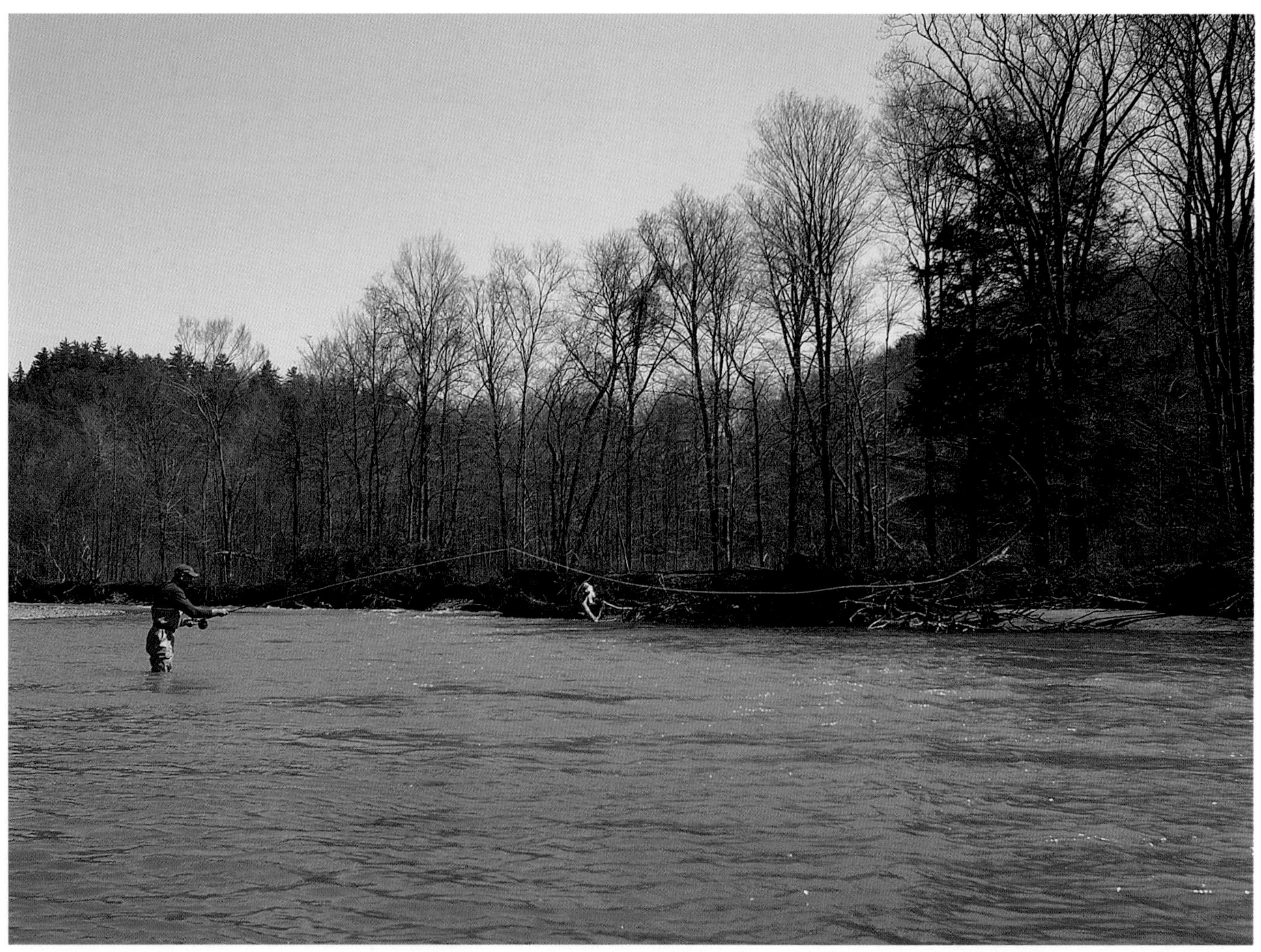

A weighted fly will improve presentation in faster currents by allowing the fly to sink as fast as the sinking-tip or even faster.
NICK PIONESSA PHOTO

feet with a Skagit system and a heavily weighted fly allows me to attain the greatest depth in water with moderate to fast current speeds. The longer leader and weighted fly setup may also allow a stealthier approach in low, clear water. My good angling friend Jim Wilson feels that this setup provides a distinct advantage in getting the fly down quickly.

The sinking-tip or sinking leader selected for each piece of water should readily and consistently take the fly down into the bottom third of the water column. However, placing the fly near the bottom won't be quite as important when water temperatures are in the mid-40s and 50s, when a steelhead will be more likely to move farther for a fly. Ideally you'll be able to fish a pool or run all the way through with one sinking-tip. You may have to change the tip while working pools or runs that have significant variations in the current speed or depth from the beginning to the tailout. Keep a variety of tips in an easily accessible pocket to facilitate a quick change. Slight variations in the current speed or depth of a pool or run can usually be handled by controlling the angle of the cast or through mending.

Selecting the proper tip is an art in itself. Experience along with trial and error are the best tools for finding the right tip. Maintaining notes on which tips have been successful on particular pools or rivers under certain conditions can be extremely useful and eliminate guesswork. Determining whether a tip is reaching the desired depth usually takes a bit of analysis. Estimate the depth of the water, examine the angle that the line takes as it enters the water, and watch the angle of the line as you remove the fly from the water for the next cast for clues.

The best feedback that the fly is fishing at the proper depth is multiple takes or pulls from steelhead, sure signs that a number of things are going right with the presentation. Conversely, if the fly is continually scraping or hanging on the bottom, then the tip is simply too heavy. Hanging up on the bottom disrupts the swing of the fly and eliminates its enticing powers. I have found that when steelhead are fairly aggressive, the same tip can often be applied to a range of pools and runs within a river by making simple adjustments of fly weight or casting angle.

Most of the time when I'm fishing the wet-fly swing, I wade to the depth of my upper calves or lower thighs. I want my fly to swing out entirely and hang in water that has enough depth to hold fish or where I would be comfortable enough to chase the fly and take at the end of the swing. I wade in shallower water in low light or when the water is off-color, since steelhead can position themselves in shallow water under such conditions. Other times I may need to wade to my upper thighs to cover more water or attain the desired swing.

The wet-fly swing presentation begins with an across-stream cast. You can control the depth of the fly somewhat by the angle of the cast: A slight upstream angle will allow the fly to dig deeper, whereas a downstream angle has the opposite effect. The effectiveness of the upstream angle is limited to maybe 5 or 10 degrees. Too great of an upstream casting angle will make it difficult or impossible to set up the swing portion of the presentation.

You can also control the depth of the fly through mending. An exaggerated upstream mend immediately following the delivery of the fly takes tension off the sinking-tip and allows it to sink at a faster rate. The mend sets up a deeper swing and can be especially effective when allowing a tip and fly to sink through the surface tension of swifter water. The upstream mend can also include some stack mends, as discussed earlier in the chapter.

For attaining even greater depth, add slack line immediately after the cast. Do this by pulling more running line from the reel than you need for the cast. When you complete the cast, feed the extra running line into the drift, taking tension off the head and tip of the line and allowing for a greater sink depth during the setup of the swing.

I also add slack in the line by overcasting my desired target and pulling back on the line by raising the rod tip and then returning it to the normal fishing position. This motion creates slack that feeds into the setup of the swing. The amount of slack is determined by how much you pull the rod tip back. Pointing the rod directly up so that it is perpendicular to the water's surface creates the most slack.

After the cross-stream cast, the fly will initially be presented in a broadside manner as its materials flow and undulate in the current. You may need to make an extra mend or two to get the fly down or to control a downstream belly in the line, which can pull at the fly, forcing it to swim quickly downstream. Fish rarely take a fly that is swimming toward them. Occasionally a steelhead takes the fly in this broadside phase of the presentation as the fly basically drifts with the current. I have received more takes on the broadside presentation while fishing faster runs and slots.

As the fly reaches an angle approximately 45 degrees to the casting position, it will begin swimming or swinging across the current. At this transition point, the fly picks up some speed and creates the illusion of fleeing or swimming away. This motion often triggers an instinctive response from a steelhead. The key to the presentation at this point is to control the speed of the fly. While the fly should be swinging the entire time, it should also remain accessible to the fish. In other words, a fly that swings too fast generally will not elicit as many strikes, especially in colder water. You can control the fly's swing speed by manipulating the line. The key is to avoid a large downstream belly that forces the fly to swing rapidly.

In some pools and runs where the current softly tapers to the inside edge, very little or no line manipulation is required for a consistent swing. But uneven currents working on the floating portion of the fly line that rests on the surface will often create a large belly. Soft upstream mends can reposition the floating portion of fly line and control the speed of the swing. The mend should move the floating line without pulling on the tip or impeding the swing of the fly. Two-handed rods make it easy to control the line and remove any belly that develops. I prefer to limit my mending, and when the swing is right I make an entire presentation without mending at all. Excessive mending can interfere with the seductive fleeing motion of the fly and reduce the effectiveness of the presentation.

While mending is used to eliminate excess line downstream, occasionally it can be to your advantage to add a downstream belly to extend the swing. When you have extremely

Wet-Fly Swing

Start the wet-fly swing by casting across the river. In this case the cast should cover the deep water along the bank.

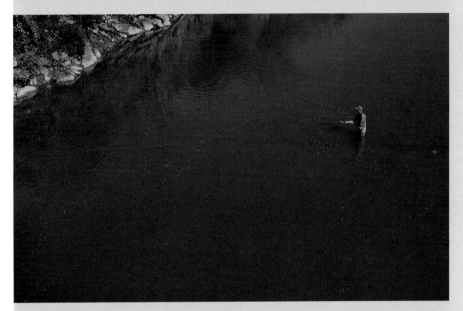

Make an upstream mend using two hands to allow the fly to gain greater depth.

With the standard swing, keep the rod tip low and pointed at the fly.

The fly begins its swing as it reaches a point approximately 45 degrees to your casting position.

Steelhead often take the fly as it begins to pick up speed.

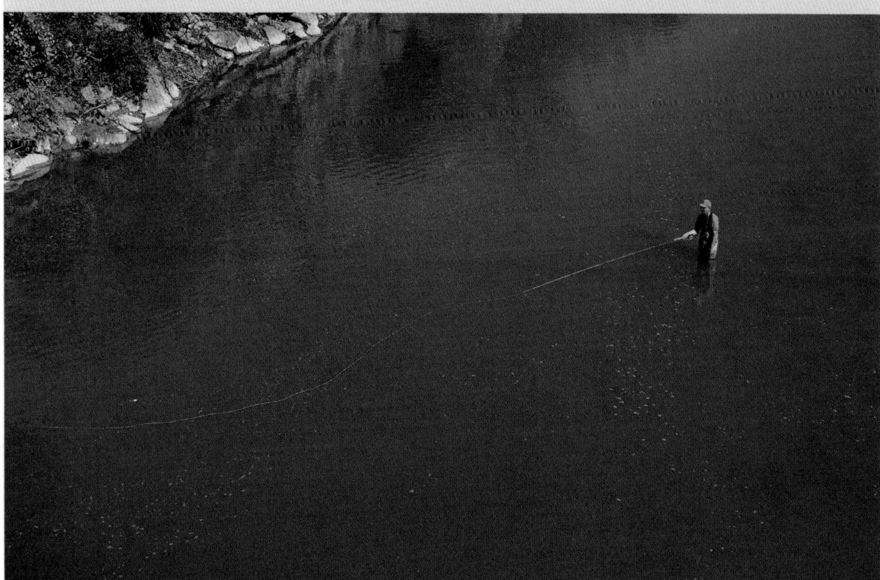

You can use an upstream mend to reduce a downstream belly, which can cause the fly to swing too fast, especially in water with a quicker current speed.

As the fly swings out, steelhead will often follow and take as the fly begins to slow. Only react to the weight of a fish that has entirely taken the fly.

Allow the fly to swing to a point directly below the casting position and hang there for a few seconds. Many takes come at this point, especially in cold water.

NICK PIONESSA PHOTOS

soft water below your casting position, the swing of the fly will often halt before it reaches a point directly downriver. A downstream mend can pull the fly just a little farther and entice a steelhead resting in the soft water.

The fleeing motion of the swung fly plays upon the instincts of a steelhead. That is why it is important for the fly to be continually swimming away. Great Lakes anglers who have spent years pursuing steelhead with small flies and dead-drift techniques may be skeptical of a technique that uses big flies and a taut line. But you must remember that steelhead are top-of-the-food-chain predators that make a living chasing down baitfish and other food sources in lakes. It should be no surprise that this aggressive behavior carries over into rivers during their migration.

Once the fly begins to swing, the chance for a take from a steelhead increases significantly. The take can come at any time, but a high percentage of takes occur just as the fly begins to pick up speed during the swing. Steelhead often follow the fly as it swings, striking at any point including after the fly has completed the swing and hangs in the current below the casting position. This point is often referred to as the "hangdown," and it is important to allow the fly to sit in this position for a few seconds before beginning the next cast. I have hooked numerous fish over the years as the fly simply hung in the current at the end of the swing. This is especially true in coldwater conditions. Steelhead can even strike as you strip line in for the next cast.

You can control the angle of the swing by the position of the rod tip. The angle of the swing impacts the speed of the fly and how the fly presents itself to the steelhead. If you point the tip toward the middle of the river, the swing slows down and the fly is presented tailfirst as it moves across the current. This

Controlling the Speed of the Swing

As an alternative to the standard swing, you can control the fly's speed more acutely by changing the rod angle. Here the rod is pointed at the opposite bank.

A mend that angles across and upstream takes tension off the fly line and allows the fly to sink and swing slowly in the current.

Holding the rod out reduces and controls the speed of the fly as it passes across the width of the river.

The rod tends to follow as the swing slowly makes its way toward the near bank.

An exaggerated reach can reduce the swing to a crawl, which can be effective on lethargic steelhead that won't react to a faster swing.

With this approach, the swing is complete with the rod pointing slightly out.

NICK PIONESSA PHOTOS

angle also keeps a tighter line and may pull the fly up in the water column.

Pointing the rod tip at the fly or angled downriver allows for a more broadside presentation. Proper line control is required to keep the fly from moving too rapidly across the current. I prefer more of a broadside look, since it gives the fish a more substantive view of the fly and forces more of an instinctive reflex response.

No matter the angle at which the fly is fished, it should swing continuously to create an enticing target. Some anglers prefer to add some action to the fly as it swings. Making a 3- or 4-inch strip and then allowing the fly to drop back repeatedly through the swing has brought about a number of takes for me over the years. This approach is a good trick for lethargic fish or to create a different look when making a second or third pass through a pool or run.

I also strip the fly in extremely slow tailouts. Sometimes the current is so subtle that a constant slow strip is required to keep the fly moving. In this situation you have to pinch the line against the cork and strip the line in as the fly makes a gradual movement through the water. Another approach for any type of water is to crawl the fly with a one-handed retrieve by slowly stripping the fly. This allows you to add a little speed as desired or when the swing changes. The crawl can help control depth and entice stubborn steelhead.

Wide variations on a swinging fly can be required for certain circumstances. Flies tend to swing quickly in high-water conditions. Speed combined with trouble sinking the fly in heavier flows calls for some adjustments to the approach. One step toward slowing the fly's speed in faster flows is using a shorter line. Wading deep to take a position as close to the water being fished as possible results in less line beyond the rod tip and provides more acute control over the speed of the fly.

A day fishing with expert steelhead guide and angler Jeff Liskay gave me a living illustration in using a short line. We were fishing an Ohio river that was right on the edge of being too high to fish. Combine this with cold water temperatures and a stain to the water, and the deck was clearly stacked against us. Jeff used very aggressive wading to put himself into position to use a short line with a weighted fly. This position allowed for more precise mending and eliminated almost all the downstream belly in the line by keeping much of the line off of the water. With this approach, Jeff caught a couple impressive fish in softer seams that were surrounded by heavier flows.

Another step for controlling speed is to dramatically change the angle of the rod. Pointing straight out toward the opposite bank can dramatically slow the swing since this angle prevents the fly from quickly slicing across-current. The effects of this approach are maximized when using a short line. The rod angle holds back the swing of the fly and allows it to hang

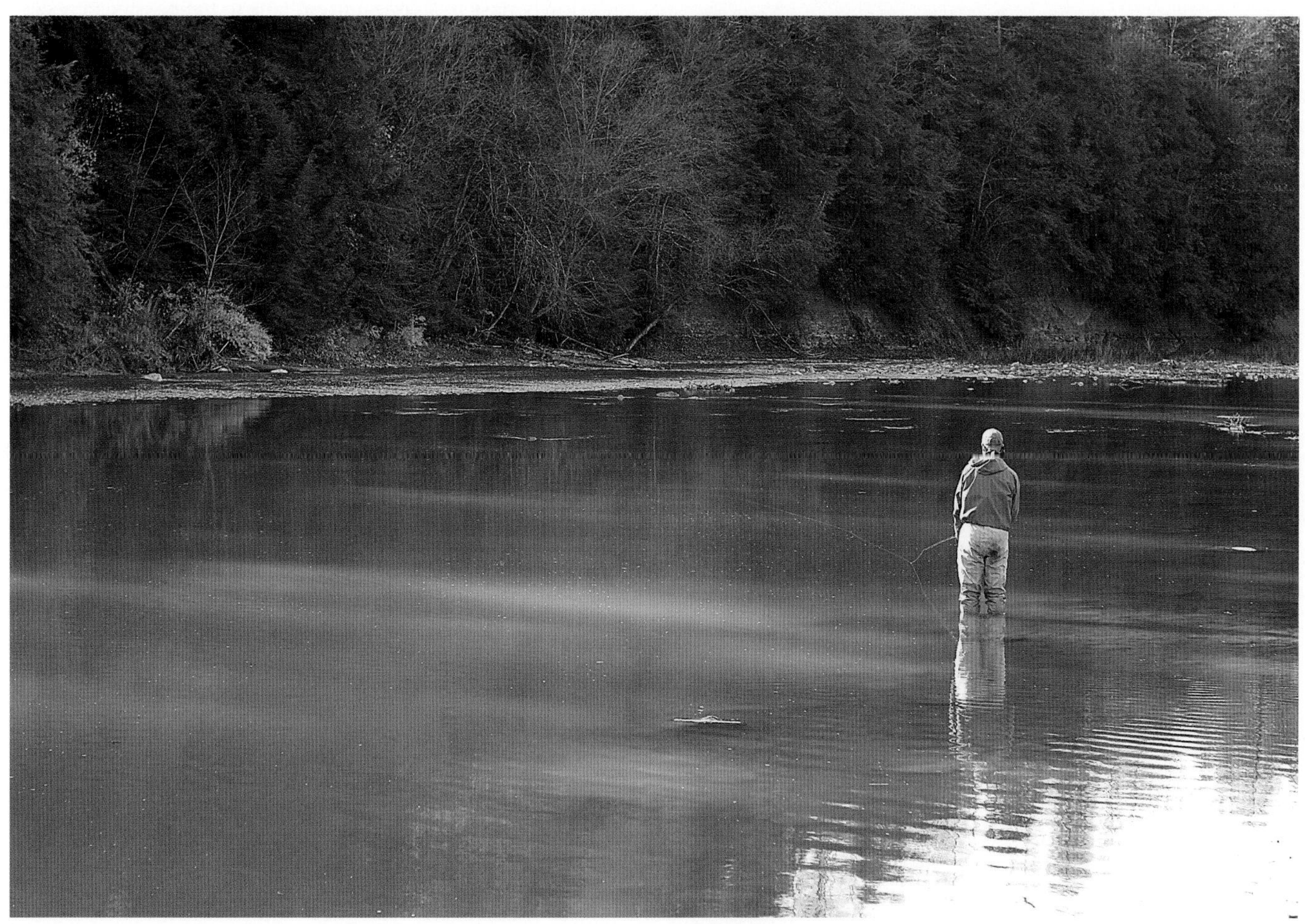

When you are fishing tailout water with a slow flow, you may need to strip the fly to maintain the swing. NICK PIONESSA PHOTO

Aggressive wading allows an angler to improve line control and presentation.

and slowly pass from one current lane to the next in an accessible and seductive manner. Aggressive mending immediately after an across-angle cast will help sink the fly quickly. This is a great approach for fishing in colder water temperatures.

A steelhead can take a fly at any time during the wet-fly swing, but the majority of takes come as the fly is swimming across the current lanes. The strike can be violent, nearly pulling the rod from your hand as the steelhead catapults above the water's surface. But others can be subtle, as the line is pulled backward, or you may just feel a heavy weight as the swing is interrupted by the mouth of a steelhead. It is important not to react too quickly to a take and to ensure that the steelhead has completely eaten the fly. Often a steelhead will follow a fly a great distance prior to the take. Sometimes you can feel the fish tapping or plucking at the fly as it swings.

Floating Line and Monofilament Leader

An alternative to fishing with a sinking-tip or sinking leader is to use a floating fly line and a monofilament leader. Use a leader the same length as the length of the rod, constructed so that it can easily turn over a big fly. The basic presentation is the same as for the sinking-tip, but the floating line and long leader allow for variations in the presentation to meet certain conditions and opportunities.

When water temperatures are in the optimum range, Great Lakes steelhead can be more surface-oriented on some rivers.

Nick Pionessa reaches to tail a tired steelhead.
NICK PIONESSA PHOTO

In early to mid fall and then again in the spring it is not uncommon to bring steelhead to the top of the water column to take a fly. Rigging with a floating line and an unweighted fly can be an exciting way to fish when steelhead are aggressive. Cast across-stream or angled slightly down and begin fishing the fly immediately. You can add an upstream mend after the cast to sink the fly, but with the pull of the fly line, the fly will not fish much deeper than a foot into the water column. Line control is the same as when fishing with a sinking-tip—control the speed of the fly by limiting the downstream belly. Takes will often be forceful as a steelhead rises up and turns on the fly.

Success with a floating line and unweighted fly depends on water that is clear enough that the fish can easily see the fly while positioned along the bottom. The floating line approach works especially well on rivers with natural reproduction. Adult fish in these rivers have leftover instincts from their days of living in a stream or river as a juvenile and depend on surface feeding in the spring and summer as a main source of food. A variety of flies work with this approach, but I have had my best success on small patterns with natural colors.

A variation of the approach with an unweighted pattern is to add a riffle hitch to the fly. A riffle hitch is simply two half hitches added to the front of the fly. You must tie the fly on an up-eye hook. The riffle hitch then lies on the return wire of the hook. For the flies that I tie to be used with the riffle hitch, I leave extra room at the head for the two half hitches to seat. When the dual half hitches are completed, the tippet should lead from beneath the hook toward the casting position as the eye of the fly faces upstream. The knot has to be positioned this way to give the fly the desired effect. This means that you have to retie the hitch when you fish the opposite side of the river. Draw the double half hitches as tight as possible so that the knot doesn't loosen and untie while casting.

When you use the riffle hitch, the side pull exerted by the tippet positioned under the hook shank and at a 90-degree angle forces the fly to present in the surface film. The fly swings while plowing through the surface tension and creates a disturbance on top of the water. The disturbance gives the impression of something lifelike struggling on the surface. But more important, the commotion grabs the attention of a steelhead positioned below. When you fish the riffle properly, you can see the wake of the fly and the fish's take, which adds another element of excitement to the presentation.

Vince Tobia caught this big buck using a long leader.

A heavy copper tube and long leader were used to attain the proper depth to fool this steelhead. NICK PIONESSA PHOTO

In order for the fly to keep moving through the surface film, you must maintain tension from the side. This can require more line manipulation and control than the standard wet-fly swing. A slight downstream belly may be required, and it is common to lead the fly with the rod. You may need to adjust the rod's angle in relation to the water throughout the presentation as well. Lifting the rod tip will allow the fly to speed up, and moving the tip toward the near bank will allow the hitched fly to wake all the way into the hangdown position. It is common for a steelhead to follow the fly all the way to the end before taking with a bulging riseform. For visual takes, make sure you can feel the weight of the fish before setting the hook.

A more versatile use of the floating line and long monofilament is to match this rig with a weighted fly. Bead heads, cone heads, and dumbbell eyes not only dress up a fly, but also allow it to reach depths where a steelhead will more likely strike. While this rig may be more cumbersome to cast, it clearly has some tactical advantages in certain situations. In low, clear water, the long monofilament leader provides a low-profile alternative to a sinking-tip. You also get more acute depth control with this rig and can slow the swing better.

For the most part, a fly fished on a sinking-tip or sinking leader is a very effective approach, as a steelhead keys in on the movement of the fly and is not spooked by the short monofilament leader section. But experience has shown that in very clear water, especially on smaller rivers, a weighted fly and a floating line can increase takes from steelhead. Stealth is important with this approach. Small, subtle patterns of olive and brown are particularly effective. Sometimes I cover a pool in this fashion after fishing it through with a sinking-tip or sinking leader to coax a reluctant steelhead.

Since the weighted fly is unencumbered by the larger diameter of a sinking-tip or sinking leader, it is able to sink quickly when you use a long monofilament leader. This is an advantage for fishing quick runs and deep slots. If you make an upstream mend just after the cast, a heavily weighted fly can freefall to significant depths. This approach can be quite effective for lethargic steelhead holding along ledges and in deep drop-offs. The fly can be fished in a deep broadside manner on a tight line for a distance before starting to swing. You can cover this same water with a sinking-tip or sinking leader and a weighted fly, but the monofilament leader will allow the fly to sink quicker and provide for more acute control of the fly.

I recall one particular day that proves the effectiveness of this approach. I fished the upper reaches of one of my favorite rivers with friend, professional guide, and outfitter Vince Tobia. I was rigged with a sinking leader and a slightly weighted fly, and Vince used a Beadhead Woolly Bugger fished on a long monofilament leader. The falling water had the steelhead holding tight to structure, particularly along some ledges, and his rig fished the structure more effectively than mine. Vince hooked and landed a number of good fish while I had a rather frustrating outing.

The weighted fly and long monofilament leader approach also has its place in moderate to slower currents. The presentation is different from that of a sinking-tip as the angle to the water is more dramatic when using the monofilament leader rig and the diameter of the leader is lower than that of a sinking-tip. Both factors add to the ability of gaining greater control over the speed of the fly. This becomes a significant advantage when fishing to lethargic steelhead or in cold water. The speed control results from the lower-diameter leader more effectively cutting through the tension of the current. A slower presentation makes the fly more visible and accessible to a steelhead for a longer period of time, which is important when coaxing fish that are not aggressive.

A weighted fly and a long leader provide for a stealthy approach and can be used effectively along ledges and drop-offs.

If you make an upstream mend after the cast and hold the rod more in a high-stick mode, you can fish the fly in a broadside, dead-drift manner for a significant distance. While some fish take at this point, more take just as the fly begins to swing. Because of the low-diameter leader, the turnover point where the fly goes from drifting to swimming is not as dramatic or as fast as with a sinking-tip. The fact that a fish with a slowed metabolism does not have to move far or fast to intercept an enticing, swimming fly presented in this manner is at the heart of this method's effectiveness. The fly swings out in a slowed presentation all the way to the hangdown position. The approach combines elements of the wet-fly swing and high-stick nymphing presentations, causing one of my fishing partners, Dave Mosgeller, to call it "swymphing." Flies that work best with this approach look like food sources while drifting and come alive with seductive movement when swinging.

Transitioning from Dead-Drift to Swing Techniques

With the advent of Spey gatherings and an increase in available information regarding casting and fishing techniques, more new anglers are experiencing the fishery with a switch or two-handed rod than ever before. For many steelhead anglers in the Great Lakes region, their initial efforts with a fly have been with the dead-drift approach. But each year more anglers show an interest in catching a fish on a swung fly. In my opinion, using the swing approach exclusively makes you a better angler through a deeper understanding of steelhead and their behavior and greatly increases the experience through more direct contact with the water. But it has taken me many years to reach the level where I am comfortable exclusively fishing with this approach, and it has taken a change in perspective to arrive at this point.

The first step in the transition is to understand that the wet-fly swing may not produce the same quantity of fish as the dead-drift approach. As fly fishers, we accept the challenges and limitations of our sport. One of the attributes of fly fishing is that it forces you to hone your skills. Fishing the wet-fly swing with a switch rod or two-handed rod is simply an extension of what makes fly fishing a lifetime pursuit for many anglers. It is this drive to learn and experience all that the sport has to offer that has fueled my passion for more than 30 years. How an angler catches a steelhead doesn't really matter as long as it is done in an ethical manner. But as a guide and fly shop owner, I have known anglers who became complacent and almost bored with catching steelhead with highly effective techniques and were reluctant to try other alternatives. Some of these anglers lose interest in steelhead fly fishing.

Making a transition from dead drift to the wet-fly swing can be a significant undertaking. There is much to learn about lines, casting, and presentation. The number of hookups can be significantly lower at the beginning of the process. But like learning to fly-fish for the first time, making a commitment to this style of fishing will shorten the learning curve. Using the wet-fly swing only when no other techniques are working because of the poor conditions or lack of fish will not help to

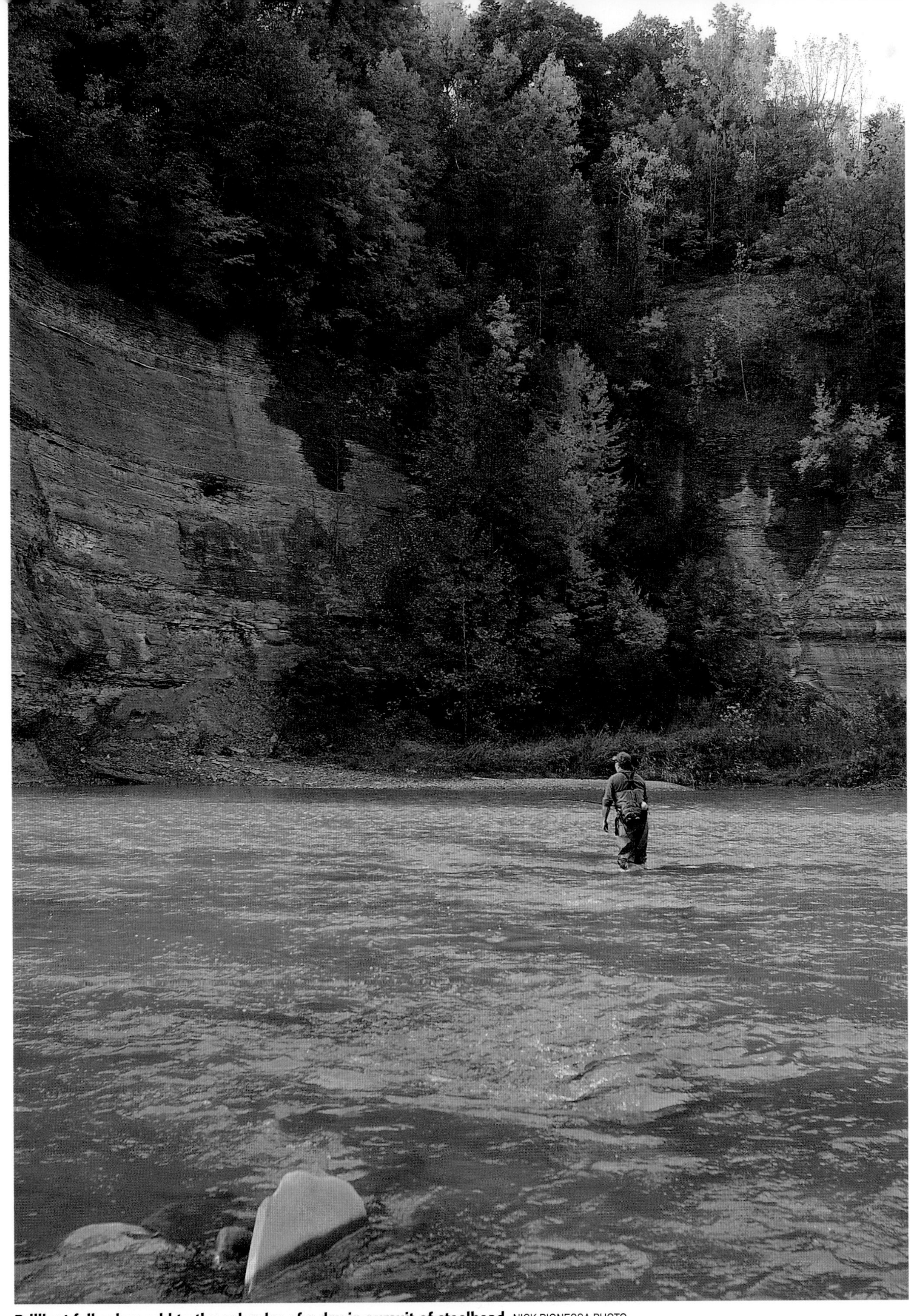

Brilliant fall colors add to the splendor of a day in pursuit of steelhead. NICK PIONESSA PHOTO

Last light is often a magic time to be on the water.
NICK PIONESSA PHOTO

boost confidence or refine skills. Fully committing forces you to learn and improve. Admittedly it can be difficult to stay the course when other anglers are successful with other methods—especially when those other anglers are your fishing partners. Today's lighter switch rods and longer one-handed rods make it easy to change techniques on the water. The swymphing technique described above is a good way for a dead-drift angler to become comfortable with the swing approach.

Ultimately it is about the overall experience. The constant connection to the water and the explosive takes common with the wet-fly swing make it the only approach for me. I am always in search of and waiting for the next pull of my swung fly by a steelhead. Many anglers in the Great Lakes region have developed a passion and appreciation for this style of fishing over the last 10 years, and I suspect the popularity of the wet-fly swing and Spey fishing will continue to grow at a steady pace.

Working a Pool with the Wet-Fly Swing

Fishing through a pool with the wet-fly swing is a process. The starting point is the head or riffle where the pool begins and the ending point is the lowest part of the tail section capable of holding steelhead. Properly implemented, the wet-fly swing completely and methodically covers the water. You create an imaginary grid to show the fly to every fish in the pool. By casting across the river, allowing the fly to swing out, and then taking a step or two downriver, you'll cover the entire pool in quadrants. The key is to make the same cast each time and to take a step of a similar distance after each swing. I may move farther downriver after each cast when the water is clear and water temperatures are in the optimum range because I anticipate that a steelhead will move farther to intercept a fly. Conversely, I would make a shorter movement down in dirty or cold water since a steelhead will not see as far or move as far to the fly. I may also move more deliberately through the prime part or bucket of the pool.

I normally wade until I am calf or knee deep before making my first cast, although I sometimes fish the water before wading it when I am the first angler through in the morning or when the water is off-color. My first cast is only 10 or 20 feet long, and I lengthen each cast by 5 feet or so before making the next cast from the same position. Once the cast reaches a distance to cover the width of the pool or to the point of a comfortable, repeatable cast, it is time to start working downriver after completing each swing. It is best to stay within the bounds of your casting ability. While long casts cover a lot of water, it is the repeatable cast that covers the most water in an efficient manner.

While you can catch Great Lakes steelhead in all levels of the water column, working the fly in the lowest foot is the most productive approach. However, you don't want the fly so deep that it scrapes the bottom. Getting to know a particular pool is a significant advantage and gives you a knowledge base for selecting the sink rate of the sinking-tip or sinking leader. But you can make simple adjustments to fly depth by changing the angle of the cast and by mending. A greater upstream angle fishes the fly deeper and a greater downstream angle keeps the fly higher in the water column.

I prefer to set up my rig so that it is slightly lighter as opposed to slightly heavy. I can fish the fly slower and allow it to be more accessible to a steelhead when the rig is lighter, and it allows for cross-river casts. Casts angled downriver tend to swing a little faster, and in some cases too fast to induce a strike. You can manage depth best by changing the angle of the cast when a pool has a varied bottom structure.

Longer pools can take an hour or even two to cover thoroughly. But in a beautiful pool with the proper speed, the minutes and hours simply melt away, especially when you are fairly confident of hooking a fish.

Once you have worked through the entire pool you have to decide whether to cover that pool again or to move on. Sometimes the decision is easy: If other anglers have moved into the pool, I typically look for open water. But if the pool remains open or if other anglers are fishing by rotating, then I consider fishing the pool a second or even third time.

Waiting for the pull. The most exciting element of the wet-fly swing is feeling the take and instant connection to a steelhead.

The advantage of covering the pool again is the familiarity gained by fishing it the first time. You can assess whether you need to make adjustments to cover the water more effectively. However, my decision to cover the pool again will normally be based on the existing evidence of steelhead in the pool. I analyze the clues, such as whether I witnessed other steelhead being caught, how many takes or hookups I had on the previous pass, and whether I saw any visible evidence of fish rolling on the surface. I also may spend more time in a pool that I know has been especially productive during the current season or in pools that have traditionally produced more fish in past seasons.

When making a second pass through a pool, I may make an adjustment to my rig or fly to change up the presentation. I rely on adjustments mainly when I know that steelhead are present but didn't show much interest in my offering on an earlier pass. But my philosophy is to keep changes to a minimum and to fish a rig and fly that give me the most confidence. Sometimes it is a matter of just the right cast or fishing the pool at that magic hour when the fish simply turn on. This often happens in the lower-light periods of the day. When fishing behind other anglers in a rotation, I try to vary my rig, fly, or presentation from theirs to show the fish something different, often with good results. Covering a pool properly is an art in itself. And a certain satisfaction comes with fishing the fly properly and knowing that a pool has been covered from top to bottom.

A happy Suzanne Pionessa poses with a perfect steelhead before its release. NICK PIONESSA PHOTO

Lake-run brown trout can be a welcome surprise when using the wet-fly swing for steelhead in the Great Lakes region.

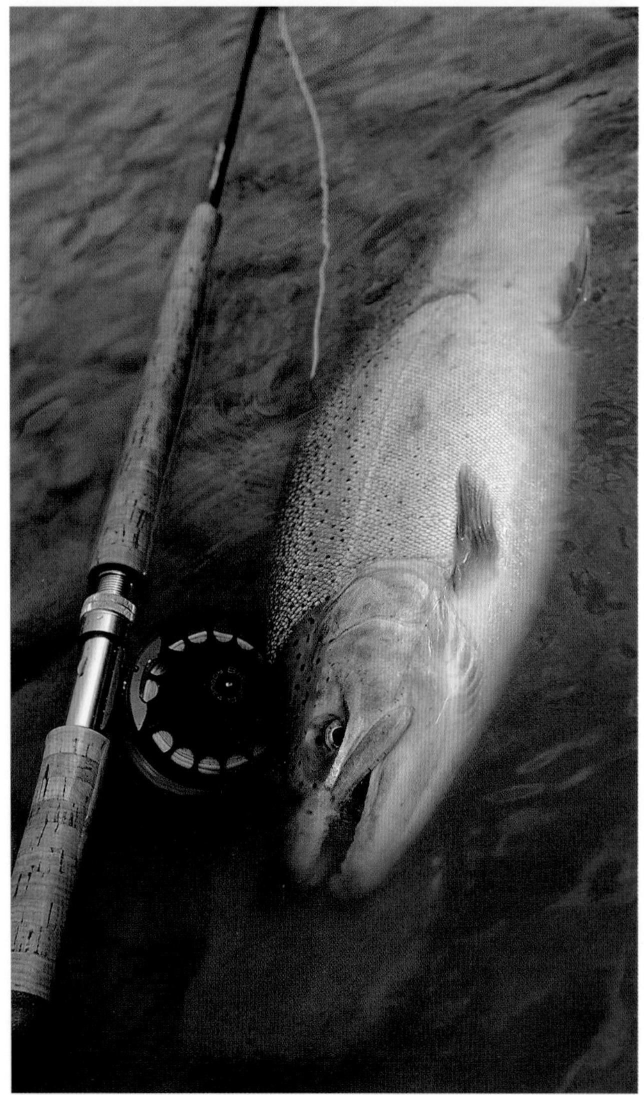

Big male steelhead are capable of strong, exciting battles. NICK PIONESSA PHOTO

Working a Steelhead That Shows an Interest

A steelhead commonly shows an interest in the presentation without actually taking the fly when you are using the wet-fly swing. This feels like a tap or lazy pull of the fly. Occasionally a steelhead follows the fly a great distance while continually tapping. And at times the pulls are quite dramatic—to the point where it is difficult to believe that the fish didn't get hooked. Steelhead strike or nip at the rear of the fly, which translates to taps and pulls on the angler's end. A steelhead can also cause these effects by positioning itself right behind the fly and discharging water through its gills as it attempts to feed. Due to the taut line of the swing, the fly is pulled slightly but not enough to enter the fish's mouth. While a tap or pull without a hookup is frustrating, it provides clear evidence that you have found a relatively active fish that you can still catch.

The interaction with an interested fish is a very exciting part of fly fishing for steelhead. It often reminds me of working a rising trout with a dry fly. It is important not to set the hook on a mere tap or pull, but rather to hold off until you can feel the weight of the fish. Setting the hook too early alerts the fish and makes it less likely that it will return. When I feel a pull from a steelhead, I typically entice that fish into a solid take approximately a third of the time.

When I receive a pull from a steelhead with no hookup, I plant my feet so that I can cover the same water again, normally with the same pattern. If that doesn't work, I'll try a couple other fly patterns, normally smaller ones. If there are no other anglers in the rotation, I may take a couple steps upriver and try my original fly again, thinking that the steelhead may have repositioned slightly after the initial pull. If that doesn't work, I may wait a few minutes to allow things to settle down and then slowly work down through the water again. There have been times that I hooked a fish a few steps below where the original pull occurred; it is likely that the fish backed down slightly after its initial interest.

Sometimes the fish will pull a second or even third time. At that point I typically remain with the pattern the fish has

Changing to a sparsely tied pattern can entice a reluctant fish into taking. NICK PIONESSA PHOTO

Early to mid fall is one of the best times for dry-fly fishing. NICK PIONESSA PHOTO

shown interest in and slow down the presentation with upstream mending. It seems that the chance of hooking the fish goes down with each time the fish pulls and doesn't take, but I have caught aggressive steelhead in the Great Lakes that pulled the fly on as many as five casts before actually committing to a take.

When I encounter a fish that doesn't come back to the fly, I make a mental note of its position. If I make another pass through the pool, I work that area slowly and thoroughly, as a rested fish will be likely to move to the fly again. This is especially true as the evening light advances on the day. Hooking a steelhead after it has shown for the fly on previous casts is a fun, captivating, and challenging aspect of the wet-fly swing.

Dry-Fly Opportunities

While most steelhead in the Great Lakes region are hooked in the lower portion of the water column, there are opportunities to bring fish to a surface fly. You can fish on the surface when water temperatures exceed 40 degrees F, but fishing is even better when the mercury rises into the upper 40s and low 50s. These water temperature ranges occur in early to mid fall and mid to late spring.

Steelhead that are pooled up and holding tend to be better candidates for the dry fly than those that are actively migrating. And water clarity should be sufficient for a steelhead that is resting on or near the bottom to see the fly on the surface. Dry-fly fishing opportunities are also more consistent on rivers with natural reproduction. I suspect that wild fish have a leftover response from the first year or two of their lives when surface feeding on aquatic insects and terrestrials made up the majority of their diets. But good dry-fly fishing also occurs on some of the more heavily stocked streams and rivers along the Lake Erie shoreline.

The best time to try a dry is during low, clear water conditions in the fall. Low water seems to keep fish from being motivated to move. Your best bet is on holding fish in a pool or tailout with a water depth of 2 to 4 feet and a slow to moderate current flow. In extremely clear water conditions, steelhead can often be visible while holding. This creates another element of excitement, and you can observe how the fish react to the fly.

In the fall, the best approach is to use a waking fly. Patterns that work well with this approach are those tied on an up-eye hook and constructed from spun deer hair and closed-cell foam or sparsely tied flies with elk or deer hair wings. A riffle hitch (see page 59) and dry-fly floatant will keep the fly on the surface.

Patterns tied on tubes and constructed so that the tippet enters through the sidewall allow the fly to wake on the surface as well as or even better than a riffle-hitched fly. Use a full floating line and a leader 10 to 12 feet long with a stiff enough butt section to turn over big, wind-resistant flies. The tippet should be constructed of 10- to 12-pound-test material.

When waking a fly on the surface, make the cast angling slightly downstream. As with the riffle-hitched wet-fly approach, the tension of the tippet pulling off to the side keeps the fly on the surface, cutting a visible V as it moves across the top of the water. Control the speed of the fly with side tension and by changing the angle of the rod. Raising the rod will speed up the fly and keep it working on the surface.

It is critical that you are able to see the fly through the entire presentation. When the water's surface has a gray, oily look to it, dark patterns tend to show up best. However, when

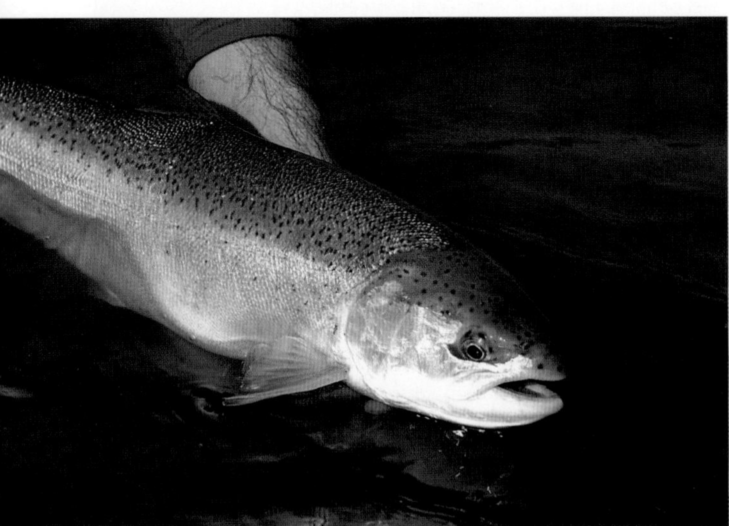

In the springtime you can catch steelhead on early-season insect hatches using the dead-drift approach.

the water looks dark, white and other brighter colors tend to be more visible. Part of seeing the fly is knowing what to look for and where to look. Experience creates a trained eye. On small rivers and streams it is much easier to see the fly since the casts are shorter.

Takes can come in the form of a large boil or the fly simply disappearing into a barely discernible riseform. More often than not, a steelhead will show for the fly without actually taking. There are a number of strategies you can use with fish that show for a dry. My approach is to repeat the cast with the same fly. If the fish doesn't take, then I'll try a smaller dry followed by a riffle-hitched wet fly. The riffle-hitched wet often gets a reluctant fish to commit, but if it doesn't, I will go back to the fly in which the steelhead originally showed an interest. Working a fish that has shown for a dry is often the most exciting part of dry-fly steelheading.

Another type of dry-fly fishing for steelhead typically occurs in the spring and coincides with early-season insect hatches on streams and rivers with high water quality. Spawned out steelhead dropping back to the lake often hold and feed in preferable lies in an effort to quickly build up their bodies after the rigors of the reproductive process. On some streams and rivers, this movement back to the lake occurs at a time when prolific insect hatches such as *Ephemerella subvaria*, commonly known as the Hendrickson, are at their peak. Sometimes steelhead can be found readily surface feeding on duns and spinners. This type of feeding activity is most common on the rivers of Ontario and Michigan, usually on rivers that have runs of wild fish.

This opportunity requires a dead-drift approach with a long leader and a fly that is at least a reasonable representation of the natural insect. Use a much lighter tippet of 2X or even 3X for this presentation than you would with a waking fly. Total leader lengths up to 15 feet, including tippet lengths of 4 to 5 feet, aid in placing slack in the leader and allowing the fly to drift naturally with the current. I normally use a single-handed rod when dead-drifting dry flies for steelhead.

Finding rising steelhead is not easy. It requires the perfect combination of a strong hatch or spinnerfall, good numbers of drop-back steelhead, and low, clear water conditions. Blind casting is a possibility, but your chances are greatly improved if you can find actively feeding fish. Search in the midsection down through the tailout of a pool. Tails with slow current and boulders are the best places to find surface feeding. Actively feeding steelhead are usually not hard to miss; look for a significant push of water with a surface rise.

When you find a rising steelhead, carefully get into position and make a cast as soon as possible. A steelhead may not feed or stay in the same place for long, so time is of the essence. If the fish has a cadence or rhythm, deliver the fly when it is likely to feed next. An up-and-across cast can work well, but I prefer to take a position slightly up and across from the fish's position. From either angle, I use a stop or a dump cast to deliver slack to the leader and gain a drag-free drift. Slack also allows the fish to suck in the fly as it takes. Be sure the fly disappears before the hook is set, and set with finesse as an 8- to 10-pound steelhead can break even a modest-size tippet if you are not careful.

Stripping Streamers

The lower end of a stream or river where it flows into a lake usually has very little current or almost no movement at all. Since current won't help move the fly as part of the presentation, you must provide the action to entice a take. Stripping a baitfish pattern in this slow estuary water can be quite effective.

Steelhead located in the estuary water at the beginning of their migration likely have more of an urge to feed on bait and other food sources than fish located miles upriver. Because of this, some aggressive strikes can be experienced. Steelhead do not tend to hold well in this type of water, but rather move through to hold in water with some current. But when water levels are low and the upstream migration becomes temporar-

Using streamers in the lower end of a tributary near the lake can produce fresh, aggressive fish. NICK PIONESSA PHOTO

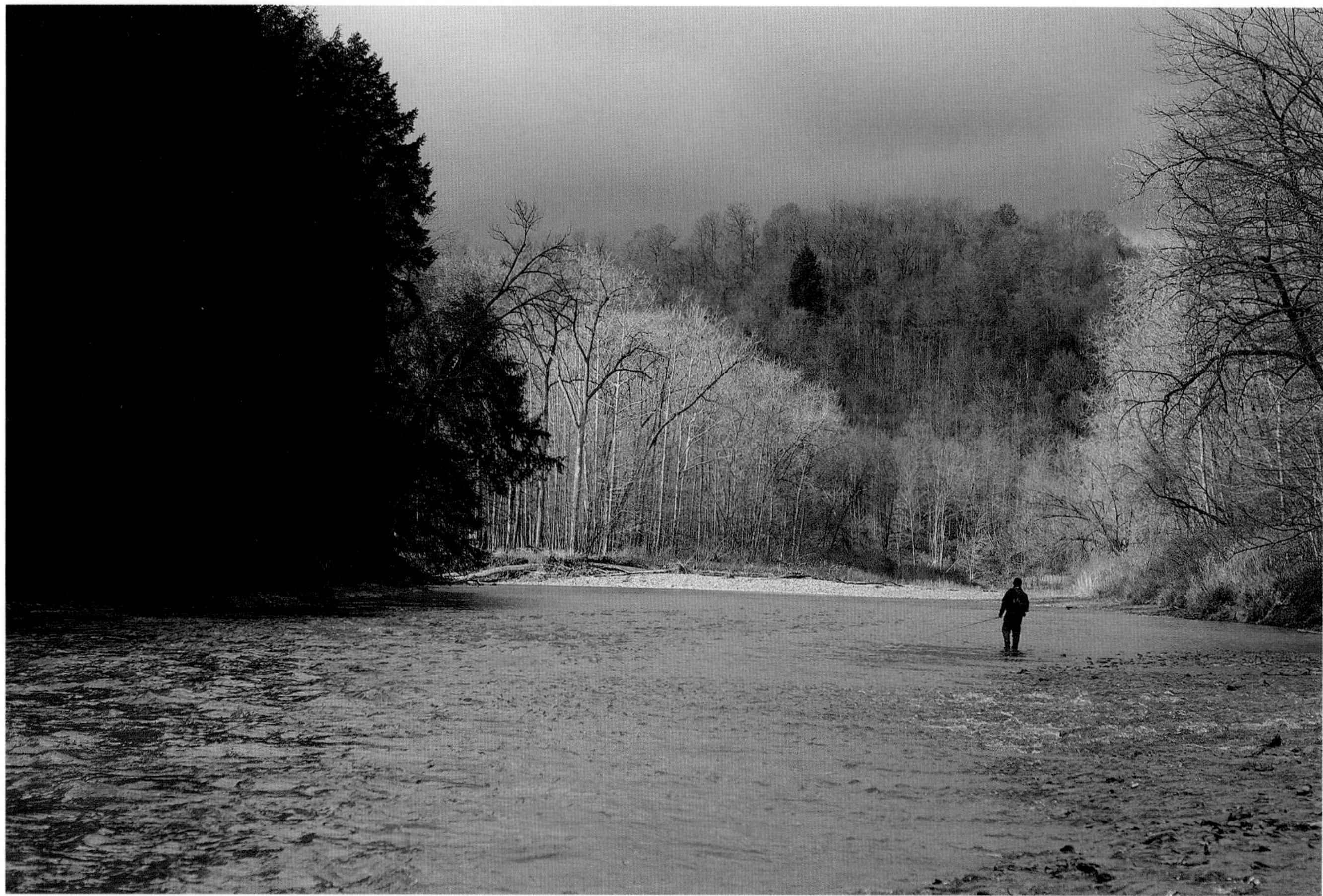

Ominous skies announce that a change in the weather is on the horizon. NICK PIONESSA PHOTO

ily postponed because of the difficulty or impossibility of moving through skinnier water, steelhead can mill around in estuary water for days at a time. Often the fish found in the estuary water are fresh from the lake and explosive fighters. Also, this type of water and fishing is not likely to attract much of a crowd and offers an opportunity to separate from the pack on days of heavy angling pressure.

Another stillwater opportunity exists in the lake itself. Steelhead congregate at the mouths of streams and rivers in the fall and spring before beginning their ascent. The water right at the mouth and along the shoreline near the mouth can produce exciting fishing for anglers in a small boat or personal watercraft or even those wading along the shoreline.

Flies tied to represent baitfish and other swimming aquatic life forms can produce well in stillwater situations. Adding movement to the fly by stripping line with the line hand is the only way to effectively fish the estuary and lake waters. Pinch the line between your fingers and the cork of the handle and then strip line from behind the point where it is pinched against the cork. The speed and cadence of the strip impart action to the fly. Dumbbell eyes also impact the way the fly swims. I prefer a retrieve with a fairly steady, moderate speed that gives the fly the impression of fleeing prey but isn't so fast that a steelhead may not bother giving chase.

You can also strip line to add action to a swinging fly in water that has current. The erratic motion caused by the strip can entice a reluctant fish and is worth trying on a fish that has shown an interest but hasn't taken the fly. I have also caught a few steelhead by stripping streamers through eddies along fast currents.

A single-handed rod generally works best when stripping streamers while wading or fishing from a boat or personal watercraft. The single-hander makes it a bit easier to lengthen the line after the retrieve and to control the rod while stripping line. While a full two-hander is a bit cumbersome for stripping flies, a light switch rod is quite versatile and useful for this type of fishing. When using a switch rod, you can make an overhead cast or a forward Spey cast.

Hooking and Landing a Steelhead

After a steelhead takes the fly, whether that fish is eventually brought to hand depends on your reaction to the take and how you handle the fish after it is hooked. Reaction to the take varies depending on whether you are using the dead-drift approach or the wet-fly swing or a waking dry. The way you handle a steelhead often depends on how much room you have to fight the fish, water temperature, and tippet strength.

When a steelhead takes a dead-drifted fly, it will often be subtle, as the fish simply opens its mouth to intercept the drift of the fly. A steelhead can quickly spit out a fly when it dis-

When using the wet-fly swing, you have to feel the weight of the fish before setting the hook. NICK PIONESSA PHOTO

covers what it just ate was a fake. A quick, decisive hook set is critical the instant you detect a take. Sharply raise the rod or raise it while sweeping it at an angle downstream for the best possibility of a solid hook set. It is quite common for a dead-drifted fly hookup to occur along the edge of the fish's mouth. Since this area of a steelhead's mouth can be hard, the set of the rod needs to be sufficient for the hook to penetrate and to compensate for the power lost as the rod flexes.

The hook set when using the wet-fly swing is very different, and in this case patience is key. You'll detect the take by feel when using a subsurface fly. It is critical to feel the weight of the fish before setting the hook; never react to a mere bump or tug of the fly as that will most likely only pull the fly from the fish's grasp. Once you detect the weight of the fish, make a sweeping hook set toward the near bank to set the hook in the side of the fish's mouth.

The percentage of fish landed is much higher when they are hooked in the side of the mouth than when they are hooked on the edge of the mouth. Being patient and reacting to the weight of the fish is also very important when fishing a waking surface fly or riffle-hitched wet. If you set the hook on the sight of the take, you will usually pull the fly from the fish's grasp.

Some anglers prefer to hold a few inches of loose line pinched off between the index finger and cork grip of the rod, keeping a loose loop ready to feed to a steelhead when it takes the fly. Another approach is to maintain a very loose drag or to use a reel with a simple spring tension drag so that the fish can actually pull line off the reel as it takes the fly. After the fish has taken a foot or two, pinch the line briefly to add tension. The loose line allows a steelhead to firmly grab the fly in its mouth since there is no tension initially on the take.

With both of these approaches, the fish practically hooks itself as it takes the loose line. Most steelhead would still be hooked without the loose line, but sometimes the fish drops the fly because of the tension. Also, a steelhead expels water through its gills to assist in sucking in a fly. Without the loop or a loose drag, the fish may not take the fly deep enough for a solid hookup.

Once a fish is hooked, the real fun begins. Steelhead are known for their exciting runs and acrobatic leaps. The intensity of a steelhead's fight will generally be greater when optimum water temperatures exist.

The approach to fighting a steelhead will vary based on the amount of room available to play the fish. I generally opt for a fairly loose drag setting when fishing a big pool with no obvious obstructions. This approach allows a steelhead to run freely and tire itself out quickly. The loose setting also provides less drag for the quick, explosive start to a run. When fighting a steelhead in a fairly open area, I sit back and let the fish run when it wants and I get line back when possible.

Always keep a taut line to the fish, as slack in the line or leader can let a steelhead wrestle the fly free. Quick pickup with the reel is critical when a steelhead does a 180-degree turn and shoots right back at you. I use everything I can to keep the line tight, including sweeping the rod toward the near bank or quickly backpedaling and even running up onto the bank while reeling.

You'll need a looser setting when using lighter tippets along with the dead-drift approach. A reel with ultralow startup inertia when a steelhead begins a run is critical for protecting light tippets. The rod can play an important role as well: A rod with a softer, smoother action throughout its length will act more as a shock absorber than one with a faster action. When you are forced to put the brakes on a steelhead while battling it with a light tippet, the softer action is a significant benefit.

Fighting a steelhead in confined areas or in pools with obstructions creates a variety of challenges. One of my favorite steelhead runs is just above a long stretch of fast, turbulent water. It is treacherous and even dangerous to follow a fish down through its churning current. It can be done, but I avoid it at all costs. While this one run comes quickly to mind, I have fished numerous pools where I couldn't follow a fish when I hooked it. In this situation, I use a tight drag and heavy tippet, forcing a steelhead to fight for every inch of line.

I have found time and time again that steelhead generally do not want to leave the pool when hooked. But when the drag is too loose at the beginning of the fight in a confined area, a steelhead is likely to rocket downriver out of the pool on its initial run. When fishing my run, it is critical to survive the first few minutes of the fight. This can be especially challenging when the fish is hooked near the tailout. I attempt to firmly stand my ground, and I know the breaking point of my rod and tippet.

If a steelhead can be kept in the pool initially, it normally will stay there for the duration of the fight. And while I'll apply maximum pressure at first, lightening up on the amount of pull exerted on the fish by the rod seems to relax a steelhead. On numerous occasions I have been able to slowly move a steelhead upriver by exerting a minimal amount of pressure, usually just enough to keep the line tight. My brother Jerry and I have termed this technique "walking the dog." Once the fish has moved up the run or pool, the fight can resume with plenty of room to reach a successful conclusion.

Logjams and big boulders create their own challenges when it comes to landing a steelhead. A fish that is hooked near the security of timber extending into the water will often fight to get back to the logjam and find sanctuary in its branches and limbs. It is imperative to use a tight drag and side pressure, holding the rod parallel to the water to pull the fish away from impending doom. You'll need a heavy tippet when pulling a fish away from an obstacle like a logjam.

Do not let a fish wedge the fly line or leader under a large boulder during the fight. Holding the rod high to place the line at a more perpendicular angle to the water makes it less likely that the line will wrap around a rock or boulder. Wading deeper into the river to maintain a shorter line also reduces the possibility of losing a fish on a rock. Even if a fish does become wedged, not all is lost. I have rescued a few fights over the years by wading out as close to the obstruction as possible while keeping the line tight and reaching out with my arm to dramatically change the angle and free the line.

When fighting a steelhead in a spot that doesn't have an obstruction, I generally keep the rod fairly low and nearly parallel with the water's surface to create side pressure, which is

Maintaining a lighter drag setting when possible allows a steelhead to tire.

It is important to maintain a taut line and a strong bend in the rod when fighting a steelhead. Here, Larry Halyk fights a fish on a broad tailout.

A fresh steelhead makes a run downstream. Often a fish will stay in the pool if you apply enough pressure. NICK PIONESSA PHOTO

more effective in controlling a fish than applying pressure from the top. A high rod position generally results in more lost steelhead since it is easier for a fish to create slack in the line with the high angle. The high angle creates pressure in a direction that is more likely to pull the fly from the fish's mouth.

A low rod angle is especially important toward the end of the fight. Applying side pressure when the fish is in close will assist in steering and guiding the steelhead to the shallows. As the fight nears its conclusion, be ready for a steelhead to make a final run or two.

A large net with a catch-and-release bag will help you wrap up the fight quicker and promote a successful release. But unless you are fishing with the aid of a drift or jet boat, large nets usually aren't practical to carry along a river. Typically, it is not too difficult to land a steelhead without a net. When a fish is tired and guided into the shallows, it will normally turn on its side, and you can grasp it firmly just in front of the tail. Gloves that provide extra grip when tailing a fish can be useful.

I tail the fish with my right hand and gently slide my left under the steelhead's belly to gain control. If there isn't a shallow area to land the fish in near proximity, the next best place is an eddy or lee in the current. Even if this water is fairly deep,

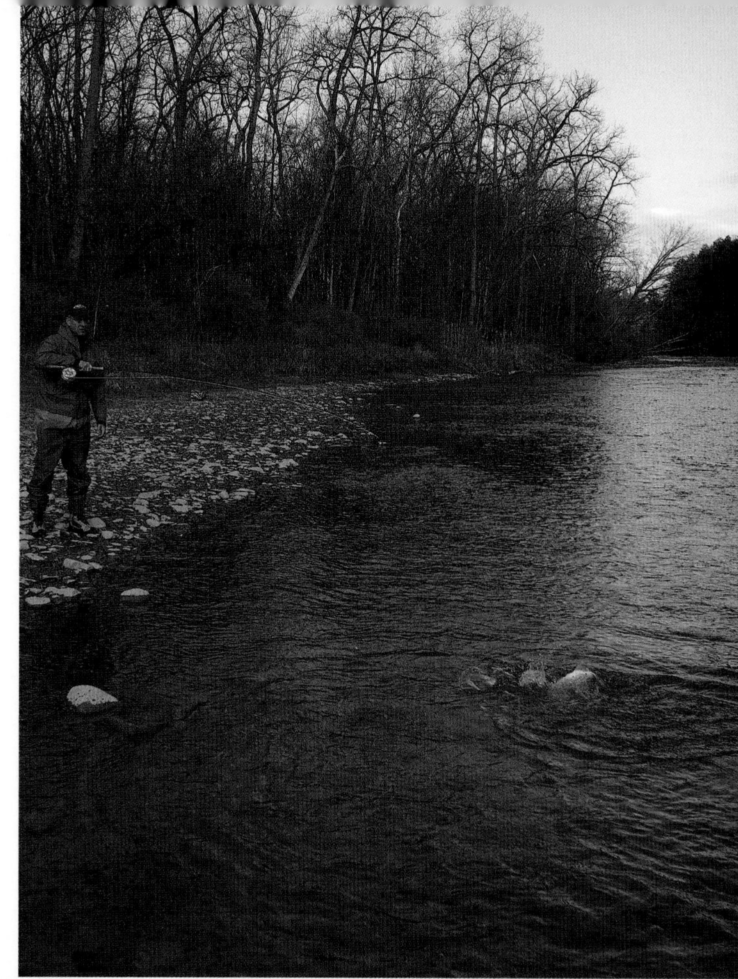

Keeping the rod low allows me to direct a steelhead into the shallows for a successful landing. NICK PIONESSA PHOTO

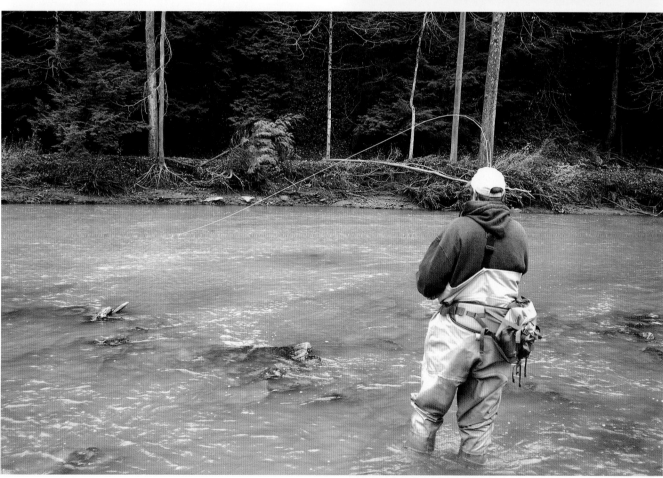

It is important to keep the rod tip high when fighting a steelhead in water with large boulders.

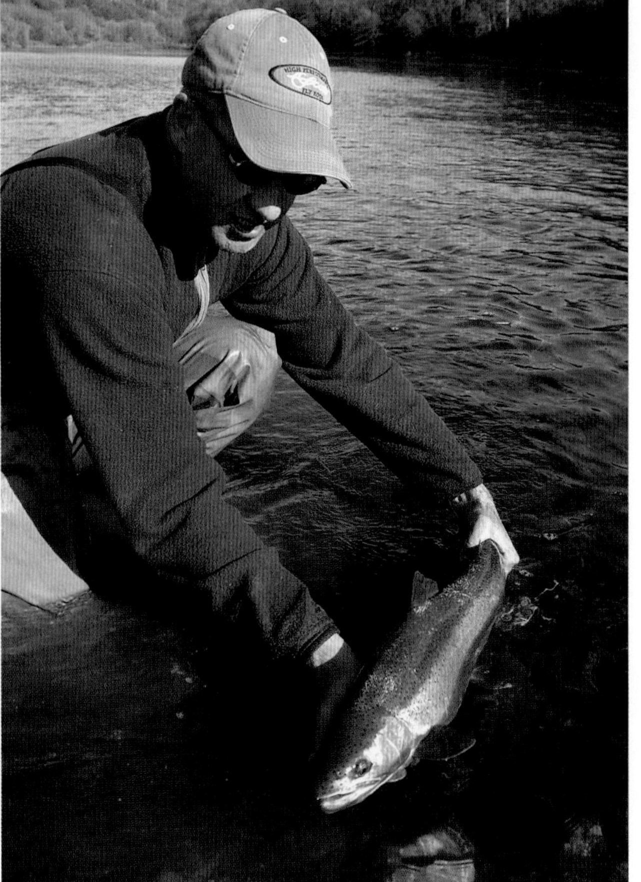

***Above:* Be prepared for a steelhead to run out some line when the fight gets close to the bank. *Left:* Careful handling of a steelhead is critical to a successful release.**

a steelhead will turn on its side when tired, giving you the opportunity to grasp its tail.

Two-handed rods create some difficulties when landing a steelhead. The rod's length makes it difficult to get close to the fish. This normally does not pose a problem when there are shallows to roll the fish up onto, but landing a fish in deeper water with a two-hander can be more of a challenge. Do not place the rod at too steep an angle when the fish is in close as this places stress on the rod's tip and you can easily wind up with a broken rod. When the fish is sufficiently played out, loosen up on the tension applied to the fish, grab the fly line between the rod tip and the fish, and slowly guide the steelhead close enough to be tailed. Place the rod under your arm so that both hands are free. This approach requires a stout tippet, and you have to let the fish run if it still isn't ready to land.

Successfully releasing a steelhead requires proper handling of the fish during and after it is landed. A steelhead should be kept in the water as much as possible. Don't let it flop on the bank or wallow in sandy or dirty water. When taking photographs, keep the steelhead in the water except for a quick lift to be caught on camera with your smiling face. Before it is released back into the river to continue its journey, make sure it has regained most of its strength and is able to hold or even move forward in the current.

CHAPTER 4

Strategy

An angler finds winter solitude.
NICK PIONESSA PHOTO

While presentation and perseverance are the most important aspects of success in just about any type of fly fishing, having a plan is nearly as critical. An understanding of the quarry and the water that it swims in are the building blocks for forming a strategy that leads to encountering steelhead and to an overall quality experience. The basis for developing a successful strategy includes observations and conclusions from previous times on the water, research of current river conditions and opportunities, and personal preferences as to which waters will provide a desired experience.

During the prime steelhead season, I am always steelhead fishing. I analyze run densities and water conditions to determine when and where the next outing will occur, using notes and memories from past outings as a guide. Sometimes decisions are made based as much on instinct as on science. Instincts become honed with experience, and over the years the decision-making process becomes easier. Many aspects of strategy involve making a plan before ever heading out to the river.

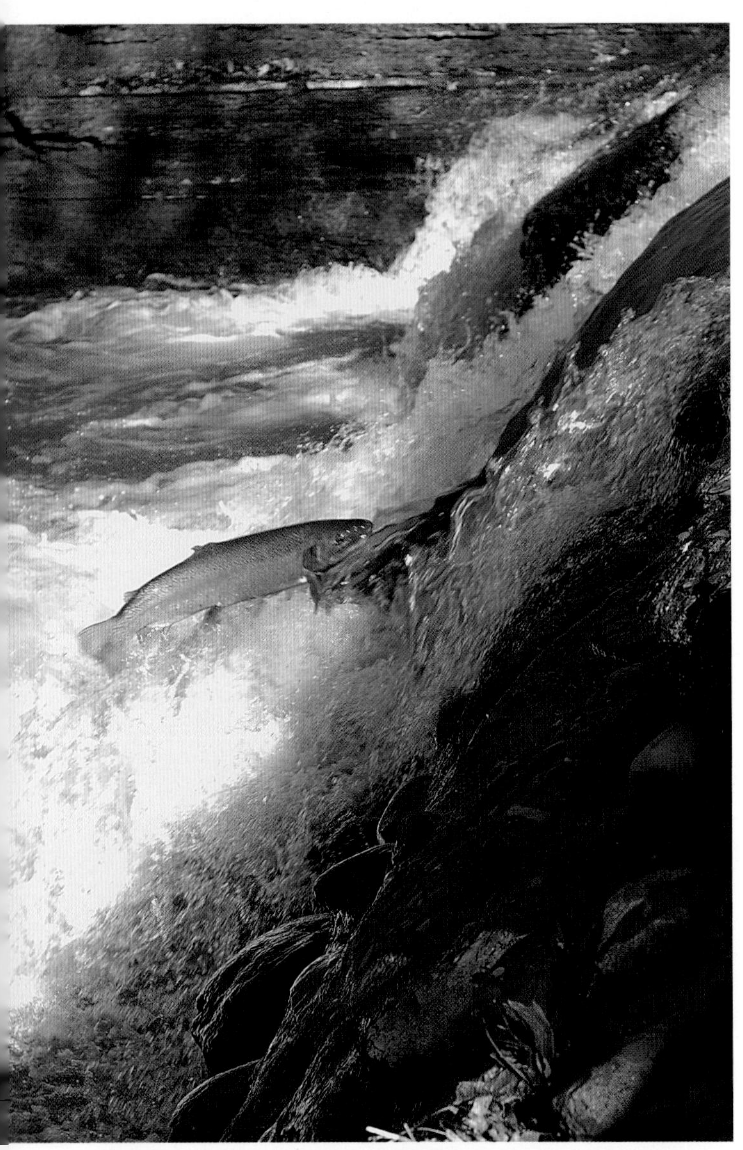

Steelhead will use their strength and leaping abilities to bypass small falls and low-head dams. NICK PIONESSA PHOTO

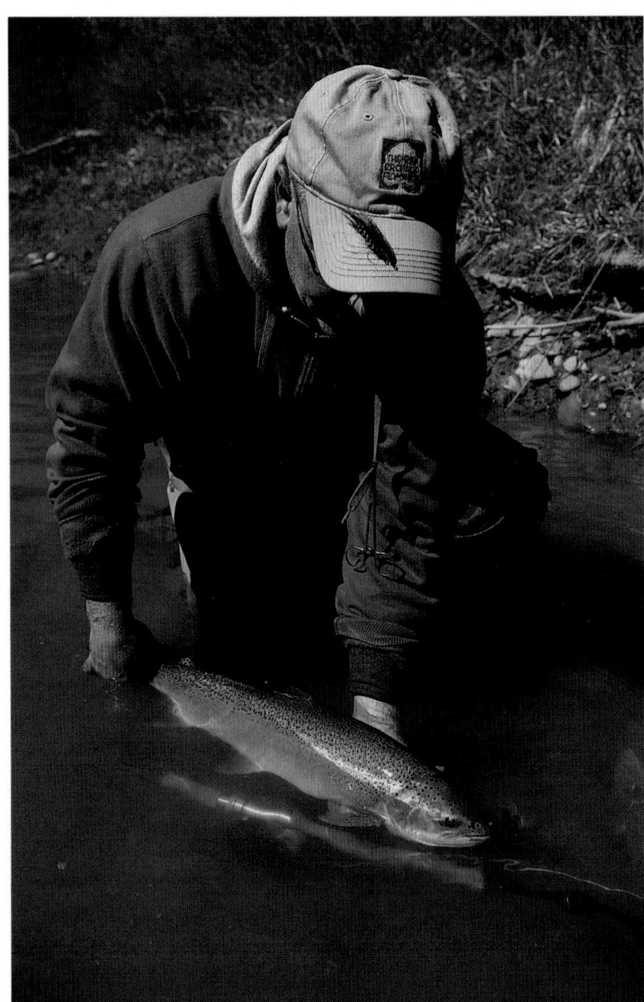

Bill Ingersoll releases a fresh-run steelhead. NICK PIONESSA PHOTO

Understanding Steelhead Behavior

Understanding what makes a steelhead act the way it does will help you anticipate the activity on a river on any given day. But understanding behavior really means understanding steelhead tendencies because no rules are written in stone. In fact, a run comprises many individual steelhead that demonstrate a wide range of behavioral traits. This section looks at some of the key factors that impact the manner in which a steelhead acts or reacts to stimuli.

Run Timing

A steelhead is a migratory rainbow trout. A migratory fish begins its life in one body of water such as a river or creek, escapes to a larger body of water, and then returns to its point of origin to spawn and propagate the species. Hatchery steelhead that have been planted in a river as smolts have this same migratory urge. However, the instinctive ability of a fish to return to the river of its origin is much greater in wild fish than in hatchery steelhead. For anglers, understanding the migratory process is critical.

Steelhead migrations in the Great Lakes region are mainly composed of winter-run fish. Winter-runs begin to migrate in the fall and spawn in the late winter and the spring of the following year. As a general rule for the Great Lakes, the peak months for steelhead runs are October and November. Almost all rivers in the region receive some degree of a run in this period, and for most rivers this is the height of the season. But each river has its nuances—some regularly receive good numbers of fish in September, and others may not see a consistent number of fish until December. Steelhead are most aggressive in this autumn time frame, and since they have just spent the summer feeding in one of the forage-rich Great Lakes, fish at this time of year are normally in prime shape. It is for this reason that October and November are my favorite months for steelhead fishing.

Fish enter rivers that remain open all winter even during the coldwater months. Steelhead ascending the rivers and streams in winter combine with fish that have already moved up in the fall to provide great fishing opportunities throughout the region's nastiest season. Fish usually trickle in during winter migrations, but I have experienced great waves of steelhead, particularly in late winter as active spawning nears. Winter fish generally lack the aggressive nature of an autumn steelhead, but fish fresh from the lake are usually quite active even in the cold water.

March through May marks the height of the steelhead spawning activity. The actual occurrence varies widely among rivers, mainly because of differences in water temperature and annual variations in water conditions. As active spawning

***Right:* Early-autumn fish can be aggressive and acrobatic.**

October and November typically provide some of the best steelhead opportunities.

nears, the remaining steelhead that have not moved out of the lake or those that ascended earlier and backed out are now drawn into the rivers and streams. The steelhead that wintered over become more active too. Spring fish move toward the gravel areas of a river and stream and are often distracted by the spawning process. Spring steelhead often migrate with a sense of urgency as the instinctive urge to procreate drives them and results in wide fluctuations in the number of fish present from day to day. The ability to find steelhead, especially those willing to take a fly, becomes a little more hit-and-miss in the springtime.

Spring steelhead will often linger in the rivers and streams for a time after the spawn is complete. If water temperatures remain under 60 degrees F and there is a viable food source, post-spawn fish may not be in a hurry to go back to the cooler waters of the lake. Instead postspawn steelhead use the opportunity to begin the process of building up their bodies after the rigors of the spawning run. Postspawn or drop-back steelhead can be very aggressive and provide explosive takes on a swung fly.

Throughout the Great Lakes region, a few rivers host summer-run steelhead. These fish are genetically programmed to begin their ascent in the summer months. Since not many of the region's streams and rivers maintain cool enough temperatures during the summer months for steelhead to survive, summer-run fish are not widely distributed. And even in rivers where they can survive, summer-run conditions are at their best during cool, rainy summers. Summer-run steelhead can show up as early as June but more often will arrive in the first part of July, and fish can trickle in throughout the summer. Runs of summer steelhead are typically maintained through hatchery programs. The strain of steelhead that provides most of the summer-run activity in the Great Lakes is the Skamania strain.

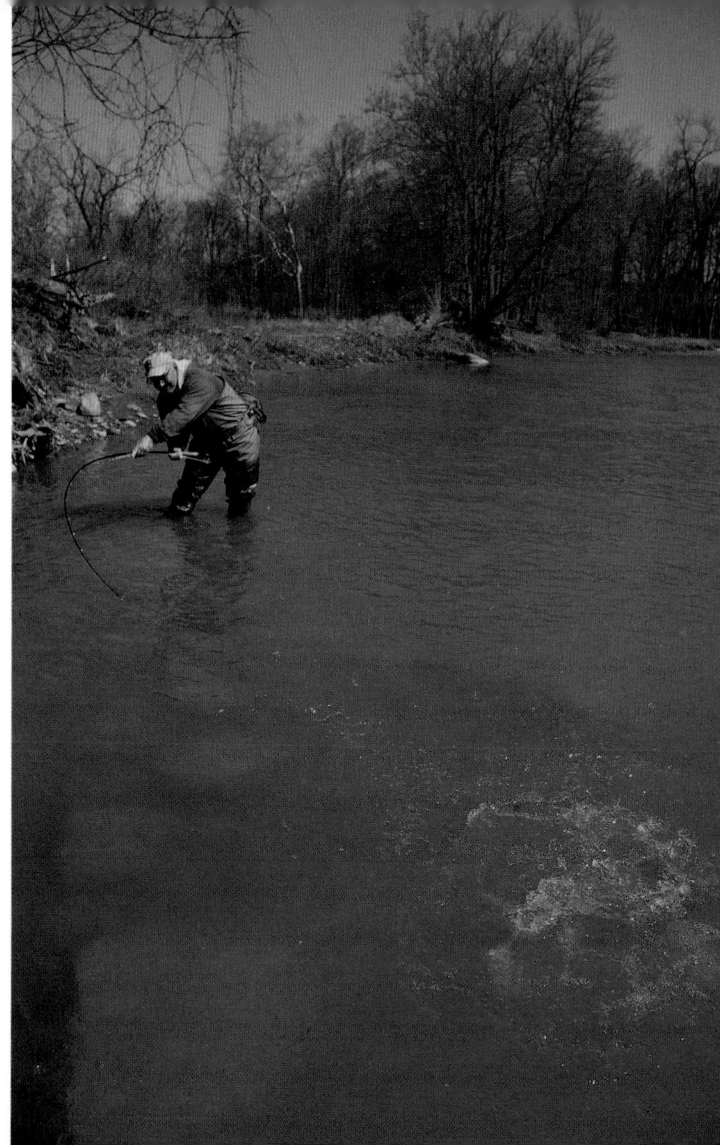

The optimum water temperature range for steelhead is 42 to 58 degrees F. NICK PIONESSA PHOTO

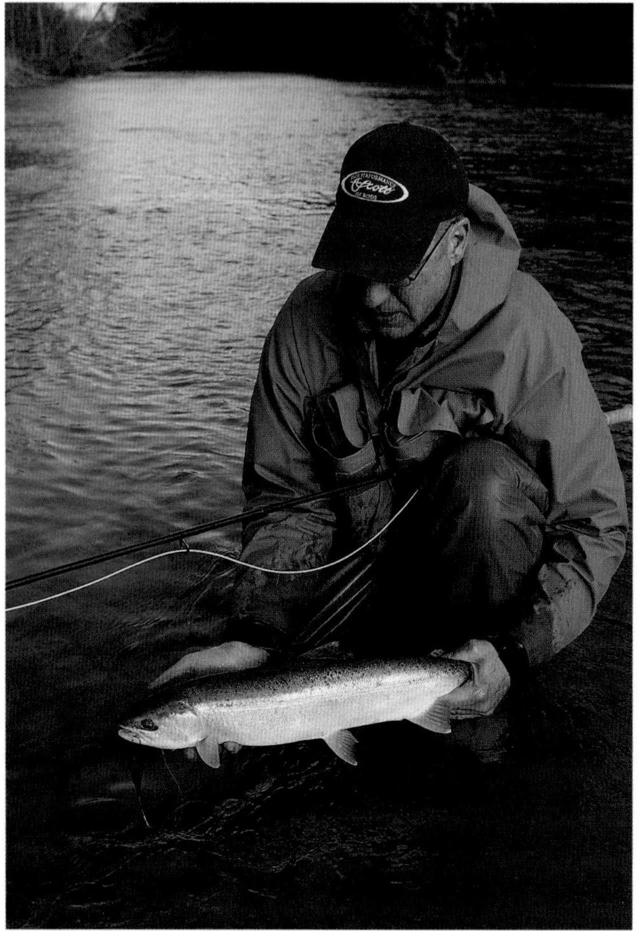

A postspawn spring steelhead. These fish can be very aggressive and provide explosive takes on a swung fly. NICK PIONESSA PHOTO

Water Temperature

When I first started steelhead fishing in the Great Lakes region, I fished mostly during the winter months. Cold water complete with shelf ice and floating slush were the typical conditions that I faced on a weekly basis, forcing me to draw some inaccurate generalizations about Great Lakes steelhead behavior. The thing that struck me most is that fish of this region didn't seem as active as their Pacific coast counterparts. But as my range of experience increased it became clear that water temperature had a direct impact on steelhead activity and aggressiveness. I now feel as though water temperature is the most important factor associated with steelhead behavior, and it also figures prominently into the timing of migration and spawning. A thermometer is an important piece of a steelheader's equipment and will help to unlock some of the mysteries of a river.

The optimum water temperature range for steelhead is 42 to 58 degrees F. Within this range, 50 to 55 degrees is ideal. What this means to an angler is that within the optimum range, steelhead tend to be most aggressive and capable of moving a long distance to intercept or chase a fly. This temperature range can be found on most Great Lakes rivers from late September through November. That is why I prefer that time of year for steelhead fishing. In the fall, steelhead are spread throughout the river in a wide range of water and are susceptible to a range of angling techniques. Normally, fall water temperatures need to fall into the mid to low 60s before steelhead enter the stream or river.

But actual water temperature does not always tell the entire story. The direction of the mercury often has a greater significance. Cold fronts that blow through the Great Lakes region can reduce air temperatures by 20 degrees in a short period of time, causing water temperatures to drop by 5 to 10 degrees or even more overnight. Streams and rivers with a predominance of bedrock are particularly susceptible to wide temperature changes. Rivers that have more groundwater influence or that run out of an impoundment or large body of water may not have such dramatic changes.

A significant decrease in water temperature will slow steelhead activity. Therefore, fishing is often more difficult after a cold spell, especially for swinging flies, so I try to avoid fishing the early-morning hours after a cold night. A number of times a cold front has moved through in the late morning or early afternoon while I was on the river, and as the water temperature dropped throughout the afternoon, so did the number of fish interested in taking a fly.

Rising water temperatures have the opposite effect. Even a small to moderate increase in the water temperature can have a positive impact on steelhead activity. Based on the notes in my fishing log and my observation, some of the best steelhead fishing coincides with stable or rising water temperatures. I try to time my outings to meet such conditions. After a very cold night, I prefer to fish the late morning and afternoon, allowing the water temperature to recover. I also do my best to select days to fish when temperatures will be on the rise as opposed to falling.

You can still find quality steelhead fishing even when the water temperature isn't in the optimum range. During the winter months, you can seek out solitude on most rivers, and an understanding of water temperature can play an important part in your success. When water temperatures drop into the 30s, a steelhead's metabolism begins to decrease. This generally causes steelhead to hold in slower water or flows that are out of the main current.

Steelhead can remain quite active during the winter months, especially when the water temperature is fairly stable. The slow presentation of a dead-drifting fly can be very productive in coldwater situations, but I have also had good success swinging flies in 33- to 35-degree water that has held stable for a time. Given the fish's slower metabolism, presenting a swinging fly in a slow, controlled fashion will work best in the winter. Steelhead will generally not chase a fly as far or with the same aggressive manner as they do when temperatures are in the optimum range.

Some rivers will draw fish in all winter, particularly in the late-winter months as the spawning activity nears. The fresh-run winter fish can often be more aggressive. A very slight increase in water temperature caused by a moderate, sunny winter day can significantly improve steelhead activity. I have had some incredible winter steelhead fishing in the middle of a mild afternoon.

As water temperatures drop into the 30s, a steelhead's energy for upstream migration drops. Cold water can stall or even halt migration on streams or rivers with small falls or low-head dams. However, the pools below these obstructions can hold concentrations of fish during coldwater periods.

Later in winter and in spring, as the water temperatures rise consistently into the high 30s, steelhead activity will increase as well. This rise in temperature, more than any other factor, seems to trigger the onset of spawning behavior. It will create a certain urgency, forcing steelhead to migrate, at times quickly, to spawning gravel. You'll find fewer steelhead in the slower, deeper runs and pools. Rather, they will concentrate in shallower riffle water and the runs and pockets below and adjacent to these areas.

Steelhead are often preoccupied with spawning during the spring months, especially once the spawn is in full swing. At times these fish may not be as likely to take a fly as in the fall. You can find late spawners in a river and fish dropping back to the lake until the water temperatures are consistently in the mid 60s. Keep an eye on spring water temperatures—70 degrees or greater can prove lethal to a steelhead.

A fresh hen perfectly lit in the late-afternoon light.
NICK PIONESSA PHOTO

Doubleheader: steelhead action can heat up when the conditions are favorable. NICK PIONESSA PHOTO

Water Flow

After the time of year and water temperature, the main factor influencing steelhead migration on a day-to-day basis is water flow. An increase in flow after a rain or runoff will bring steelhead into the rivers and streams from the lakes and also motivate fish that have ascended the rivers to continue their journey. Increases in water flow make many rivers easier for steelhead to negotiate and also dislodge fish from certain holding lies, forcing them to move. An increase in flow at the right time is capable of drawing waves of steelhead into a river or stream.

On the downside, an increase in flow can make the water too high or too stained to fish. On some rivers, these conditions may last for days, while other rivers clear quickly. As a river or stream falls back into shape, fishing conditions can be excellent. I put significant effort into meeting these conditions head-on throughout the steelhead season. However, perfect conditions present themselves only some of the time. Adjusting to high and dirty or low and clear water is very important.

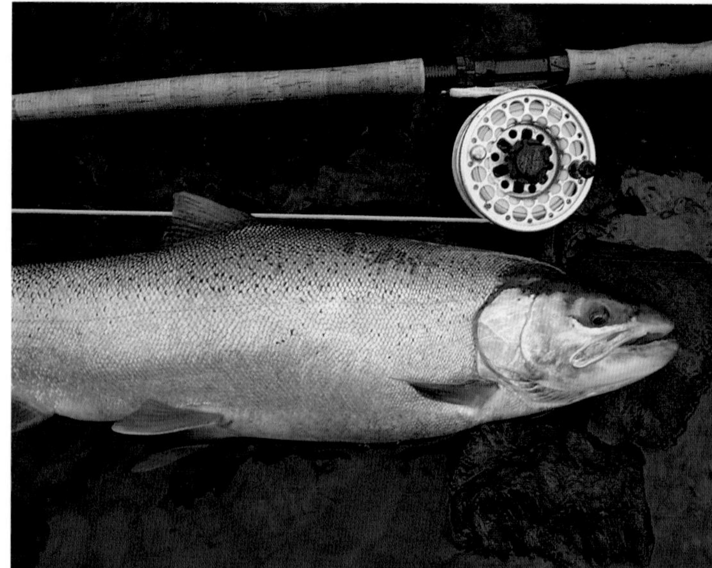

This fresh steelhead was caught after a rise in water level.

While high and dirty water can be intimidating, fishing water in this condition is not a guaranteed failure. High water often accompanies dirty conditions, and the extra flow poses more of a problem than the stain. But as long as the river remains in its banks, you can turn these conditions to your favor.

Before you fish in heavily stained water, assess the situation. Your first concern is safety. Whether you can wade the river and fish safely is always the key question. I can determine this more readily on a river that I regularly fish, and for those rivers that have monitoring gauges I keep notes on my experiences at various water levels. Dirty water has its limits. Sometimes the water can be so opaque that visibility is near zero. I like to be able to see the fly at least 3 to 4 inches deep in the water column before I'll start fishing.

One of the advantages of dirty water is that it keeps most other anglers at home or on smaller creeks. Fishing a river that isn't in top shape is one of my tricks for finding space or solitude on heavily pressured water. I have had my best success in dirty conditions on familiar stretches of water. Another advantage is that the rise in level associated with dirty water will draw in fresh steelhead from the lake that can be very aggressive and put up an incredible fight when hooked.

On the other hand, low and clear water presents its own set of challenges. These conditions tend to make steelhead dour. They move less, and migration slows. Steelhead often concentrate in certain pools but also tend to be much less aggressive to the fly.

Low and clear water conditions can still provide great fishing opportunity, though. Fishing can be best during the low-light periods of the morning and evening. Dark, overcast days are also good when the water is low. A slight increase in water temperature can also activate steelhead sulking in a pool. Since the low water tends to concentrate the fish into condensed areas, if steelhead do become active during these conditions, you could see multiple hookups.

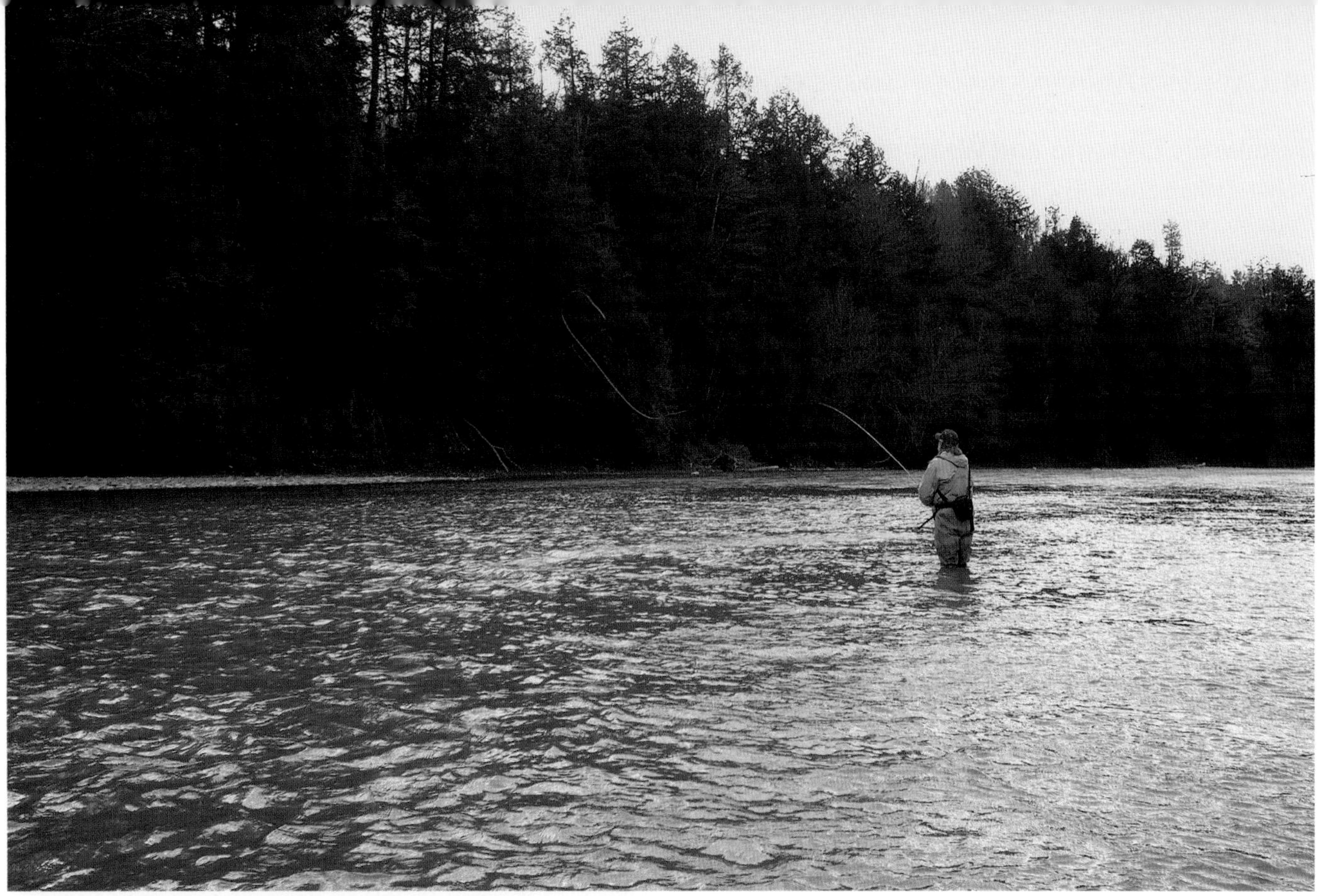

Steelhead fishing can often be at its best just as the water begins to clear.

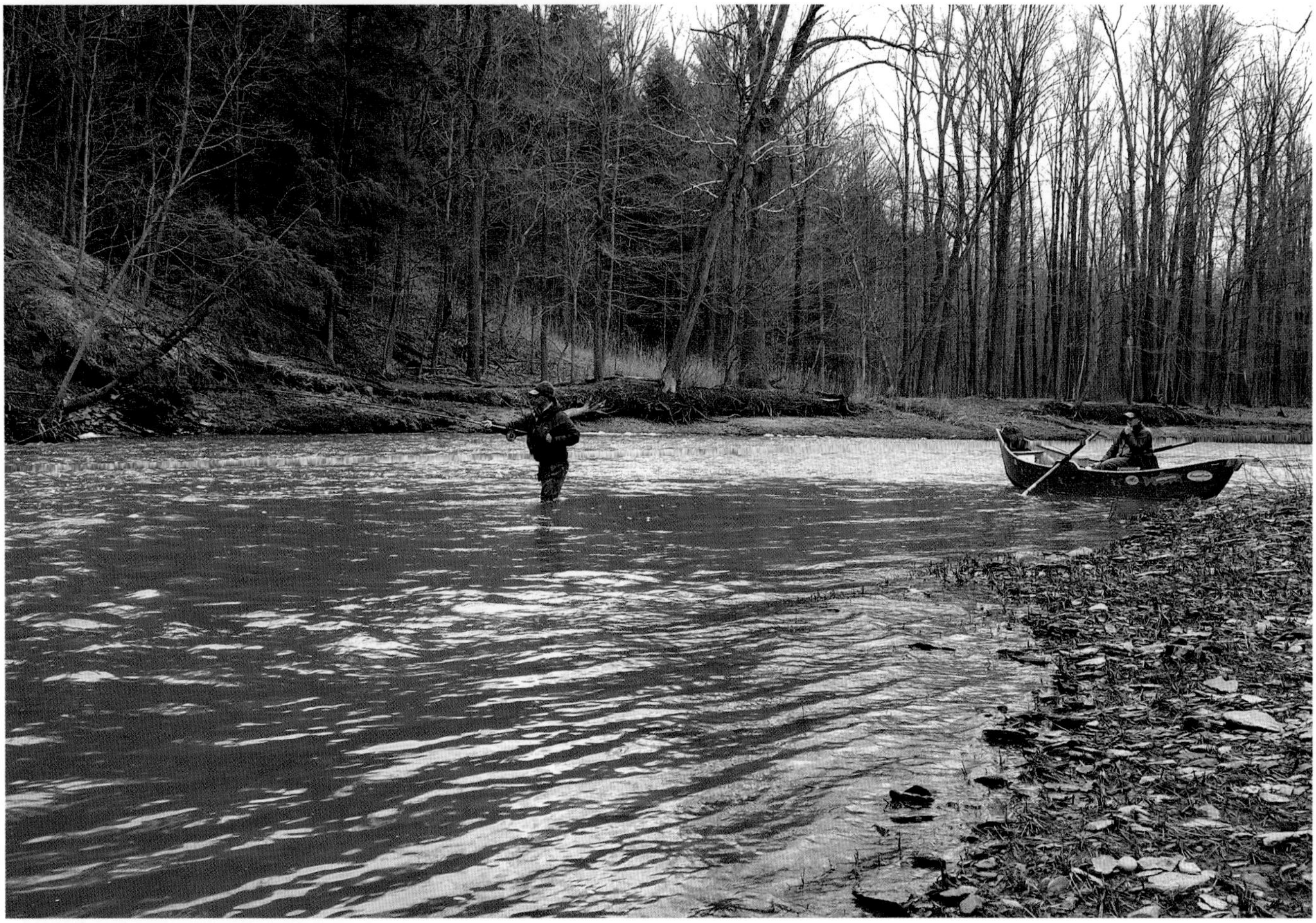

Steelhead can be quite aggressive in stained water.

Barometric Pressure and Weather

Another natural force that has an impact on steelhead behavior is barometric pressure. My research in this area has not been scientific, but I have reviewed barometric pressure readings after enough good and poor fishing outings to observe some correlations.

I have found that days with a relatively steady barometer tend to be good for steelhead fishing. In fact, some of my best days in terms of fish activity have been during stable weather patterns. This has proven especially true in the winter months. Stable weather combined with optimum water temperature and flow can create the perfect conditions for steelhead.

I have also seen a significant increase in steelhead activity during a falling barometer ahead of a substantial weather front. It seems as if these conditions create an urgency that generates movement and aggressive behavior in steelhead. Other fish and wildlife also exhibit this behavior, most likely an instinctive activity to prepare for what may follow. Activity usually drops off dramatically once the front passes.

Good steelhead fishing is also associated with a barometer that is on a slow rise. But steelhead activity tends to taper off in periods of extreme high or extreme low pressure.

Cloudy weather conditions are almost always better than bright, sunny skies for steelhead fishing. Fish tend to be comfortable away from direct sunlight. A light rain can create the perfect situation. Rain adds oxygen and nitrogen to the water and seems to supercharge a steelhead, resulting in more aggressive behavior. But too much of a good thing can ruin the fun—rapidly rising water from excessive rain eventually puts a halt to aggressive movement as steelhead will hunker down to protect themselves.

Sunny conditions aren't necessarily a negative factor and have much less impact when the water is stained. Also, later in the fall and through the winter, the angle of the sun is such that its light becomes softer and not nearly as illuminating. Besides, some direct sun can help warm the water temperature in the late morning and afternoon, which can result in an increase in steelhead activity.

Stable weather patterns create good steelhead conditions.

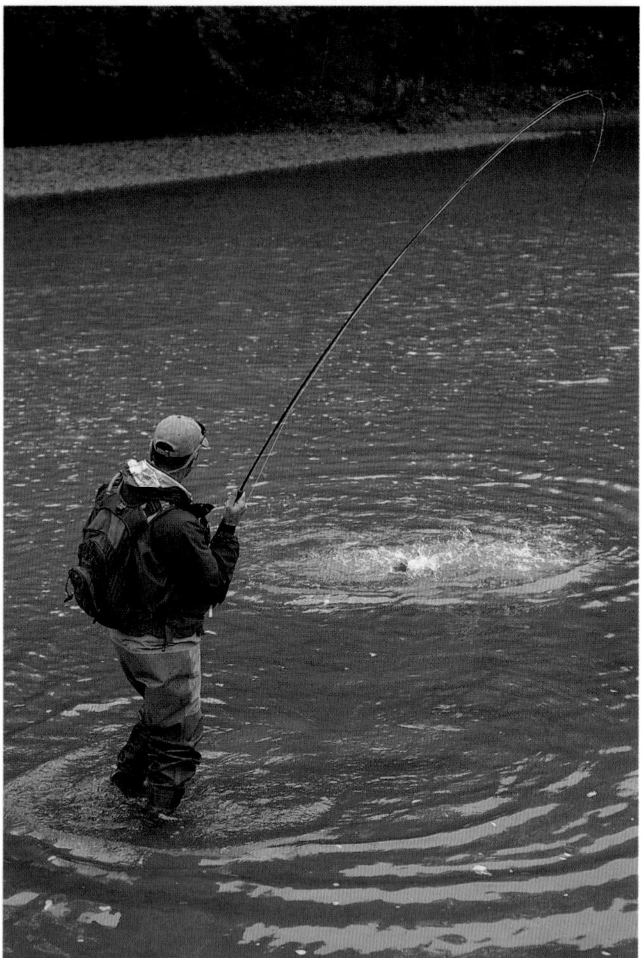

Steelhead are often quite active on lightly rainy days.
NICK PIONESSA PHOTO

Sun will have its most ill effects when it is angled directly onto the pool. Such intense, direct light makes it difficult for a fish to see the fly, and steelhead sulk when these conditions are present. I search for shaded pools when the sun is high and bright. I prefer pools where the shade comes early in the afternoon because of a gorge wall or tall, thick trees lining the bank. Steelhead activity often increases dramatically the instant the direct sun leaves the water.

Fishing Pressure

The number of anglers fishing a river or stream has a direct effect on its steelhead activity. Those rivers or streams that have a strong historic catch-and-keep ethic are improved by reducing kill limits. But reductions in kill limits over the last 10 to 20 years combined with greater education regarding reducing harvest has led to a strong catch-and-release ethic on many if not most of the region's rivers.

Even where catch-and-release is prevalent, fishing pressure can significantly influence steelhead behavior. The mere presence of anglers walking along the banks or wading in the water will force fish into more secure holding lies. This is especially the case on smaller rivers and streams. Sloppy wading can

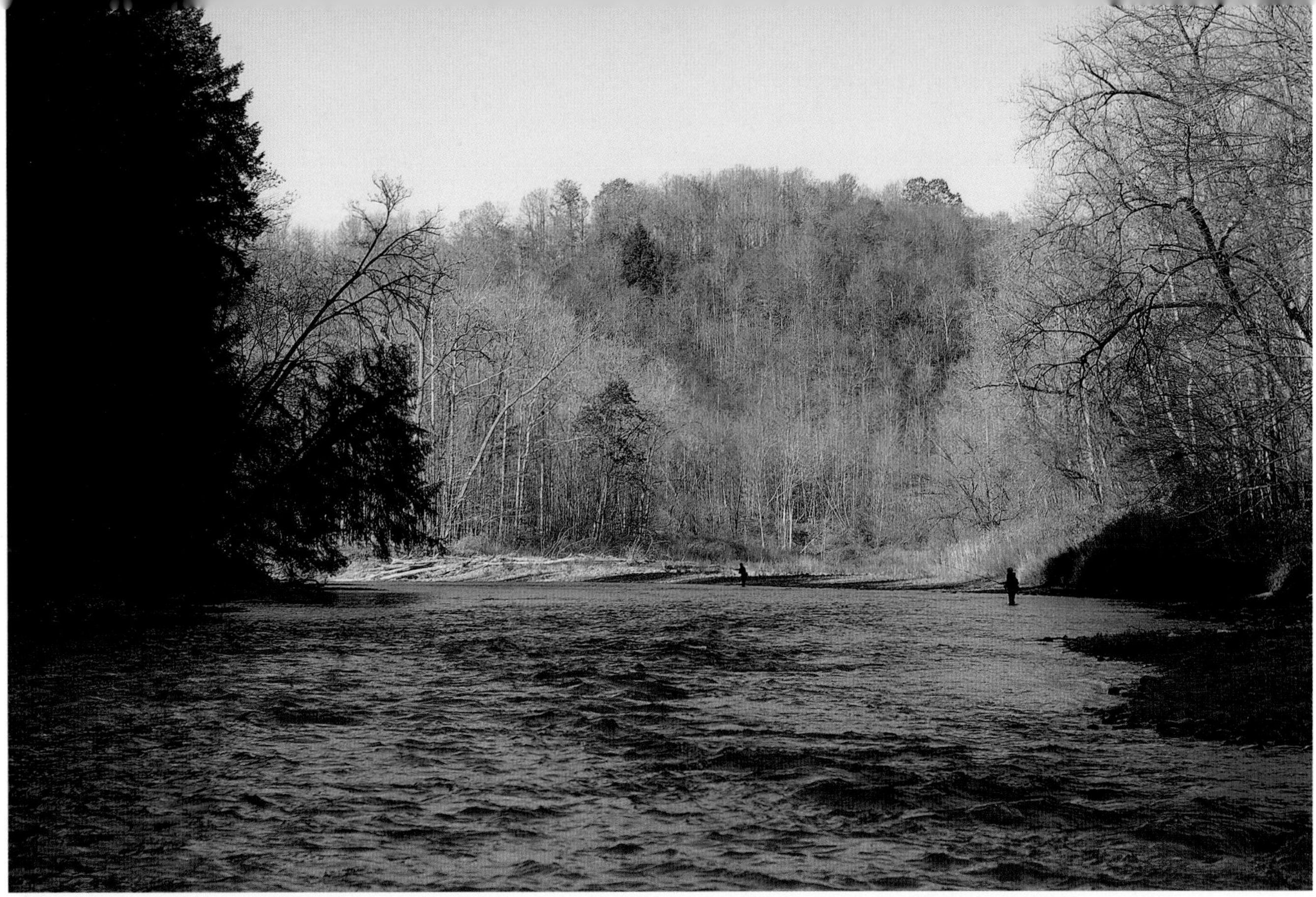

On sunny days, locating water that is in the shadows is often the key to finding active steelhead. NICK PIONESSA PHOTO

Moving away from fishing pressure can bring you greater success and enjoyment. Here Chris Garcea holds on for the ride. NICK PIONESSA PHOTO

force steelhead to hold close to boulders and overhangs, and to find the deepest pools. Steelhead are less likely to take a fly after being forced into a secure lie. Many times I have found steelhead holding in heavy water after being forced out of the more popular pools by heavy fishing pressure. Working the off-beat areas of a river can be very productive.

Fishing pressure has its greatest impact when other anglers are hooking and landing steelhead. Even with catch-and-release, a fish that has been caught once is less likely to take again, and even if it does, the fight will be diminished. I have, however, hooked and landed the same fish within hours on a few occasions. Anglers fighting a steelhead in a pool, particularly in low, clear water conditions, can also cause the remaining fish to be less aggressive and move closer to secure lies. But a continual movement of new fish from the lake or from lower on the river can reenergize a pool and provide good fishing even during periods of heavy fishing pressure. And sheer numbers of fish will also diminish the impact of fishing pressure. Some of the most popular pieces of water in the region still produce good catch rates because of the volume of steelhead from aggressive hatchery programs.

Some of the most detrimental fishing pressure to fly anglers is the highly effective and efficient use of bait, light leaders, and bobbers some anglers throughout the region use. This approach is so successful that anglers experienced in this method can hook incredible numbers of steelhead. In the process, they leave few that will still be interested in taking a fly. I think all steelhead anglers have a responsibility to share the resource, and when one approach severely limits the opportunity of others I question its fairness.

Since fishing pressure is so important, I tend to fish rivers that receive less attention from anglers. Normally the impact of fishing pressure on steelhead behavior is minimized by focusing on the first and last hours of daylight.

Wild vs. Hatchery Steelhead

A number of rivers throughout the Great Lakes region have sufficient water quality to support populations of naturally produced or wild steelhead. Most of this high-quality water runs through Ontario and Michigan, while small areas of naturalized populations exist in New York, Wisconsin, and Ohio.

Being on the water at dusk has many rewards. NICK PIONESSA PHOTO

From an esthetic standpoint, wild fish are clearly superior to hatchery fish. Their improbable journey starts with emergence from an egg, continues through running a gauntlet of predators on their way to and while in the lake, and then years later resumes when they return to their natal river to propagate the species. They are the true embodiment of the steelhead spirit.

Wild steelhead generally have a cleaner, more regal appearance and typically have a stronger fight. While it is impossible to determine a wild fish strictly by appearance, the structure of its fins will often provide sufficient evidence. The fins of a wild fish are generally fully formed with distinct edges. This is especially true of the dorsal fin. Hatchery fish can have fins that are rounded or deformed, and in some rivers the hatchery fish are marked with a fin clip.

I strongly prefer fishing for wild steelhead when possible—even though rivers that have runs composed entirely of wild fish hold numbers that are typically much lower than on rivers supported by hatchery fish. I believe that the difference between wild and hatchery fish also impacts their behavior. Most of this difference seems to stem from growing up in a truly natural environment as opposed to controlled surroundings in a hatchery.

In addition to being a hardier fish, wild steelhead learn to adapt to their nursery waters, taking advantage of available food sources. Wild fish retain some of these feeding habits upon returning as adults. Wild steelhead seem more likely to lock in on a natural source peculiar to their home rivers or streams. You are more likely to bring a naturally produced steelhead to a fly fished on the surface too.

The difference between wild and hatchery steelhead also impacts positioning in the river. Successful spawning can occur in tributaries to the main river or in specific sections of the river. Wild fish are typically positioned near spawning water. Pools within close proximity to main spawning tributaries hold more wild fish throughout the season. While hatchery fish go through the process of spawning and in some cases are successful, a hatchery fish does not have the same draw as a wild steelhead to a particular tributary.

A handsome wild buck. NICK PIONESSA PHOTO

This appears to be a hefty hatchery fish as evidenced by the unformed dorsal fin. Hatchery programs are important on rivers where natural reproduction doesn't exist.
NICK PIONESSA PHOTO

Selecting a River

A number of factors go into selecting a river or rivers to fish for steelhead. By learning the characteristics and moods of a piece of water, you gain a significant tactical advantage. Year after year, certain patterns develop so that getting to know a river or even a particular pool will yield significant rewards. Personal preference often plays a role in selecting a river. Factors other than success in terms of numbers of fish hooked and caught draw anglers to certain rivers, and the steelheader's spirit for exploration fuels travel to a variety of streams and rivers.

Proximity

Proximity to your home is probably the most common consideration in selecting a river, and because it allows you the greatest opportunity to become intimately familiar with the water, it makes a lot of sense.

Those living in the Great Lakes region would be hard-pressed to drive more than an hour without passing some steelhead water. While getting to know the closest river has the advantage of reducing drive time, anglers living near one of the lakes often have a handful to choose from that are within an easy day trip. Choosing a river then becomes a matter of personal preference often dictated by the size of its run. But getting to know two or three rivers, especially of various sizes, can be extremely important as conditions vary throughout the season. Familiarity with more rivers provides options so that you can decide on a particular day which river is likely to have perfect conditions or at least avoid water suffering from poor conditions. Establishing a repertoire of streams and rivers means that you will almost always have somewhere to fish except during the heaviest rains or most significant droughts.

For anglers who live well outside the Great Lakes region, selecting the river with the shortest possible drive is one approach. However, if you are making a long trip, it probably

A fresh hen from my home river. NICK PIONESSA PHOTO

makes good sense to also consider streams and rivers that have consistent runs with fishable conditions for a majority of the time during a typical year. Quality lodging and guide service may also play into your decision when venturing well away from home, especially when a quality experience is more important than exploration and adventure.

Size and Character

Being blessed to be quite literally surrounded by steelhead water, I select a river to fish based on a range of criteria. The overall size and general character of a piece of water often influence my choice. I prefer big water that runs free and unencumbered by dams and man-made obstructions. Big water gives steelhead the opportunity to spread out and makes it harder to locate and hook them. Big water allows me to move around and use two-handed rods. Rivers that run free best accommodate and support the steelhead spirit, and big water gives an energetic fish a great place to dance when hooked. The experience on bigger rivers is measured by quality as opposed to quantity of hookups, and it is an appreciation that develops with time on the water and maturity as a steelheader.

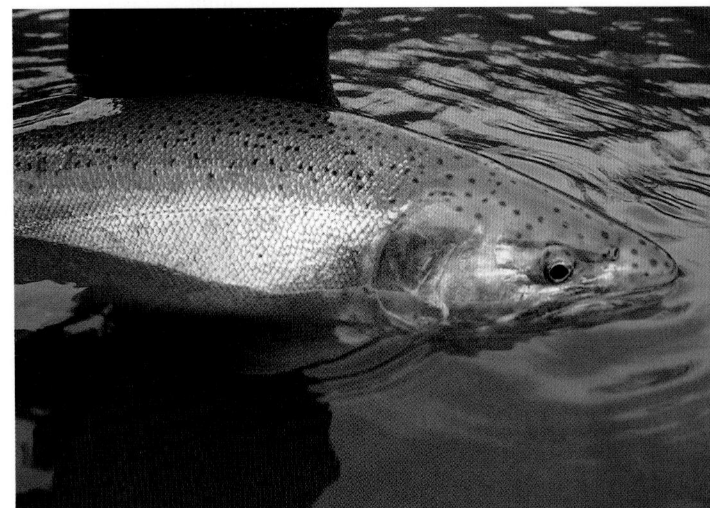

A thick-bodied steelhead is released to fight again.

Some anglers prefer the intimate setting of a smaller river or stream. This type of water allows for a closer connection, and it's easier to cover all the holding spots. Anglers who prefer fishing with a one-handed rod, smaller flies, and lighter tippets will do well to select one of the region's smaller streams or rivers. Steelhead tend to concentrate in the prime holds on this type of water, making it more likely that you'll hook larger numbers of fish, which is an attraction for beginning anglers and those with limited fishing time. However, the more popular smaller streams and rivers tend to see more fishing pressure.

Wild Fish

My preference for wild fish plays heavily into my selection of a steelhead river. Most of the rivers that I frequent have at least some natural reproduction in the main river or its tributaries. Rivers that have a run composed entirely of wild steelhead have a special feel. Besides the fact that most rivers with natural reproduction run through relatively unspoiled countryside, a greater connection to the wondrous forces of nature is gained by intercepting, holding, and observing a beautiful wild steelhead.

Over the last 20 years a greater emphasis has been placed on wild steelhead—both from an esthetic standpoint and due to the fact that wild steelhead with superior genes are hardier fish with higher survival rates and can better deal with varying environmental factors. Numerous management steps have been taken to save or improve wild stocks. But such measures are often met with resistance since some individuals do not place the same value on wild stocks. Reducing kill limits, enacting closed seasons on spawning waters, improving streams to increase spawning areas, and encouraging or even putting into law catch-and-release fishing are all steps that have had a positive impact on wild fish populations in the Great Lakes.

The greatest deterrent to increasing the level of wild fish available in the Great Lakes region is the number of dams that have been constructed throughout the region. These man-made structures block fish from reaching potential high-quality

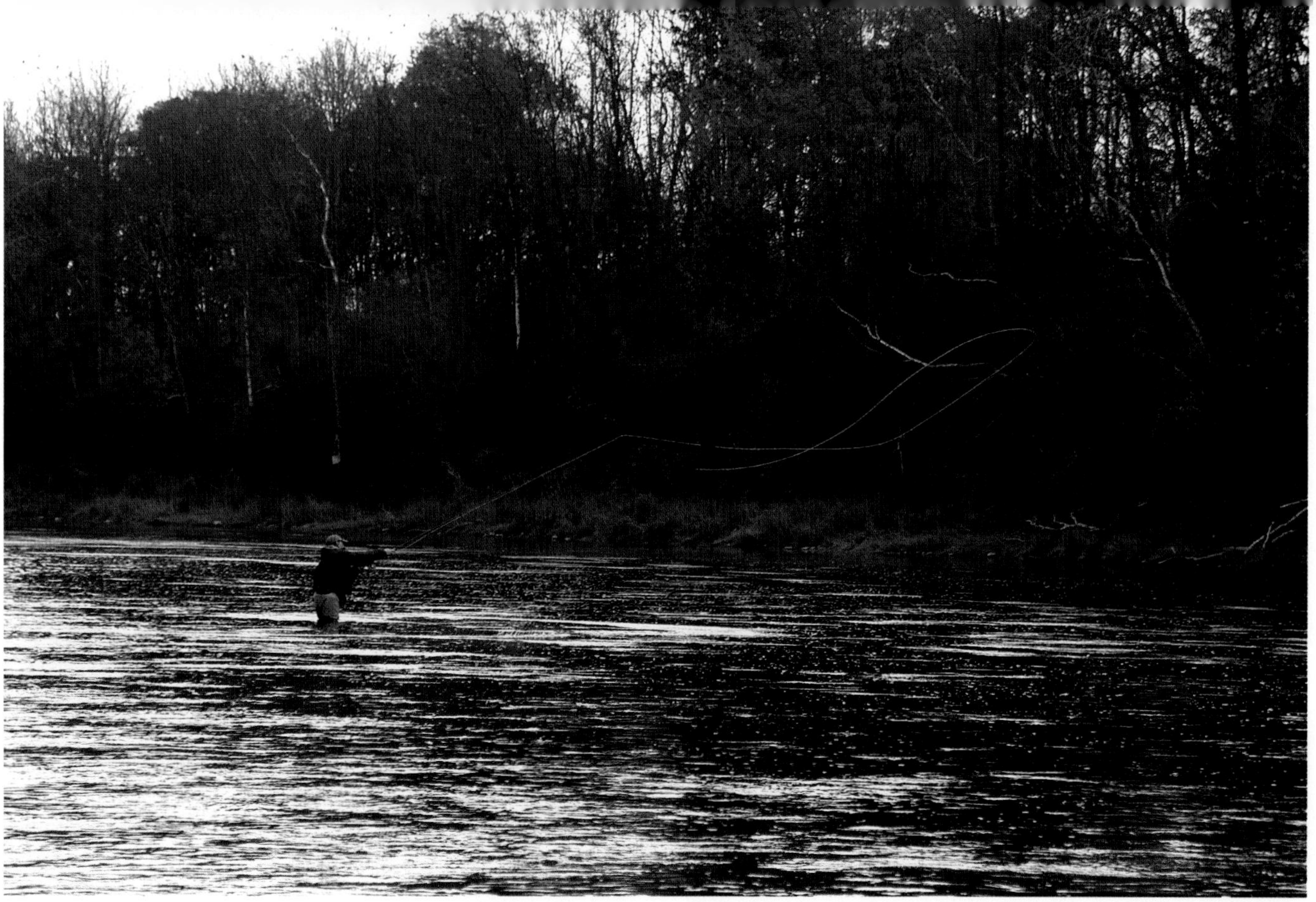

Big rivers give anglers and steelhead the opportunity to spread out.

Two-handed rods are also useful tools when only a short cast is required.

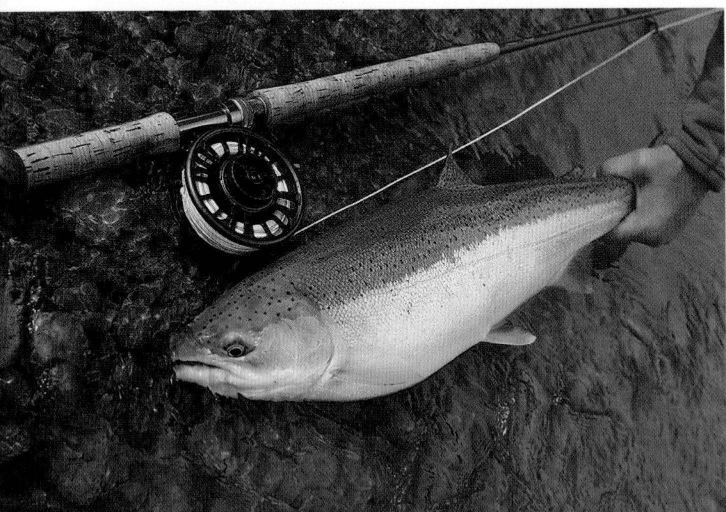

A plump wild steelhead. NICK PIONESSA PHOTO

Dams and other man-made structures create an impediment for steelhead to reach spawning water on some rivers in the Great Lakes. The removal of a dam can have a very positive impact on habitat. NICK PIONESSA PHOTO

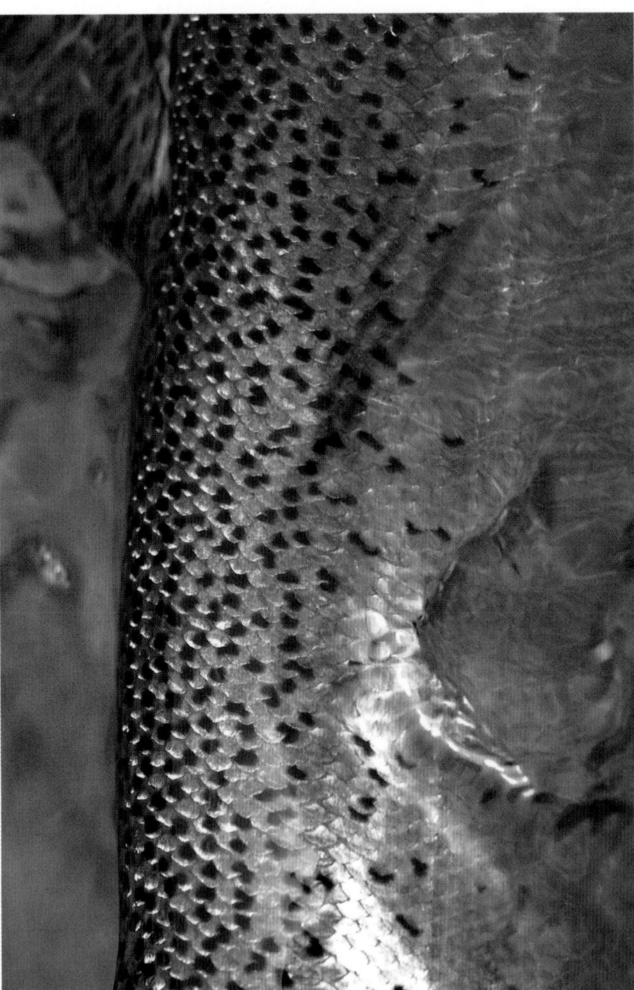

The beauty of a wild steelhead is often found in the detail.

spawning water on the upper end of the stream or river. Many of these dams are no longer used and sadly create an eyesore and a detriment to a river's true character. However, the trend is slowly being reversed as some dams are being removed or at least notched to allow fish to pass. While this process can be quite costly, it has yielded immediate dividends on tributaries with high water quality. A focused effort by concerned steelheaders who value wild fish stocks and want to increase the miles of fishable water that a river has to offer is often the driving force behind the difficult task of dam removal.

Reading Water

Reading water refers to the act or ability to distinguish the character of the water throughout its depth by observing and analyzing the surface. Some rivers give clear signs as to the water below, which allows for a short learning curve. But on many others the clues are more subtle and the true characteristics of the water can be learned only through years of trial and error. The satisfaction that comes from the success of discovering new water by recognizing its potential is a main motivating factor for me as a steelheader.

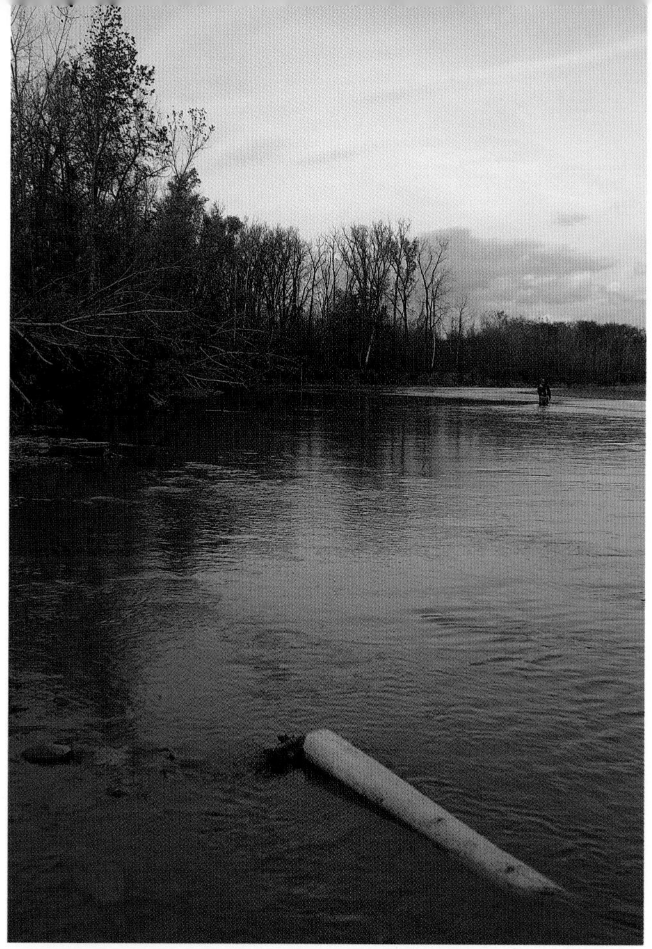

Identifying Holding Water

The ability to recognize suitable holding water for steelhead is an acquired skill and one of the most important for a proficient steelhead fly fisher. Identifying holding water is particularly critical on big rivers that have a significant amount of barren water between prime lies, but it can be equally important on smaller waters where you can find fish in unconventional lies. The main factors to consider when assessing holding water are water depth, water speed, structure, and migration routes.

Classic steelhead water is characterized by a series of runs or pools that are fairly well defined and identifiable. A typical run or pool begins with a faster flow moving over a relatively shallow area, creating an obvious riffle. As the run or pool develops, the depth increases and the current slows. Typically the river channel widens at the midpoint of the run or pool. The current is often at its slowest in the tailout and then begins to increase again as the bottom rises to meet the next riffle.

A typical run or pool commonly pushes against one bank, creating a softer seam or flow on the opposite side. The side with the softer current is preferred from a fishing standpoint. Some runs and pools are set up with the current flowing heav-

***Left:* An angler works through the middle of a placid pool.** NICK PIONESSA PHOTO

This photo illustrates a small but classic steelhead pool with a riffle giving way to a slower, deeper midsection and then flowing into a broad tailout. NICK PIONESSA PHOTO

iest through the middle and tapering off on each side. In this type of pool, you can present a fly effectively from either side.

A good steelhead pool can hold fish throughout its entire length. Steelhead prefer the softer seam at the head of a run or pool and tend to spread across the pool toward the middle and through the tailout. Water depth, speed, and structure determine a run or pool's capacity to attract and hold steelhead.

Generally a run or pool that's 3 to 5 feet deep is ideal, as it provides sufficient security for a steelhead and yet can be easily covered by fly-fishing techniques. Steelhead hold in water that is shallower than 3 feet when they are not pressured or during times of extremely low water. Some fish may actually seek out shallow, fast riffle water for security during times of heavy fishing pressure.

Steelhead prefer water with a current speed that approximates a steady walk. I use this test more in the middle portion of the run or pool, as the head will generally be faster and the tailout a little slower. While there are exceptions to every rule in steelhead fishing, the walk test is a good gauge for determining the flow that holding fish prefer and can be applied to a wide range of water types, even those that wouldn't be considered classic steelhead water.

Structure may be the most important element when it comes to a piece of water's ability to hold steelhead. Structure provides both security and a break from the main flow of the current. Drop-offs, ledges, and boulders provide the perfect structural elements that steelhead seek out as prime holding lies.

Some of these types of structure will be indicated by the disturbance on the water's surface caused by a submerged boulder or better yet a series of disturbances as a result of a bottom littered with rocks and boulders. I have caught countless steelhead that had been holding in the soft water created by a rock or boulder.

Drop-offs and ledges are often indicated by a change in the color of the water. Steelhead seek out this type of water because it allows them to rest below the heavier current flows overhead. Polarized glasses will help you spot water color changes. Also preseason scouting during low-water conditions will often provide valuable information on what lies beneath.

Logjams and overhanging brush provide a more obvious type of structure that consistently holds steelhead. I have found steelhead to particularly prefer logjams and deadfalls during periods of low water. Overhanging brush is a key security element on smaller rivers and streams.

The type of water both upstream and downstream from a run or pool can have a direct impact on the pool itself. Heavy rapids or a small falls upriver from a run or pool can sometimes accumulate fish as they wait for the right conditions to traverse the upstream water. On the downstream end of a run or pool, a series of long, fast riffles leading into the tail of the pool is the perfect resting water after a fish has fought through

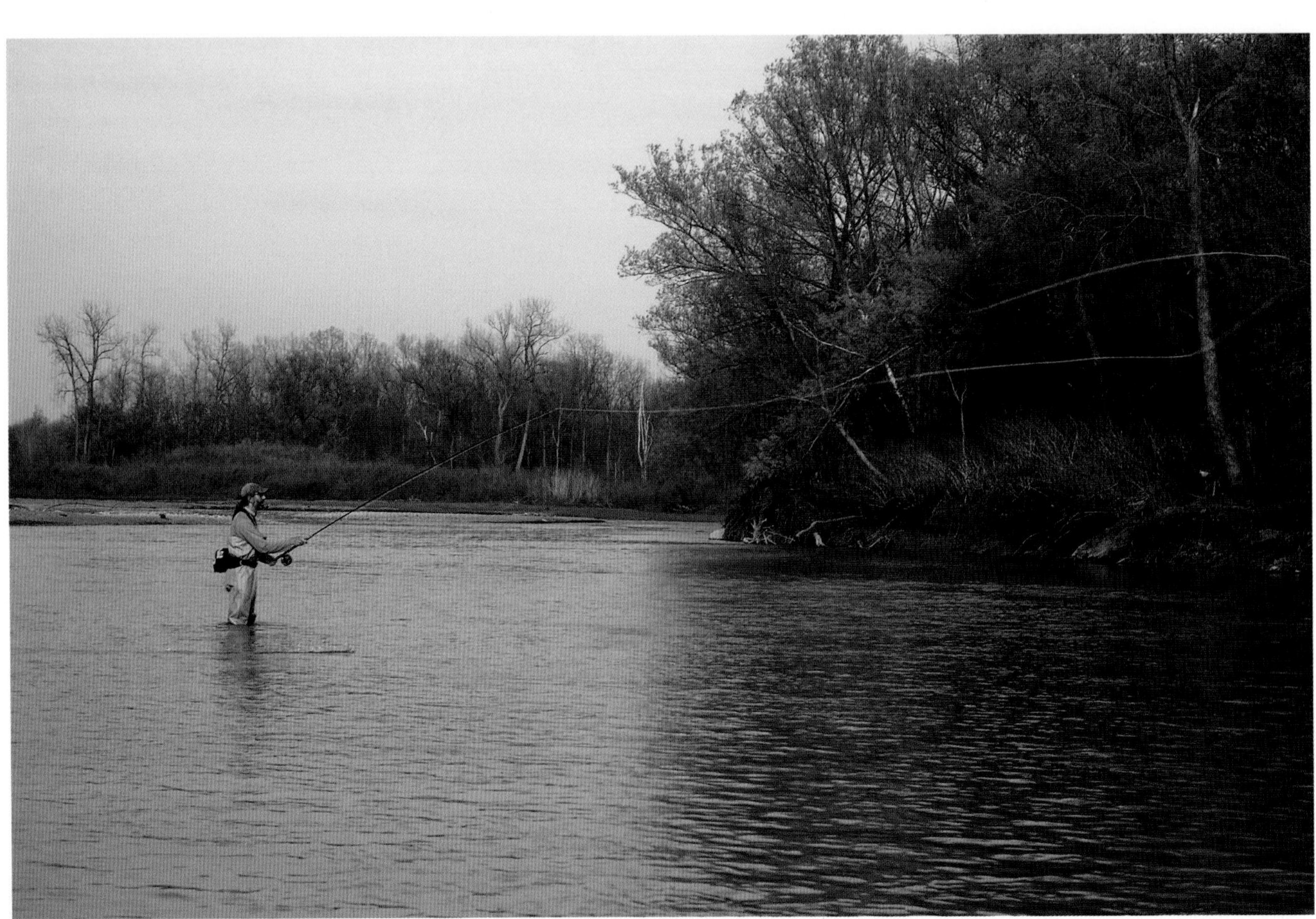

The middle part of the pool where the current begins to slow can be a good place to find fish.

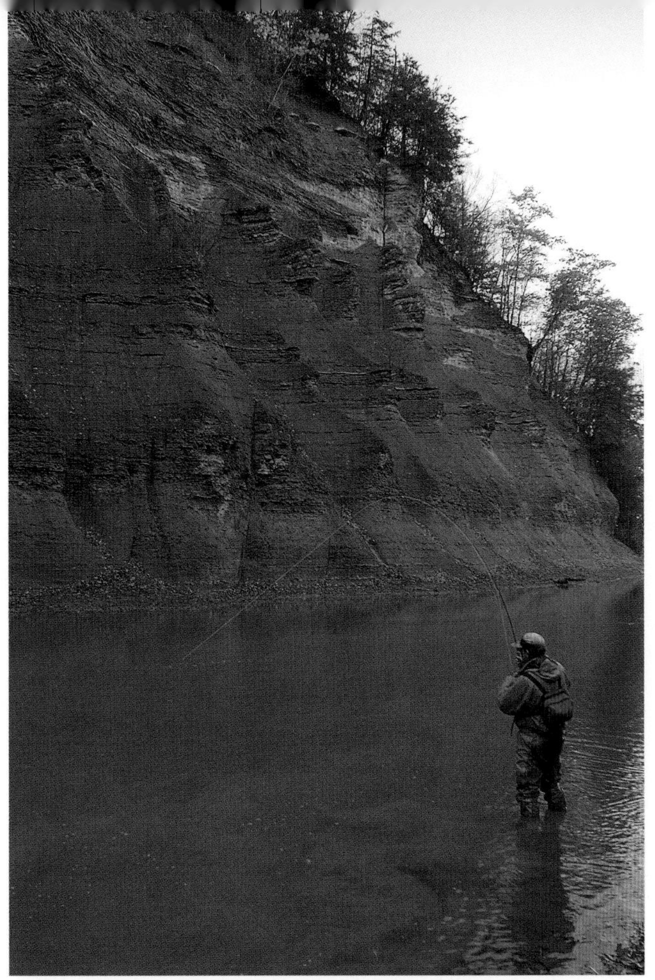

the heavy current. If the tailout contains boulders that further block the effects of the current, it can be a prime lie. Softer currents tend to dictate travel routes that steelhead use during their migration. Visualize travel routes to find areas with higher concentrations of steelhead and to help uncover unlikely holds.

I cover a classic steelhead run or pool from top to bottom. (More on the concept of pool rotation later in this chapter.) My favorite type of run or pool has a soft seam on the inside, or from the side that I am fishing, and where the current gently tapers off. This tapering effect allows fish to spread out across most or all of the width of the pool and allows for a long, seductive presentation with a swinging fly requiring little or no mending. Steelhead will often be positioned near the head of the pool in times of heavy fishing pressure, in low water, or in the low-light periods of the day.

Normally the prime part of the run or pool is where the current slows and the depth increases. The fly will begin to fish at a slower pace that is more accessible to a steelhead. Steelhead congregate in this section of the pool, and if it has rocks, boulders, and other structure, you'll find fish the width of the run or pool. In pools and runs with heavier flows toward

***Left:* Tailout water above a heavy riffle is often quite productive.** NICK PIONESSA PHOTO

Soft inside seams are high-percentage holding areas.

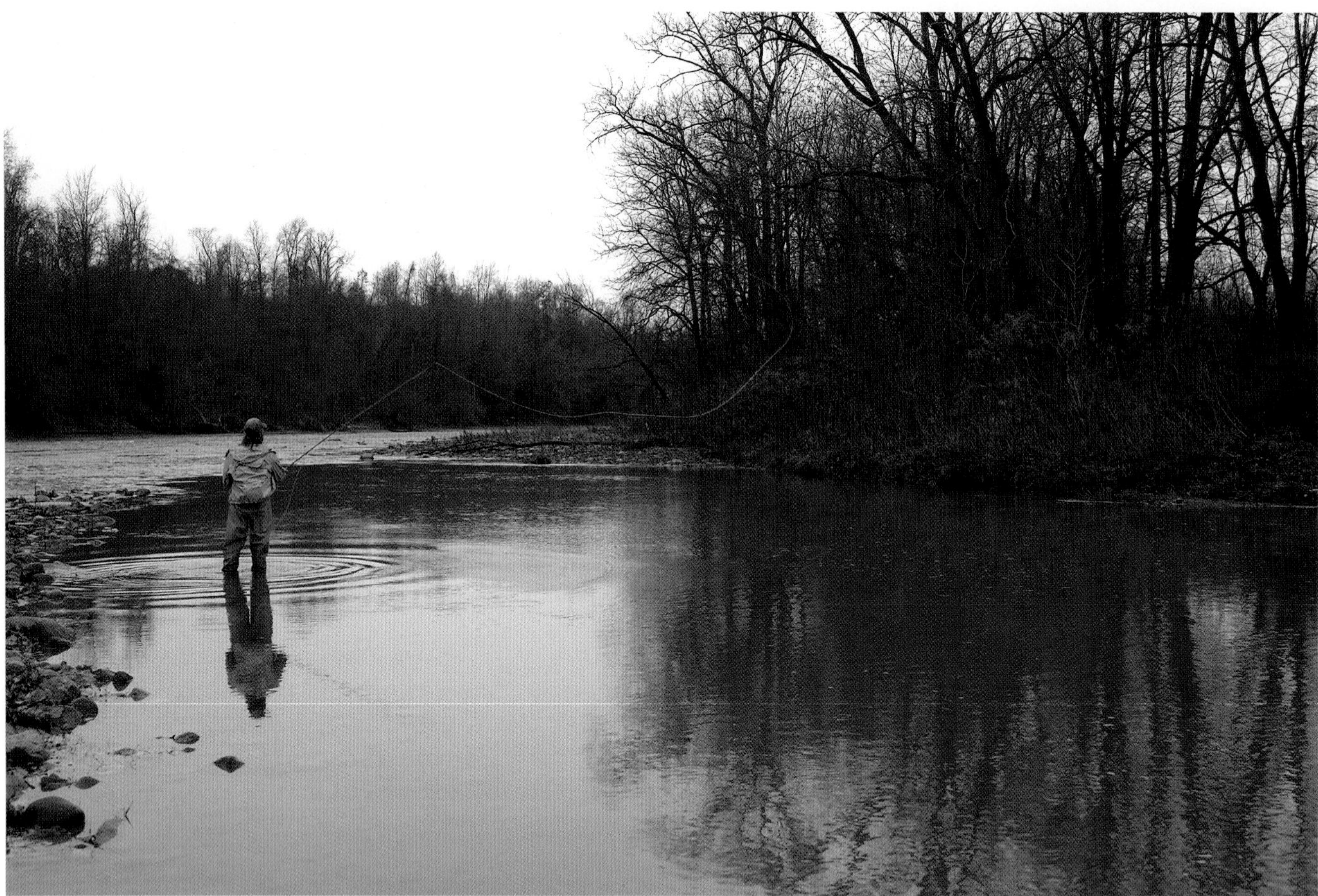

Steelhead readily hold in the slow, placid flow of the tailout of a pool.

the opposite side and in the middle, the inside seam has more holding steelhead.

Tailouts can also hold significant numbers of steelhead. The slower flows of a tailout offer the perfect spot for a steelhead to rest while using minimal energy. Tail sections of pools that are strewn with boulders are prime holding water. It took me a while to become confident fishing the slow currents of a tailout, but once I developed the patience to fish this type of water thoroughly I realized the potential these slower currents hold. Even tailouts that barely have a flow but have the proper depth and structure can provide holding water for aggressive steelhead. Presenting a fly slowly through water with only a slight current can result in a subtle take or an explosive strike. Deep, slow tailouts can be especially productive in low-water conditions.

Some Great Lakes rivers, particularly in the Midwest, have a more channelized and uniform flow on the surface. Classic pools and holding water are disguised by the lack of obvious distinguishing characteristics. Many of the same structural elements that attract and hold steelhead elsewhere exist on these rivers, but it is much more difficult to read the signs. Normally this type of water is composed of a moderate flow over a relatively consistent depth. Pools are formed by drop-offs in the river bottom. It takes more trial and error and a few more lost flies to learn this type of water, but once you find good holding water, you have valuable information that other anglers may not know about. When searching this type of river, finding water that increases in depth, has a slow to moderate current, and contains structural elements such as rocks or boulders will often pay dividends.

Changes in water flow because of rainfall or snow runoff can have a tremendous impact on the character of a river. Some rivers are better equipped to handle a wide range of flows than others. In almost all rivers, a greater flow will increase the average current speed. For some rivers and streams that run through a confined channel, this greater current speed will make it difficult to effectively fish a fly in a majority of the water. However, rivers that allow higher flows to spread out a bit can simply shift the best holding water. It is critical to find the soft water during higher levels—this might mean fishing a fly near a rock that you were standing on a week earlier in lower water.

The one river that comes to mind when I think of adjusting to water flow is the Salmon River in New York. I have successfully fly-fished this river for steelhead in flows that have ranged from 275 to 1,500 cubic feet per second. The river normally remains clear even in higher flows, and the character of the river and the prime water changes dramatically with the level. The lower flows tend to congregate fish into the more defined runs and pools, whereas the higher flows push fish into a wider range of holding water or pools that have sufficient depth only during periods of higher levels.

Any steelhead river or stream has a fair amount of water that doesn't fit into the category of a classic run or pool. On

Changes in water levels on rivers such as New York's Salmon River impact the character of steelhead holding water.

Delivering a cast to the deep trough along the far bank. NICK PIONESSA PHOTO

higher-gradient rivers, typical runs and pools are at a minimum. You need to be able to recognize holding water that isn't so obvious. The nontypical runs and pools may be the main type of water on some rivers. Also, the nontypical holding water may provide great opportunities during times of higher fishing pressure when the more recognized pools are occupied by anglers. Most of the nontypical water has faster current. Steelhead hold in fairly quick water, especially when the water is above 40 degrees F, but a holding spot where the main current is broken offers the best possibilities.

Most rivers or streams have quick runs and slots, which are characterized by a depth of 2 feet or more and caused by a drop-off of the bottom or channelization of the flow. You can identify them by their darker appearance. On the surface, this type of water normally has a fast, uniform flow, and while there may be a soft edge, it could easily be passed by because of its current speed. The key factor in faster slots and runs is simply what lies beneath. Significant drop-offs and ledges can create soft currents under the main flow that are perfect for resting steelhead. Even without a sharp drop in the bottom, surface currents will almost always be heavier than the flow near the bottom, which results in soft water in the depths of almost any run. Getting a fly down quickly and fishing it deep are the keys to success in this type of water.

Most Great Lakes rivers and streams have pocketwater created by boulders, a series of rocks, or fallen timber. This type of water can be extremely productive for a steelhead fly fisher. Pockets generally occur in the faster water between classic runs and pools. A pocket can be obvious when the obstruction creating it protrudes through the water's surface. However, a pocket can also be quite subtle, appearing simply as a slick spot on the surface current. Pocketwater can also be formed downstream in gravel patches as the river's current digs a hole in looser gravel. These pockets will show up as dark depressions in the river. The slack flow of the pocket attracts and holds steelhead during their migration. Pockets found in the middle of heavy, shallow water are often the most productive since they are among the few options for steelhead to rest in the surrounding water. While I prefer the water in classic runs and pools, I have caught some memorable steelhead that jumped on a fly as they rested in pocketwater.

A significant bend in a river or stream almost always creates soft water on the inside, which can attract steelhead. Rivers that wind through the countryside have a larger percentage of this type of water. Insides of bends can be especially important during high-water conditions, as the softer water usually still exists even in bigger flows.

Even fast riffle water between pools can hold steelhead at times. While this type of water does not have the best opportunities, you can find steelhead resting there during migration. This type of water is best when steelhead metabolism is still elevated, which will generally coincide with water tempera-

Pockets created by boulders, logs, or other obstructions can be very productive steelhead lies on some rivers. NICK PIONESSA PHOTO

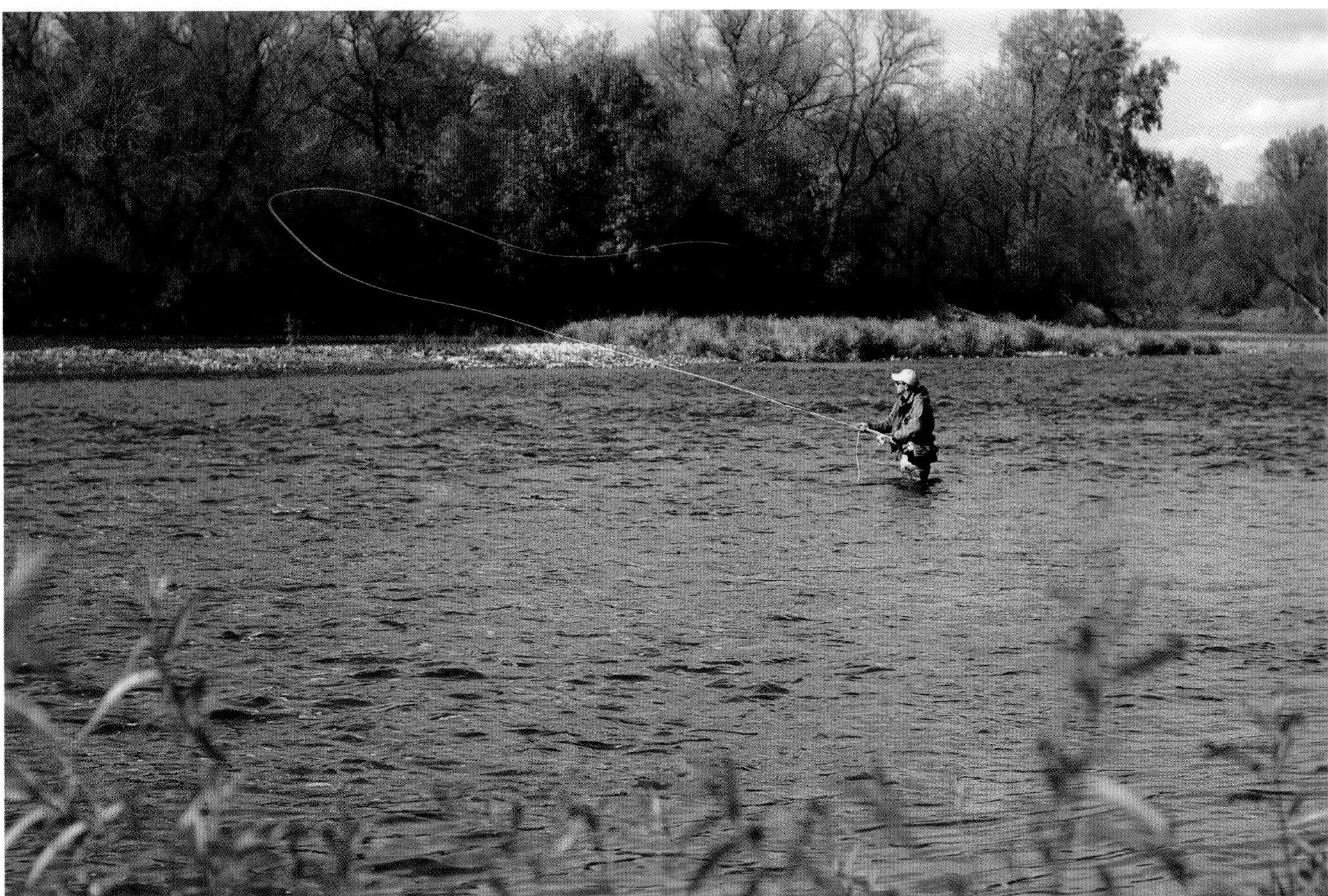

Aggressive steelhead can often be found in the riffle at the head of a pool.

ture that is 40 degrees F or higher. Steelhead found in this water tend to be aggressive. This type of water can be especially productive during periods of heavy fishing pressure as the riffles provide a level of security. Riffle water can be fairly nondescript in character. I look for subtle breaks in the main current flow and slots and depressions in the bottom. I can recall a number of days when the riffle water between the more well-defined pools saved the day, especially on some days when the more popular pools were occupied by anglers.

Certain types of bottom structure create their own sets of challenges. A number of rivers and streams in the Great Lakes region have slate and shale bottoms. Slate bottoms often prevent the water from reaching a proper depth to hold steelhead. However, cuts and drop-offs in the shale create structure and deeper water that can consistently hold fish. Often these cuts in the shale are quite obvious, especially in clear water, showing as darker areas. In deeper water, cuts in a shale bottom may be more difficult to see—experience or observation in periods of low water helps. The challenge to fishing cuts and slots in the bottom is getting the fly positioned deep enough to entice a steelhead that is resting comfortably along this secure structure.

Many anglers are intimidated by big rivers. I prefer them because anglers have the opportunity to spread out, they give steelhead plenty of room to fight, and they provide the ultimate challenge for my casting and fly presentation skills. My approach for big rivers is to break the water down into manageable pieces and use my experience and instincts to identify holding water. All the elements discussed above are present on big rivers, and focusing on the water that can be effectively covered with a fly rod is the key to success.

Most seasoned steelhead anglers know that particular pieces of water on any river hold more steelhead than others. And some might not only consistently hold more fish, but because of the characteristics of the flow may also make it easier to present the fly, making a take more likely. Some spots are so dependable that if a steelhead is positioned there, an aggressive take can almost be expected. Finding these prime holds may take years, but once you do, it will be the foundation for consistent success on any river. In fact, becoming intimately familiar with a section of river or a handful of runs, pools, or other type of holding water on a river or stream will increase your steelhead encounters and your overall fishing experience.

To learn a piece of water well, you need to not only know how it looks on the surface, but also understand what lies underneath. Determining depth, drop-offs, boulders, and other structure will unlock the key to where fish may concentrate and how to present the fly. This understanding is most important when fishing the wet-fly swing and a sinking-tip as it will form the basis for determining sink rate and for making adjustments while working through the pool. This working knowledge of a piece of water extends to condition changes and how rigging and presentation will be impacted by flow and clarity

Knowing a particular piece of water well is a key to consistent success. NICK PIONESSA PHOTO

fluctuations. Intimate knowledge of a piece of water is critical for steelheading success.

Reading the water also includes reading fish activity. The best water on the river fishes well only if steelhead are present. Because of the timing of steelhead migrations, there is a wide range in density of fish in a given section of river or stream. Reading the signs will help you determine if you are fishing in the right section of the river or even on the right river.

Information about the density of steelhead migrations comes from many sources, including secondhand from reliable shops, a network of fishing acquaintances, and up-to-date postings on web sites. But since information about steelhead runs and densities can quickly become dated, the best source is personal observation. When you are on the river, keep your senses alive. Anglers in other pools hooking up with steelhead are the simplest positive sign of active steelhead in the river. Talking with other anglers to gauge their success will provide valuable data to determine whether a section of river is worthy of fishing. Direct observation of fish moving through a riffle or sitting in a pool is possible when conditions are right. I rely heavily on watching or hearing fish rolling on the surface. I'm not exactly sure why a steelhead shows on the surface, although it is often associated with fish on the move. But it is almost always a good sign exhibited by fish that are agitated and aggressive. While it is not a guarantee, I have often hooked steelhead in pools with steelhead showing on the surface.

Sometimes you can follow the migration of a concentration of steelhead. Actually trying to stay one step ahead is the best approach. Steelhead are most aggressive after arriving in new water. Depending on water conditions, steelhead can cover considerable distances over the course of a day, but fish generally move a few miles per day in the Great Lakes region. Staying in front of a migration of fish always takes some guesswork. In the prime of the season, there is a good chance that more fish will be following behind, so it often makes sense to focus on favored pools.

Identifying the presence of steelhead statistically increases the odds of encountering them, but more importantly allows you to fish with confidence. You need to have confidence in the water you are fishing to effectively cast and present the fly to the best of your abilities for hours at a time.

Matching Technique with Water

My approach to matching my technique to the water type is fairly simple—I always fish a two-handed rod or a switch rod with a wet-fly swing. I search out water where this approach works best and make adjustments to allow this technique to fit as wide a range of water as possible.

From the standpoint of catching fish, some techniques work better with specific types of water. A fly has to get down through the surface tension of the current rather quickly in quick, short runs and small pockets. A weighted fly or weight added to the leader with the dead-drift or tight-line approach often works best in this type of water. This can also be true for fast riffle water and runs with deep drops and cuts in the bottom. You can also use the dead-drift and tight-line approaches in the soft seam water of more classic runs and pools. Generally the dead-drift and tight-line approaches work best for covering smaller to medium-size rivers. By matching these techniques with two-handed rods, you can increase the size of water that you can comfortably cover with these techniques. The size of the rod combined with Spey casting techniques allows you to cast and maintain line control at longer distances.

Whether you are using a single-handed or two-handed rod, I think the wet-fly swing is perfect for the classic run or pool. This approach effectively covers broad pieces of water by allowing the fly to move sideways across the pool as it swings to the inside of the current. While this approach aligns best with larger rivers, it can be equally effective and fun to fish on small rivers and streams. You can make a variety of modifications to the wet-fly swing approach to make it fit a wider range of water as well, including pockets and fast runs. The key in this water is often adding some weight to the fly and finding subtle seams to control the speed of the fly.

Steelhead often become visible in the evening when rolling on the surface. NICK PIONESSA PHOTO

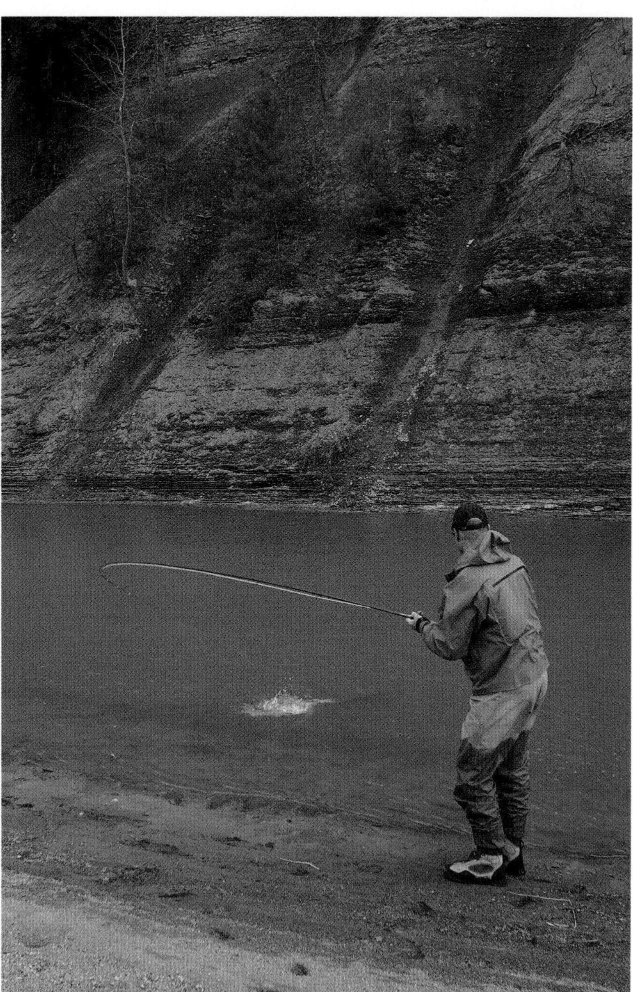

The end of a successful battle. NICK PIONESSA PHOTO

Finding Water

Finding specific water to fish generally requires some thought. The availability of steelhead, fishing conditions, and other anglers have an impact on finding water. My approach is to seek water that is away from the highest fishing pressure but also yields a good chance to encounter steelhead. Being flexible and going the extra distance almost always pay off when attempting to find steelhead water.

Developing a Plan for Solitude

Enlightened management combined with elevated promotion of the Great Lakes fishery has made the region a top fly-fishing destination. Some of the region's well-known rivers and streams receive significant fishing pressure during the peak of the season. At times, even more important than identifying the best holding water is simply finding suitable water free of other anglers. I put considerable effort into finding water away from concentrations of other anglers, even though sometimes it is difficult. Finding water away from other anglers will almost certainly add to the esthetic experience of an outing. Also, less

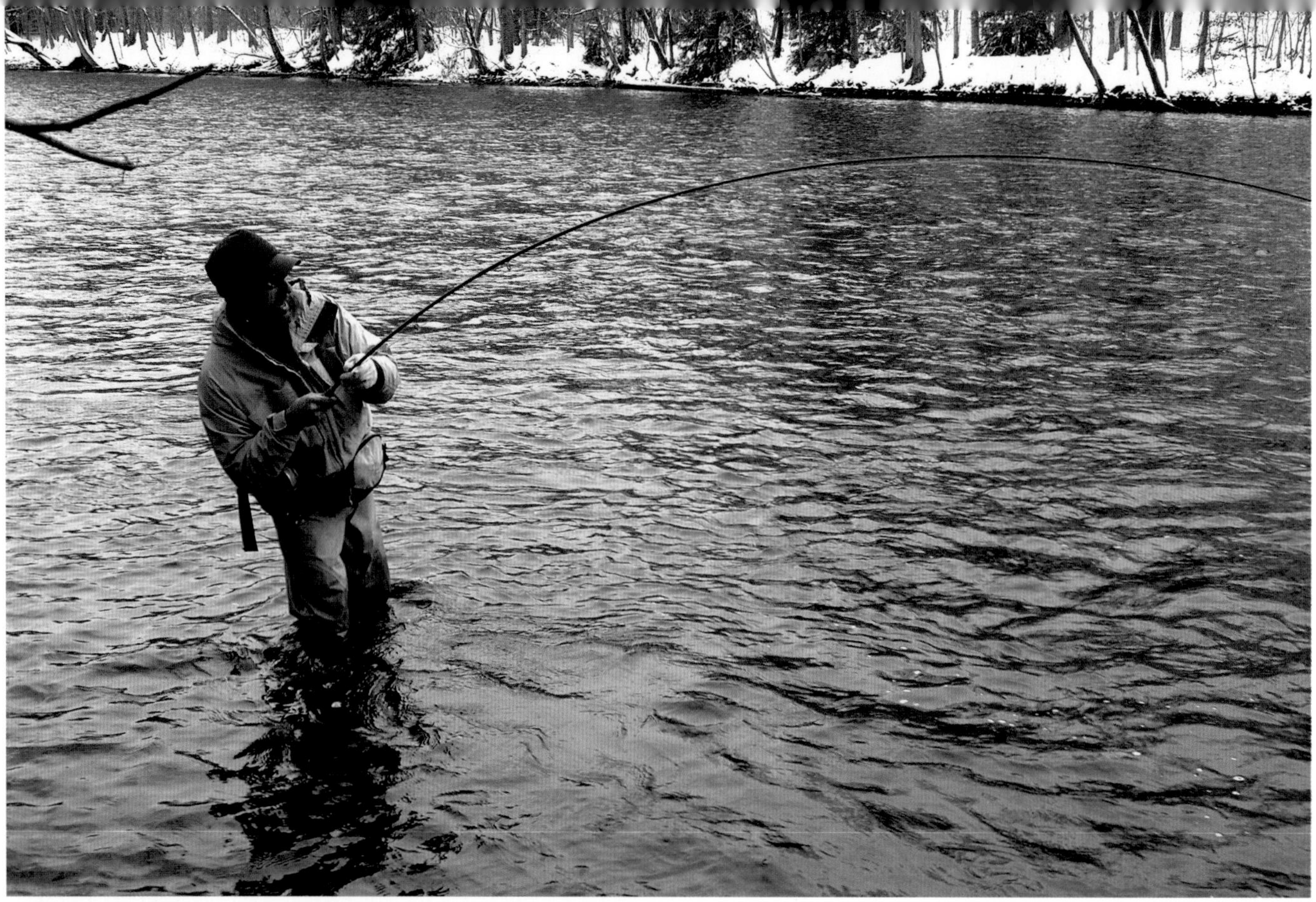

Nick Pionessa fights a strong, fresh-run steelhead hooked while using the wet-fly swing.

Early morning on a favorite piece of water. NICK PIONESSA PHOTO

pressured water will increase the possibilities of encountering more active fish. Having a plan that considers other anglers is a key part of developing an overall strategy for success.

For those anglers who are restricted to fishing weekends on more popular waters, dealing with angling pressure head-on during the peak of the season is common. Finding water with enough room to comfortably work a fly may come down to identifying holding areas away from the popular pools. Getting to the water at sunup and fishing to last light may provide the opportunity to work over more popular runs and pools.

For me, searching out solitude both increases the overall experience and improves my odds of catching steelhead. And despite the popularity of the fishery, I can normally find lightly fished water with a bit of effort. The strategy for finding solitude on a Great Lakes steelhead river depends on when you fish and where you fish. The key is to take a contrarian view and to approach the water in a manner that is different from that of other anglers.

You can commonly find good numbers of steelhead from September until the following May on most Great Lakes rivers and streams. A few rivers even produce from June through August. This gives the Great Lakes steelheader a wide range of times to pursue his quarry. When you fish during this period often determines how many other anglers you'll encounter. Fishing pressure is at its greatest when the runs commonly are at their peak. This normally occurs in October and November and then again in March and April. I often take advantage of this by fishing the weeks bordering prime time. Fishing pressure is often light in September on rivers that do not receive runs of chinook salmon. Pressure is also light in May after the best fishing has passed.

The keys in these shoulder times are water conditions and temperature. For September fishing, look for cool, rainy periods that bring fish into the lower ends of the rivers. Look for similar conditions in late April and May. It is important to keep an eye on your thermometer when fishing during these periods. When water temperatures reach 70 degrees F, the steelhead's activity slows and the likelihood of a successful release is greatly reduced. Temperatures in the 50s and 60s often produce aggressive steelhead, and the quality of the take and fight compensates for the lack of numbers at this time. Some of the fish in late April and May are dropping back to the lake, but on rivers where the temperatures remain cool, I have encountered fresh fish well into May.

The cold weather and less active fish of the winter months usher in another period of light angling pressure. With the technologically advanced clothing available today, steelhead fishing can be a wonderful way to spend a winter's day. Flexibility is important in the winter months. I do not enjoy fly fishing in drastic subfreezing temperatures; instead I look for breaks in

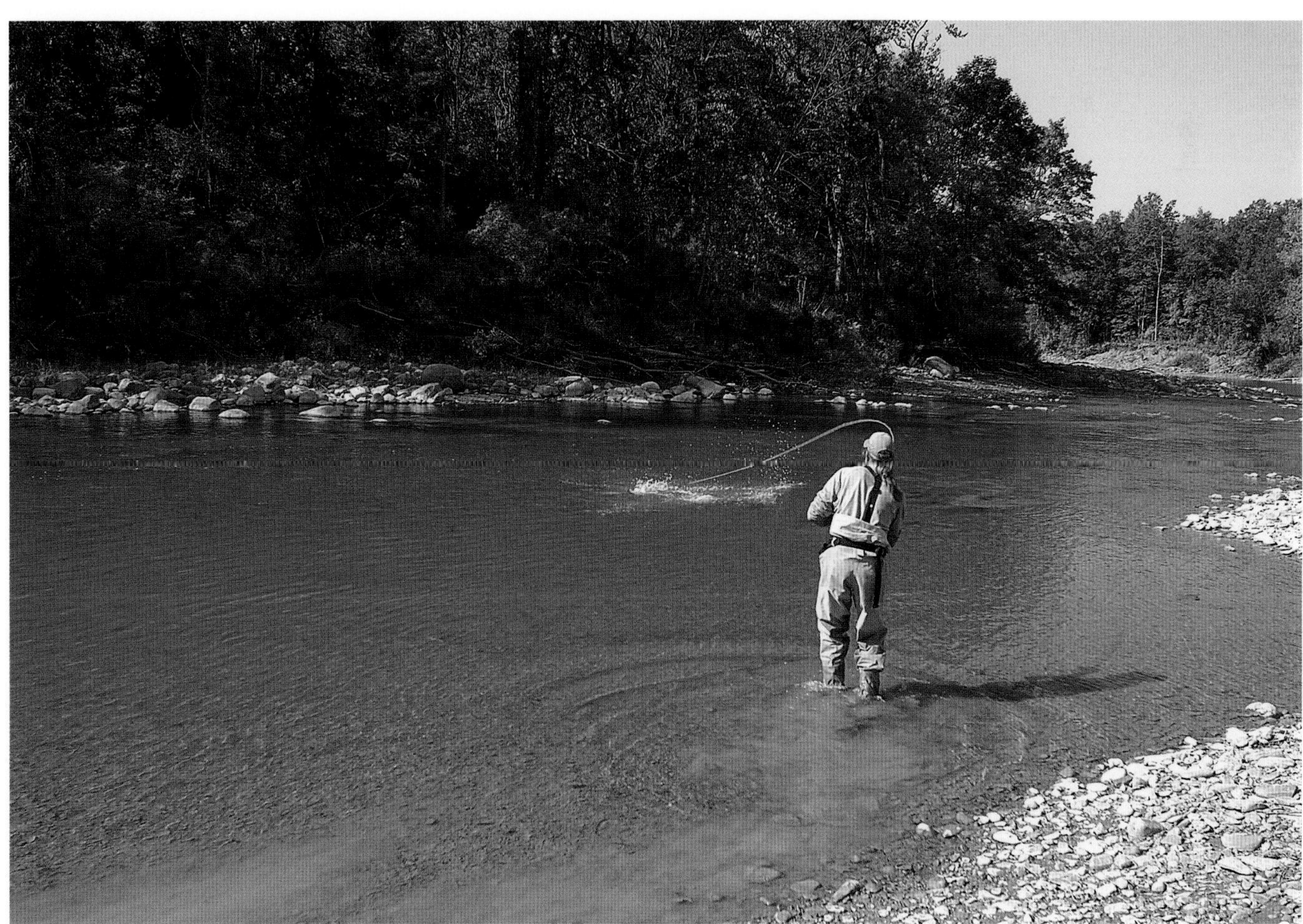

Late-summer or early-fall steelhead can be incredibly strong and put up a memorable fight. NICK PIONESSA PHOTO

Angling pressure diminishes dramatically during the winter season.

High water with a milky stain can still be quite productive as long as there is a foot or so of visibility. NICK PIONESSA PHOTO

the weather that produce temperatures in the high 20s and 30s. I keep a constant eye on the weather. Predicting Great Lakes weather is always difficult, and in the winter it can be quite frustrating. Often the breaks in the weather are short and come without much notice.

Not all rivers and streams fish well during the winter. Many ice over unless the winter weather is extremely mild. The best winter rivers are the larger waters that have a higher gradient or that are fed from a reservoir. Winter fishing takes a more methodical and patient approach. It is important to fish the fly deep and slow while focusing on water with a slow flow or out of the main current.

During the peak run months, I look for conditions that discourage other anglers. Except for a few drainages in the Great Lakes, moderate to heavy rains bring levels up and color the water. When the rain is heavy enough, it renders the river or stream unfishable for a time. After the water begins to recede and visibility increases by a foot or two, some of the best fishing of the year can occur. If you have a flexible schedule, you can fish popular pools with little or no angling pressure as the river drops back into shape.

I do not shy away from water that is still up and dirty either. I have found that steelhead will take a fly in water that has only a few inches of visibility. Dirty water has a disorienting effect, so you will find steelhead in areas that would not normally hold fish. Look for any soft current on the inside of a seam or up along a bank. Steelhead often feel comfortable in the shallows under dirty water conditions. Some pools maintain their character in high water and continue to hold fish in high, stained water as they do under normal flows. Such places are good starting points when you are searching for steelhead in high, stained water. I use big, dark flies that cast a solid silhouette when the water is off-color.

Most anglers are intimidated by dirty water, but these conditions are a good match for the type of fishing that I enjoy most—prospecting the water with a wet-fly swing. Finding plenty of water for yourself takes little effort during these times.

Extremely clear, low water conditions typically make steelhead lethargic and dour, which also tends to keep anglers off the rivers and streams. However, you can always find a few active fish if you are patient and persistent. Under these conditions, the low-light periods of the day will often be the most active.

I am fortunate to live in close proximity to steelhead water and have discovered one approach that almost always results in solitude during the prime months. Fishing pressure always seems to be at its highest on Great Lakes rivers and streams during the morning hours. On days when I have only a few hours to fish, I time my outing for the afternoon and evening. I can usually find open water with little effort in the last two to three hours of the day. The bonus to this approach is that steelhead normally become quite active at the end of the day. Almost nothing is more peaceful than standing in one of my favorite pieces of water as the waning light fades into night.

With careful planning, selecting where to fish can lead directly to finding room to spread out. While I prefer larger rivers, many smaller, less known tributaries throughout the region can be the perfect options for steelhead solitude. Most anglers fish the rivers that receive the bulk of the steelhead runs. One of the advantages of the current fishery is that there are steelhead returning to almost every drainage. Enlightened management has created runs of fish on rivers that until recently saw very few steelhead. Even though some of the runs are marginal by Great Lakes standards, they provide the opportunity for the committed angler to hook steelhead in relative obscurity. I find a great challenge in hooking fish in rivers that have lower return numbers.

Longer rivers provide solitude too. The farther you move from an access point, the more likely you'll find empty water. Long rivers with miles between such points are perfect. Hiking to the river through a remote access or walking along its banks can separate you from the crowds. I enjoy hiking into areas that require long, challenging treks, and I often gain a great sense of accomplishment in simply completing the walk itself. It is certainly a good way to keep in shape. Some of the most foreboding hikes to other anglers are those that entail a descent into one of the many gorges that have been formed in the Great Lakes region. Always respect landowner rights when hiking in to steelhead water.

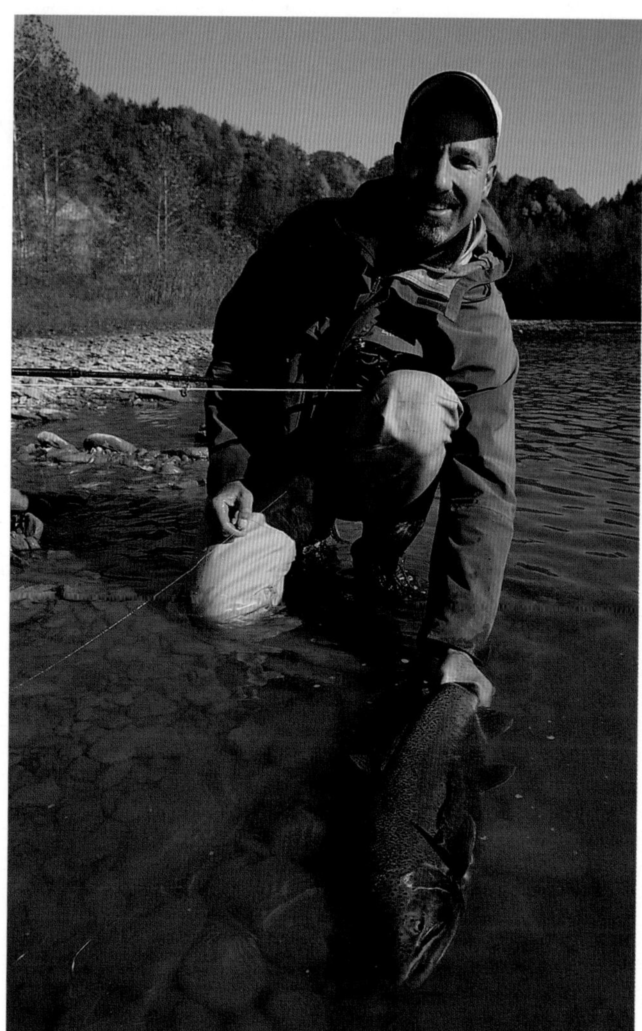

A nicely marked buck with a perfect red stripe on its body.
NICK PIONESSA PHOTO

Extra care should always be taken when wading or crossing a steelhead river. Here the angler has selected the broadest part of the river where the bottom is visible most of the way across. NICK PIONESSA PHOTO

When packing in or along a river, make sure to take enough food and drink to stay fueled and hydrated. When making a hike that is remote and possibly a little risky, let somebody know your plans. But in order to keep some places remote, it may be necessary not to tell anyone at all.

Many Great Lakes rivers are large enough for drift boats, rafts, or personal watercraft. Floating a river from one access point to another is a great way to separate from the crowds on water with limited walk-in access. The upside to floating a river is that you can cover a large number of pools. And on some larger rivers, you can cover water that can't be fished from shore. But floating a river takes careful planning or you'll spend more time riding in the boat and less time fishing the water.

I prefer shorter floats that maximize fishing time. I have had mixed experiences with watercraft on Great Lakes rivers. On some outings, floating has worked perfectly—a spring day on an Ohio river with my friend Jerry Darkes clearly stands out. After paddling around anglers crowded into the popular water near the launch point, we found one pool after another devoid of anglers and full of steelhead. It was an epic day and the perfect use of a boat.

Other times it hasn't worked as well. I have battled difficult weather and fishing conditions made worse by being committed to the river for the day because of the float. When selecting a watercraft to use in the Great Lakes region, carefully consider where you will use it. While some rivers have good boat access, many do not. The most versatile style of boat may be a kayak or other ultralight raft that can be launched and pulled out of the water just about anywhere along the river. This opens up options and adds to the strategic advantage.

One of the best strategies for fishing well-known waters with significant runs is to pass by the popular areas and concentrate on the water in between. Certain pools usually become popular for consistently holding fish throughout the steelhead season, and the popularity increases if there is easy access. The best holding pools usually contain all the key elements that attract and hold steelhead. But some of these elements exist in the water between the popular pools. With careful observation and exploration, you can discover subtle holding areas in water that other anglers pass right by.

Ultimately, the key to finding good steelhead water is to identify the type that you most enjoy fishing and develop a plan to gain access. As I mature as an angler, the act of fishing has become as important as catching fish, if not more so. If I am going to spend hours upon hours in pursuit of steelhead, it is mostly likely going to be in water that has some charm, some challenge, and that I enjoy covering with a fly. Most of the water that I enjoy fishing has been found over numerous seasons on a particular river.

Using Resources and Technology

I am a bit old-fashioned when it comes to combining technology with steelhead fishing. In my early years of fishing for steelhead, up-to-date information on fishing conditions could only be gained from a network of fishing friends and acquaintances. A series of nightly telephone calls provided information that varied widely in reliability. Gathering information in those days was more an art form than science.

Today a wealth of information that can be applied to the pursuit of steelhead is at every angler's fingertips. Many rivers have flow and level gauges monitored by the United States Geological Survey (USGS). On the USGS web site (www.usgs.gov) a map shows all the monitoring stations by state. A simple click lets you access near real-time charts on the flow measured in cubic feet per second (cfs) and a height level, which varies by river. Once you determine the optimum range in both flow and level for the rivers that you frequent, you can use this information to select where to fish. The charts also give you a way of estimating when a river will be fishable after heavy rains. I also make detailed notes of the sinking-tips I use on specific pools at various levels so that I can use the data on the USGS site to help select the proper rigging on a given day.

Weather web sites allow you to plan ahead as well. The weather changes quickly in the Great Lakes region. Real-time conditions, forecasts, and maps can provide the information to help you determine the best days to fish or the best rivers given the near-term or long-range forecast. This updated weather information is especially valuable in the winter months, when it is critical to be prepared to take advantage of any break in the conditions that Mother Nature serves up.

Many fly shops and sports stores keep updated web sites for the rivers in their proximity. The reliability of this infor-

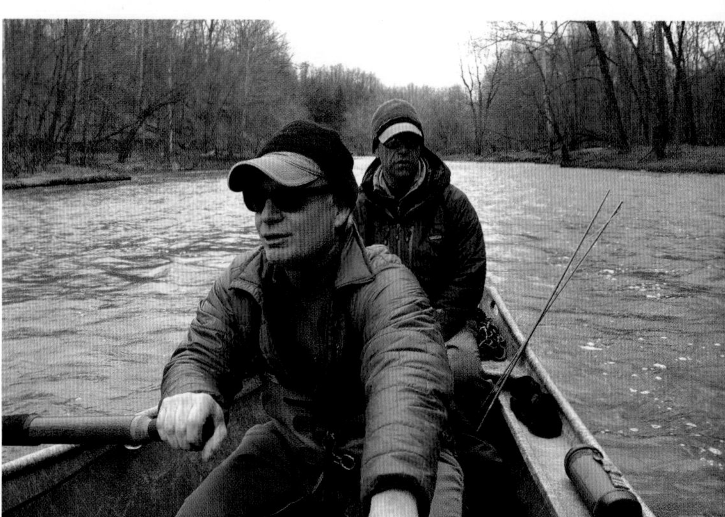

A drift boat, raft, or other floating device allows you to get away from fishing pressure on some rivers.

An angler battles an explosive fish, the result of executing a good plan. NICK PIONESSA PHOTO

Lake trout, a native Great Lakes species, are a bonus catch on some rivers throughout the region. NICK PIONESSA PHOTO

Analysis of water flow graphs assisted in landing this early-fall buck.

mation varies by shop, but in time you can determine how consistently accurate they are. Many sites also provide links to the USGS site for the rivers nearby and a link for the local weather forecast.

I would never have thought that I would have become so reliant on technological advancements and the ever-evolving level of information they make available. But now I find myself using a handheld device to retrieve up-to-the-minute flow and weather info while standing thigh-deep in a river. One of the more sensible reasons for carrying a cellular phone or other wireless device is that it allows for contact in case of emergency and could be a lifesaver when fishing remote areas. And while I prefer the word-of-mouth method that I grew up with because it kept me more personally connected to my fishing partners, the technology has provided an efficiency that can benefit all anglers.

Searching for a Quality Experience

Searching for quality in all aspects of life seems to come with maturity. At some point most steelheaders realize that there is more to the sport and the pursuit than simply racking up numbers of steelhead. Quality can be measured in many ways, such as the beauty of a river, fishing in solitude, or catching a fish with a challenging or favored technique. To me an important part of a quality experience is the ability to cover the water in my style and at my own pace. Finding solitude certainly helps me work the water on my own terms. But typically other anglers are present, and how we all interact will have a direct impact on the experience.

A serene hush surrounds a steelhead river in the snow-filled winter months. NICK PIONESSA PHOTO

Pool Rotation and Sharing the Water

A concept that is well entrenched in the tradition of Atlantic salmon fishing is pool rotation. An angler begins at the head or the top of a defined run or pool and works downstream a step or two after each cast. This is an approach that works well with the wet-fly swing and when done in a systematic method allows for complete coverage of the water. From a strategic standpoint, rotating through the pool provides an angler with the best opportunity to intercept any aggressive fish that might be positioned in that run or pool. From an esthetic standpoint, rotating through a pool provides more anglers an opportunity to fish the water and is a fair and equitable way to split up a run or pool.

While rotating a pool is practiced on every Atlantic salmon river—on many rivers it's the regulation—and it's practiced extensively on Pacific coast steelhead rivers, it has been slow to catch on in the Great Lakes. The region has a history of stationary anglers working small pieces of water in a first-come, first-served approach. This concept is more in line with working a run or pool while fishing an inland trout stream. And since many anglers who fish Great Lakes steelhead rivers had their first salmonid experience on an inland trout stream, this approach has been carried over. Since some of the Great Lakes rivers and streams are smaller and can have high concentrations of fish, this stationary approach can be highly effective.

I began my steelhead career as a stationary angler working a run or pool slowly while moving upstream with a dead-drift approach. This approach kept me well satisfied because of the big numbers of fish in those days. However, by the late 1980s I began to read and learn about Pacific coast steelhead fishing. The idea of rotating a pool made a lot of sense. Covering more water increased the opportunities to find aggressive steelhead, and the renewed hope gained by each step downriver made steelhead fishing even more interesting and captivating. I have been fishing with this approach for well over 20 years.

Finding water to rotate through isn't always easy. Stationary anglers can make it difficult unless they are greatly spread out. Most of the thoughts on finding water so far in this book have been geared toward searching for ample room to work the water. However, when all anglers in a pool are rotating, everyone gets an opportunity and the main pools can accommodate more anglers.

The concept of pool rotation is catching on slowly and is clearly more popular on larger rivers with more of a Spey fishing following. On one Ontario river that I frequent, which does not have a relatively long steelhead history, rotating a pool is the norm. It is clear evidence to me that this approach will continue to gain in popularity.

Rotating a pool gives each angler a fair opportunity to fish the entire run or pool. Successful anglers are those who learn to fish the fly in a productive manner over a range of water. It is very common to catch fish after following a number of anglers through a pool by using a different fly, sinking-tip, or simply varying the technique. I feel that rotation and working the water improve an angler's odds since covering more water increases the odds of finding aggressive, fresh-run steelhead.

The concept of rotation simply allows more anglers to enjoy and experience the water. The continued evolution of this style of fishing depends on education. I invite other anglers to rotate through a run or pool that I am fishing any time I have the opportunity. I have found that most anglers are willing as long as each angler in the pool is essentially on the same page. The idea of pool rotation is now readily discussed and presented at Spey gatherings and other fly-fishing forums throughout the Great Lakes. The word is spreading, and I see the evidence of this on the water.

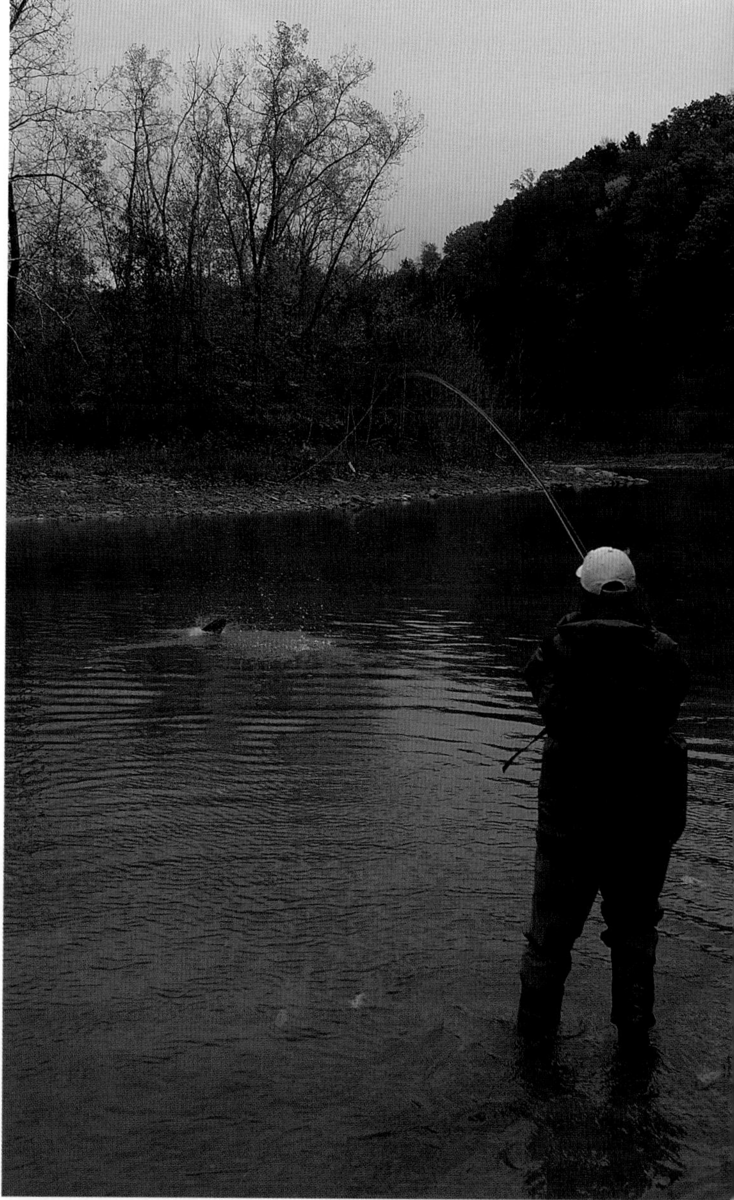

Suzanne Pionessa battles an energetic steelhead on a perfect fall day. NICK PIONESSA PHOTO

Rotation completes the act of fishing with a two-handed rod or switch rod, but also works well with a single-hander. Each cast is made with hope as new water is constantly being explored. The rhythm of this approach simply melts the time away while on a river like nothing else I have experienced. And you'll gain satisfaction from knowing that you have covered the water carefully and completely.

Ethical Considerations

Ethical issues that impact the fishery are a concern for every steelheader. We have a responsibility to respect the resource and fellow anglers. Respect for the resource goes a long way toward protecting and improving the quality of a fishery. Respect for other anglers is an integral ingredient in creating a quality experience for everyone. If we use the resource, then we have the responsibility to give back in one form or another.

Being aware and getting involved are the best ways to support a fishery. Every river or region faces its constant set of challenges. Most also have opportunities to expand and improve. A complete steelhead angler takes the resource personally and acts as a steward and an ally. Stewardship can come in the form of simple acts like practicing catch-and-release, respecting spawning areas of wild steelhead, and making sure that a river is left in the same condition as it was found. Becoming active in conservation and fishing organizations that support a river or region is critical. Such groups are a direct link to professional fisheries managers and a pipeline for current information and news concerning a fishery. In the world of fisheries management, there is strength in numbers, and more anglers becoming involved at a grassroots level can help pass new regulations or support progressive management initiatives such as dam removals, significant river improvements, or regulations that protect wild steelhead. Even without formal memberships or clubs, letters and emails to lawmakers in support of important improvements can make a significant difference.

In order for anglers to coexist on rivers and streams, we need to consider the rights of other users of the resource. Don't crowd or infringe on the space of another angler. This is entirely subjective. What is too close for one angler may be fine for another. Give each angler enough room to work his or her water, which includes fishing the opposite bank. An angler entering the water should not significantly restrict an angler who is already fishing.

The most certain way to not crowd another angler is simply to ask before entering the water. Clarifying how much space another angler wishes to have or determining which direction he or she is working the water will always alleviate any chance of a conflict. This interaction may also provide the opportunity to develop a rotation. A positive exchange between anglers helps keep everyone relaxed and creates a more sporting atmosphere on the river.

In Atlantic salmon fishing and all other rivers or pools where rotation is used, it is considered poor sportsmanship to enter a pool downstream of an angler who is rotating through the same pool. In the Great Lakes region, many conflicts develop in this way, most often because anglers do not know the rules of pool rotation or are unaware that an angler is working through. In some cases an aggressive angler attempts to fish a prime part of

Rotating through a pool gives each angler a fair opportunity to fish the water. NICK PIONESSA PHOTO

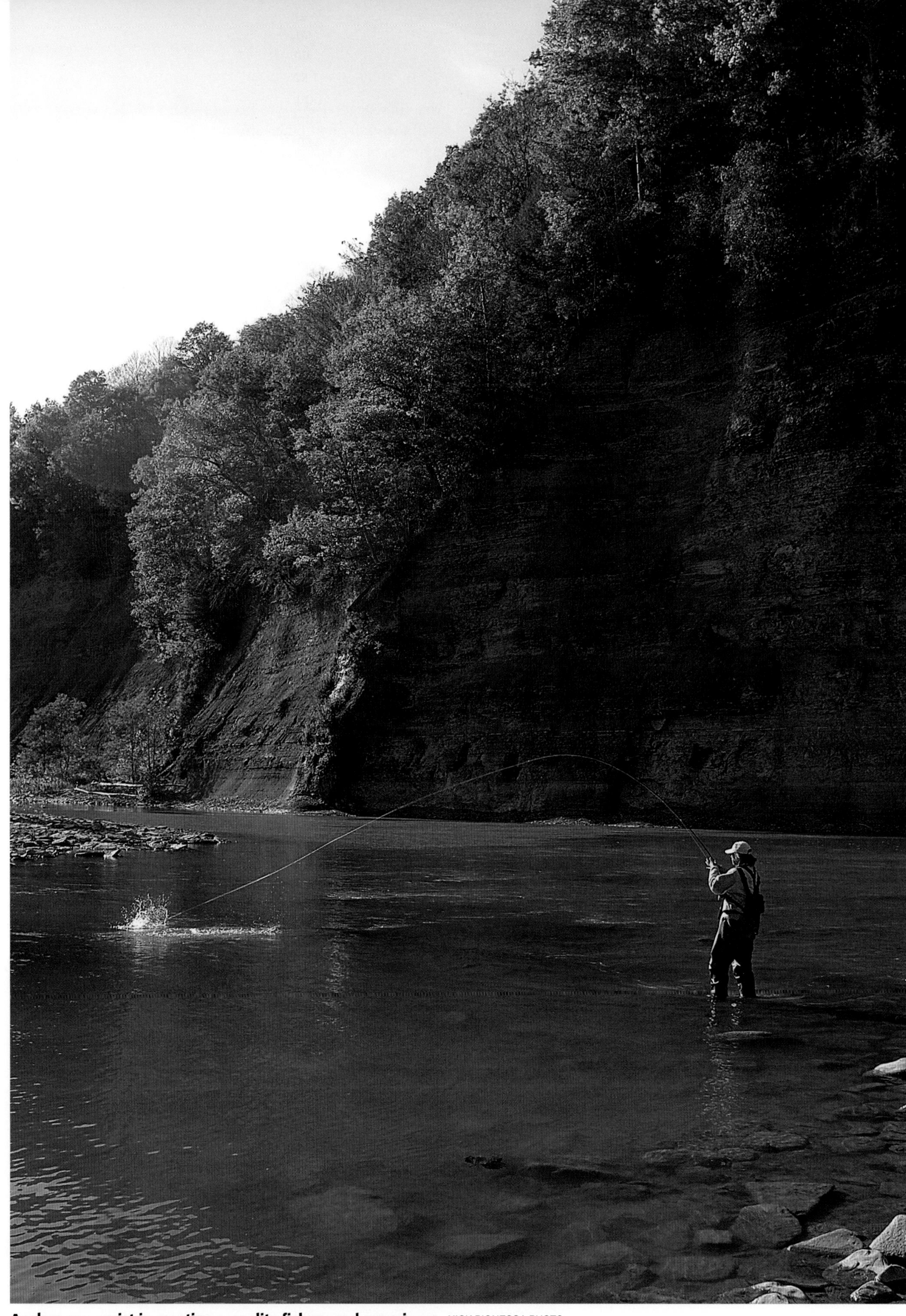

Anglers can assist in creating a quality fishery and experience. NICK PIONESSA PHOTO

Sporting opportunities in the Great Lakes region have increased dramatically in recent years. NICK PIONESSA PHOTO

the run before other anglers. Pool rotation is becoming popular enough on many rivers that most anglers should be aware of it. You can eliminate these types of conflicts by communicating with the other anglers in the pool. When someone cuts in below, I usually take the opportunity to explain the manner in which I am fishing the pool. Often this approach is met by curiosity and acceptance. Other times it can lead to an unpleasant exchange. But education is the key to changing attitudes.

Over the last 30 years, sporting techniques have improved significantly on Great Lakes rivers. When Pacific salmon were first planted in the region, most states allowed blind snatching or snagging. At the time it was believed that chinook and coho salmon would not actually take a fly, bait, or anything else once they migrated from the lake to the river. Pacific salmon die after spawning and their feeding mechanism begins to shut down as that time nears. But it has been proven that chinook and coho will take a fly and other offerings, even if it is mainly out of aggression or a leftover instinctive response.

Fishery managers admit that allowing snagging in the first place was a huge error. Not only were steelhead and migratory brown trout part of the snagging catch, but snagging also taught a terrible lesson to a generation of anglers that allowed unethical behavior to overflow into their steelhead angling. While many tried to disguise it, illegal lifting and lining was commonly practiced on fish that would readily take an offering presented with a modest amount of skill. This type of behavior gave the Great Lakes fishery a black eye for years. Time has a way of changing things. Unsavory behavior and characters still exist in concentrated areas of some rivers, but the movement toward a more sporting ethic has been remarkable.

In some ways the movement toward legal and ethical fishing has almost gone too far. Effective use of techniques with bait under a float or bobber can become so deadly that they limit the opportunity for other anglers. Single eggs or small egg sacs fished on light tippets using center-pin reels are capable of efficiently hooking nearly every fish in a pool, leaving little opportunity for those who prefer a more challenging approach. Personally I have nothing against any sporting means of catching a steelhead, but when one approach significantly takes opportunity away from other anglers, there does seem to be something that borders on the unethical about this type of behavior. Many fly fishers are calling for a ban on bait or a catch-and-release limit like that found on Quebec salmon rivers. As we grow and mature as steelhead fishers we want to explore all that steelhead fishing has to offer, such as new and challenging ways in which to encounter fish. As a fly-fishing steelheader who prefers to swing flies in a more traditional manner, I have modest expectations. But I feel cheated when a fellow angler severely limits my ability to fully enjoy a fishery.

Rivers that support wild runs of steelhead are dear to my heart. Protecting and enhancing these runs is a multistep process that is directly impacted by anglers' behavior. Each angler has a responsibility for leaving behind a limited footprint. Catch-

A beautiful wild Great Lakes steelhead. NICK PIONESSA PHOTO

and-release is an extremely important step toward enhancing steelhead populations, especially on wild-fish rivers. You have to handle the fish properly during the catch-and-release process. Keep the fish in the water during the entire process except for a quick lift for photos. Remove the hook by applying very little pressure, if any, to the fish's body. Removing the hook with a pair of forceps while the fish is lying in the water is most effective. Barbless hooks assist in a quick hook removal.

It is best to photograph a steelhead while it is still partially in the water, but lifting the fish up is fine provided it is not kept out of the water very long. Always support a steelhead when you lift one. Grasp it firmly around the tail with one hand and support the fish's body behind its head near the pectoral fins with the other. Never lift a live steelhead by its jaw.

Another step that anglers can take toward preserving wild stocks is to avoid actively spawning steelhead. Fish that have survived the many obstacles to arrive at the spawning gravel should be given an uninterrupted ability to propagate the species. Seasonal closures on some rivers and tributaries assist in this objective, but it is largely up to each angler. Spawning steelhead are usually quite visible and tempting targets, but allowing these fish to go unmolested will go a long way toward enhancing wild runs of steelhead.

I caught this wild steelhead on a perfect autumn morning after a long hike to the river. NICK PIONESSA PHOTO

Higher gradient rivers like Ontario's Jackpine provide an exciting challenge. SCOTT EARL SMITH PHOTO

Fitness

Keep yourself physically fit in order to have a quality experience while on the water. My weekly fitness plan includes strength training, cardio exercises, and a diet that is relatively low in fat and full of grains, protein, fruits, and vegetables. Being in shape allows me to enjoy all types of fly fishing and other physical activities and I hope will continue to do so well into my later years. Physical fitness increases circulation, strength, and stamina, which are all important for meeting the demands of fly fishing for steelhead. My ability to make long hikes to lightly fished water, make long casts from sunup to sundown, and wade and stand thigh deep in the water for as long as it takes can all be directly attributable to maintaining good physical condition. It is a good plan for life.

My weight training focuses on my leg muscles for strong wading, as well as core exercises, which are critical for balance and overall strength. The body's core is the basis of strength and power, critical when casting a two-handed rod. I also have a weight program for my arms, since they are typically the most active part of the body during a daylong outing. You should develop your own fitness regimen. There are numerous books, magazines, and web sites dedicated to fitness.

Staying in peak condition and being able to handle the rigors of a full day on the water also rely heavily on nutrition and keeping the body fueled. My body works more efficiently when it is fueled consistently throughout the day as opposed to eating one big meal in the middle of the day. I pack such items as granola, high-protein energy bars, trail mix, nuts, and fruits when fishing all day. I eat when walking between pools or even as I let my fly swing through the water. Equally important, if not more so, is proper hydration, and it is just as important on a cold day as on a hot one. Dehydration leads to fatigue and reduced body core temperature, and it inhibits the body's recovery from a long day on the river. I drink about 64 ounces of water during a full day and add an energy drink with electrolytes at the end of the day.

CHAPTER 5

Flies

An angler contemplates the choice of the right fly.
NICK PIONESSA PHOTO

Why exactly a steelhead takes a fly is a bit of a mystery. While some immature fish may voyage into the lower ends of a river or stream to forage, adult steelhead ascend a river with the specific purpose of propagation. A steelhead's mood clearly impacts its willingness to strike a fly.

Most veteran steelheaders would agree that steelhead take a fly for a variety of reasons. Aggressive territorialism and an instinctive reaction to stimuli are two of the main factors behind a steelhead striking a fly. And while steelhead may not search out food sources while in the river, they don't shy away from food when it exists. Steelhead can be opportunistic feeders.

I have seen a steelhead lash out at a fly that invaded its space. I have also seen a steelhead chase a fly as it swung away in a clear move to attack fleeing or helpless prey. And on a number of occasions I have watch steelhead actively feed on baitfish or intercept drifting spawn at the rear of a salmon or brown trout redd. These observations support the idea that steelhead take flies for different reasons at different times.

It seems to follow that if steelhead take flies for a variety of reasons, it is important to have a variety of patterns. And while I feel that is true to a degree, I also feel that developing confidence in a small nucleus of patterns allows an angler to fish most efficiently and not spend an inordinate amount of time making fly changes. Most seasoned steelhead anglers would agree that strategy, presentation, and perseverance are more important than the fly pattern and that an individual steelhead will take a wide range of flies when it is in the right mood. But having the fly that provides high confidence for the conditions or a particular river is essential.

I break patterns for steelhead roughly into three categories. The first is flies tied with materials that move and undulate when in the water. These patterns are not designed as much to represent a particular food source as to be seductive in the water, inducing a strike through their lifelike movement. Almost all of my patterns that fit into this category include marabou, rabbit strip, or arctic fox and a small element of flash.

These seductive patterns range widely in color from white to hot pink to purple and black. Color preference often depends on the river as some colors just seem to work better in certain watersheds. I usually default to black and purple because they are productive colors on most rivers. My seductive patterns are typically larger and create a significant silhouette, especially when fishing stained water. A good portion of the time I spend swinging a fly for steelhead is done using larger patterns with lifelike movement.

The next group is tied in a manner consistent with traditional salmon and steelhead flies. Most are tied in a Spey-fly or wet-fly style, and their elegance is an art form in itself. Many argue that a fish as noble as a steelhead should be caught only on such a beautifully constructed pattern.

Flies constructed of materials that create movement in the water, like marabou, rabbit strip, and arctic fox, work well with the wet-fly swing. A black-and-purple marabou Spey tube fly fooled this fish.

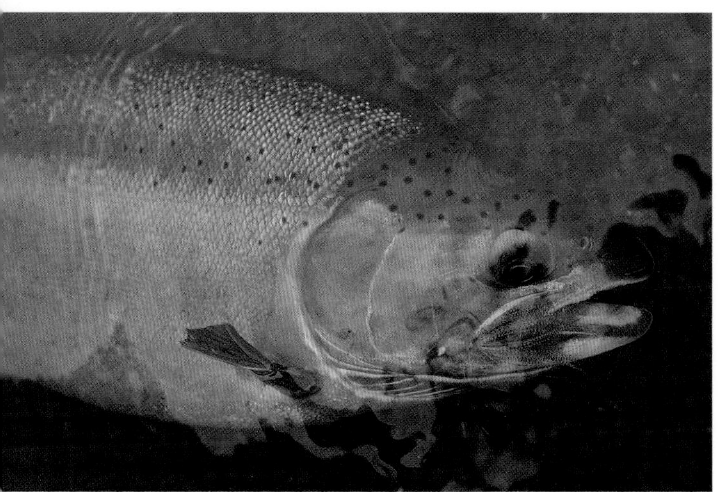

Olive and brown patterns work well in clear water conditions.
NICK PIONESSA PHOTO

Spey flies originated on Scotland's River Spey. The original Spey flies used very particular materials, most of which are illegal to possess today. But the main feature of this style is the long, flowing hackle fibers, which have been incorporated into modern patterns using a variety of substitutes for those used on the original patterns. Spey flies commonly have a folded hackle wound through the body of the fly and a wing constructed of feather or hair. Spey flies are usually tied on size 4 hooks and larger. By contrast, wet flies are usually tied on smaller hooks. This style of fly also features a folded hackle wound in at the head of the fly. Most wet flies also include a wing.

I use Spey flies when I am in the mood to catch a steelhead on an elegant fly. I also prefer Speys when it seems as though my large, seductive flies are providing too much stimuli and steelhead are shying away. Spey flies often give a more subtle movement and appearance in the water. Wet flies provide an even more subtle and stealthy look and are good for low, clear water or spooky fish that do not seem interested in larger patterns. A small wet fly makes a good follow-up pattern after a steelhead makes a short take on a larger fly.

The third group of flies is those that are tied to imitate an exact food source. Patterns that imitate baitfish, aquatic insects, and drifting spawn fall into this category. These patterns are constructed for rivers where the steelhead seem to key in on specific sources of food. In the dead-drift approach, the flies often match the common food sources of the river. Those tied to represent specific insects such as stoneflies, *Hexagenia*, and caddis larvae, along with a variety of more generic mayfly patterns, can be extremely effective on many rivers and streams.

Flies tied to represent naturally occurring insects seem to work best on clear, heavily fished waters where a stealthy approach pays off. Egg patterns can be tied in a variety of colors, and often the best colors vary by river. The color of eggs from other spawning fish vary by species among yellow, orange, and red after being freshly deposited. The general theory is to use brighter colors when other fish are in the spawning process. Naturally occurring eggs tend to lose their color quickly, and therefore more muted tones are a good match for drifting spawn that has been in the water for an extended period. Varieties of pink and cream represent older spawn. Some colors work well on a particular river even if that color is not naturally occurring—I suspect it is simply how that color shows to a steelhead on that river. (Remember, fish see differently than humans.)

Flies tied to represent specific bait that is prevalent in a river have become an increasing trend in the Great Lakes fishery. One of my home rivers, the Niagara, has a significant baitfish population. Small rainbow smelt are in the river from fall through the following spring, and patterns that mimic them are extremely effective for the entire steelhead season. Many steelhead rivers in the region host a significant population of sculpins. Olive, brown, and gold sculpin patterns with deer and wool heads are very effective on some Michigan and Ontario rivers. The combination of the subtle colors and natural look makes this fly a good choice in clear water conditions.

Fly Styles

The style of flies used for Great Lakes steelhead varies widely by river and region. These patterns can be loosely divided into a handful of styles. A number of anglers with years of Great Lakes steelhead experience have contributed to the fly section of this book, providing varied perspectives and a wide range of successful fly patterns.

Tube Flies

Tube flies have become very popular for steelhead and salmon anglers, and this style is quickly growing among Great Lakes tiers. What is a tube fly? you might ask. Instead of the fly being constructed on the shank of the hook, it is tied on a hollow tube made of plastic, aluminum, or copper. To fish with a tube fly, you insert the tippet through the tube from the head of the fly

Weighted tube flies are capable of reaching deep into the water column.

The short-shank hook used with this tube assisted in landing this bright hen. Hooks with short shanks make it less likely to lose fish. NICK PIONESSA PHOTO

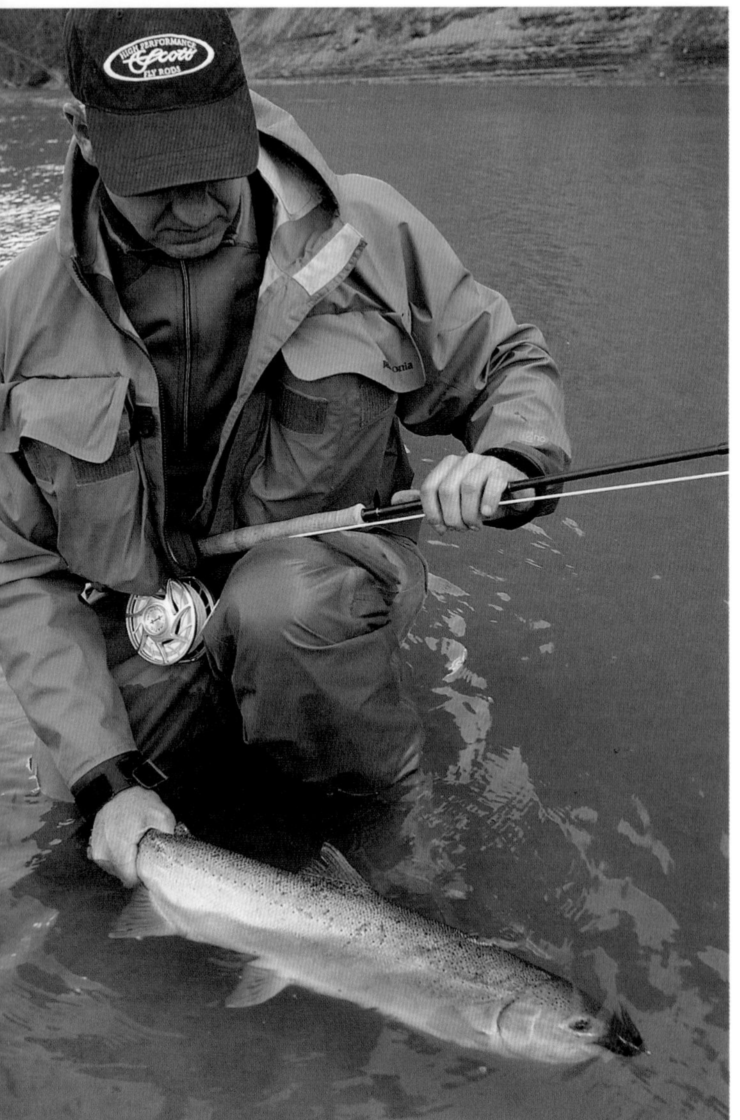

A spring steelhead that fell for a black-and-purple marabou tube fly. NICK PIONESSA PHOTO

to the tail and tie it to a single straight-eye hook using your favorite knot. You then insert the eye of the hook either into the tube or into another short piece of plastic tubing just large enough to fit snugly over the tube the fly is tied on, and slide it over the butt of the main tube. The short piece of tubing is referred to as junction tubing. Softer plastics have become more prevalent in steelhead tube-fly design, greatly reducing the use of junction tubing except for tying rigid tubes like aluminum and copper. Another method for securing the hook is to use an up-eye hook and allow the knot section of a loop knot such as a surgeon's loop to be drawn into the tube. This allows the hook to be less rigid.

Tube flies are tied in a special vise or using an attachment to a standard vise. The special vise or attachment has a steel rod slightly smaller than the inside diameter of the tube. You insert the rod through the tube and secure it in place so that it is similar to tying on a hook shank. Many different types of flies can be tied on tubes, but the most common are streamer-type flies and those traditionally used for salmon and steelhead.

One of the advantages of the tube-fly design is that you have complete control of where the hook is positioned relative to the materials because you can change the length of the tube. A longer tube will place the hook to the rear of the pattern. My experience with steelhead has been that a hook positioned at the rear increases the chance of hooking a fish that subtly yanks on the tail of the fly. Lethargic or uninspired steelhead commonly tug on the fly halfheartedly. A rear hook position connects with some of these fish.

The second advantage of tube flies is that the ratio of steelhead hooked and landed increases significantly when using a tube fly with a short-shank hook. Since the fly is built on the tube, the length of the hook shank does not control the length of the fly. You can use hooks with short shanks on all tube flies. Long-shank hooks result in more lost fish as the shank length creates greater leverage, allowing the fish to twist it more easily from its mouth. A short-shank hook will more consistently stay firmly affixed in a steelhead's mouth or jaw.

A cone on this tube fly allowed the fly to get to the proper depth in heavy water. NICK PIONESSA PHOTO

Another advantage of the tube design is that the fly generally slides up the leader when a fish is hooked. Less damage occurs to the fly during the fight, and it is out of the way when you extract the hook from the fish. When using a conventional tie, you can damage the materials with a pair of forceps. If, in the process of fishing, a hook becomes damaged beyond the point of repair, you can simply replace a tube fly, whereas you have to discard a conventionally tied fly once the hook can no longer be sharpened. Also, since you determine the size of the tube, you can control the size of the fly easily as well and still have a short-shank hook positioned at the rear of the fly.

Weighting a tube fly is simple and versatile. Cones and beads slide over the tube or the inside tube liner. You can make some very creative designs at the tying bench this way. Brightly colored beads not only add some weight to the fly, but also can finish off a neat egg-sucking leech design. Cones and beads make your tube flies versatile as you can easily add them while on the river, transforming an unweighted fly into a weighted version in seconds. Make sure you leave enough room at the front of the fly to slide the cone or bead onto the front of the tube. First thread the cone or bead onto the leader and then the tube. Once you add the hook, the cone or bead slides up and is secured on the tube at the thread wraps of the head. I wrap the heads of my tube flies in a tapered fashion to create a solid base and tighten the connection when I push the cone or bead into position. To add a cone or bead permanently to a plastic tube, use a lighter to heat up the end of the tube so that it flares at the end and creates a secure connection.

There are various tube designs aside from the simple straight type. Some, such as the Temple Dog tube fly, influence how the fly is weighted relative to the materials, which controls how the fly looks and tracks in the water during the swing. The Temple Dog type of fly has an elongated wing that is approximately two times the length of the tube. The wing is angled up, which gives the fly a full silhouette in the water with only limited materials, reducing wind resistance and allowing for casting ease. Also, since the wing is angled up, it remains unencumbered from the body of the fly, free to undulate and move in the water as the fly swings. A teardrop-shaped tube enhances this type of fly design by counterbalancing the wing and allowing the fly to ride flat in the water.

Spey Flies

Defining what a Spey fly is is not easy. It has become more of a concept than a definitive type of fly. Original Spey flies were simple patterns tied in rather drab colors and finished with two tips of bronze mallard. The most distinguishing feature of this style of tying was the long, flowing body hackle, which displayed an undulating, seductive movement in the water. This feature has held true through many changes and adaptations over the years.

Some modern Speys still exhibit the same elements of the earlier versions right down to the teal collar, but many others vary quite widely from the originals. The original patterns featured a body hackle of the Spey cock. Heron feathers make a great Spey hackle because of their long barbules and thin

This bright steelhead fell for a classic-tie Spey fly.
NICK PIONESSA PHOTO

stems, but heron is protected and illegal to possess in the United States. A variety of other hackles provide the long, flowing look on today's patterns. Blue-eared pheasant is similar to heron, although its barbules do not have as consistent a length. It can be bleached and dyed various colors to create beautiful Spey flies.

Burnt goose feather (the burning process removes wispy underfibers), schlappen, and even marabou can also be used to tie Speys, but each of these has limitations too. The stems on goose tend to be on the thick side and can make it a bit difficult to finish the wrap. The stems can also be brittle, but soaking in water before wrapping them can prevent them from splitting.

The stems on schlappen are generally much thinner and easier to work with than the burnt goose hackles. Schlappen creates a full-looking fly that moves well in the water, and some of the feathers have quite long barbules. But schlappen can be webby—the barbules may stick together on some of the feathers, which can negatively impact both the appearance and seductive movement of the fly. Selecting the right schlappen hackle makes a high-quality pattern.

Marabou can create an elegant Spey fly. The positive attributes of marabou are that the fibers can be quite long and the stems fairly thin. However, the fibers are wispy and do not always sit well on the fly. Marabou moves extremely well in the water, though, and can create an effective and attractive fly.

I appreciate the elegant appearance of the Spey fly. Most of the Spey flies that I have designed or use for Great Lakes steelhead blend traditional elements with simplicity and fishing effectiveness. Two of my favorites, the September Spey and October Spey, use hackle tips or arctic fox for the wing, which adds to the movement in the water. I prefer a long body hackle and a collar of guinea or teal. Jungle cock eyes give a Spey fly a regal finish.

Spey fly colors are often selected to match fishing conditions or to match a specific color that has proven to be productive on a particular river. As with the original Spey flies that were developed specifically for one river, Spey flies often evolve in the Great Lakes region in the same way—patterns are developed to match a certain size and color that are known to be productive on a certain river.

While many Spey flies are designed and tied to be framed and never fished, I prefer those that have a beautiful appearance but can be constructed in a reasonable amount of time—in other words, fishing flies. I also tie some Spey flies on tubes, and I include in this group of flies a series of marabou Speys that have proven extremely productive wherever steelhead swim. The marabou Speys are missing most of the elements of the original patterns, but their long, sweeping construction resulting from folded marabou creates an attractive Spey-like appearance. Great Lakes tiers such as Bob Blumreich, Charlie Dickson, Brian Slavinski, Rick Whorwood, and Neil Houlding have been designing and tying Spey flies for the region's rivers for many years. Most of these patterns exhibit a combination of artistic and practical fishing elements.

Wet Flies and Soft-Hackles

This style of fly is characterized by its simplicity and size. The main element is a soft hackle folded and tied in as a collar. Most wet flies also have a wing. This style of fly includes many patterns that have traditionally been used for steelhead and Atlantic salmon. Most of the wet flies that I use in the Great Lakes are smaller, ranging from size 6 to 10.

I mainly use smaller wet flies when a stealthy approach is required. Clear water conditions can often be fished effectively with low-profile wets as steelhead seem more likely to commit to something smaller when in a less aggressive mood. I also switch to a small wet fly to change up the pattern after a steelhead shows an interest in a larger fly. Going back to that same fish with a small wet fly can often result in a solid take. Wet flies tied on up-eye hooks can be riffle-hitched to ride in the surface film, and when conditions are right, they bring steelhead up for an exciting take.

Most of the wet flies I use are composed of natural, drab colors to represent aquatic insects or other common life forms. But a variety of colors are effective, and one of my most reliable wet flies is the Purple Peril.

Streamers

Streamer patterns are tied to represent baitfish. Many streamers used in the Great Lakes region have evolved as innovative tiers match a specific bait on a particular river. Others are more suggestive of a range of bait.

Sculpin patterns make very effective streamers on many rivers in the Great Lakes region. Sculpins are common on most rivers that have good water quality. The most effective patterns for steelhead are commonly constructed with wool heads to absorb water and take the fly down to the bottom. Michigan guide Kevin Feenstra has been using oversize sculpin flies very effectively on his rivers for years. Many of Kevin's flies are tied with the same color tones as the natural sculpin, but others incorporate brighter colors and flashy material to match the ever-changing mood of a steelhead. Ontario guide Mike Verhoef is also a proponent of sculpin patterns on his rivers and uses his brown and olive creations as a stealthy option to other standard patterns.

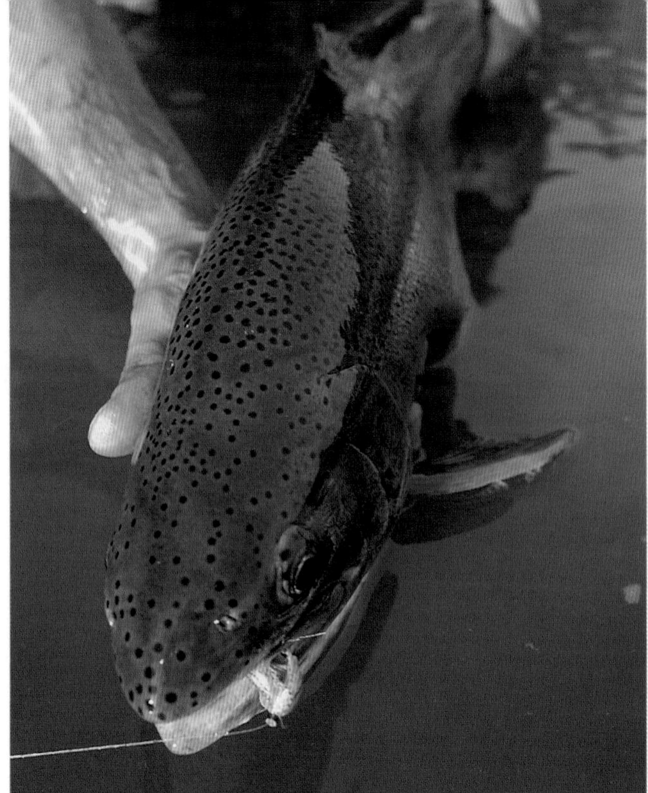

Lightly dressed flies can be very productive in low, clear water.
NICK PIONESSA PHOTO

Many of the streamer patterns that I rely on use rabbit strips to mimic a realistic swimming motion in the water. Zonker flies in a range of colors are very effective on Great Lakes steelhead. The Bunny Spey is a further adaptation of the Zonker that incorporates a long schlappen hackle at the collar. A white-winged fly with a purple body is an effective representation of smelt and a range of other bait swimming in and at the mouths of many of my local rivers. This style of fly can be tied in a wide range of colors.

Other designs using both synthetic and natural hair are easy to tie, swim well in the water, and induce exciting strikes from aggressive steelhead. Some synthetics create bulky flies with a minimum of materials. Guide and fly tackle representative Jerry Darkes of Ohio uses a variety of fairly simple streamers on Ohio and Pennsylvania rivers and streams. Small streamers tied with minimal materials can be very effective in low, clear water conditions.

Leech Patterns

Some leech patterns represent actual freshwater leeches living in steelhead rivers, and others are more generic patterns built to exhibit a wiggly, seductive movement. Most leech patterns feature rabbit strips, marabou, or soft saddle hackles. Leech patterns are generally tied in black or purple, although some include splashes of brighter colors. I have had great success with smaller patterns in brown and olive.

Articulated leeches are tied with a jointed section to give the fly extra wiggle and movement. The joints are commonly constructed of two hooks joined together with a monofilament loop off the rear of the first hook. Many anglers feel that the extra swimming motion of the joint will entice even the most stubborn steelhead to take the fly.

Another style that I lump into the leech category is the Intruder. This style of fly is designed to impart a seductive movement in the water. The Intruder is often tied 3 to 5 inches long, and the hook is placed at the rear of the fly. While you could use a long tube to place the hook at the rear of the fly, the tube makes the fly more rigid. The key to the Intruder is that a short-shank hook positioned at the rear using a heavy length of monofilament allows the materials to snake through the water. The hook is attached with a loop connection so that the point rides up. With the flexibility of the monofilament and the hook riding point up, the Intruder is designed to snag less frequently than other patterns.

Some leech patterns are very easy to tie. I have had good success with patterns that are simply tied with a rabbit strip tail and the rabbit palmered forward to the head of the fly. I usually add a little flash to the tail of this pattern. The Egg Sucking Leech is basically a Woolly Bugger with an egg formed at the head with chenille, dubbing, or a fluorescent bead. I like to use a bead to add some weight to the fly. Simple Woolly Bugger patterns make great steelhead flies and account for many caught fish each year in the Great Lakes. Small Woolly Buggers in brown and olive have been my most reliable pattern when fishing low, clear water and for following up on fish that have just tugged or bumped a larger fly. Beadhead and Conehead Woolly Buggers provide for a stealthy approach when swinging flies and fishing pockets with a long monofilament leader.

Nymph Patterns

Nymph patterns play an important role on many Great Lakes rivers. Nymphs commonly are used with the dead-drift approach, and some of the larger patterns can also be used with

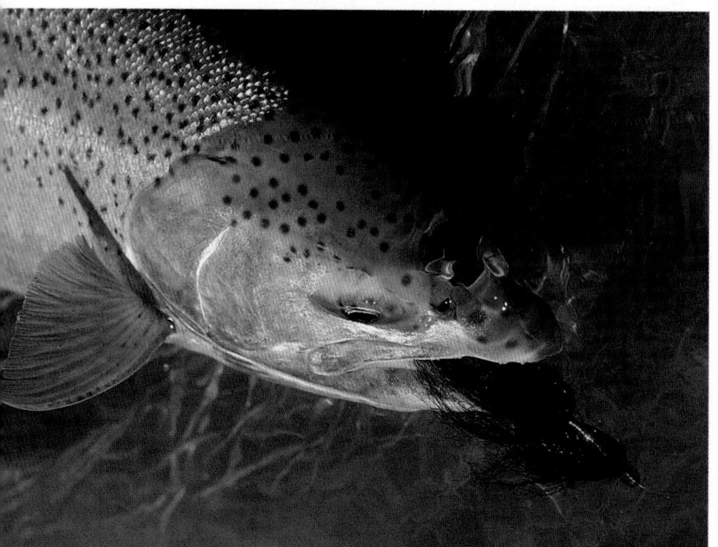

Most leech patterns have a seductive movement in the water. NICK PIONESSA PHOTO

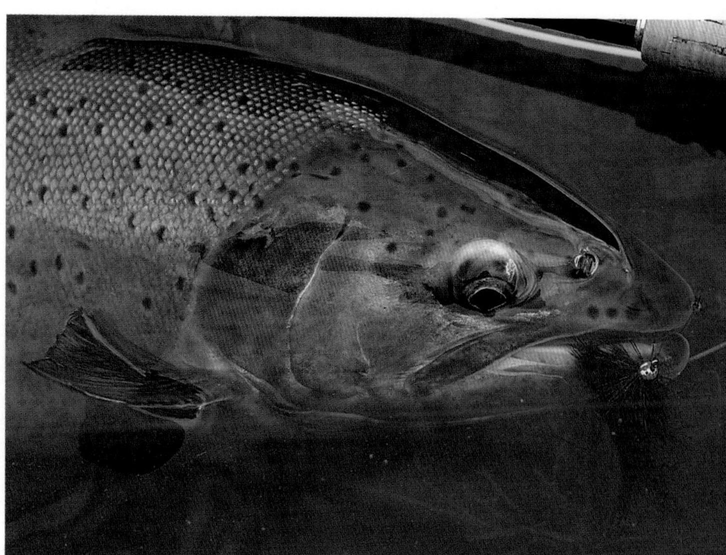

Fluorescent beads not only add weight to the fly, but also create an enticing contrast in colors. NICK PIONESSA PHOTO

the wet-fly swing. Rivers with significant insect populations may require specific nymph patterns. *Hexagenia* patterns can play an important role in Midwestern and Ontario rivers, especially in the spring. Stonefly nymphs account for steelhead on many watersheds throughout the region, including some of the rivers in New York. Other specific mayfly patterns can be effective on particular rivers that require a more match-the-hatch mentality because of low, clear water conditions.

On rivers and streams that don't have high water quality, nymph patterns can still be an important option for dead drifting. Generic patterns such as the Hare's Ear, Squirrel Tail, Prince Nymph, Pheasant Tail, and caddis larvae are productive patterns throughout the region. This is true for some of the Ohio and Pennsylvania waters where, despite significant insect hatches, these patterns have their place when a stealthy approach is required.

Egg Patterns

There have been many attempts over the years to improve upon the single egg Glo Bug. And while there have been innovative patterns that seem to produce better in some circumstances, the single egg is still the mainstay for many dead-drift anglers. You choose to make the egg any size you want, and the smaller patterns tend to work well in low, clear water. The Glo Bug is simple to construct by tying in Glo Bug or similar yarn to the top of the hook, pulling it all straight up, and cutting it with a very sharp pair of sewing scissors. You can use various colors for a marbled effect or a small amount of a second color for a dot to represent the egg yolk. Small egg patterns with a dot make realistic imitations of naturally occurring spawn.

Egg cluster flies have gained popularity over the years in the Great Lakes region. The most common is the Sucker Spawn, which originated as a trout fly in Pennsylvania but over the last 25 years has become a favorite fly of anglers dead-drifting a fly for steelhead.

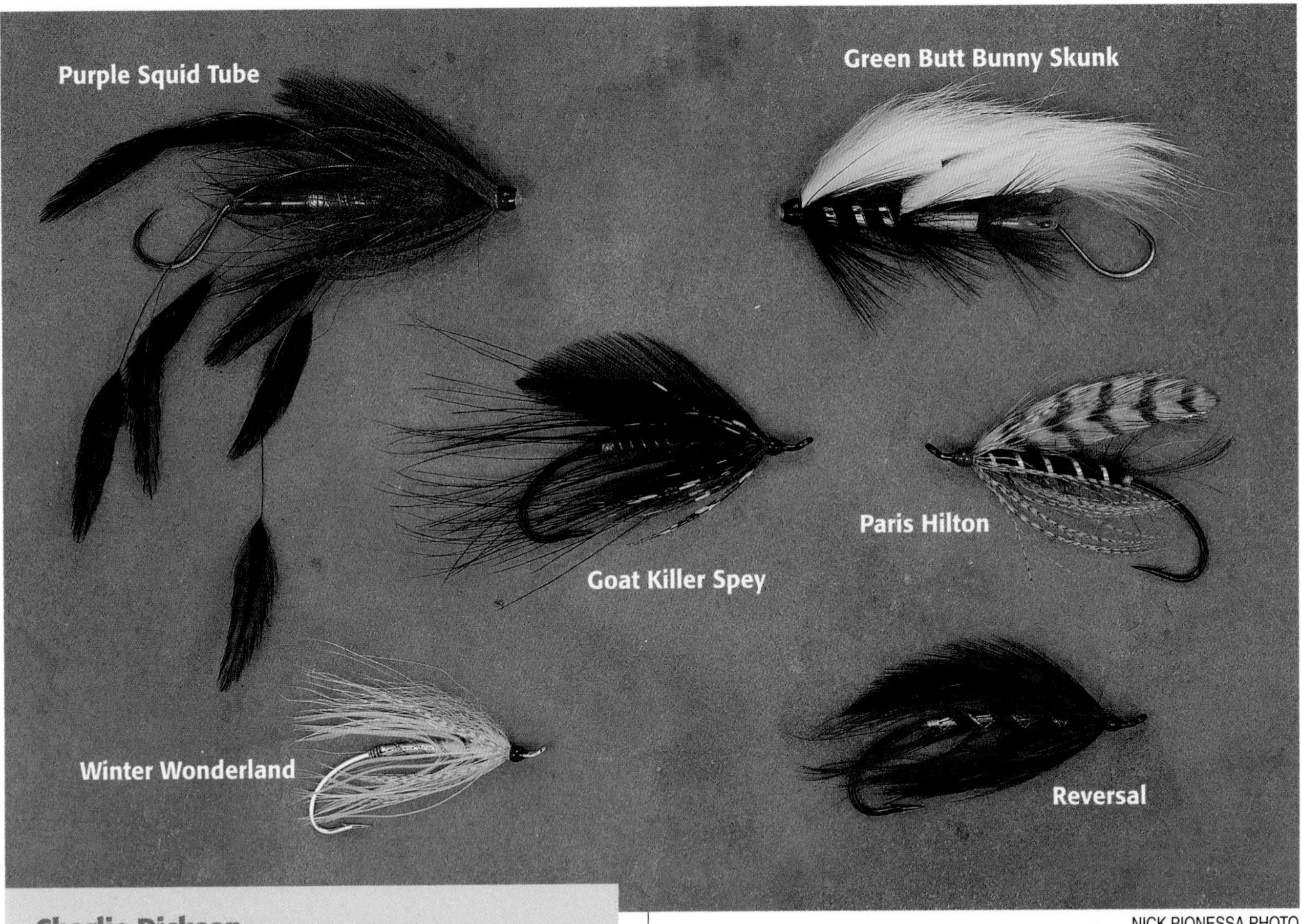

NICK PIONESSA PHOTO

Charlie Dickson

Charlie is a western New York angler and tier of high-quality innovative patterns. Charlie is a dedicated angler well into his third decade of pursuing migratory fish in the Great Lakes region. He brings both a practical and artful eye to his award-winning tying.

PURPLE SQUID TUBE

Tier:	Charlie Dickson
Tube:	1½-inch aluminum or copper
Tag:	Fine oval silver tinsel
Body:	Rear half pink floss; front half pink, then purple SLF spun in a dubbing loop
Rib:	Purple flat braid with fine oval silver tinsel on either side, over the back half only
Hackle:	Purple burnt goose midbody
Feelers:	Nine grizzly saddle hackles dyed purple, stripped, except for the tip tied in randomly in the front half of the body
Collar:	Mallard or teal dyed pink
Wing:	Two purple hackle tips inside two pink hackle tips
Head:	Red

GREEN BUTT BUNNY SKUNK

Tier:	Charlie Dickson
Tube:	Copper, brass, or aluminum
Tag:	Oval silver tinsel
Tail:	Red cock hackle swept back
Rear rib:	Fine oval silver tinsel
Rear body:	Fluorescent green floss
Joint:	Black cock hackle swept back
Rear wing:	White rabbit strip
Front rib:	Medium oval silver tinsel
Body:	Black dubbing
Front hackle:	Black cock hackle swept back
Front wing:	White rabbit strip
Head:	Black

PARIS HILTON

Tier:	Charlie Dickson
Hook:	Up-eye salmon
Tag:	Flat silver tinsel
Tail:	Pink hackle fibers
Rib:	Oval silver tinsel
Body:	Black seal substitute
Wing:	Grizzly hackle tips with pink flash material in between
Hackle:	Mallard or teal
Head:	Pink

Note: This fly was created by western New York angler Tim Voigt.

REVERSAL

Tier:	Charlie Dickson
Hook:	Up-eye salmon
Rib:	Flat pearl Mylar and oval silver tinsel
Body:	Rear third black floss; front two-thirds black seal dubbing
Body hackle:	Red schlappen, one side stripped
Throat:	Black schlappen and red guinea
Wing:	Four black hackle tips
Head:	Black

Note: This is a deviation of a fly called the Mahoney invented by Pacific Coast steelhead guide Dec Hogan.

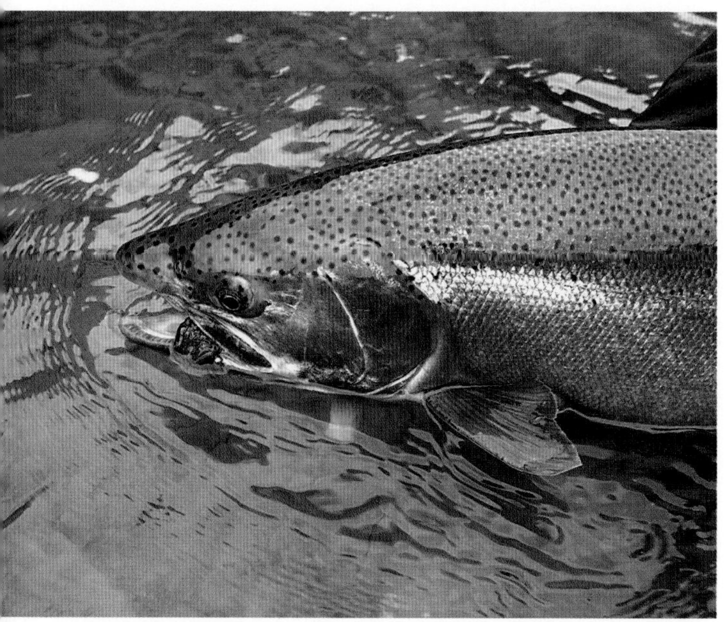

Developing faith in a handful of patterns helps to streamline the fly selection process.

WINTER WONDERLAND

Tier:	Charlie Dickson
Hook:	Up-eye salmon
Tip:	Oval green tinsel or green wire
Rib:	Oval green tinsel or green wire
Body:	Black half flat silver tinsel; front half white dubbing
Body hackle:	White schlappen over front half of the body
Hackle:	Mallard
Wing:	White polar bear or substitute
Head:	Red

Note: This is a very productive winter steelhead pattern.

GOAT KILLER SPEY

Tier:	Charlie Dickson
Hook:	Up-eye salmon
Tag:	Fine oval silver tinsel
Rib:	Fine oval silver tinsel over red floss and red flat braid over the dubbing
Body:	Rear third red floss; front two-thirds purple goat dubbing
Body hackle:	Spey-type hackle such as pheasant rump dyed purple
Throat:	Natural guinea
Wing:	Two red hackle tips enveloped by two purple hackle tips
Head:	Red

Note: This is a Syd Glasso–style pattern I created for fishing Great Lakes tributaries. While this is a relatively simple fly to tie, the wing can be a bit tricky. The hackle tips used in its construction should be tented over the body. Flattening the stems of the hackles at the tie-in point, and slightly twisting them with a pair of flat-nosed pliers or tweezers before tying them in, can help to achieve this.

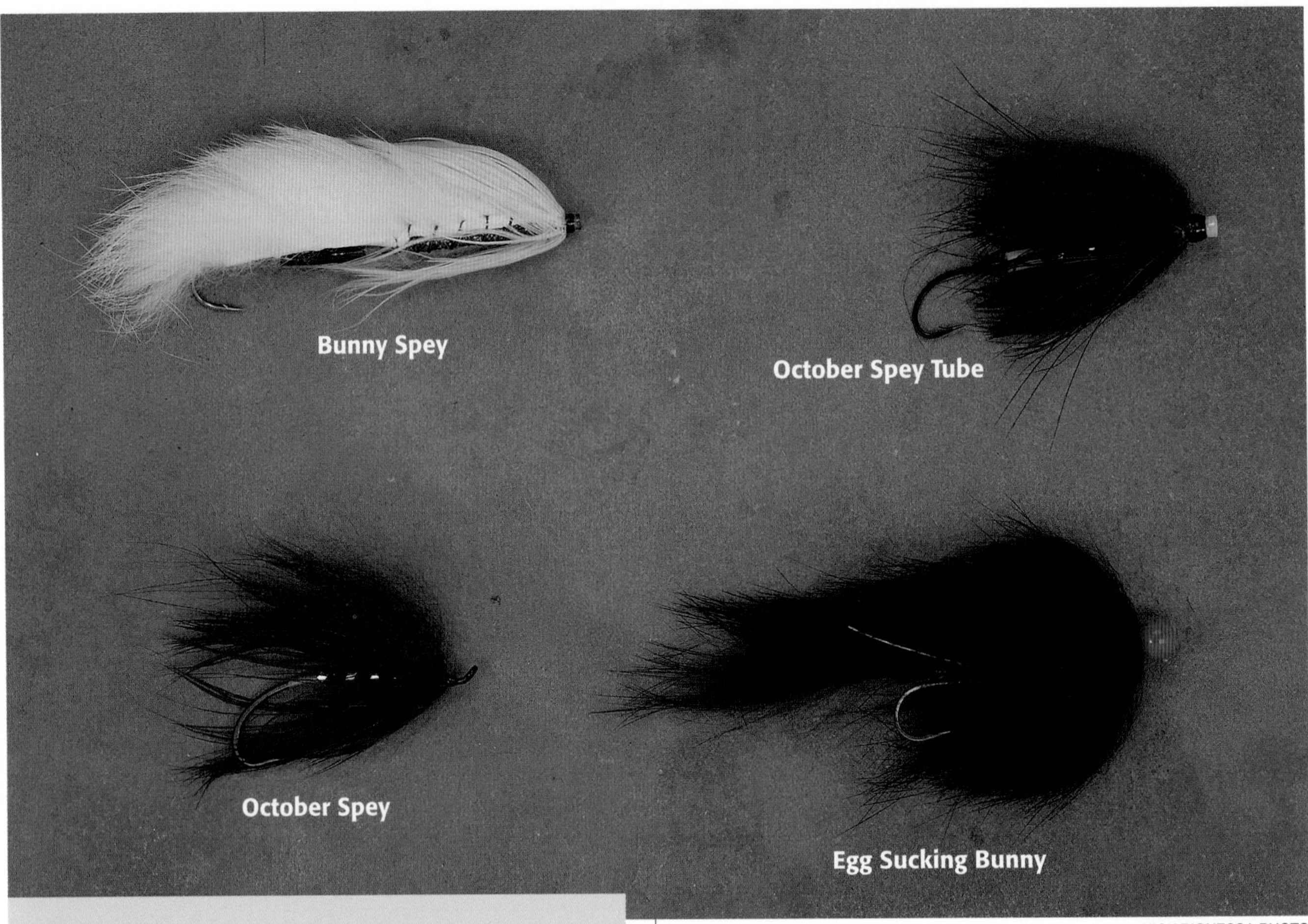

NICK PIONESSA PHOTO

Rick Kustich

I stick to a pretty basic repertoire of patterns for my steelhead fishing. I like using tube flies for versatility and effectiveness. All my patterns incorporate marabou, rabbit strip, or arctic fox to create a seductive movement. I make adjustments to size and color based on conditions.

BUNNY SPEY

Tier:	Rick Kustich
Tube/hook:	Copper or plastic 1½ to 2 inches in length or #3 Daiichi 2051
Thread:	Red or black 8/0
Tail and wing:	White, black, or purple rabbit strip
Body:	Purple Haze SLF
Rib:	Red copper wire carefully worked through the rabbit fibers
Hackle:	A long schlappen hackle

Note: This pattern has long been one of my best producers for steelhead and other lake-run species. It has an enticing and seductive movement in the water.

OCTOBER SPEY TUBE

Tier:	Rick Kustich
Tube:	Fluorescent green or orange flexible or junction tubing
Thread:	Purple 8/0
Body:	Purple Haze SLF
Rib:	Medium flat silver tinsel
Body hackle:	Long purple schlappen with a thin stem wrapped forward from the third wrap of tinsel
Front hackle:	A few turns of blue-eared pheasant folded and stroked to the rear of the fly
Wing:	Arctic fox dyed purple

Note: This is the tube version of a pattern that I also tie on a hook. It has more options for weighting the fly.

EGG SUCKING BUNNY

Tier:	Rick Kustich
Tube:	Plastic cut to length
Thread:	Black 6/0
Tail:	Black or purple rabbit strip cut long enough to wrap as the body and tied in at the end of the tube with a few strands of holographic Flashabou
Body:	Black or purple rabbit strip wrapped forward with the fibers pulled back before each wrap
Head:	Unweighted craft bead or fluorescent tungsten bead

Note: You may need to use a liner tube with the tungsten bead. This is a simple but very productive pattern.

OCTOBER SPEY

Tier:	Rick Kustich
Hook:	#3 Daiichi 2061
Thread:	Purple 8/0
Tag:	Orange UNI-Floss
Body:	Purple Haze SLF
Rib:	Medium flat silver tinsel
Body hackle:	Long, purple burnt goose wrapped forward from the third wrap of tinsel
Front hackle:	A few turns of extra-long guinea dyed purple
Wing:	Arctic fox dyed purple

Note: This pattern provides a more subtle presentation than some of my larger marabou-and-rabbit-strip flies. It is a good pattern when covering a pool for the second time or when a fish has showed interest.

Experienced anglers can visualize the way a fly will be presented in the water and select a fly pattern to fish a certain way given the water structure.

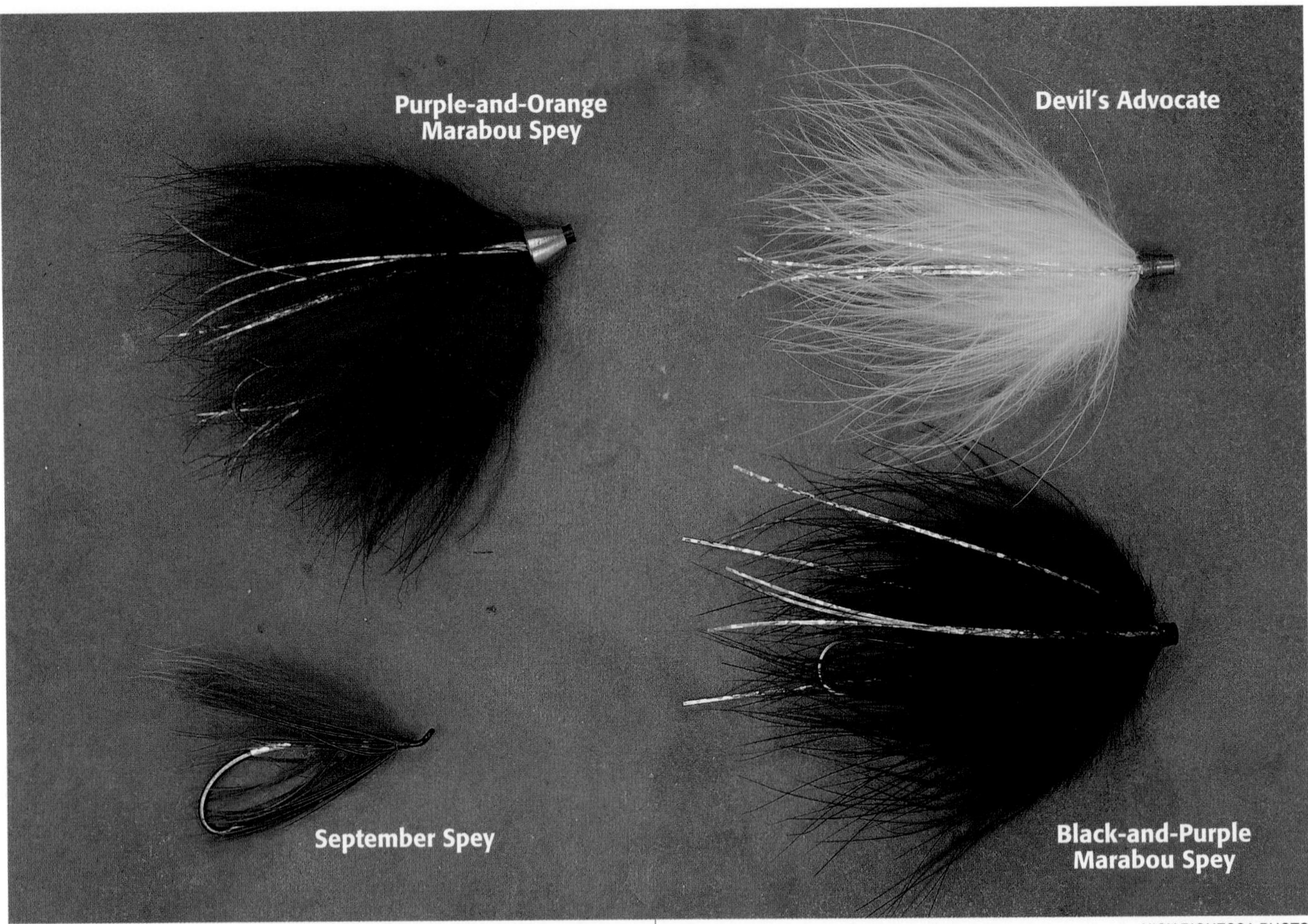

NICK PIONESSA PHOTO

PURPLE-AND-ORANGE MARABOU SPEY

Tier:	Rick Kustich
Tube:	Plastic cut to length of fly
Thread:	Purple 8/0
Body:	Purple Haze SLF in a dubbing loop to create a full body and a wider silhouette
Hackle:	Purple marabou blood quill over orange
Flash:	Four or five strands of holographic Flashabou tied in on sides
Head:	Cone slid over the tube

Note: You can add the cone on the water. Being able to add weight to the fly while on the water can help you make the proper presentation.

DEVIL'S ADVOCATE

Tier:	Rick Kustich
Tube:	Copper tube 1½ or 2 inches in length
Thread:	Red or gray 8/0
Body:	Purple Bodi-Braid
Hackle:	Two white marabou blood quills
Collar:	A few turns of natural guinea (optional)

Note: This is a great pattern when good numbers of bait are in a river. This deep version fished with a heavy tip can cover significant depths and is my main fly on my home Niagara River.

BLACK-AND-PURPLE MARABOU SPEY

Tier:	Rick Kustich
Tube:	Purple flexible plastic or junction tubing cut to length of fly
Thread:	Black 8/0
Under-hackle:	Purple schlappen
Hackle:	Purple marabou blood quill over orange
Flash:	Four or five strands of holographic Flashabou tied in on sides

Note: This is my go-to fly on most of the rivers that I fish.

SEPTEMBER SPEY

Tier:	Rick Kustich
Hook:	#3, 5, or 7 Daiichi 2051
Thread:	Olive 8/0
Tag:	Medium flat gold tinsel
Body:	Medium olive SLF
Rib:	Medium flat gold tinsel
Body hackle:	Long olive schlappen with a thin stem wrapped forward from the third wrap of tinsel
Front hackle:	A few turns of blue-eared pheasant folded and stroked to the rear of the fly
Wing:	Arctic fox dyed olive

Note: This has been a great pattern in the low, clear water that is common early in the season on Lake Erie tributaries.

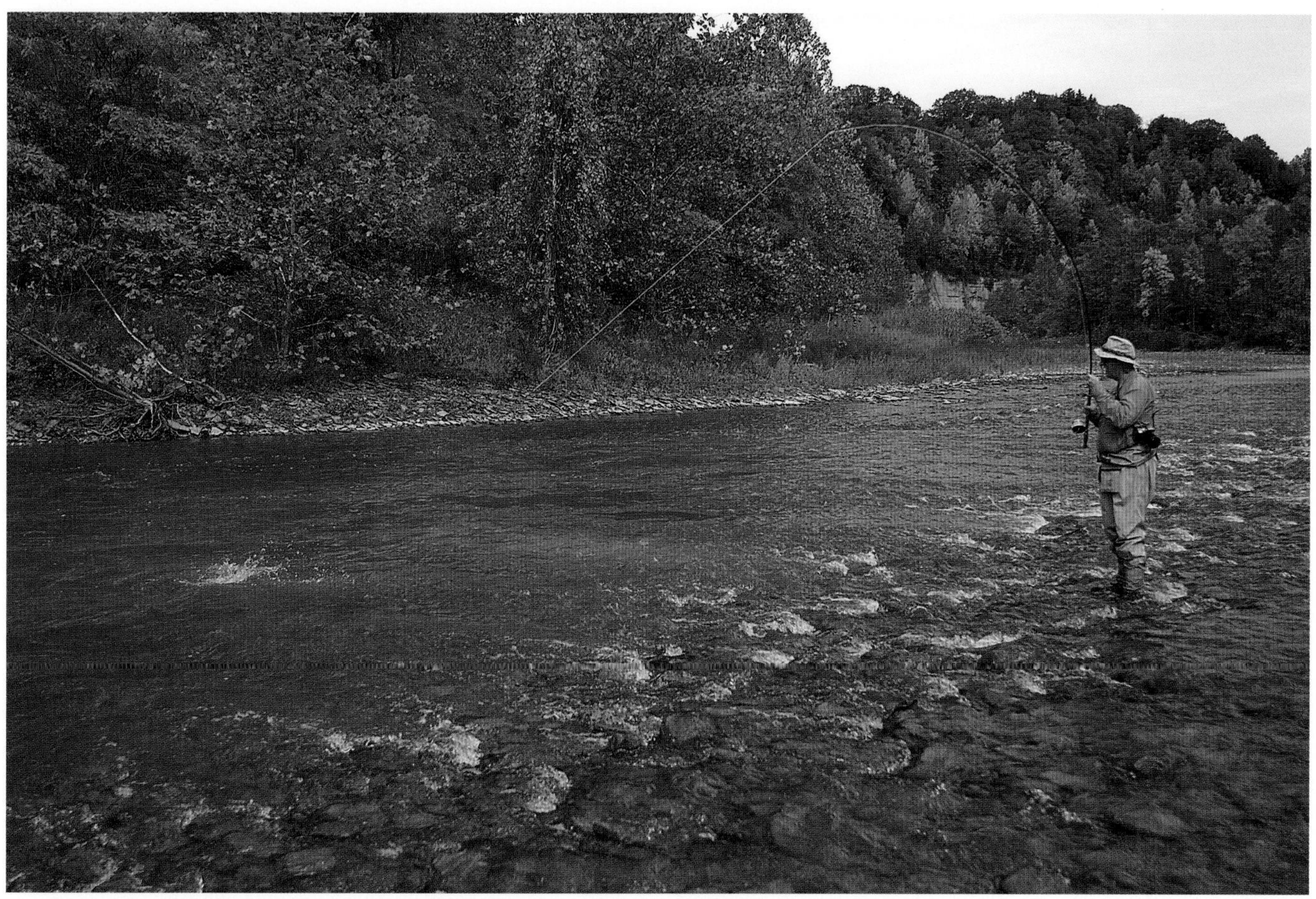

Smaller, understated fly patterns work well in low, clear water conditions. NICK PIONESSA PHOTO

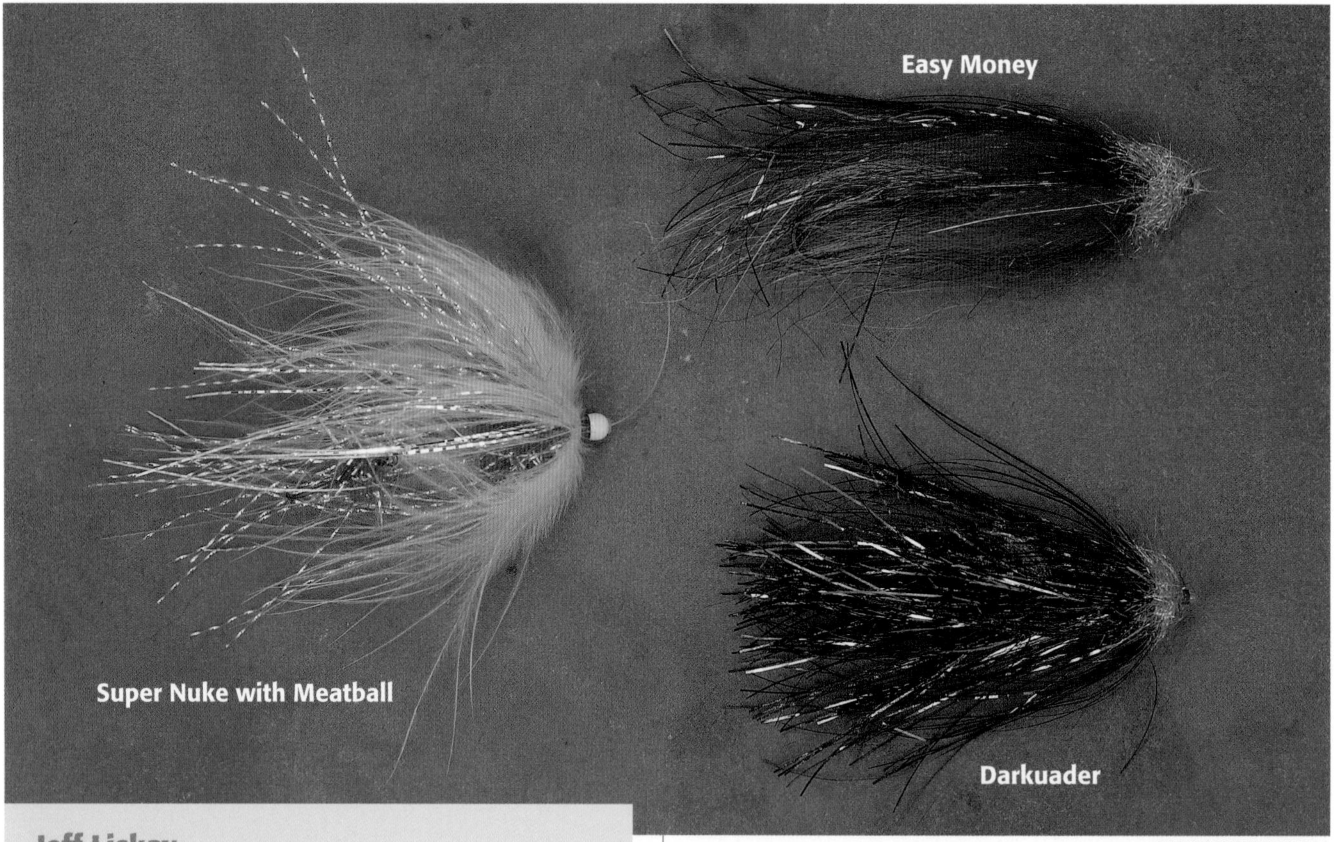

NICK PIONESSA PHOTO

Jeff Liskay

Jeff is a part-time guide and avid Spey caster and steelheader from Ohio. Jeff is a talented fly fisherman who approaches the sport with a dedicated tenacity combined with an appreciation of the fishery and other anglers.

SUPER NUKE WITH MEATBALL

Tier:	Jeff Liskay
Tail:	#4 octopus hook dressed with egg or flash material
Body:	Ball tube with Cactus Chenille
Flash:	Krinkle Mirror Flash mixed with Krystal Flash
Undercollar:	Schlappen
Collar:	Marabou

Note: Red marabou is best for tannic water. A purple and pink combination is a good all-around choice.

EASY MONEY

Tier:	Jeff Liskay
Tube:	2-inch plastic
Tail:	Bucktail
Body:	Diamond Braid or Sparkle Braid
Undercollar:	Dubbing ball with bucktail or chenille with arctic fox overlay and hanked Lite Brite mixed in
Collar:	Schlappen
Wing:	Flashabou
Head:	Ice Dub

Note: This has been a consistent producer throughout the Great Lakes region.

DARKUADER

Tier:	Jeff Liskay
Tube:	2-inch plastic
Tail:	Cactus Chenille dubbing ball with Flashabou or Krinkle Flash
Body:	Ice Dub/Diamond Braid or Sparkle Braid with Ice Dub butt
Collar:	Cactus Chenille dubbing ball with Flashabou or Krinkle Flash
Head:	Ice Dub or Senyo's Laser Dub

Note: This is the Great Lakes version of the Intruder.

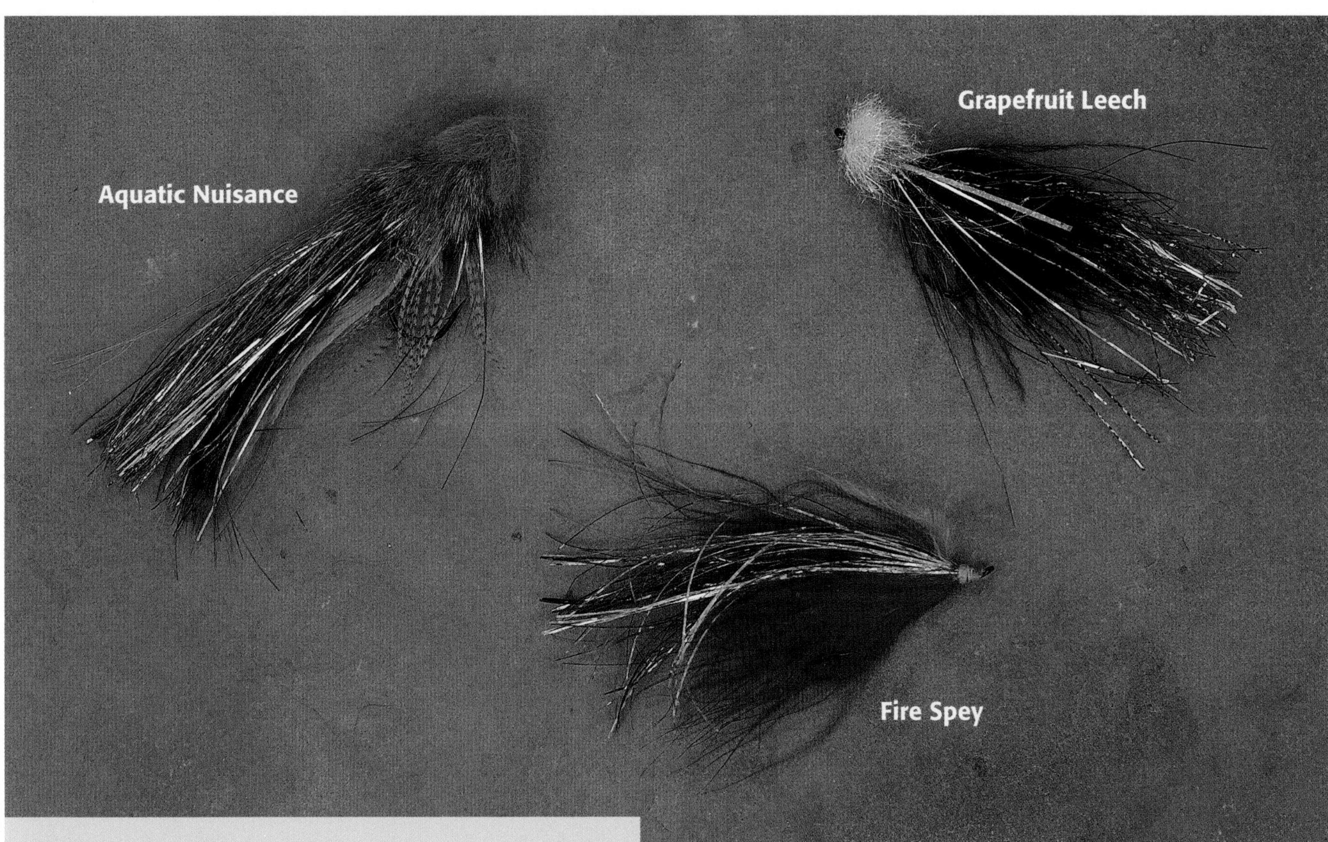

NICK PIONESSA PHOTO

Kevin Feenstra

Kevin is a well-known, successful full-time guide and outfitter in Michigan. Kevin is also a contributing writer and photographer for a number of publications. He has been a longtime proponent of two-handed rods and swinging flies. His offbeat patterns have proven very productive on his home waters.

AQUATIC NUISANCE

Tier:	Kevin Feenstra
Hook:	Large streamer hook
Tail:	Dark olive, black, or chocolate rabbit strip
Body:	Peacock or black Ice Dub wound through three-quarters of the body
Hackle:	Dark schlappen wound through the body
Flash:	Copper Flashabou topped with green or blue Polar Flash or kelly green Flashabou
Head:	Australian possum, natural, tied in a clump around the hook

Note: Some clients call this a "casting nuisance," but they have no problem with it on the line when it catches fish.

GRAPEFRUIT LEECH

Tier:	Kevin Feenstra
Hook:	#1 or 2 streamer hook, 3XL
Eyes:	Hourglass-shaped eyes
Tail:	Black marabou
Body:	Olive or purple Ice Dub
Hackle:	Duck flank or schlappen wound through the body
Legs:	Fibers from Limber-Legs Spinnerbait Skirt
Flash:	Silver, pink, and blue Flashabou
Head:	Pink Ice Dub behind eyes, with a clump of chartreuse in front of eyes

Note: This is an indispensable pattern for coldwater steelhead fishing. Use a higher concentration of blue Flashabou for the winter months.

FIRE SPEY

Tier:	Kevin Feenstra
Hook:	#2 or 4 up-eye salmon
Underwing:	Red Flashabou
Hackle:	Red marabou
Body:	Front third hot orange Ice Dub
Overwing:	Orange marabou topped with copper and Fire Tiger holographic Flashabou

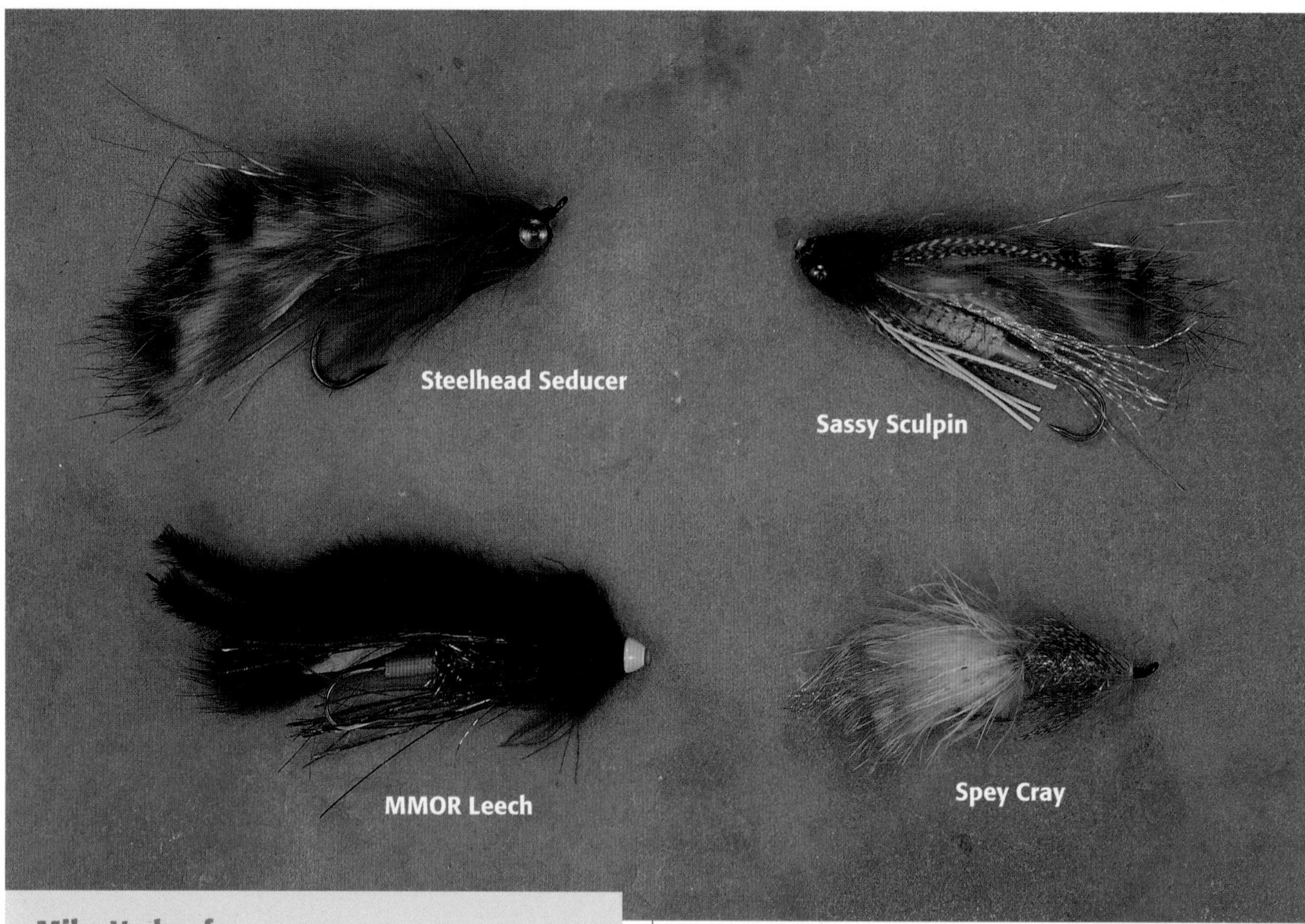

NICK PIONESSA PHOTO

Mike Verhoef

Mike is a highly experienced guide and casting instructor in Ontario. An accomplished angler, Mike guides and fishes on some of the most appealing Spey water in the Great Lakes. His patterns reflect natural aquatic life forms that entice steelhead on the clear waters of his home rivers.

STEELHEAD SEDUCER

Tier:	Mike Verhoef
Tube/hook:	Plastic tube or up-eye Spey hook
Body:	Micro UV Polar Chenille (olive) on rear two-thirds of the shank
Underwing:	Four strands of tan Krystal Flash
Wing:	Gold variant barred rabbit strip and 6 to 8 strands of copper Flashabou tied in on top and side of rabbit strip
Eyes:	Hourglass eyes for desired depth
Hackle:	Gold variant barred schlappen wrapped behind and in front of eyes

SASSY SCULPIN

Tier:	Mike Verhoef
Tube/hook:	Plastic tube, #1/0 Spey hook, or 4XL streamer hook
Body:	Chenille wrapped forward two-thirds of tube or shank
Underwing:	4 to 6 strands of light brown Krystal Flash extending beyond tube or hook
Overwing:	Gold variant barred rabbit strip and 4 to 6 strands of copper Flashabou
Underside:	2 white rubber strands of two hook lengths doubled over to make 4 strands one hook length
Hackle:	2 to 3 wraps of mallard flank dyed tan
Eyes:	Small dumbbell on bottom
Head:	4 clumps of rag wool dyed brown tied in on top, bottom, and sides, pulled back, whip-finished in front, and trimmed

SPEY CRAY

Tier:	Mike Verhoef
Hook:	#4 or 6 Spey hook
Tail:	Two ½-inch pieces of barred ginger rabbit strip tied on each side at rear with a few strands of Krystal Flash
Body hackle:	Partridge feather
Body:	Brown Micro Cactus Chenille stopping a quarter of the way from the eye
Front hackle:	Partridge feather
Head:	Peacock dubbing wrapped to make a head finish behind eye

MMOR LEECH

Tier:	Mike Verhoef
Tube/hook:	Plastic tube, #1/0 Spey hook, or 4XL streamer hook
Egg:	¼-inch hot orange bead for hook; orange cone for tube
Body:	Purple Cactus Chenille wrapped three-quarters of the way to the eye
Underwing:	10 to 12 mixed bright color strands of Flashabou around shank/tube
Overwing:	Purple rabbit strip topped with 5 to 6 strands of black ostrich herl
Hackle:	Three wraps of purple schlappen tied off and whip-finished tightly behind bead

An ideal autumn day for steelhead fishing. NICK PIONESSA PHOTO

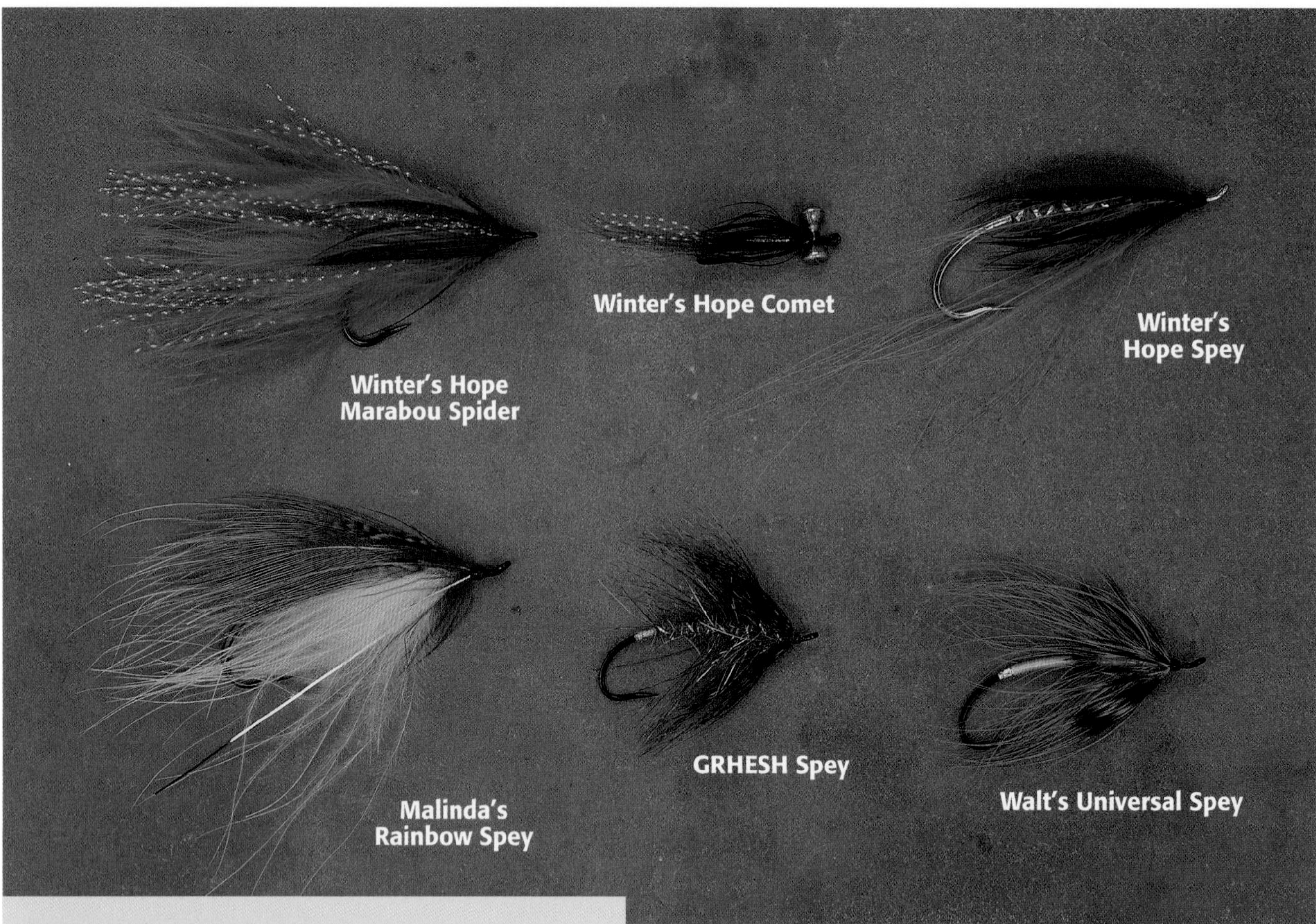

NICK PIONESSA PHOTO

Bob Blumreich

Bob is an experienced steelhead and trout guide in Wisconsin. He has been a longtime proponent of Spey fishing in the Great Lakes region. Bob's tying is inspired by the classic patterns, and the flies he presents here are tied with a color theme that works well in the stained waters of his home rivers.

Walt Geryk and Malinda Barna

Walt has been guiding on eastern Lake Ontario rivers for many years. Malinda is a fly shop owner and operator in New York State. Both have promoted traditional angling and Spey fishing for many years. These patterns were tied by professional tier Vern Burm.

WINTER'S HOPE MARABOU SPIDER

Tier:	Bob Blumreich
Hook:	#1-2 Daiichi 2151
Tail:	Clump of hot orange marabou with orange Krystal Flash on each side
Body:	Kingfisher blue marabou tied in by the tip, doubled, and wrapped forward with smolt blue Krystal Flash on each side
Collar:	Mallard flank dyed purple
Thread:	Wine 12/0

WINTER'S HOPE COMET

Tier:	Bob Blumreich
Hook:	#6-8 TMC #7999
Tail:	Clump of hot orange polar bear or goat with orange Krystal Flash on each side
Body:	Flat silver tinsel
Eyes:	Nickel-plated dumbbell or silver bead chain tied on top of hook
Collar:	Purple over blue schlappen
Thread:	Wine 12/0

WINTER'S HOPE SPEY

Tier:	Bob Blumreich
Hook:	#1½ Alec Jackson
Tag:	Fine flat silver tinsel
Body:	Kingfisher blue wool or seal substitute
Rib:	Five turns medium oval silver
Counter-rib:	Silver wire
Hackle:	Kingfisher blue marabou, stripped on one side, tied in by the tip from third turn of rib
Throat:	Purple schlappen
Wing:	Hot orange goose or turkey set low and tented
Thread:	Wine 12/0

MALINDA'S RAINBOW SPEY

Tier:	Vern Burm
Hook:	#1½ Daiichi 2051
Thread:	Black 6/0
Tip:	Medium silver oval tinsel
Body:	Fluorescent pink flat wax nylon or UNI-Floss
Rib:	Medium silver oval tinsel
Spey hackle:	White blood quill marabou
Throat:	Red mini marabou
Wing:	Golden yellow pheasant rump laid flat with two strands of Opal Mirage Flashabou laid on each side

GRHESH SPEY

Tier:	Vern Burm
Hook:	#5 Daiichi 2051
Thread:	Rusty brown 6/0
Tag:	Chartreuse holographic tinsel
Counter-rib:	Fine gold tinsel
Abdomen and thorax:	Wapsi Whitlock Fox Squirrel Nymph-Thorax Dubbing
Body hackle:	Coq de leon rooster saddle stripped down one side
Collar:	Coq de leon rooster saddle

WALT'S UNIVERSAL SPEY

Tier:	Vern Burm
Hook:	#3 Daiichi 2051
Tip:	Medium flat holographic silver tinsel
Butt:	Flat wax nylon or floss
Joint:	Peacock herl
Body:	Flat wax nylon or floss
Hackle:	Burnt goose
Collar:	Grizzly hackle

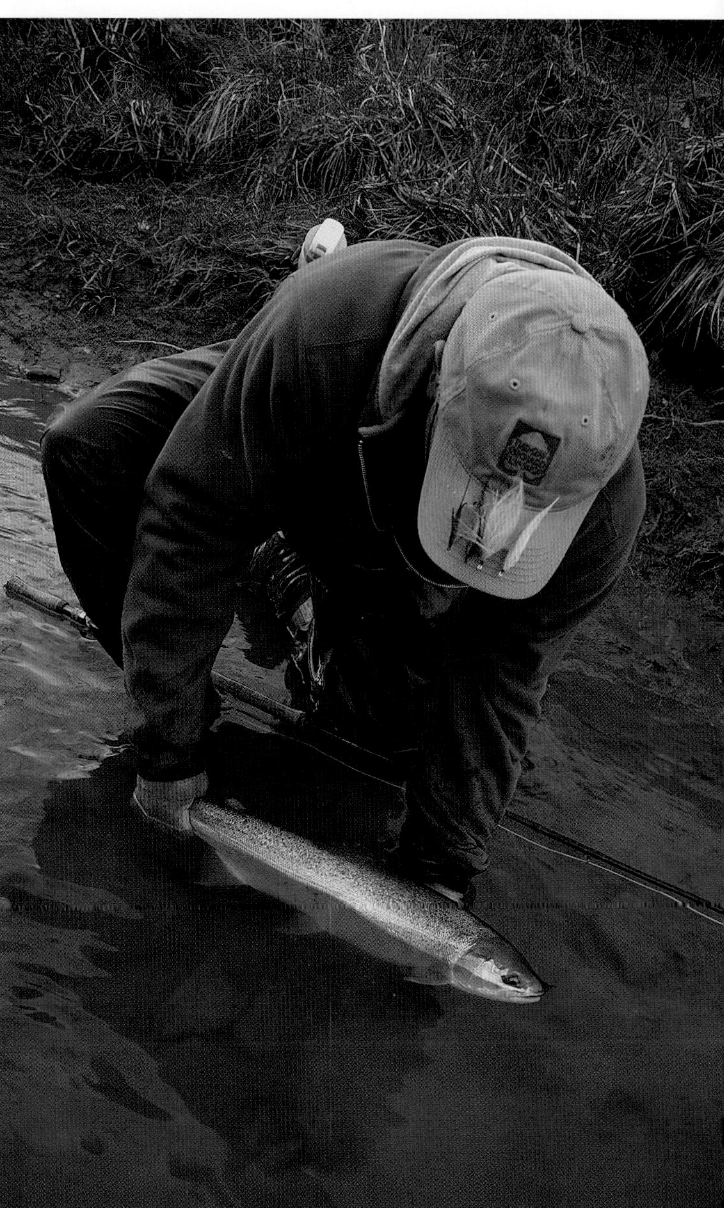

If a steelhead shows an interest in a pattern but does not take, switching to a smaller fly can seal the deal. NICK PIONESSA PHOTO

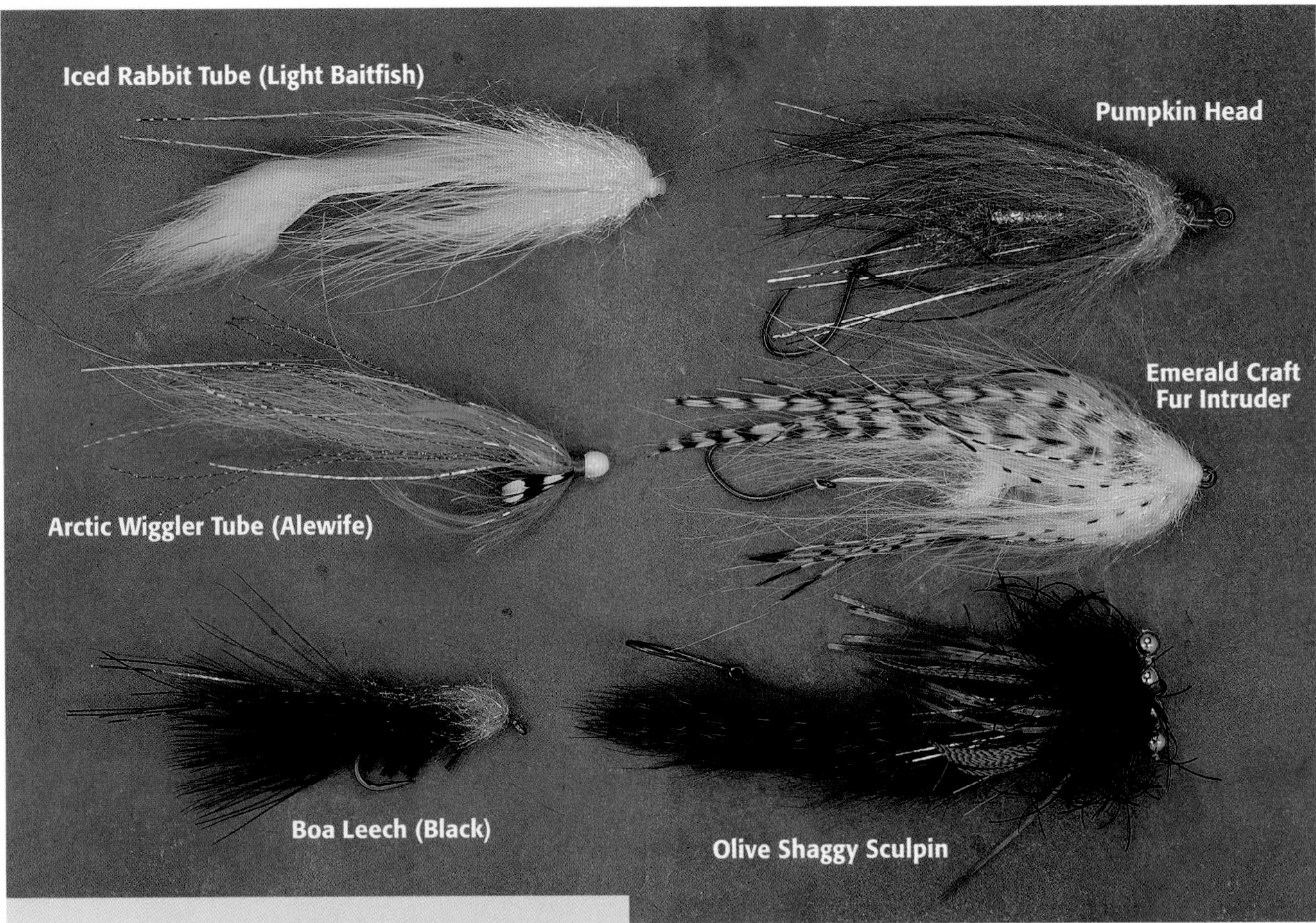

NICK PIONESSA PHOTO

Jerry Darkes

Jerry has worked in the fly-fishing industry full-time for many years as a guide, writer, seminar speaker, and successful fly-tackle sales representative. His patterns, each incorporating enticing movement, have been designed for the rivers of his home state of Ohio as well as neighboring states.

Greg Senyo

Greg is a guide, outfitter, and commercial tier. His guiding focuses on the rivers and streams flowing into Lake Erie, and he uses traditional and Spey techniques. Greg has developed a series of Intruder-style flies to meet various conditions.

ICED RABBIT TUBE (LIGHT BAITFISH)

Tier:	Jerry Darkes
Tube:	1-inch-long plastic
Thread:	UTC 140D
Hackle:	White marabou
Wing:	Blue and white rabbit strip
Topping:	Pearl Krinkle Mirror Flash
Head:	Pearl Ice Dub, single clump spread around hook and tied down in the middle

Note: This is a quick and simple tie, but it catches fish. Good color combinations are endless and limited only by your imagination.

ARCTIC WIGGLER TUBE (ALEWIFE)

Tier:	Jerry Darkes
Tube:	17 mm Eumer Ballhead
Thread:	Gray UTC 140D
Wing:	Gray arctic fox with pearl Krinkle Mirror Flash
Topping:	Peacock Krystal Flash
Body:	Pearl Estaz
Head:	Gray schlappen with Shad Gray Palmer Chenille in front
Eyes:	Jungle cock or golden pheasant tippet (optional)

Note: Tie this in baitfish, leech, and attractor colors. It has great movement in the water and can be swung or cast and stripped.

BOA LEECH (BLACK)

Tier:	Jerry Darkes
Hook:	#2-6 Daiichi 1710
Thread:	UTC 140D
Tail:	Black Marabou
Body:	Black Boa Yarn or Gala Yarn
Topping:	Black holographic Flashabou
Head:	UV shrimp pink Ice Dub

Note: This is an updated version of a classic steelhead pattern. The body material, also called eyelash yarn, is found in most craft stores. You can also tie a purple version with a fluorescent pink head.

PUMPKIN HEAD

Tier:	Greg Senyo
Shank hook:	#2/0 Mustad 3191 cut off at bend
Trailing hook:	#2 VMC drop shot
Connector:	4 inches of Berkley Fire Line
Thread:	Orange 6/0 UNI
Butt:	Hareline Pheasant Tail Ice Dub
Body:	Gold Diamond Braid
Underwing:	Hareline Pheasant Tail Ice Dub
Wing:	Eumer Morrum arctic fox, 10 strands gold Flashabou
Collar:	8 to 10 strands orange Lady Amherst tail feather
Head:	Shrimp pink Hareline Ice Dub
Egg:	8 mm tangerine Trout Bead

EMERALD CRAFT FUR INTRUDER

Tier:	Greg Senyo
Shank hook:	#2/0 Mustad 3191 cut off at bend
Trailing hook:	#2 VMC Drop Shot
Connector:	4 inches of Berkley Fire Line
Thread:	White 6/0 UNI
Butt:	Pink and chartreuse Hareline Ice Dub
Body:	Rainbow or silver Diamond Braid
Underwing:	White Senyo's Laser Dub
Wings:	White marabou and extra select white Hareline Craft Fur
Overwing:	A pair of chartreuse and black Euro hackles
Collar:	8 to 10 strands natural Lady Amherst tail feather
Head:	Pearl green Hareline Ice Dub

OLIVE SHAGGY SCULPIN

Tier:	Greg Senyo
Shank hook:	#2/0 Mustad 3191 cut off at bend
Trailing hook:	#2 VMC Drop Shot
Connector:	4 inches of Berkley Fire Line
Thread:	Black 6/0 UNI
Tail:	Olive brown Hareline rabbit strip
Body:	UV copper Hareline Polar Chenille
Collar:	Yellow or tan mallard flank feather
Rubber legs:	Mottled pearl olive brown
Head:	Black Senyo's Shaggy Dub
Eyes:	Copper Hareline Beady Eyes

Weighted flies work well in faster current flows or when using a long monofilament leader.

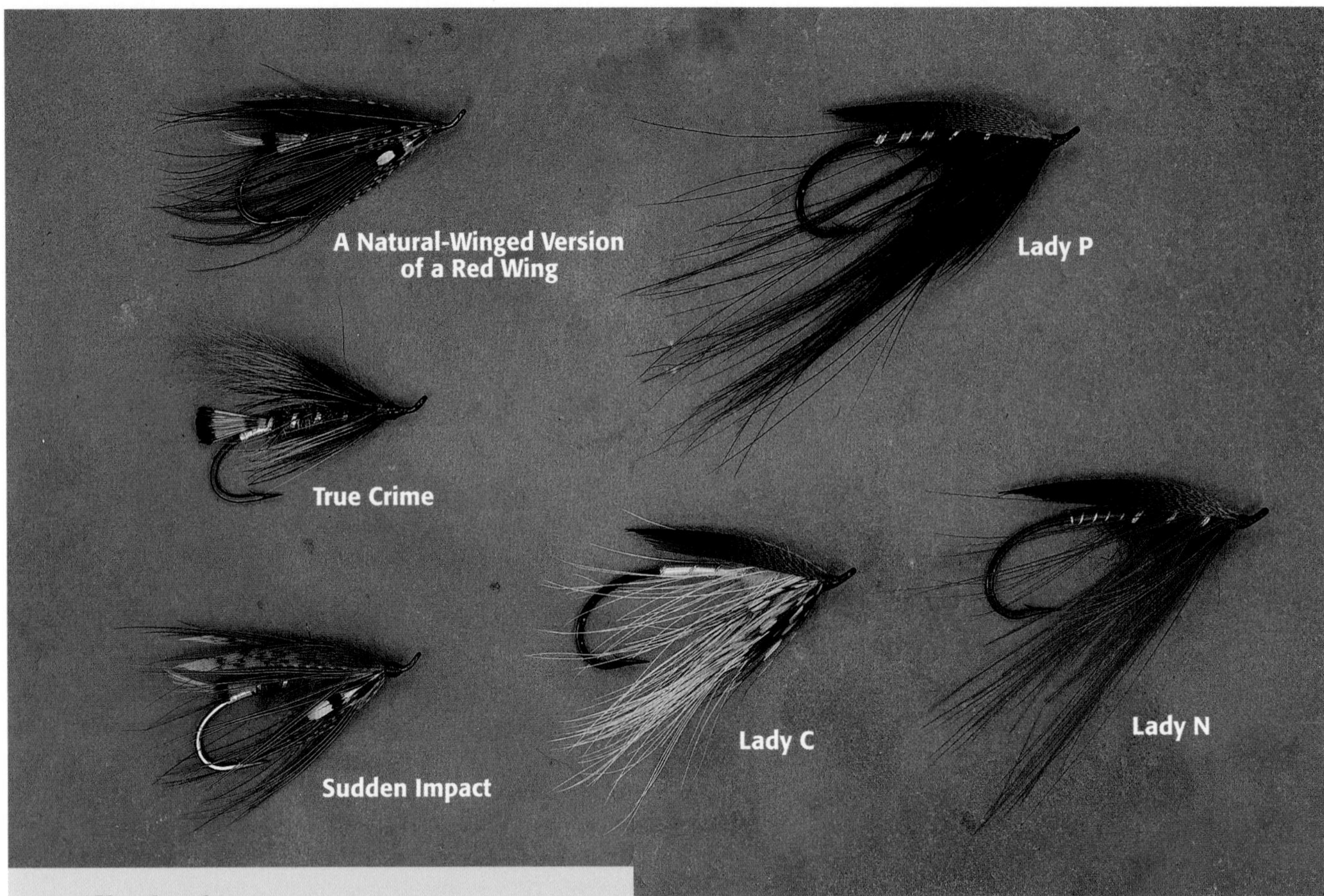

NICK PIONESSA PHOTO

Geoff Schaake

Geoff is an experienced Spey fisherman from New York State. He organizes and runs Spey Nation, an annual Spey gathering on the Salmon River, which has been instrumental in expanding this style of fishing. The natural tone of his flies is effective for clear water and pressured fish.

Rick Whorwood

Rick is a Federation of Fly Fishers master casting instructor for single-handed and two-handed rods. He is a well-traveled angler and lives in Ontario. Rick is also an accomplished tier with a special fondness for classic salmon flies. It is this classic style that he brings to his steelhead patterns.

A NATURAL-WINGED VERSION OF A RED WING

Tier:	Geoff Schaake
Tag:	Silver Holo tinsel
Tail:	Golden pheasant tippet and golden pheasant crest
Body:	Rear half blue angora and blue SLF dubbing, mixed; front half purple angora and purple SLF dubbing, mixed
Hackle:	Blue-eared pheasant
Collar:	Natural teal
Wing:	Natural goose shoulder
Cheek:	Jungle cock

TRUE CRIME

Tier:	Geoff Schaake
Tail:	Golden pheasant tippets
Tag:	Silver holographic tinsel
Body:	Peacock herl
Rib:	Silver holographic tinsel
Hackle:	Golden pheasant body
Wing:	Red squirrel tail
Collar:	Peacock body

SUDDEN IMPACT

Tier:	Geoff Schaake
Tag:	Copper tinsel
Tail:	Golden pheasant tippet and golden pheasant crest
Body:	Olive, olive-brown angora, and copper SLF dubbing, mixed
Rib:	Copper tinsel
Hackle:	Blue-eared pheasant
Collar:	Gadwall
Wing:	Mottled turkey slips
Cheek:	Jungle cock

LADY P

Tier:	Rick Whorwood
Hook:	Up-eye salmon
Body:	Rear half purple silk with fine silver or gold rib; front half purple seal's fur with medium silver or gold rib
Body hackle:	Blue-eared pheasant hackle dyed purple
Throat:	Guinea or golden pheasant dyed purple
Wing:	Bronze mallard

LADY C

Tier:	Rick Whorwood
Hook:	Up-eye salmon
Body:	Rear half yellow silk with fine silver or gold rib; front half yellow seal's fur in the front with medium silver or gold rib
Body hackle:	Blue-eared pheasant hackle dyed yellow
Throat:	Guinea or golden pheasant dyed yellow
Wing:	Bronze mallard

LADY N

Tier:	Rick Whorwood
Hook:	Up-eye salmon
Body:	Rear half red silk with fine silver or gold rib; front half red seal's fur with medium silver or gold rib
Body hackle:	Blue-eared pheasant hackle dyed red
Throat:	Guinea or golden pheasant dyed red
Wing:	Bronze mallard

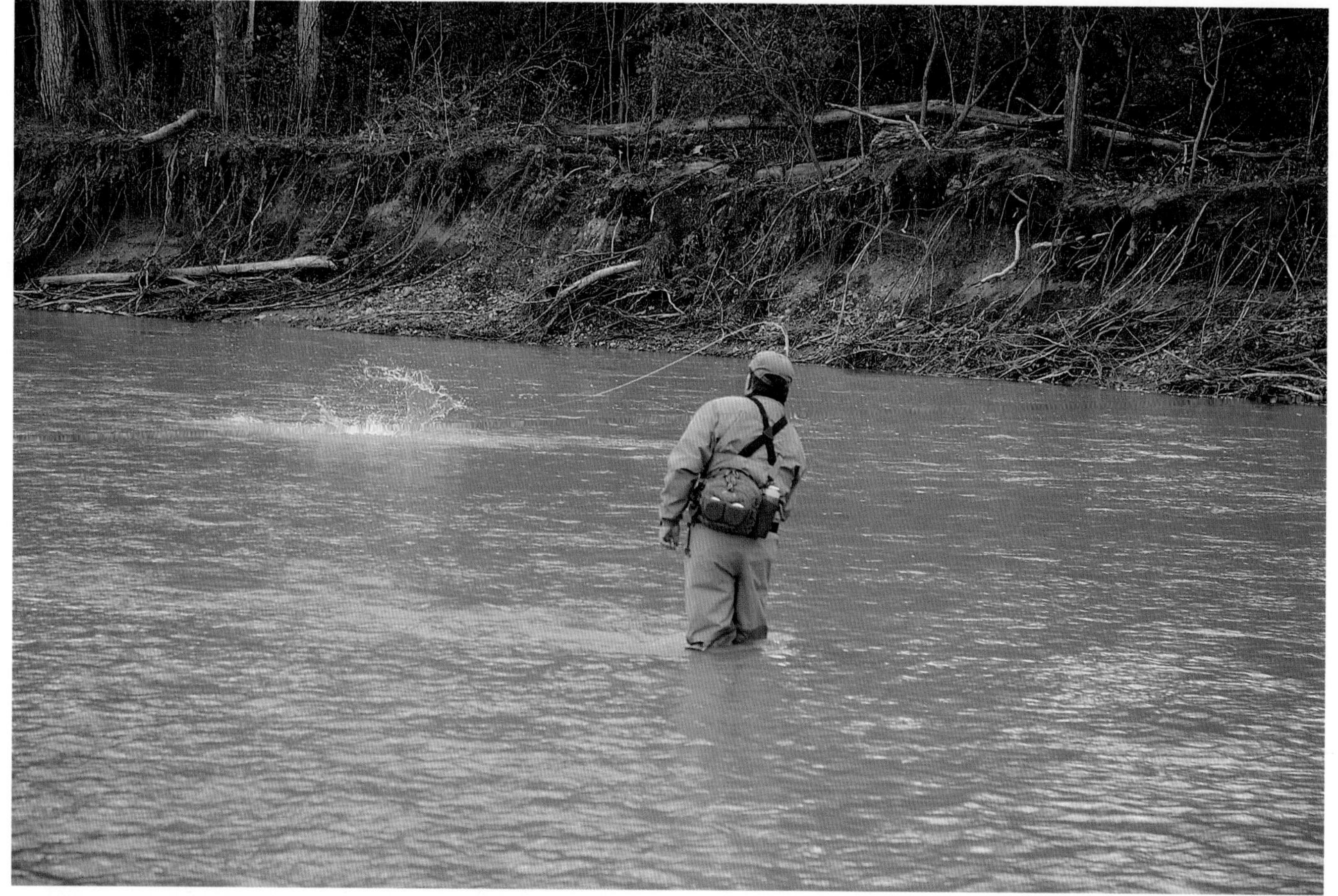

The tube fly design increases the percentage of hooked and landed fish. NICK PIONESSA PHOTO

NICK PIONESSA PHOTO

John Nagy

John ties meticulous, effective flies for steelhead. John has guided in Alaska and has been a well-known guide on the Lake Erie tributaries for 20 years. He is also a writer and photographer, and his *Steelhead Guide: Fly Fishing Techniques and Strategies for Lake Erie Steelhead*, now in its fourth edition, is an essential guide to the Lake Erie tributaries.

LAKE ERIE RAINBOW SMELT TUBE FLY

Tier: John Nagy

Tubes: Clear, transparent Canadian Tube Fly Co. FlexTube (1 1/2 inches long), extra small (.60 grams) Wurm Micro Tungsten bottle tube, and 1/16-inch OD, clear, stiff, plastic Wurm liner tubing (2 inches long)

Thread: White 8/0 UNI-Thread

Tail: 5 strands pearl Orvis Krinkle Mirror Flash extending 2 inches beyond end of FlexTube

Body: Pearl Hareline Ice Dub loop dubbed over front of FlexTube and Wurm bottle tube

Wing: Krinkle Mirror Flash, white T's Fur, silver Angel Hair, white T's Fur, plum Angel Hair, Wapsi multicolor smolt blue SLF Hank, plum Angel Hair, dark olive T's Fur, rusty olive Angel Hair, and 8 peacock herls tied on small-diameter tubing from bottom to top

Head: Polar pearl Lite Brite and 3/16-inch holographic eyes

Note: The Lake Erie Rainbow Smelt has a compact Wurm bottle tube just behind the wing (on small-diameter plastic tubing) camouflaged under dubbing. This balances the fly nicely on the swing while providing enough weight to sink it without interfering with its lively action. The wing uses T's Fur, an extremely soft and semitransparent natural fiber material that is completely free of stiff guard hairs and excess underfur, providing superb action in the current flow. The fly is about 4 inches long.

CRYSTAL INTRUDER TUBE FLY

Tier:	John Nagy
Tube:	Clear, transparent Canadian Tube Fly Co. FlexTube (1½ inches long)
Thread:	White 8/0 UNI-Thread
Rear hackle:	White schlappen feather, olive Lady Amherst center tail feather
Body:	Crystal Chenille palmered with stiff white hackle
Front hackle:	Chartreuse Mirror Krystal Flash, olive Lady Amherst center tail feather, and white schlappen feather
Wing:	Two pairs of yellow Keough grizzly saddle feathers tied into sides
Head:	Silver dumbbell eyes

Note: The combination of movement and reflection provided by the Crystal Intruder often proves irresistible to steelhead. This fly is about 3¾ inches long. Blue-and-white, blue-and-black, and orange-and-yellow versions also work well.

EMERALD SHINER WAKE-UP CALL TUBE FLY

Tier:	John Nagy
Tube:	40 mm and 10 mm Clear Pro FlexiTube
Thread:	White 8/0 UNI-Thread
Rear cone:	Fluorescent red plastic Pro Soft Disc (XL) enlarged to fit 40 mm tube
Body:	Bass Pro Bullet Weight slid onto 40 mm tube behind tie-in point of wing; UV Polar Chenille wrapped up to weight
Legs:	Yellow chartreuse or green chartreuse Hot Tipped Sili Legs
Wing:	White rabbit fur strip, chartreuse Angel Hair, and chartreuse Krinkle Mirror Flash, top to bottom
Collar:	White schlappen feathers or soft saddle hackle
Cheeks:	Jungle cock (optional)
Front cone:	Silver Pro ConeDisc (medium) or clear plastic Pro SoftSonic Disc (XL)

Note: The Wake-Up Call works well stripped or on the swing (particularly in higher or stained flows), not only for steelhead, but also for smallies, brown trout, and salmon. The finished fly measures 3½ to 4 inches from cone to tail, but it can be tied in smaller versions for low-water steelhead and inland trout. You can also tie it in Black 'n' Blue and UV Olive versions.

BLUE AND WHITE TEMPLE DOG TUBE FLY

Tier:	John Nagy
Tube:	Silver Eumer brass tube (large) and Eumer .07-inch OD, clear, stiff plastic liner tubing (2 inches long)
Hook connection:	Clear vinyl or silicon junction tubing (¼ inch)
Thread:	White 12/0 Bennechi
Tail:	Red or orange Fluoro Fibre
First wing layer:	Silver Angel Hair, white T's Hair or bucktail (1½ inches long), silver Fire Fly, stiff white saddle feather, silver Angel Hair, bottom to top
Second wing layer:	White Temple Dog fur (2½ inches long), silver Fire Fly, stiff white saddle feather, blue Krinkle Mirror Flash, bottom to top
Third wing layer:	Kingfisher blue T's Fur (3½ inches long), peacock Fire Fly, kingfisher blue teal flank feather, bottom to top
Fourth wing layer:	Dark blue T's Fur (3¾ inches long), peacock Fire Fly, black ostrich herl (just under 4 inches long), bottom to top
Cheeks:	Jungle cock

Note: This fly combines the innovation of a tube fly design and the beauty and effectiveness of a Scandinavian Temple Dog–style wing. The silhouette of the wing, the movement of the soft wing materials, and the jungle cock cheeks (suggesting eyes on a baitfish) make the Temple Dog fly design very effective for imitating Great Lakes baitfish. The Blue and White Temple Dog (which is approximately 4 inches long) works well on sunny days because of its predominately white coloration and flash that reflect sunlight.

I sometimes select a pattern to mimic the natural food sources in a river. NICK PIONESSA PHOTO

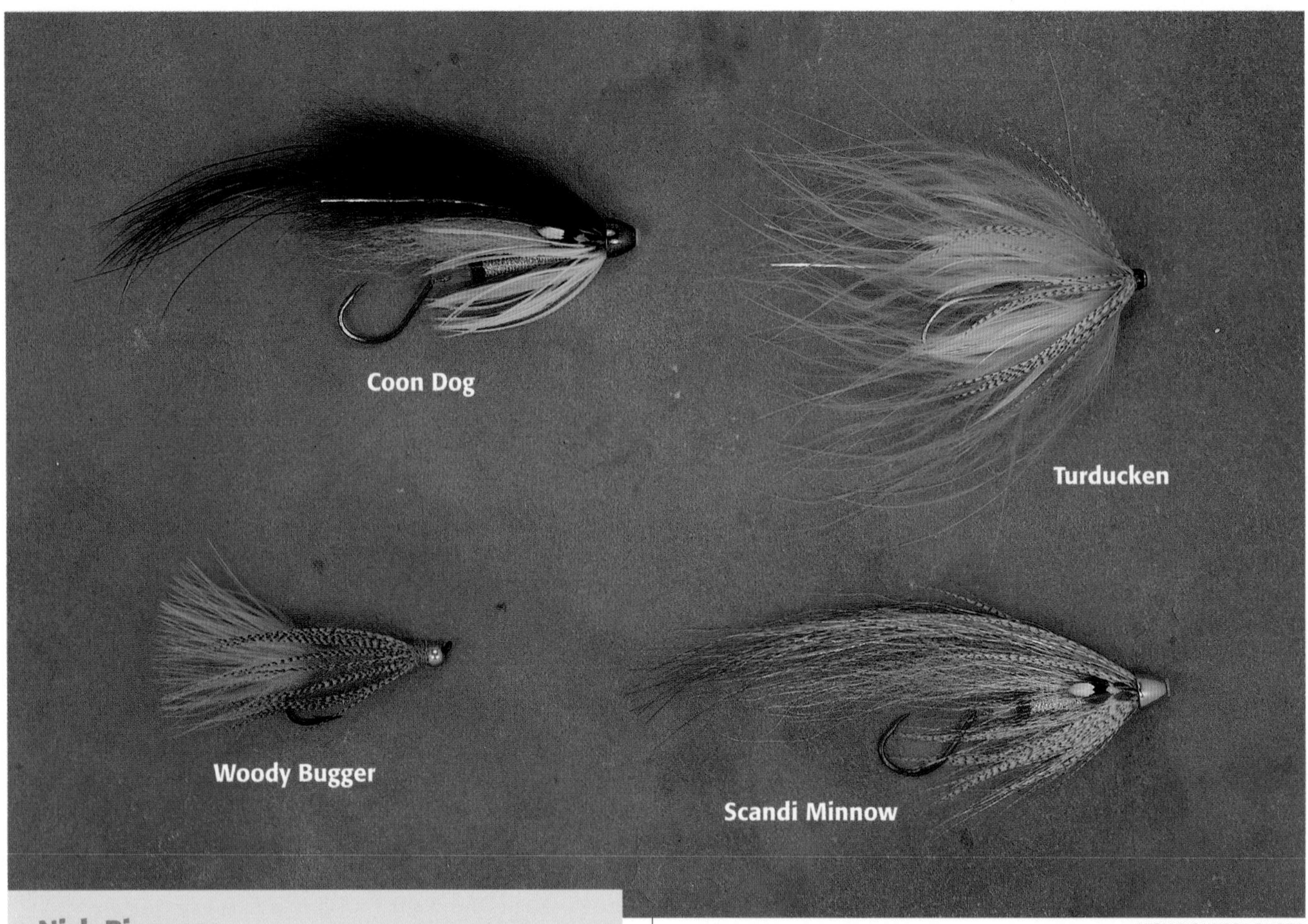

NICK PIONESSA PHOTO

Nick Pionessa

Nick is an experienced fly angler and one of the nation's top commercial tiers. His patterns combine elegance and functionality. Nick also applies his artistic approach to his photography, which appears throughout the book.

COON DOG

Tier:	Nick Pionessa
Hook:	#4 Daiichi 2553
Tube:	1- or 1½-inch plastic
Thread:	White 8/0
Butt:	Red dubbing
Body:	Bodi-Braid
Underwing:	Arctic fox tail
Hackle:	Schlappen
Flash:	Flashabou
Overwing:	Finn raccoon
Eyes:	Jungle cock
Head:	Large cone to fit over liner tube

TURDUCKEN

Tier:	Nick Pionessa
Tube:	½-inch copper
Thread:	Red 8/0
Body hackle:	Whole schlappen feather tied in by the tip
Flash:	Flashabou
Front hackle:	Marabou blood quill tied in by the tip
Collar:	Duck flank folded

SCANDI MINNOW

Tier:	Nick Pionessa
Hook:	#4 Daiichi 2553
Tube:	1- or 1½-inch plastic
Butt:	Red dubbing
Body:	Bodi-Braid
Underwing:	Arctic fox tail
Body hackle:	Thin arctic fox tail, spun in dubbing loop
Flash:	DNA Holo Chromosome Flash
Overwing:	Cashmere goat
Collar hackle:	Mallard flank
Eyes:	Jungle cock
Head:	Large cone over liner tube

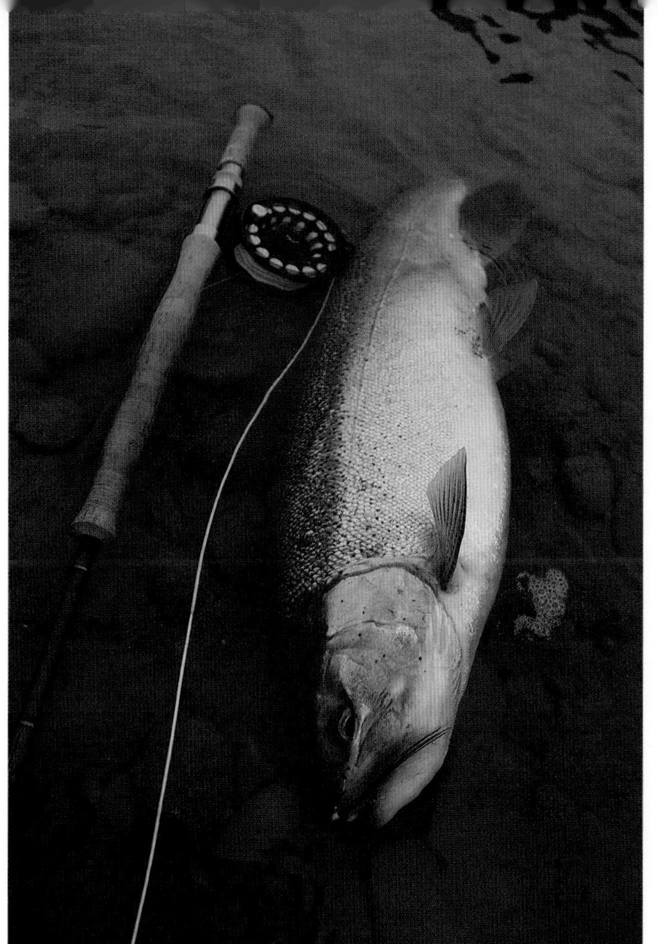

WOODY BUGGER

Tier:	Nick Pionessa
Hook:	#6 Daiichi 2421
Bead:	5/32-inch copper
Thread:	Olive or tan 6/0
Tail:	Ginger marabou
Rib:	Medium oval copper
Body:	Summer duck SLF
Hackle:	Wood-duck flank folded
Head:	SLF dubbing

Steelhead tend to be attracted to flies that have a seductive movement in the water—something to keep in mind when you fish the wet-fly swing. NICK PIONESSA PHOTO

Tom Cornell puts the finishing touch on a fresh steelhead. NICK PIONESSA PHOTO

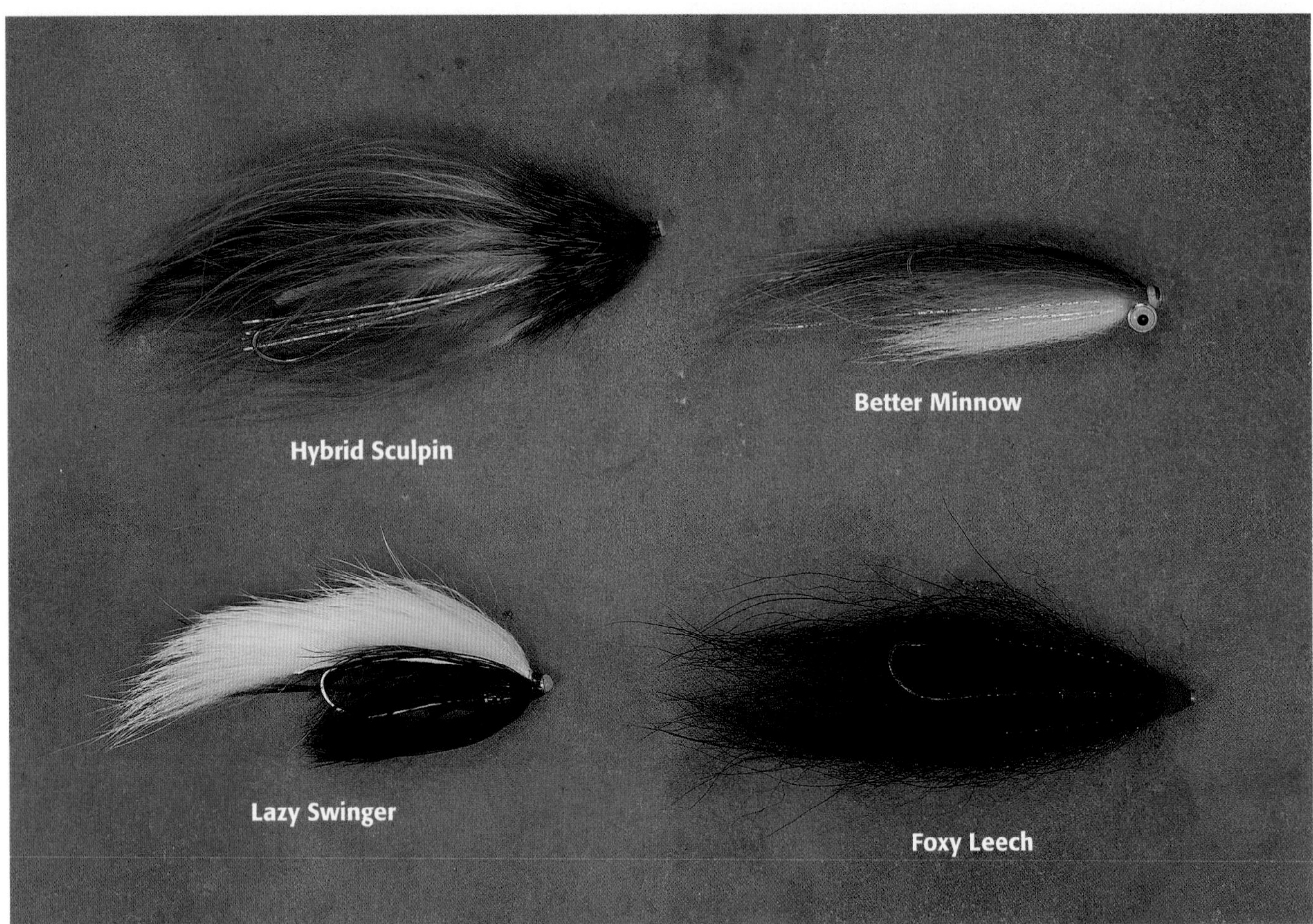

NICK PIONESSA PHOTO

HYBRID SCULPIN

Tier:	Nick Pionessa
Hook:	#4 Daiichi 2553
Tube:	1-inch-long, 3/32-inch-diameter copper 1 1/2-inch hybrid tubing
Thread:	Olive 6/0
Wing:	Olive Zonker strip
Flash:	Gold Holo Flashabou
Hackle and body:	Olive marabou blood quill
Head:	Olive Zonker strip in dubbing loop

BETTER MINNOW

Tier:	Nick Pionessa
Hook:	#6 Daiichi 2450
Tube:	1- or 1 1/2-inch plastic
Body:	Arctic fox tail, spun in dubbing loop
Eyes:	3/16-inch Real Eyes
Flash:	DNA Holo Chromosome Flash
Wing:	Finn raccoon
Topping:	3 to 6 natural gray ostrich strands

FOXY LEECH

Tier:	Nick Pionessa
Hook:	#6 Daiichi 2450
Tube:	1- to 1 1/2-inch, 3/32-inch-diameter copper
Thread:	Red 6/0
Tail section:	Arctic fox tail, spun in dubbing loop
Body section:	Bodi-Braid
Front section:	Arctic fox tail mixed with Krystal Flash and spun in dubbing loop
Head:	Fox or rabbit fur dubbing

LAZY SWINGER

Tier:	Nick Pionessa
Hook:	#6 Daiichi 2450
Tube:	Shumakov bottle tube
Thread:	Red 6/0
Flash:	Flashabou
Hackle:	4 turns of schlappen
Wing:	Thin bunny strip

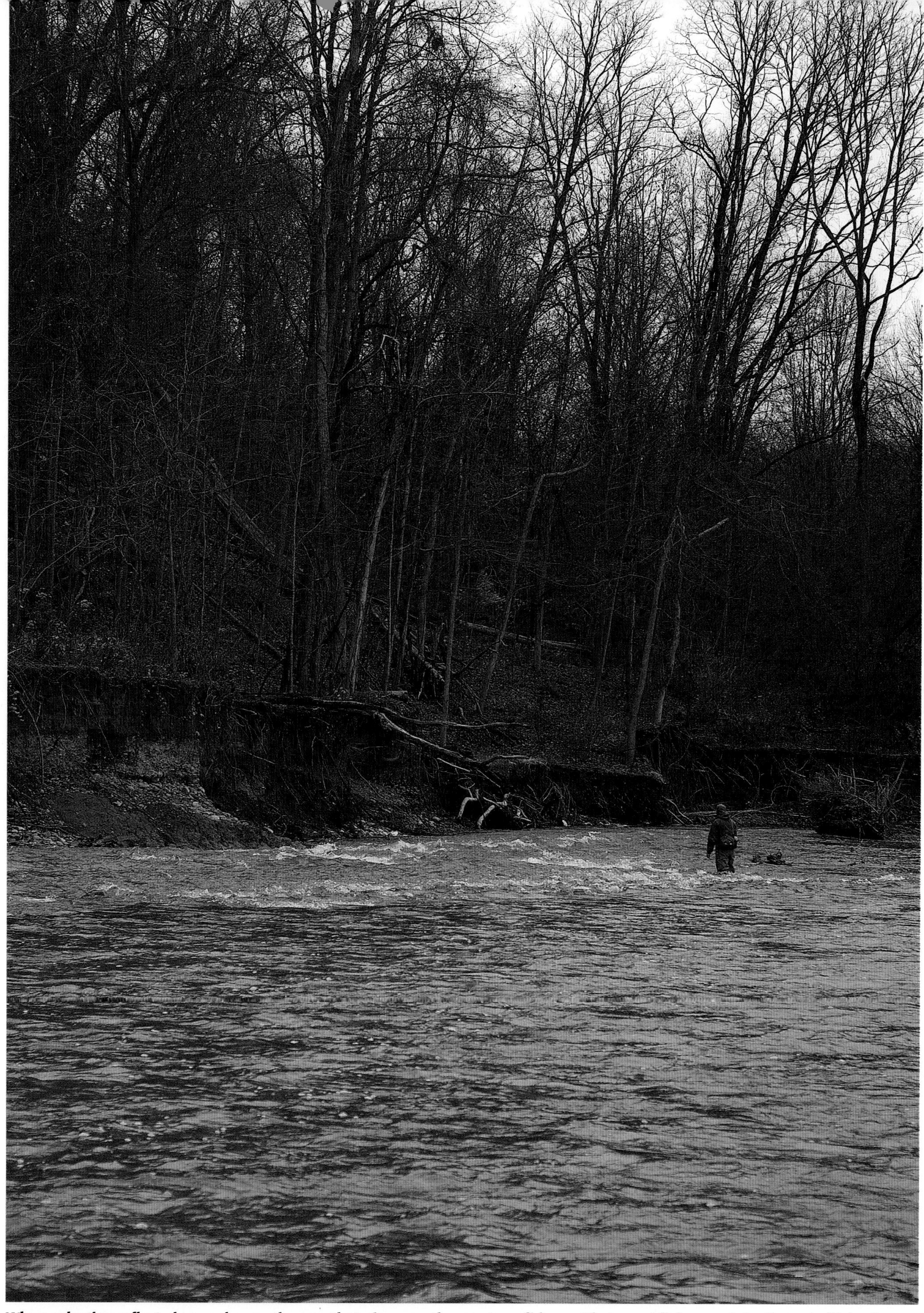

When selecting a fly, I always choose the one that gives me the most confidence. That way I fish more intently and efficiently.
NICK PIONESSA PHOTO

NICK PIONESSA PHOTO

Vince Tobia

Vince is a full-time guide, outfitter, fly-fishing travel host, and accomplished angler. His guide operation focuses mainly on steelhead in New York. Vince has found that some basic, versatile patterns are essential for consistent success.

Justin Damude

Justin is a dedicated fly angler who uses a stealthy approach for clear water conditions, which includes fishing natural patterns on a long leader.

Gerri Moore

Gerri is a talented professional tier whose flies have filled the boxes of anglers in the Great Lakes region for more than 30 years.

OLIVE WOOLLY BUGGER

Tier:	Vince Tobia
Hook:	Daiichi 2220
Tail:	Marabou and a few strands of green Krystal Flash
Body:	Olive chenille with Krystal Flash tied in along the side
Hackle:	Grizzly olive saddle wrapped through the body
Bead:	Gold

Note: The Woolly Bugger has consistently been an important steelhead pattern in the Great Lakes for many years. It is a key fly for Vince's guiding operation. I have found it to be a very effective pattern for enticing dour fish into a solid take. Brown is my favorite color for this pattern.

BEAD HEAD HARE'S EAR

Tier: Justin Damude
Hook: Daiichi 1120
Tail: Squirrel body hair
Body: Hare's ear dubbing
Rib: Fine copper wire
Wing case: Brown Swiss Straw for length of the body
Bead: Gold

BLACK STONEFLY

Tier: Gerri Moore
Hook: Daiichi 1720
Tail: Black biots
Body: Black dubbing
Rib: Dark brown vinyl rib
Wing case: Turkey tied in and folded
Hackle: Black hen soft hackle

BIG BIRD HEX

Tier: Nick Pionessa
Hook: #7 Daiichi 2051
Eyes: Small black bead chain
Tail: Natural ostrich
Abdomen: Ginger ostrich herl
Thorax: Natural emu
Rib: Copper wire
Wing case: Rear half natural ostrich; front half mottled turkey wing

ROLLING STONE NYMPH

Tier: Jerry Darkes
Hook: #8-14 Daiichi 1120
Thread: Black UTC 70D
Tail: Black or dark brown goose biots
Rib: Black wire
Abdomen: Black stone dubbing blend
Thorax: Black stone dubbing blend, spun in a loop and brushed out
Wing case: Black or peacock Krystal Flash

STEELHEAD SCUD

Tier: Justin Damude
Hook: Daiichi 1120
Tail and body: Wapsi Sow Bug Dubbing
Top: Orange Scud Back
Rib: Black wire

SCRAMBLED EGGS

Tier: Vince Tobia
Hook: Daiichi 1530
Body: Glo-Bug yarn tied in loops

CARROT TOP NYMPH

Tier: Jerry Darkes
Hook: #10-14 Daiichi 1530
Thread: Black or olive UTC 70D
Body: Black or peacock Ice Dub
Head: Pinch of UV shrimp pink Ice Dub, trimmed short
Bead: Gold or copper

SPARROW NYMPH

Tier: Ed Riederer
Hook: Daiichi 1260
Tail: Natural ring-necked marabou
Dubbing: Olive
Rib: Fine copper
Hackle: Natural pheasant rump
Head: After shaft of natural pheasant

Note: This pattern was created by fly-fishing legend Jack Gartside and has proven to be an effective steelhead pattern in clear water.

I.E. EGG

Tier: Nick Pionessa
Hook: #12 Daiichi 1120
Thread: Fire orange 6/0
Body: Glo-Bug yarn

MICRO EGG

Tier: Justin Damude
Hook: Daiichi 1120
Body: Two turns of small chenille
Dot: Waterproof marker

WHITE WOOLLY BUGGER

Tier: Vince Tobia
Hook: Daiichi 2220
Tail: Marabou and a few strands of pearl Krystal Flash
Body: Pearl Micro Cactus Chenille
Hackle: White saddle wrapped through the body
Bead: Gold

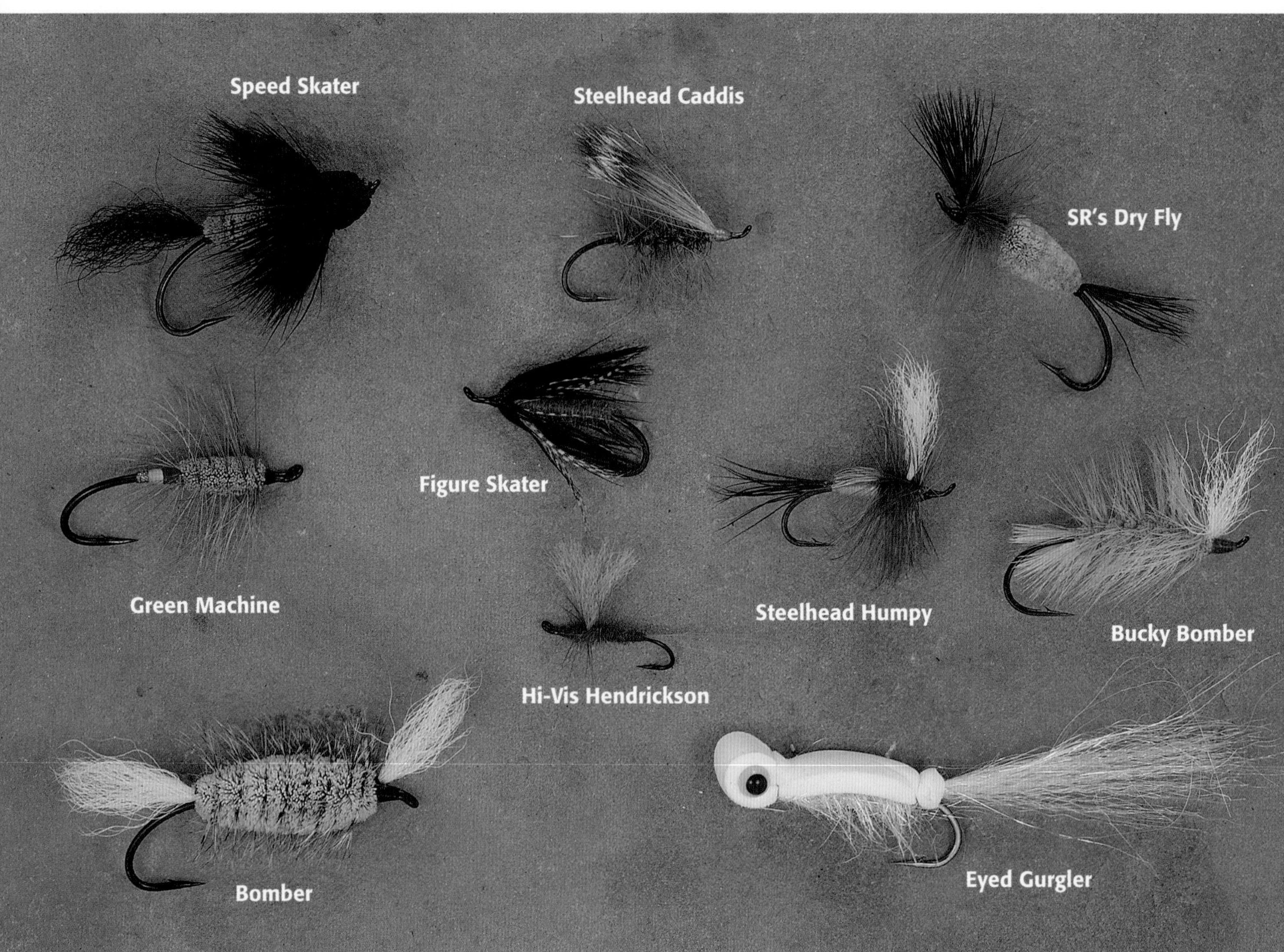

NICK PIONESSA PHOTO

SPEED SKATER

Tier:	Nick Pionessa
Hook:	#5-7 Daiichi 2051
Tail:	Black calf tail
Body:	Gray deer hair, spun
Collar and head:	Black deer hair, spun

STEELHEAD CADDIS

Tier:	Rick Kustich
Hook:	#10-12 Daiichi 2421
Body:	Burnt orange dubbing
Hackle:	Brown or grizzly wrapped through body
Wing:	Natural deer or elk

SR'S DRY FLY

Tier:	Nick Pionessa
Hook:	#5-7 Daiichi 2051
Tail:	Moose body
Body:	Gray deer hair, spun
Wing:	Moose body hair
Hackle:	Dark dun dry fly

GREEN MACHINE

Tier:	Charlie Dickson
Hook:	#4-12 Daiichi 2421
Tag:	Oval silver tinsel
Butt:	Chartreuse and red floss
Body:	Green deer hair, spun
Hackle:	Brown dry fly

Note: This fly was created by Rev. Elmer Smith.

FIGURE SKATER

Tier: Rick Kustich
Hook: #6-8 Daiichi 2421
Body: Burnt orange dubbing
Underhackle: A few wraps of natural teal
Overhackle: Black saddle folded

STEELHEAD HUMPY

Tier: Charlie Dickson
Hook: #8-12 Daiichi 2421
Tail: Moose body
Back: Moose body hair butts
Body: Chartreuse floss
Wings: Calf tail
Hackle: Furnace dry fly

BUCKY BOMBER

Tier: Bucky McCormick
Hook: #4-8 Daiichi 2421
Tail: Yellow calf tail
Wing: White calf tail
Body: Orange deer hair, spun and trimmed to a low-profile shape
Hackle: Yellow saddle

BOMBER

Tier: Nick Pionessa
Hook: #2-6 Partridge CS42
Tail and wing: Calf tail
Body: Natural deer hair, spun
Hackle: Grizzly saddle

Note: This fly was created by Rev. Elmer Smith.

HI-VIS HENDRICKSON

Tier: Rick Kustich
Hook: #12 Daiichi 2421
Tail: Microfibetts
Body: Dark Hendrickson dubbing
Wing: Dun Aero Dry
Hackle: Gray wrapped both in front of and behind wing, trimmed on bottom

EYED GURGLER

Tier: Nick Pionessa
Hook: #4-10 Daiichi 1720
Tail: White Super Hair with pearl Lite Brite
Back and head: 3 mm white craft foam same width as hook gap
Body: Pearl Lite Brite dubbed
Eyes: Solid doll eyes

Note: This fly was originally created by Jack Gartside.

Steelhead patterns do not have to be complicated; simple patterns can be very effective. NICK PIONESSA PHOTO

CHAPTER 6

Rivers and Streams

A lone angler fishing one of the many rivers of the Great Lakes region. NICK PIONESSA PHOTO

The rivers and streams running into the Great Lakes are truly wide and varied. Some run only a few hundred yards from the lake before meeting either a natural or man-made barrier. Others stretch relatively unencumbered for long lengths—in some instances 100 miles or more between the headwaters and the mouth. Some rivers have considerable width, providing the character and feel of a Northwest steelhead river, and others have the intimate setting of a trout stream. Some run through somewhat urban areas where shorelines may be lined with houses and commercial buildings, but many more run through undeveloped woodlands and fields in esthetically pleasing settings that are at the very heart of a quality experience. Some of my favorite rivers have high gorge walls rising 300 to 400 feet, providing spectacular backdrops and extending the shadows on the water for hours.

I like a steelhead river with personality, a river that has the ability to draw a steelhead well away from the lake and that still flows mainly in its natural state. And while I prefer larger rivers that allow for longer casts and the ability to spread out fishing pressure, many intimate streams throughout the region provide a quality outing well away from the pressures of everyday life.

The Great Lakes region offers anglers a steelheading bounty throughout its states and provinces. In the following pages I give an overall analysis of the management style of each area, followed by a more detailed description of particular rivers or streams and the opportunities of each. I'll describe the character and quality of the water as well as factors that make it special or limit its potential. Rivers of special interest to me are those that readily accommodate two-handed rods and Spey fishing. With lighter two-handed rods and switch rods, more and more rivers can be fished in this manner.

The Great Lakes fishery continues to develop as proactive management has become valued. I think a complete steelhead angler should understand the fish and its environment and be involved in the significant issues and decisions concerning regularly fished waters. Knowing the issues impacting the quality or future of a watershed will help you gain a greater understanding and appreciation of steelheading. My hope is that this information will inspire greater involvement and assist anglers in their personal pursuit of steelhead.

The following information is designed as a general guide—public access points can change from year to year. If anglers are lucky, public access to Great Lakes rivers and streams will increase over time. Access issues will continue to be one of the challenges the fishery faces in the future. But it is your responsibility to know the water access laws on the rivers you are fishing and to make sure you gain proper access. If you are in doubt, ask the landowner. Respecting landowner rights will go a long way toward preserving and expanding public access opportunities.

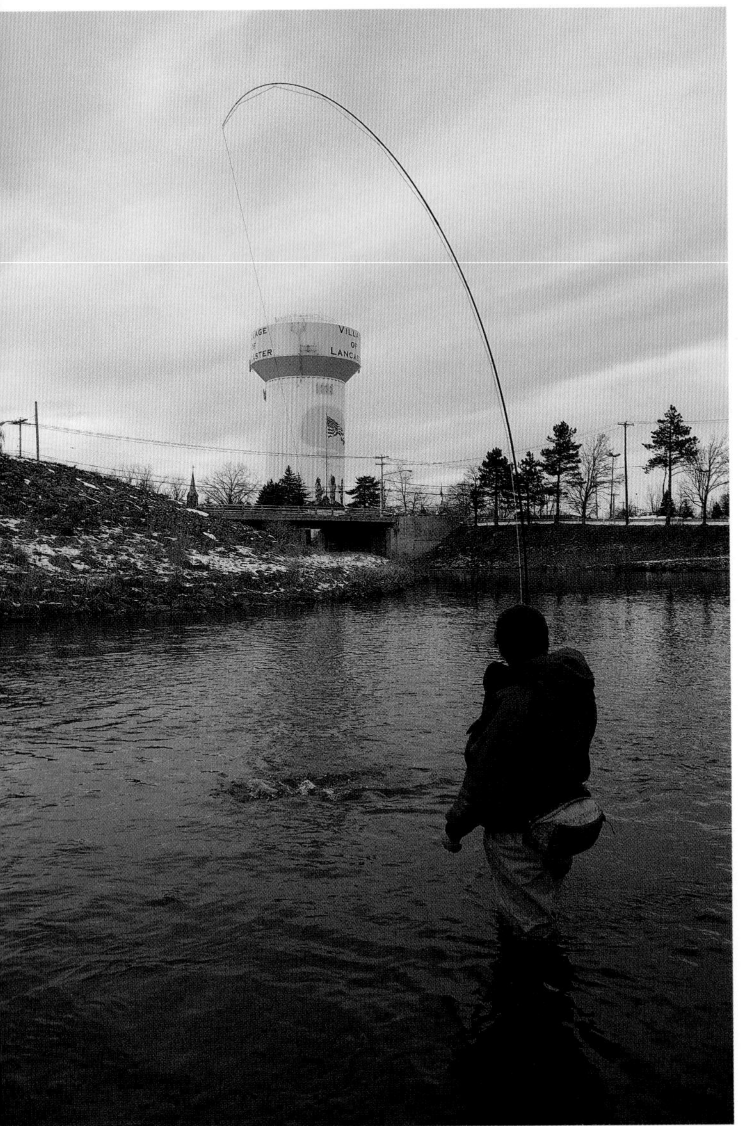

Good water can be found in the many towns and even cities that border the rivers and streams of the Great Lakes.
NICK PIONESSA PHOTO

New York

My home state of New York is host to a tremendously diverse set of steelhead rivers, from small, intimate streams to big, brawling rivers. Some are quite short, suffering from the shortsighted desire of our predecessors to dam up our flowing waters. Others flow for miles, giving anglers the opportunity to spread out and explore. There are at least a dozen significant rivers and streams running into New York's shoreline of Lake Ontario and another eight running into Lake Erie—a few of which are considered some of the top rivers in the region.

Most of the runs on New York's rivers are supported through annual stockings. Planted steelhead are generated from Chambers Creek lineage at the state-of-the-art hatchery along the Salmon River as well as a couple other state facilities. Pockets of wild fish also add significantly to the total run on at least two rivers. Both the Salmon River and Cattaraugus Creek have tributaries that produce wild steelhead. Efforts to place special restrictions on these tributaries to protect spawning fish have been met with mixed public opinion, but at least some closures have been evidence of New York's interest in wild stocks.

Part of New York's management to improve opportunity for steelhead anglers has been the reduction of kill limits over the years. This has been especially important on Lake Ontario, where the lake's carrying capacity has diminished over the years because of a shift in the forage structure.

At the eastern end of Lake Ontario is the most heralded of New York's steelhead water—the Salmon River. The headwaters of the Salmon are filled with brook trout and begin in the near-wilderness environment of the Tug Hill Plateau region. It is a beautiful, brawling river with a fairly significant gradient drop over its last 15 miles. Some parts of the river are difficult to wade because of large, round rocks and slippery boulders, so a healthy respect for the river and its flow is essential.

The Salmon River got its name from the tremendous runs of native Atlantic salmon that once occurred on the river. Sadly these native stocks were extirpated in the late 1800s from overfishing and a lack of foresight. There is currently a program in place attempting to reintroduce Atlantics to the river, but it has met with only limited success. Now the river's annual return of stocked and wild chinook salmon brings throngs of anglers to its banks.

The steelhead runs can also be significant, and an ever-growing number of fly anglers pursue them. Many of these steelheaders now wield two-handed rods to cover many of the river's large, picturesque pools. Spey Nation, an annual Spey gathering on the river, has grown dramatically each year since its inception. The army of experienced and would-be Spey anglers who attend this event are evidence of the growth in this aspect of fly fishing. The event provides a great opportunity to learn from experienced Spey fishers and to try all the latest rods and lines.

The center of action for the river is the small town of Pulaski, which is bisected by the lower end of the river. Lodging is plentiful in town and up along the river. There is outstanding access as state lands and easements provide ample parking and trails to and along the river. The Salmon features two short fly-fishing-only sections on the upper end of the river. These areas typically receive substantial fishing pressure, so I focus my efforts on the many pools, runs, and pockets downriver from the special-regulation areas. There is a fee for access on the lower river that controls the number of anglers on a daily basis. While the fee controls the angling pressure, the maximum number of anglers is quite large and can still result in significant angler pressure during the prime weeks.

Angling pressure is always a consideration on the Salmon. Positioned at the eastern end of the lake, it is the closest steelhead river to the population centers of Boston, New York City, New Jersey, and Philadelphia. Fishing on weekdays and hiking to some of the less popular pools can help mitigate the impact of angling pressure. But even this may not be enough from late September through early November. I usually fish the Salmon for steelhead after the crowds have thinned. Late fall and winter are great times to fish the river.

The steelhead run on the Salmon comprises both hatchery and wild fish. The contribution of wild steelhead produced by Trout Brook and Orwell Brook has not been quantified, but the presence of naturally produced fish provides an extra esthetic element. The Salmon River has always had a reputation for big steelhead as well. While the average size of the typical Lake Ontario fish has decreased over the years, some big steelhead still show up each year, including a few exceeding 20 pounds.

An early-morning Salmon River steelhead.

The Salmon is composed of a series of classic pools, pockets, riffles, and slots. Great Spey fishing can be found in the main pools and in some of the lesser water that generally receives lighter pressure. Dead-drifting techniques will often produce greater numbers of fish, especially in the deeper pockets and slots. Two dams, the first approximately 15 miles from the lake, control the water flow and play an important role in fishing strategy. Typical flows range between 350 and 1,000 cfs. It is possible to still fly-fish the river when it exceeds 1,200 cfs, but it becomes increasingly difficult above this point. You'll need to adjust your rigging to sink a fly at the various flows. I keep detailed records of successful rigs to prepare for each flow level. The current flow can be found on the USGS website and is monitored by the fly and tackle shops located on the river.

Winter-run steelhead begin to show by early September and can be found in the river until the following May. Because of the water flowing from the impoundments behind the dams and the high gradient of the river, the Salmon usually remains free of significant ice during the winter. For this reason, December through February can be a great time to fish the river, especially during milder periods. The river's steelhead will take a swung fly in water that is near the freezing mark.

The Salmon is also stocked with some Skamania strain summer-run fish, which you'll find during cool, rainy periods from June through August. Chinook salmon begin their ascent on the river by late August and represent one of the better opportunities in the Great Lakes for big, bright salmon on a fly.

North of the Salmon River along the eastern shoreline of Lake Ontario is the Black River. It is a large, powerful river 200 feet wide that remains a bit of a mystery from a steelhead-fishing standpoint. While the Black receives a significant stocking each year, it has evidence of a good contribution of wild fish as well. Wading can be difficult or treacherous, so take care.

Dave Mosgeller works the head of a pool on the Salmon River.

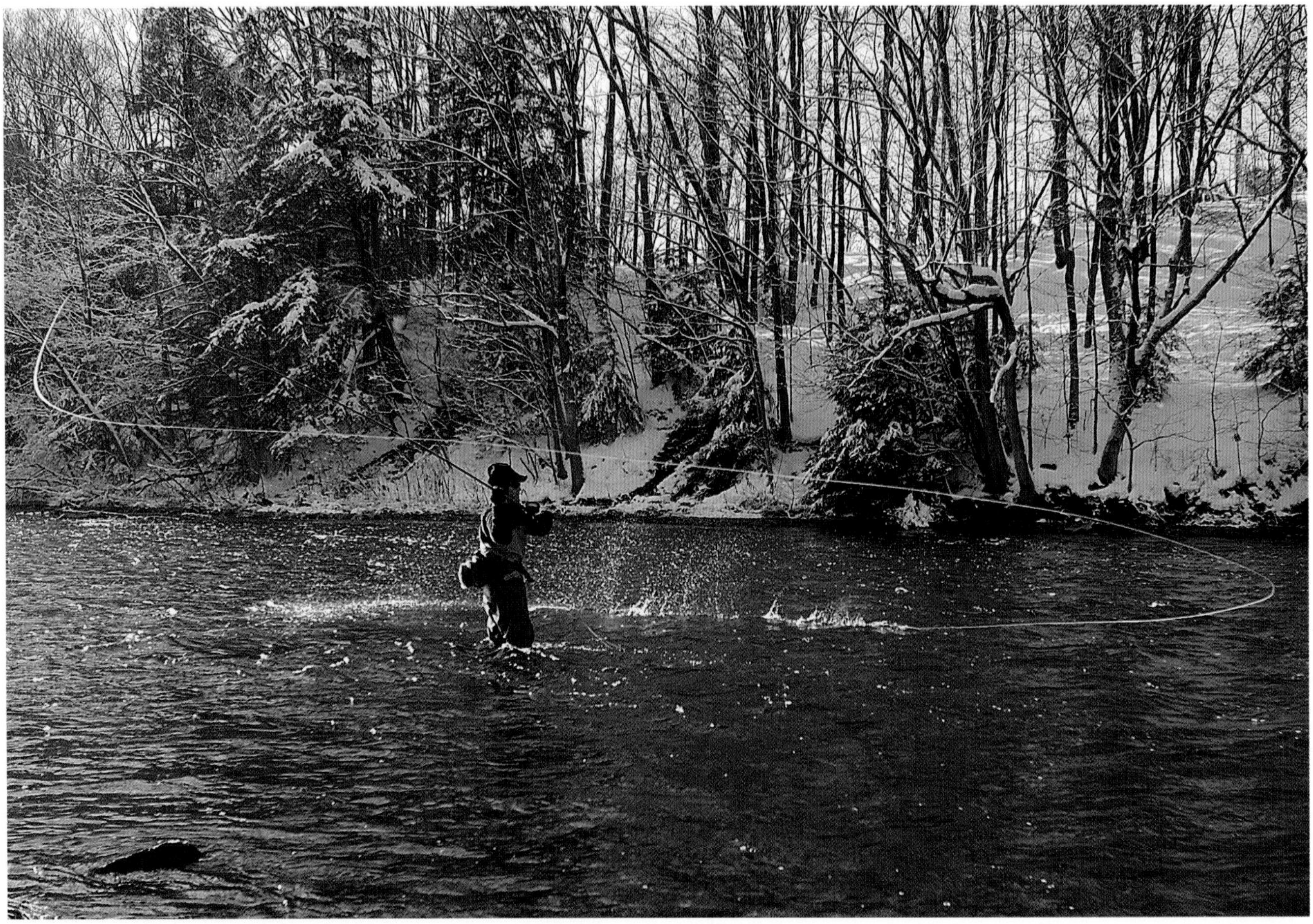

Good Spey-fishing opportunities can be found on a number of New York's rivers. NICK PIONESSA PHOTO

The Black flows through Watertown and enters the lake at Henderson Harbor. Historically, access to the river has been very limited, but it has expanded recently. The Black is a good river for a two-handed rod, which is beneficial for fishing its defined pools or working the less-defined softer currents along the river's edge. The Black produces some large steelhead and is a river worth exploring.

Between the Black and the Salmon are two medium-size bodies of steelhead water that receive fishable runs of steelhead, including some wild fish. South Sandy and Sandy (known locally as North Sandy) Creeks offer an opportunity to fish when the Black or Salmon is too high or when you just want a change of pace from the bigger waters. Both have good public access. Located to the southwest of the Salmon River is a picturesque stream called Grindstone Creek, which enters Lake Ontario at Selkirk Shores State Park. The Grindstone has a nice feel for fly fishing, and a swung fly can be a productive method of fishing with either a single-handed or light switch rod. Upstream migration is limited by a dam in Fernwood.

New York's south shore of Lake Ontario has a number of rivers and streams with steelhead runs, but almost all of these are short or fragmented. Unfortunately, man-made dams have cut off access to over 100 miles of steelhead water. Some quality fishing still exists on these bodies of water, though. While the dams concentrate and condense the fish into a smaller area, they also do the same for fishing pressure.

The Oswego River, located some 15 miles to the west of the Salmon River, is big water, but the fishable water is restricted to about a mile because of a dam. The Oswego receives good runs of steelhead and salmon, and there is good access to most of the water. Because of its size, it is probably best fished from a boat. Maxwell Creek enters the lake just west of Sodus Point. The fishing here is limited to about 2 miles but is good for traditional fly-fishing methods. Maxwell can receive a good run of brown trout in the fall as well.

There are a few good options near Rochester. The most notable is the Genesee River, which runs right through the city. And while the parking areas are in an urban setting, the hike to the river puts you in a pleasant gorge that has a more remote feel. There is some great water here for the two-handed rod, and I have experienced some quality steelhead fishing on Spey flies and leeches. However, the water is limited to about a mile because of a dam and a natural falls.

The Genny is a wide river at this point and is too deep and forceful to cross but has great swing water on both sides. You can access the gorge on the west side by parking at a city park and following the rather challenging trail to the bottom. Exercise care, especially in rain or snow. Access on the east side is a bit easier—follow a service road off Seth Green Street. Wading the Genesee can be very tricky as slick, angular rocks often make it impossible to gain a firm footing.

You can find steelhead in the river from October through the following May, and you can catch fish on a swung fly during that entire period if the winter is mild. The Genesee flows a long way—its headwaters begin in Pennsylvania. Since it drains such a significant area, it can take a long time to clear after a rain or runoff event. Timing can be everything on this river.

An alternative in the Rochester area when the water is too high and dirty on the Genesee is the Irondequoit Creek, which enters Lake Ontario in Irondequoit Bay. This is a considerably smaller piece of water that typically receives heavy fishing pressure. But the Irondequoit does produce some wild fish, and with some effort, you can find quality water away from angling pressure. There are both public fishing rights and a handful of public parks with good access to the water. Steelhead migrate up into the headwaters, giving fish access to over 20 miles of water, although in the upper reaches the creek is fairly small. Some big steelhead have been taken from the Irondequoit over the years.

Moving west along the Lake Ontario shoreline, you find a handful of steelhead waters between Rochester and New York's western end of the lake. Oak Orchard Creek is the most well known even though its waters extend only a few miles from the lake before a dam in Waterport blocks farther upstream passage. The dam lies about 5 or 6 miles from the point where the creek dumps into the lake at Point Breeze, but sufficient current for fly fishing runs for only about 2 miles at best below the impoundment. This is a real shame because a beautiful 12-mile stretch of water exists above the dam.

The Oak has gained a reputation for substantial runs of salmon, lake-run brown trout, and steelhead. It is a good size for fly fishing, and a light switch rod can work well to cover the creek's mix of small pools, runs, and pockets. I used to fish it, but its lack of length and high levels of fishing pressure have kept it off my annual list of steelhead rivers to visit for quite some time now. But I caught my first steelhead on a fly there, and I can still readily remember days when the angling pressure was limited to only a handful of anglers.

You can access the Oak at the dam and a few access points through private land down below. A creek hardly worth mentioning that suffered the same fate as the Oak is Eighteen Mile Creek. A dam at Burt blocks upstream migration to some attractive water above. The water below the dam is anything but picturesque and holds no interest for me, but its runs can produce some fast-paced fly-fishing action.

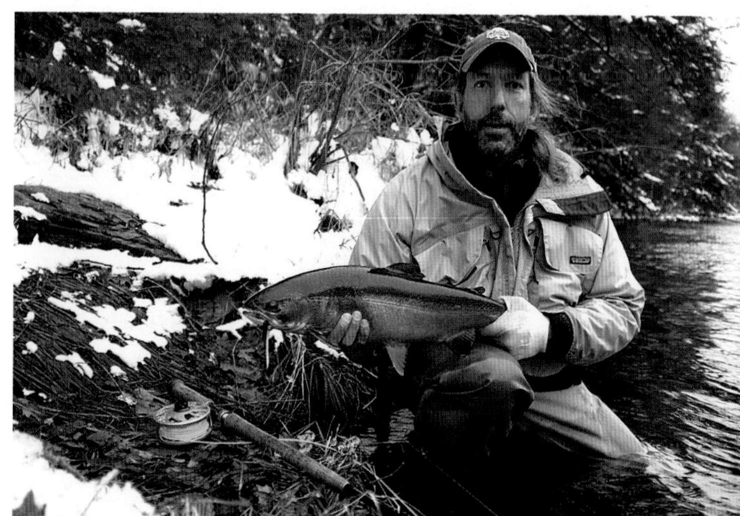

Winter steelheading can be quite productive on some Lake Ontario tributaries.

One of a handful of smaller tributaries found along Lake Ontario's south shore. NICK PIONESSA PHOTO

There are a couple other streams of note in New York's western section of Lake Ontario. Twelve Mile Creek enters the lake at Wilson and is a small stream that can save the day when other waters are running high after a rainfall. Johnson Creek, located near Oak Orchard, has about 6 or 7 miles of fishable water until a dam blocks upstream migration at Lyndonville. It is a low-gradient stream with a few nice pools.

Sandy Creek in Monroe is a bit of a jewel. It runs free of dams and has an inviting character as it winds through farmlands and small woodlots. Sandy's steelhead runs can be sparse, but it is quality water for a switch rod. There are some stretches with public fishing rights on each of these three streams. All of the western New York rivers and streams receive some runs of lake-run brown trout that can reach trophy proportions.

At the far western end of the state, and forming the border between the United States and Canada, is my home river, the mighty Niagara. While it is best known for its spectacular falls, which draw visitors from around the globe, the river also has a dedicated following of anglers in pursuit of its runs of steelhead and salmon. The Niagara is huge—200,000 cfs. Some portions of the river are calm and gentle, while others can only be described as raging torrents that are both treacherous and deadly.

The Niagara connects Lake Erie with Lake Ontario, which technically qualifies it as a strait. The falls essentially cut the river in two and create a distinct character for each section. The river above the falls is more placid and provides outstanding warmwater fly fishing. Some steelhead drop out of Lake Erie and are caught sporadically throughout the upper river. But the most significant steelhead activity exists below the falls for the fish migrating up from Lake Ontario.

While you can fish the lower river from a boat by both swinging and stripping streamers, fly fishing from the bank is best. Most of the lower river runs through a stunning, steep gorge. True wading can be done in only a few select areas of the river. For the most part, it is fishing along the bank and only stepping in to about ankle deep. The river drops off so quickly that wading any deeper can be dangerous.

The Niagara is a two-handed river since the gorge walls make a traditional backcast impossible in most areas. The two-hander is also instrumental in handling the heavy tips and flies needed to cover the depths of the river's forceful flows. For the

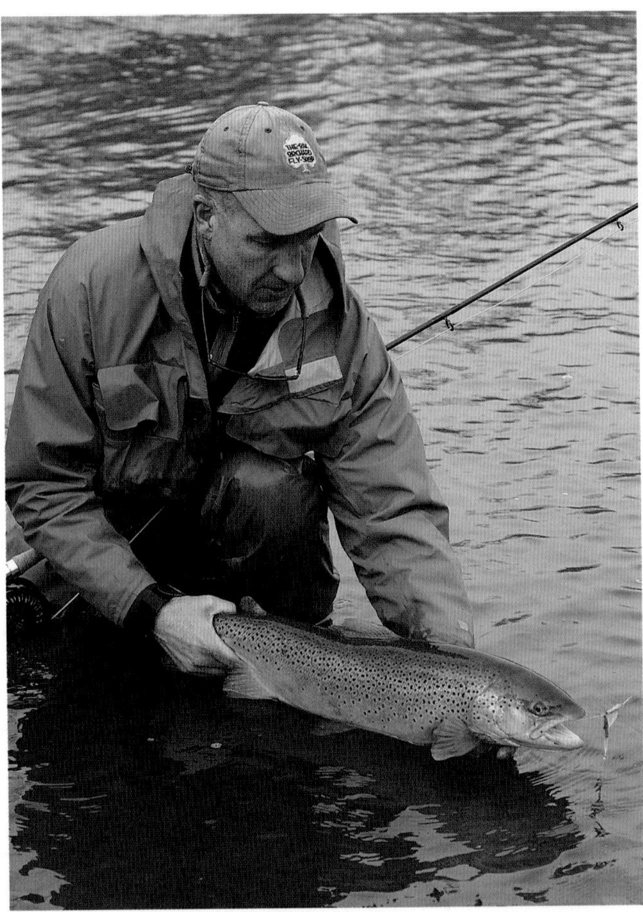

Many Lake Ontario tributaries are known for their returns of lake-run brown trout. NICK PIONESSA PHOTO

most part, the bottom drops off quickly along the bank, so a cast of only 40 to 50 feet is most effective. I always use a heavy tip, a heavily weighted fly, and a long, 6 to 8 feet monofilament leader section to increase sink speed and depth. A cast angled up with stack mends and loose line helps get the fly deep. Steelhead tend to hold closer to the bank when the water has limited visibility after runoff or heavy wave action on Lake Erie.

You generally won't catch many steelhead along the banks of the Niagara. But tangling with even one fish in its powerful flows will bring joy to any angler. You can access the lower river on the New York side via four different state parks and two boat ramps. Access roads, trails, and boat ramps provide access to miles of river on the Ontario side as well.

New York also boasts a significant shoreline along Lake Erie. The Cattaraugus Creek is the premier fishery from a Spey fishing standpoint. "Creek" is a bit of a misnomer as it has the character of a small river and is perfect for a light two-hander or switch rod. The Catt's gentle flows and its combination of pools, runs, and riffles make it the perfect place to swing a fly, and steelhead on the Catt generally respond very well to this presentation. In fact, it's a shame to fish the Cattaraugus with any other approach.

The Catt has some 40 miles of steelhead water from a dam near Springville to the lake. The dam itself has generated much discussion in recent years. Its days of electric generation are long past, and the dam no longer serves a purpose. There are preliminary plans to remove the dam entirely, breach a portion of it, or create a fish ladder. Proponents of these plans see the incredible potential for this fishery. Not only would allowing steelhead to pass upstream from the current dam site open up another 20 to 30 miles of steelhead water to spread out angling pressure, but it would provide fish access to a handful of prime nursery waters. These upper waters could produce a level of natural reproduction that could establish the Catt as an entirely wild fishery. Some opponents of the proposed changes point to the potential harm to the resident trout population in the upper Catt and its tributaries, because adult steelhead would compete with residents for the same spawning areas, and juvenile steelhead would compete with residents for food. While it is a serious concern, considering that this upper water is home to a special wild trout fishery, before the dam the river ran free, and restoration to this state would seem to be the natural resolution to the situation. Currently, approximately 20 percent of the Catt's run is composed of wild fish that are mainly generated by a few tributaries below the dam.

The lower 15 miles of the river run through the Cattaraugus Indian Reservation, which requires a separate license. Steelhead begin to show in the lower section by September. There are a number of unmarked access roads to the river throughout the reservation. Above the reservation is a combination of state

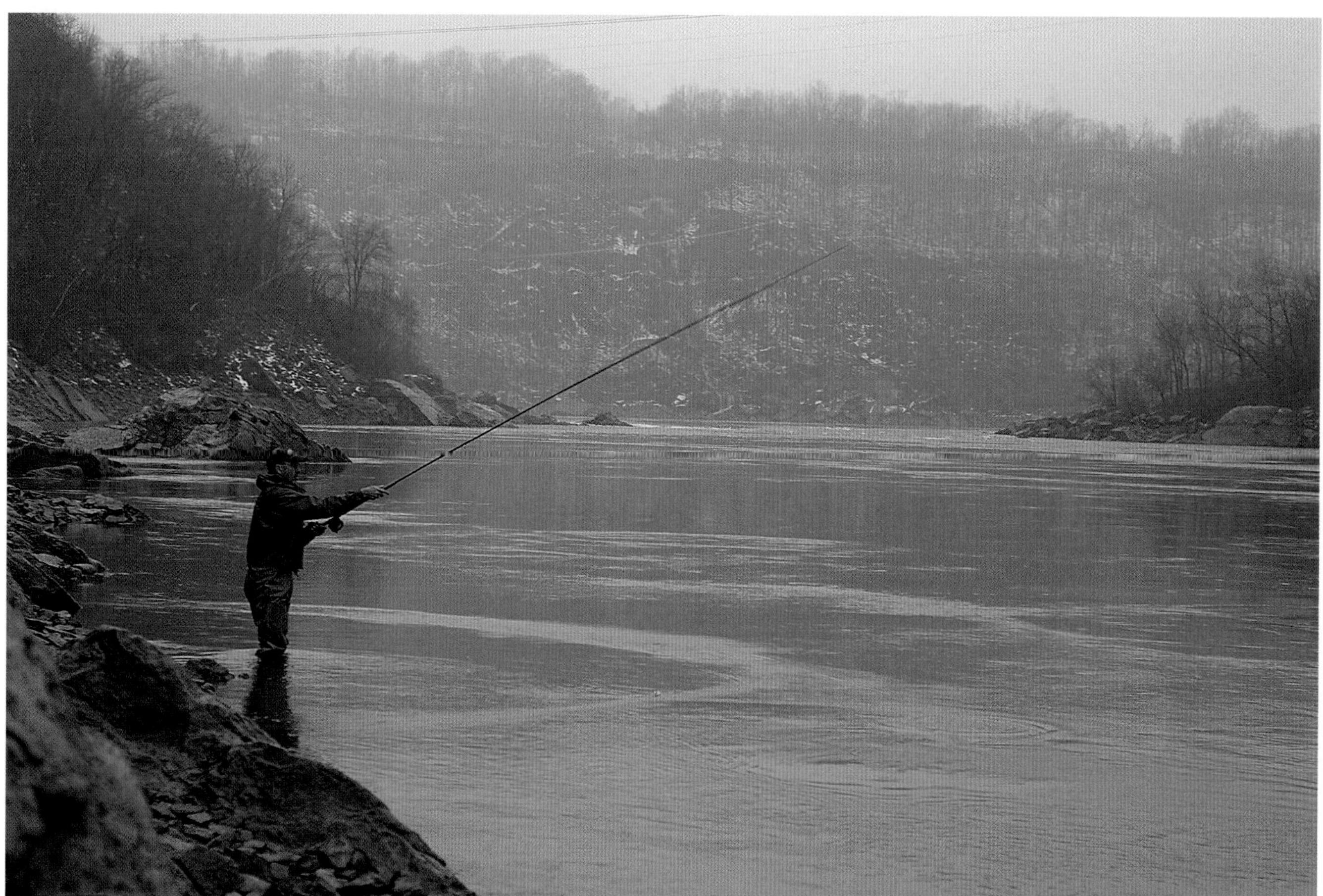

I lay out a cast on a damp winter morning. December can be a very good month in New York to encounter aggressive steelhead and lighter fishing pressure. NICK PIONESSA PHOTO

There are many picturesque settings along New York's section of Lake Erie. NICK PIONESSA PHOTO

land, public fishing access, and private lands up to the dam. The middle river winds through a picturesque gorge.

But the Catt may be known best for its unpredictability. The upper river and its tributaries flow through areas with long stretches of clay banks. In addition, the entire drainage collects a significant amount of water. After even moderate rains, the Catt can rise and turn muddy and be out of commission for days at a time. In an autumn with above-average rainfall, you need to carefully monitor water levels and clarity to determine whether conditions are fishable. The Catt is best in the fall, as it generally ices over in the winter, and spring runoff usually creates only a short window. It receives a sparse run of wild chinooks.

A fresh, wild steelhead from New York's Cattaraugus. NICK PIONESSA PHOTO

When the Catt isn't fishable or for anglers searching out a more intimate setting, three other, smaller waters can provide a quality experience. Eighteen Mile Creek near Hamburg, which runs through a pretty gorge, has some public fishing rights and a special-regulation section. It is just large enough to accommodate swinging flies and a switch rod. Canadaway Creek and Chautauqua Creek are both smaller and have a mix of pocketwater, small runs, and pools. The upper reaches of Chautauqua Creek produce some wild steelhead. Both creeks flow through a combination of countryside and small towns. Near Buffalo there are three more streams that receive sporadic to modest annual runs of steelhead. Buffalo Creek, Cayuga Creek, and Cazenovia Creek are each stocked with steelhead. Public access to each of these is fairly limited. Some lake-run brown trout can be found in the fall in these streams.

Pennsylvania

Moving southwest along Lake Erie, you enter Pennsylvania, its modest 40 miles of shoreline home to a series of creeks and streams that receive significant runs of steelhead. There is some natural reproduction on the waters that stay cooler in the summer. But Pennsylvania has a somewhat manufactured fishery—that section of Lake Erie is flooded with up to a million smolts per year. While this approach results in incredible runs, to many anglers' delight, it has also created a somewhat distorted view of steelhead fishing. Some fisheries biologists have expressed concern that such large annual stockings could eventually affect the overall balance of predator and prey in the lake and that the lesser-quality stock Pennsylvania uses will stray

A big steelhead goes airborne on a picturesque Lake Erie tributary in New York. NICK PIONESSA PHOTO

and negatively impact wild stocks in other parts of the lake. But the equation has worked so far, and Pennsylvania has a large following of anglers who pursue big numbers of fish.

The biggest and most notable of Pennsylvania's waters is Elk Creek. It is a moderate-size creek that flows through a beautiful ravine and over a bedrock and slate floor. Elk has runs, small pools, pockets, ledge drops, and crevices in the bedrock. In prime season, every piece of water that is more than knee to thigh deep is capable of holding fish. When the water is in ideal shape, any spot of dark green water is a good place to present a fly.

Most of the steelhead waters in northwest Pennsylvania are spate, meaning rains are required to provide a good flow since springs and groundwater have little impact on their water level. And this is certainly true of Elk. Understanding its flow rhythms will have a direct impact on your success. Heavy rains can raise and muddy the water rather quickly. But since Elk Creek drains a fairly short area, it can clear and drop quickly too. Finding the perfect day as the water clears can take some effort, but it can lead to some of the fastest action in terms of hookups that you'll find anywhere in the Great Lakes region.

Many of Elk Creek's pools are large enough to accommodate the wet-fly swing, and in some sections of the creek a switch rod works quite well. Dead-drifting techniques work best in the slots, drop-offs, and crevices. As the creek's level drops with no follow-up rains, the water becomes very clear. Long leaders work best under these conditions when swinging a fly. While dead-drifting, lighter tippets promote a truer drift and increase stealth.

Steelhead begin to show in Elk Creek by September when there is sufficient water flow. Its peak season is October through early December, and open water can be found in the winter months in years with moderate weather. Spring fishing generally peaks in March and April. Most of the angling

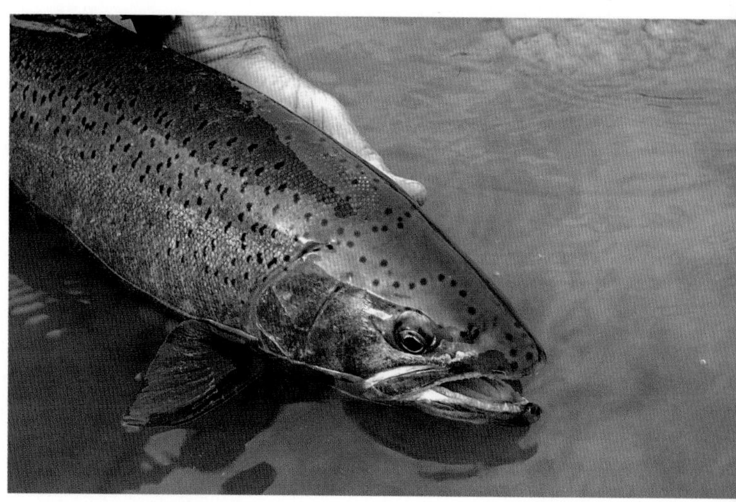

An Elk Creek steelhead.

activity centers around the town of Girard to the west of Erie. Elk has a combination of public access and private waters. Unfortunately, there has been a trend toward privatization of the access.

Elk is an excellent river for beginning steelhead anglers or for those who want an opportunity at numbers. I have enjoyed many pleasurable days there over the years. But Elk can give you an unrealistic idea of steelhead fishing with its high catch rates, and it's important to keep this in perspective.

For its relatively small amount of Lake Erie shoreline, Pennsylvania has a surprising number of streams that receive steelhead runs. Walnut Creek is the second largest, and while its general makeup is similar to Elk, it is quite a bit smaller and feels more like a creek rather than an intimate river. Walnut scan also receive incredible runs of steelhead in the fall and spring. It does not have as much room to swing flies, but some of the small pools will accommodate this approach.

Two other creeks located east of Erie are Sixteen Mile Creek and Twenty Mile Creek. Each can provide good fishing after rain or runoff, but both are smaller waters fished best with dead-drift techniques. There are a number of other smaller streams in Pennsylvania that provide steelheading in an intimate setting. Refer to John Nagy's *Steelhead Guide: Fly Fishing Techniques and Strategies for Lake Erie Steelhead* for more detail on these streams.

The large runs of fish on Pennsylvania waters understandably attract great numbers of anglers. Fishing pressure is always a consideration on these waters, and because of this anglers tend to fish closer than what I consider comfortable. Finding some space away from the crowds makes an outing more enjoyable. The future of the Pennsylvania fishery seems fairly stable except that a reduction of public fishing access is a concern. The Pennsylvania Fish and Boat Commission seems content with managing the steelhead runs as it has in the past, although budget constraints could eventually place a limit on the number of annual stockings. Steelhead comprise most of the migratory salmonids found in Pennsylvania rivers, but you can find a few lake-run brown trout on occasion.

Ohio

When I first started steelhead fishing, Ohio was never on my radar. The Buckeye State developed a significant fishery after most Great Lakes states had at least some degree of steelhead returns already occurring. A lack of sufficient habitat for any

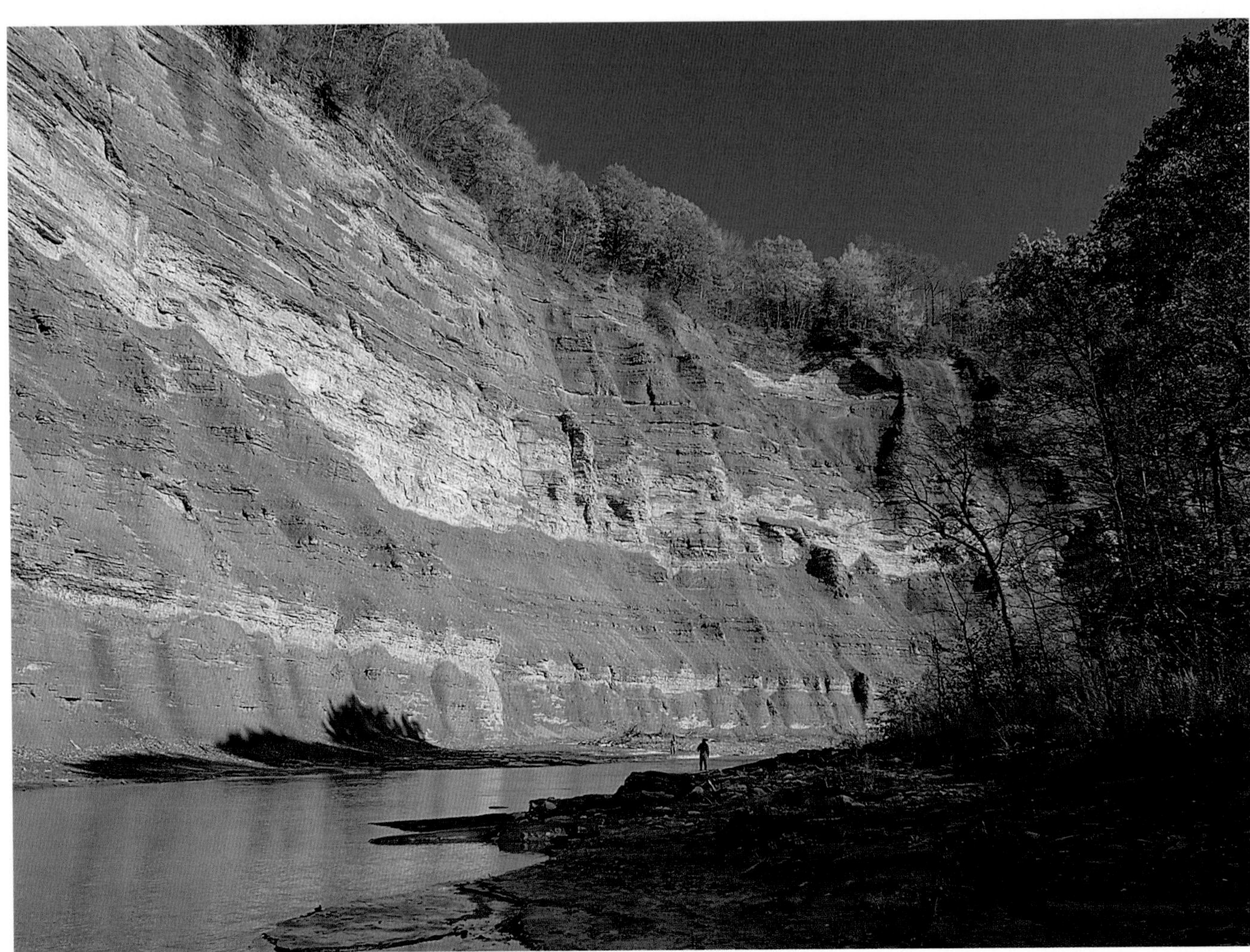

Gorge walls form a backdrop on many Lake Erie rivers and streams. NICK PIONESSA PHOTO

Jeff Liskay and a nice Ohio spring steelhead.

significant natural reproduction prevented Ohio rivers from establishing a steelhead history. While habitat improvement in recent years has increased the possibilities for some wild fish production, the state of Ohio has actively managed its rivers with planted fish for a number of years now and has established a substantial steelhead fishery.

A number of Ohio rivers have quality steelhead fishing. Most are picturesque pieces of water that meander through woodlots and agricultural lands, cutting gorge walls into the shale and bedrock. Most of the rivers are smaller to midsize and have lower gradient flows. Ohio relies mainly on the Manistee River strain to stock its rivers, which is a hardy strain developed naturally in the Great Lakes. It seems to have superior survival rates compared with the strain Ohio previously stocked. The Manistee strain has a tendency to run later in the fall and peak in the spring. Ohio only stocks its main rivers and relies on strays to fill in the lesser rivers and creeks.

Public access to steelhead waters in Ohio is impressive. Thought and foresight have been given to preserving good access in a series of parks along many of the rivers. Some recent private water closures on one Ohio river have prompted the state to be vigilant in its effort to maintain access for the public to its steelhead fishery.

Conneaut Creek enters Lake Erie at the town of Conneaut, less than 10 miles from the Pennsylvania border. The Conneaut is considered one of the top Ohio tributaries and is known for its consistent run of steelhead. It is stocked by Ohio and receives a fair number of strays from Pennsylvania. The Conneaut has the character of a small river and averages 50 to 60 feet wide. It winds through a combination of farmland and hardwood stands. The Conneaut's headwaters are located in Pennsylvania and are known to produce some wild steelhead. The creek flows to the west out of Pennsylvania into Ohio and then makes a 180-degree turn, running back to the east before turning to enter the lake.

Conneaut's holding water is composed of pockets, short runs, and placid pools. The Conneaut runs over a mix of shale and gravel. The cuts, drops, and ledges of the shale often produce some of the prime holding lies, especially in lower water. Locating the ledges can be the key to success. The cuts and ledges will not necessarily be visible when the water is a little off-color, so you have to note where they are when the water is low. Other pools that run over gravel are fairly easy to read. The Conneaut has a fairly low gradient, and its flow speed is perfect for the wet-fly swing in most of its runs and pools. The Conneaut is a great piece of water for a light two-handed rod or a switch rod. Its ample runs give an angler an opportunity for multiple hookups using the wet-fly swing.

Since the Conneaut runs through agricultural lands, it muddies after heavy rains and can take a few days to clear. It is at its best when running with a green color. You can find good runs starting in October, and they last into December. In mild winters, fishing is possible. Spring fishing normally begins in early March and lasts through April. Spring is when you'll encounter some of the Conneaut's bigger fish.

Access to the creek has remained good, although it doesn't run through as much designated public land as some of Ohio's other rivers. You can access the river at many of its crossroads. Fishing pressure can be heavy at times, especially in the lower water. Spread out to the upper river for more room to work the water.

To the west, the Ashtabula River is an option when the Conneaut is unfishable. The Ashtabula isn't currently stocked but sees enough stray steelhead to make it worthwhile. The river has a tainted past as unregulated discharge of hazardous materials during the middle of the last century polluted the lower river, but remedial actions have dramatically improved the health of the river. The Ashtabula is a pretty river of small to medium size that runs across gravel and bedrock and winds through gorge walls cut through shale. A couple of parks provide good access to the river.

Farther to the west at Painesville, Ohio's Grand River enters the lake. Many consider the Grand the premier steelhead river in the state. The Grand has both length and size, with approximately 50 miles of fishable water from a dam in Harpersfield to Lake Erie. The Grand is generally 80 to 100 feet wide and even wider in some areas. Its size, ample pools, moderate flow, and room to spread out make it Ohio's best Spey-fishing river. You'll definitely be at home with a full two-handed rod on the Grand. Bring a rod that can handle heavier tips when the water is high.

The Grand has one pool after another capable of holding steelhead under a range of conditions. Most of the pools can be easily covered with the wet-fly swing, and aggressive Grand River fish respond very well to the technique, as I have found on a few memorable days. The Grand is one of the rivers that the state stocks annually, and it has some wild fish production on some of its tributaries. Unfortunately, the river drains a large area, much of it running through farmlands. Heavy rains cause the Grand to rise and muddy, and it can take a week before it drops into a fishable condition. Waiting for the proper conditions is the key to fishing the Grand.

Access to the Grand is very good with almost a dozen parks along its banks, providing both foot and boat access. On some parts of the river, you can hike a good distance from an access

Early-morning light glistens on a stand of hardwoods along a Lake Erie tributary. NICK PIONESSA PHOTO

Getting a fish to roll on its side in the shallows is a good way to finish the fight. Here a fish is landed on the Grand River.

point to avoid fishing pressure. The Grand is also a good river to float with a small raft or kayak to see all it has to offer.

Just east of Cleveland is the Chagrin River. Because it's close to the city, it receives a fair amount of fishing pressure. The Chagrin is stocked by the state and is large enough to comfortably fish with a two-handed rod. It runs mainly over shale and bedrock, and you'll need some knowledge of the water to determine prime holding lies. A flood in 2005 washed out a dam located at Willoughby, which opened up steelhead access to some of the river's picturesque upper reaches. A part of the structure still exists at Willoughby, so the steelhead need adequate flow to jump and negotiate the remaining piece of the dam. In the winter of 2011, the previous upper limit of migration, the Gates Mills Dam, was washed out by flooding. This opens the Chagrin up to about 20 miles of steelhead water and allows access to the high water quality of the upper river. Here lies the possibility for wild steelhead production. Access to the lower river is very good through a series of parks, but access is more limited above Willoughby, although one park provides about 4 miles of public water. The Chagrin takes a few days to clear after a rain.

The Cuyahoga enters Lake Erie right in the city of Cleveland and is notorious for the burning oil slick on the lower river in the early 1980s. But the river has come a long way since then and now sees a consistent run of stray steelhead. The Cuyahoga is another river large enough for Spey fishing, and because steelhead are more spread out since it isn't stocked, the wet-fly swing allows you to prospect the water efficiently. The Cuyahoga Valley National Park south of the city provides scenic access to the river's steelhead water.

On the western edge of Cleveland runs the Rocky River. Slightly smaller in terms of flow than the Chagrin and Cuyahoga, the Rocky is a low-gradient river with pockets, short runs, and comfortable pools that flows over a shale bottom. The park system in Ohio and Cleveland had the foresight to ensure that access is preserved on the Rocky River. The entire river up to its impassable barrier—the Lagoon Dam—is accessible through the Rocky River Reservation Metropark. The Rocky is stocked annually, which provides a consistent run. It can be comfortably fished with a single-handed rod or a switch rod. The Rocky is a great fishing resource for those in and around the Cleveland metro area.

Rounding out the picturesque rivers of Ohio is the Vermilion River in the western part of the state. The river gets its name from the reddish clay found along sections of its banks. The Vermilion might very well be the prettiest of Ohio's rivers, with a rural character as it runs through heavily forested areas and some remote farmlands. Approximately 30 miles long, the main river has plenty of room to spread out, which is another reason that it is an attractive option for Spey fishing.

The Vermilion has good access near Birmingham, where Interstate 90 crosses the river, as well as good access to the upper river via a series of parks and hiking trails. Some of the trails to and along the river are remote and add to a quality steelhead experience. The Vermilion runs over a mix of shale and gravel, with some beautiful pools located throughout as well as short runs and pockets formed by cuts in the shale. In some instances there is a fair distance between pools. The Vermilion can clear a little earlier than some of Ohio's other rivers.

Jerry Darkes admires a Lake Erie steelhead.

Indiana

There is a small piece of shoreline along Lake Michigan in Indiana, and the state has some quality steelhead fishing, which has gained a following mainly because of the sheer numbers of returning adults that can be found when prime conditions exist. The state of Indiana floods its waters with a combination of winter-run fish from Michigan and Skamania strain summer-run fish to produce a near year-round fishery. Some limited reproduction has developed. Indiana has clearly made the most of the water in the state.

The most notable water is the St. Joseph River, which has headwaters in Michigan. It dips south and runs through Indiana and then cuts north back into Michigan to enter Lake Michigan at the town of St. Joseph. The St. Joe is an example of a successful reclamation project. A joint effort between the states of Indiana and Michigan as well as the U.S. Fish and Wildlife Service created fish passages in a handful of dams that were constructed in the late 1800s and early 1900s. The St. Joseph River Interstate Anadromous Fish Project opened up some of the river's best water to migrating fish and created access to a number of tributaries. A hatchery was constructed to supply a fishable return of steelhead. When the project was completed, it opened up the St. Joe to a total of 63 miles of water accessible by migrating steelhead and established a wild fish generation in tributary water.

The St. Joe is a big, broad river. It's a great river for a two-hander or a switch rod because of its size and water temperatures that often run within the optimum range. Some of the lower river is deep and slow, with little opportunity for fly fishing. However, moving upriver you will find more defined riffles and runs as the river flows through a combination of farmlands and population centers. The section of river from Mishawaka to South Bend has some good water for swinging a fly. Access to the river is quite good, with a number of authorized parking and access points in both Indiana and Michigan.

The combination of winter- and summer-run fish has created near year-round steelhead possibilities on the St. Joe and its tributaries. Water temperature is the key to the summer-run fishery. A few tributaries add cool water to the system, but fishing for summer-runs is best in late June and through the summer during cool, rainy periods. Hot summer days will raise the water temperatures in the river well into the 70s. Not only will steelhead not be active at this temperature, but it can even be a lethal level. Flexibility is the key to capitalizing on the summer-runs.

The Dowagiac River is the main tributary to the St. Joe. It is a sizable piece of water that can be comfortably fished with a switch rod. A dam blocks upstream migration at the town of Niles. If steelhead had access to this upper water, they could reproduce and establish a wild run on the river. Efforts to remove the dam or gain passage around it are gaining momentum and will hopefully come to fruition in the near future. Two other, smaller tributaries that provide a more intimate experience are Pipestone and Brandywine Creeks.

Another Indiana fishery that is certainly worth noting is Trail Creek, which enters the lake at Michigan City. Trail Creek also benefits from the state's annual stocking program. It is an unlikely looking piece of steelhead water averaging 40 to 50 feet in width. Trail Creek water is typically stained as it runs through mostly mud banks. Its relatively low gradient makes it a bit difficult to read. But let there be no doubt, Trail Creek provides a great opportunity for multiple hookups and possibly the most consistent fishing for summer-runs in the Great Lakes region. Like the St. Joe, Trail Creek fishes best during cool periods in the summer months. With a consistent migration of winter-runs as well, steelhead can be found here nearly year-round.

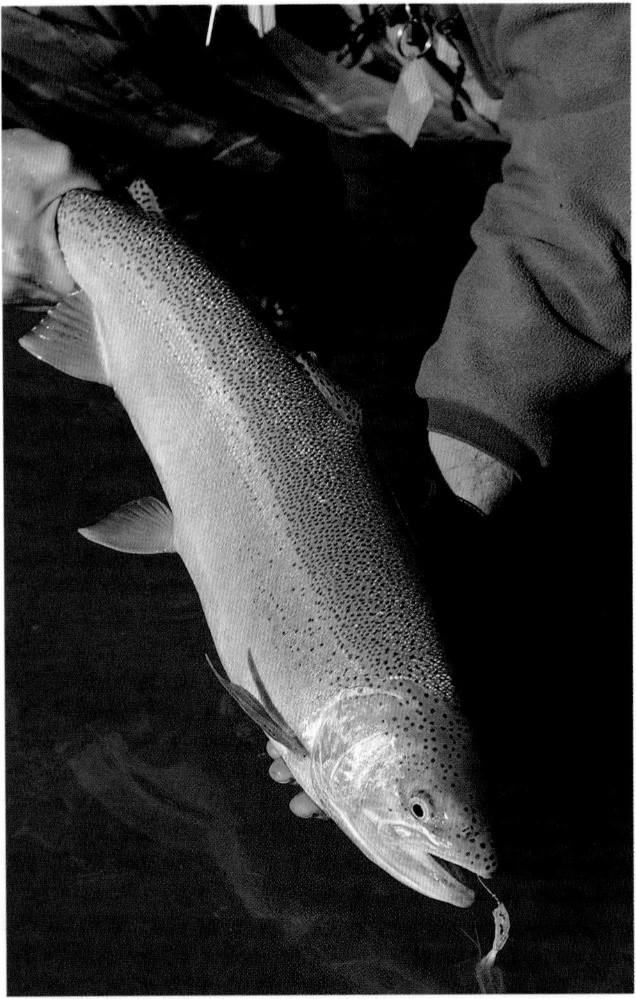

A hatchery steelhead illuminated by the morning sun.
NICK PIONESSA PHOTO

The Indiana steelhead fishery is a successful reclamation project and serves as an example for other Great Lakes fisheries, but even so, there is still much work to be done in returning some of Indiana's quality rivers to their natural state.

Michigan

Michigan's two peninsulas have shoreline that contacts four of the five Great Lakes. For its vast shoreline, beautiful rivers, and wild steelhead, Michigan is the top state for steelhead fishing. It has rivers of every size and character, many of which flow for miles through state and national forestlands. In my early years of steelheading, I spent many a day exploring the bounty that the Wolverine State has to offer and fell in love with a handful of its rivers. While I haven't spent much time there in the last few years, I have always felt connected to this special place.

Michigan's rich steelhead history is connected to its rivers' ability to produce impressive numbers of wild steelhead. A heavy influence of cool springs and groundwater seepage on many of its rivers and streams makes them capable of supporting naturally producing populations of resident trout; water quality is sufficient to rear steelhead before they escape to the lake. The Michigan or Manistee strain of steelhead is closely linked to the McCloud River strain transplanted from California in the late 1800s. The Manistee is a hearty strain that has developed over generations, adapting to the requirements of life in Lake Michigan and its rivers. For those Michigan rivers that are supported through annual steelhead stocking, eggs are collected exclusively on the Little Manistee, which according to historical records has never been stocked.

With such a great capacity for natural reproduction, Michigan manages its rivers with a significant emphasis on wild fish production. However, because of pressure from certain sectors of the angling community, the runs on a few notable rivers have been augmented with hatchery fish to produce more robust returns of adult steelhead. While this approach can result in a high number of returning adults, hatchery plantings will generally hold back a river's wild fish potential. Pressure from the public often has an influence on fish and wildlife management issues. Michigan's hatchery program aims at maintaining the genetic integrity of the homegrown strain of fish to minimize negative impact on wild fish production.

Beginning in the east and working west, the state's steelhead fishing starts out a bit slow. The Detroit River, flowing

Setting up the D loop on a Michigan river. JON RAY PHOTO

from Lake St. Clair into Lake Erie, is a diverse fishery quite similar to my home Niagara River. You can find steelhead in the Detroit, a huge piece of water best fished with a two-handed rod along current edges and shelves along the bottom.

The Huron River is a more manageable size. It flows into Lake Erie at Point Mouillee. The Huron is not a typical Michigan River in that it has more development along its banks and its run is composed mainly of hatchery fish. But this is big water made for two-handers and prospecting with big flies as steelhead have a lot of room to spread out. A park at the town of Flat Rock provides access to good fly-fishing water, and a fish ladder on the dam located in town allows steelhead to access about 13 miles above this point.

Along Lake Huron's Michigan shoreline, the most notable steelhead river is the Au Sable. Famous for its incredible population of resident trout on the upper reaches, the approximately 11-mile stretch from the Foote Dam to the lake at Oscoda is packed full of steelhead holding water. This is big water with some pockets, shorter runs, and long, sweeping pools that run over gravel. Many deadfalls are found in the river, creating both structure for steelhead and obstructions for breaking off flies. This is definitely Spey water, and the steelhead that enter the river in October and November are aggressive. Long, sweeping bend pools can take some time to cover from top to bottom. Steelhead peak on the river from mid-March through mid-May.

Wading can be a bit tricky, especially when the water is running sand-colored from recent rains. The bottom can slip out quickly, so you need to be comfortable with a run or pool before wading too far. Finding comfortable water to fish is part of the challenge here, as the river can drop off quickly, and overhanging trees and deadfalls can impede the flow of the holding water. There is some walk-in access to good water, but a great way to see the river and spread out into a range of water is to float. The Au Sable receives a run of both wild and planted fish. All the fishing occurs fairly close to the lake, meaning you can tangle with chrome-bright fish that will challenge your skills at landing steelhead. The fall also sees a run of chinook salmon.

The Rifle River to the south is another option along the Lake Huron shoreline. It is a modest-size river that you can cover with a range of techniques with either a two-hander or a switch rod. The Rifle can receive a good run in the fall, with good fishing in the spring as well. The Au Gres and Ocqueoc are two other rivers worth exploring if the Au Sable and Rifle are flowing off-color.

Across the Lower Peninsula to the Lake Michigan shoreline, starting south to north, you find the Golden Coast of Great

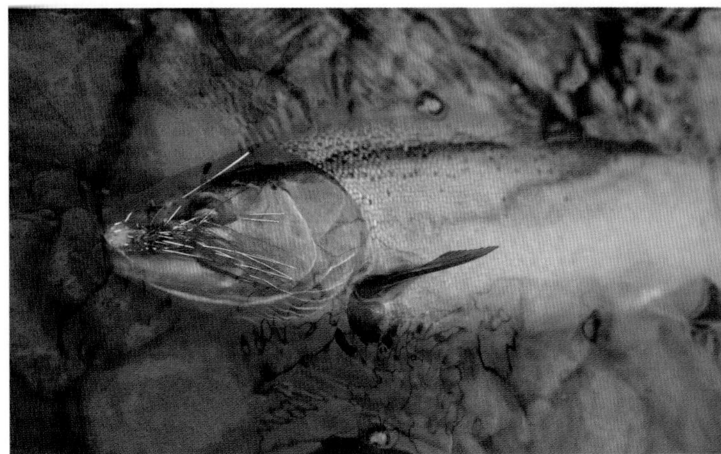

A Michigan steelhead grabbed this flashy, swung fly. KEVIN FEENSTRA PHOTO

A drift boat and a guide can be the key to success on Michigan's bigger rivers, like the Muskegon pictured here. KEVIN FEENSTRA PHOTO

Lakes steelheading. At the farthest southern point of the state is the St. Joseph River. Much of the good fly-fishing water and fish management structure are in Indiana, so I won't discuss it again here (see page 155). North of the St. Joe is Michigan's Grand River, the state's longest river and the third significant Great Lakes steelhead river with that name. The Grand travels approximately 260 miles from its headwaters above Jackson and enters Lake Michigan at Grand Haven.

The Grand is a significant piece of water that is the most heavily stocked in the state. Some natural reproduction on a few of its tributaries adds to the run. A couple of the rivers, including the Rogue and Thornapple, are respectable steelhead fisheries. The Grand is a big, low-gradient river perfect for Spey fishing. The steelhead opportunities through Grand Rapids have been well documented, and at certain times this area attracts quite a crowd. With the ability to negotiate the dams on the lower river, steelhead can migrate past Lansing. If I lived in the Grand watershed, I'd spend time in the water up from Grand Rapids that is more difficult to access. The Grand has a lifetime of water to explore.

Michigan guide Jon Ray displays a big steelhead for angler Ed McCoy. JON RAY PHOTO

There are a number of good public access points, especially near any of the river's dams. A boat, kayak, or raft is a good way to access and explore all of the river's water. Focus on the water below the river's tributaries to find concentrations of steelhead.

As you head north along the Michigan coastline, the next major river system is the Muskegon River, which enters the lake at the town with the same name. The Muskegon is a diverse fishery that many consider to be one of the best rivers in the Great Lakes to fish with a two-handed rod. The Muskegon is a big, powerful river that runs bank to bank. It is the type of river that doesn't give its secrets away to anglers simply looking at its surface. Prime holds are learned through hours of trial and error.

When wading the river, select water carefully. You can wade easily some places, while others may become too deep or treacherous. You'll find some good walk-in access points from Croton Dam, the upper limit of steelhead migration, down to Newaygo, a distance of about 14 miles. You can fly-fish most of the 50 or so miles of river from Newaygo to the lake.

A boat can be a real asset, both for transportation and to cover some of the deep runs that push against the bank. The river is generally too powerful and wide to cover the far bank by wading. Kevin Feenstra, an experienced guide on the

Muskegon, uses his drift boat to cover midriver runs and slots against the bank. He anchors the boat, and his clients use two-handed rods and sinking-tips to cover the water by swinging big streamer patterns through likely holding water. It is an approach that often results in aggressive takes. This is one river where a guide can be a significant advantage.

Steelhead begin to show in October, but the best fall fishing is usually from late November through December. Since the river flows from an impoundment, the water temperatures stay slightly higher into the late fall and early winter than those of a free-flowing river. The Muskegon can remain fishable all winter unless the air temperatures turn harsh. Spring fishing picks up in March and peaks in April. The Muskegon receives a run of both wild and hatchery fish, and some large steelhead are caught here each season. It also receives a heavy run of chinook salmon as well as enough lake-run brown to add the occasional bonus catch. The Muskegon should be on any serious Spey fisher's list.

North of the Muskegon is an enchanting piece of water just large enough to swing flies through riffled runs and quaint pools. The steelhead water of the White River runs from below the dam in Hesperia to Pine Point before it enters White Lake. The run on the White is composed of both wild and hatchery fish. This is a good river for a light two-handed rod or a switch rod. When conditions are right, White River fish can be quite aggressive.

North of the White, entering Lake Michigan at the town of Ludington, is the Pere Marquette—an iconic river from a historical perspective. The Pere Marquette is a gorgeous river that twists, turns, and winds back on itself as it flows through heavily forested banks. The river is protected for future generations under the National Wild and Scenic Rivers Act. The PM, as it is affectionately referred to, runs uninterrupted for miles from its headwaters above Baldwin all the way to the lake. The Pere Marquette has incredibly high water quality and produces a run of entirely wild steelhead.

The river's smooth flow gives it the appearance of a slow, meandering piece of water, but its channelized flow is forceful. The PM is characterized by runs, pockets formed by drops in the gravel floor, and sweeping bend pools. It can roughly be split into two sections. Most consider the Route M-37 bridge the upper end of the quality steelhead water, and the 7 miles of winding river down to Gleason's Landing is the most popular stretch on the river. This is intimate water with trees and brush growing right along the bank, making it difficult for a traditional backcast. A switch rod is perfect for the upper water because you can work the wet-fly swing in runs and pools with a moderate flow and use the dead-drift approach in quick currents and confined pockets.

Below Gleason's Landing, the river widens to 90 feet or more in spots. While a switch rod is still a good choice for this water, a light two-handed rod will more easily handle the heav-

Early morning light illuminates the bank along the Manistee. JON RAY PHOTO

ier tips and weighted flies required to fish some of the pools. The PM typically runs very clear, so a stealthy approach to rigging gives you an advantage.

Fall runs can be encountered from October into December and vary with intensity from year to year. Fall fish on the PM can be quite aggressive. The spring fishing normally picks up in mid to late March and can last well into May. The fall can also produce a tremendous run of wild chinook. The Pere Marquette is a special river capable of providing a high-quality experience.

The Manistee River, which enters Lake Michigan near the town of Manistee, is another significant steelhead fishery. Similar in size to the Muskegon, the Manistee is a full-blown Spey river that has many of the same characteristics as a western steelhead river. Its holding water is somewhat easier to read than the Muskegon. Tippy Dam near Wellston marks the top end of the steelhead water, which leaves a considerable amount of water down to the lake. As with other top Michigan rivers, the Manistee's headwaters flow from glacial sand plains, providing the river with clear, clean water.

The river has many well-defined riffles and runs and gravel flats that drop off into big, deep pockets. This dark water can hold plenty of steelhead, especially in the spring. There is some good wading access in the top 7 miles down to High Bridge. Since the Manistee is big water with significant changes in depth, you need to take special care when wading. Logjams and drop-offs can make it difficult to follow an energetic steelhead along the river's banks when hooked. A boat or personal watercraft will provide greater flexibility and access to some of the water below High Bridge that is more difficult to reach.

This is a river made for a powerful two-handed rod capable of handling heavier tips and big flies for aggressive fish. Winter-run steelhead begin to show in September and are typically aggressive, silver fish. Fall fishing continues until the weather deteriorates into the winter. Being farther north, the Manistee can have winter weather conditions that are more severe than those lower on the peninsula. Spring fishing in the upper water can be very good into May. The Manistee's run is composed of both wild and stocked fish. It is also stocked with the summer-run Skamania strain of fish, which can present some opportunities during the summer months.

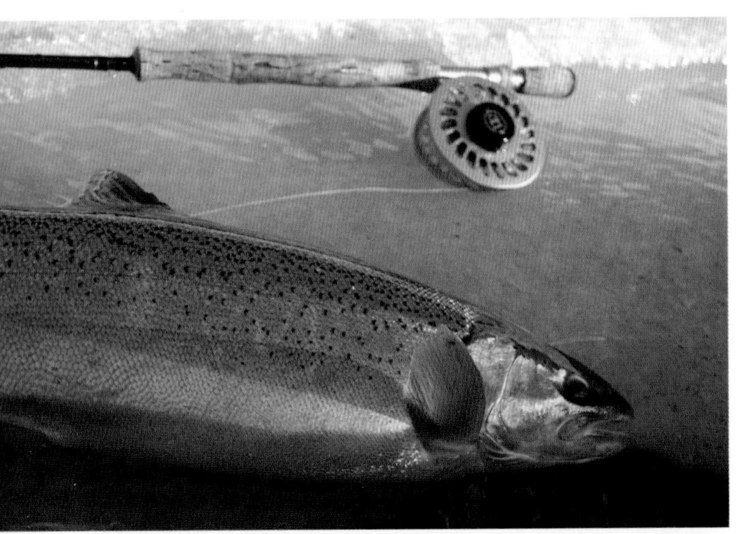

Good winter and early spring fishing can be found on Michigan rivers that remain free of ice. KEVIN FEENSTRA PHOTO

Just to the south is the Little Manistee River. Both the Manistee and the Little Manistee flow into Manistee Lake before entering Lake Michigan. The Little Manistee is a stream-size piece of water with gravel runs, small pools and pockets, and high water quality. It is a wild steelhead factory producing an incredible number of wild smolts. Returning adults are a key part of the Michigan steelhead plan as eggs collected from some of the fish are used for hatchery rearing and maintaining consistent genetics for the stocking program. Special regulations exist for the Little Manistee to protect its impressive wild steelhead resource.

In the Traverse City area, several pieces of water allow for fine steelhead fishing on a fly rod. The Betsie River is a small, low-gradient river that winds through forestland. You can easily fish it with a single-handed rod or switch rod. Its fertile waters produce a solid number of wild steelhead and provide a great opportunity for encountering fresh chinook salmon in the fall. The Platte and Boardman Rivers also offer good opportunities for steelhead fly fishing.

Moving up into Michigan's Upper Peninsula, you'll find wilderness fishing and more good runs of wild steelhead. At the eastern end of the peninsula is a unique piece of water that connects Lake Superior to Lake Huron. The famous strait is referred to as the St. Mary's River or St. Mary's Rapids. Its rather short length is defined by a vast series of riffles, pockets, and small pools across a substantial width. The St. Mary's forms the border between Michigan and Ontario.

Most of the fishing occurs along a cement wall that separates the main channel from a smaller one created for spawning purposes. The water level of the spawning channel can be controlled, whereas the main flow can vary widely. In low flow it is possible to wade well away from the wall. Steelhead begin to arrive in early October, and the fall fishing runs until a winter blast makes conditions too difficult. The St. Mary's is normally much easier to wade in the fall. The spring fishing typically begins in April and lasts through June. The St. Mary's also receives wild runs of Atlantic salmon in the summer months and chinook and pink salmon in the fall. This is great two-handed rod water as a variety of flies can be fished in the pockets, runs, and pools for aggressive fish.

The appeal of the rivers of the Upper Peninsula is the remoteness. This harsh, sparsely populated area affords a true wilderness experience. The Upper Peninsula typically receives more snow than anywhere else in the Lower 48. It has a plethora of steelhead waters of various sizes. Most are intimate rivers and streams that produce wild fish.

Possibly the most notable of the Upper Peninsula rivers is the Big Two Hearted River near Newberry. The river has the look of some of the Lower Peninsula rivers as it winds through heavily forested lands. The Big Two Hearted has a combination of broad gravel riffles and deep pools. Wading can be a little tricky because of logjams and drop-offs along the bank. The Big Two Hearted's defining characteristic is the color of the water—a nearly blood red tinge created by a high concentration of iron. Fall steelhead runs can be spotty, but the spring provides the most consistent opportunity. The peak is generally in the middle of May and steelhead can remain into June. The run is composed of a mix of wild and hatchery fish. There is good water for swinging a fly, and a switch rod would match up nicely with the river's tight-running character.

The Chocolay River near Marquette flows into Lake Superior at the village of Harvey. The Chocolay has a rich history of steelhead fishing. Its wild fish production is very good, and it typically sees a good annual run of wild steelhead. About 30 to 35 miles of river can be easily waded. The river's heavy groundwater influence keeps it running free later into the fall and winter than other Upper Peninsula rivers. It receives a run in both the fall and spring. It is a good river for a switch rod, and you can reach water away from the main access points with a canoe or kayak.

Northwest of Marquette and flowing through the Huron Mountains is the beautiful Big Huron River. The river has two branches that join together approximately 5 miles to the east of Skanee. From the falls on the West Branch downstream, you can find good fall and spring steelhead opportunities for a significant run of wild fish. The fall fish are aggressive, and the Big Huron is one of the best rivers in the Upper Peninsula for the wet-fly swing. A light two-handed rod or switch rod works well on the river, especially for the water below where the two branches meet. The Big Huron comprise a series of pockets, various-size runs, and deep pools. Some of the best pools are found on its long, sweeping bends.

Working from the town of Baraga at the bottom of the Keweenaw Peninsula, you can find a few other rivers worth exploring when visiting this remote area of Michigan. The scenic Sturgeon River enters upper Lake Michigan at the town of Nahma after running through a picturesque gorge and heavy forestlands. The Ontonagon and Firesteel Rivers can also provide respectable steelhead fly fishing.

Wisconsin

The state of Wisconsin has steelhead rivers that enter two of the Great Lakes. The state has a significant amount of shoreline along western Lake Michigan and a short section along the southwestern shore of Lake Superior. A number of rivers and streams of various sizes can be found along the Lake Michigan shoreline. This geographic area is quite reminiscent of the southern shoreline of Lake Ontario in my home state—low-gradient rivers and streams, some fragmented by dams, running through farmlands and new-growth forests, and supported largely by planted steelhead.

Wisconsin stocks winter-run Chambers Creek strain, Ganaraska strain, and even summer-run Skamania strain to spread out the available days for steelhead fishing for as long as possible. A handful of rivers in Wisconsin are capable of producing a quality steelhead experience. In addition to steelhead, you can find chinook salmon and lake-run brown trout on the Lake Michigan rivers. The rivers running into Lake Superior are few but include one of the more storied rivers in the Great Lakes and significant wild fish production. But like the other Lake Superior rivers, their wild fish have proven to be a fragile commodity.

Guide Nate Sipple displays an impressive lake-run brown caught on the big water of a Wisconsin river. NATE SIPPLE PHOTO

As you move along Wisconsin's southern border north along the Lake Michigan shoreline, you first encounter the Root River, which enters the lake at Racine. The Root River doesn't really meet my definition of quality steelhead water, but it would be remiss to not include it because of its importance to the overall Wisconsin steelhead fishery. A dam on the river restricts steelhead migration to the lower few miles. It is not a particularly attractive river, with its nondistinct water, but the Root is heavily stocked and provides significant runs to a following of anglers. Part of the reason for abundant stocking is that the Root River Steelhead Facility located on its banks was constructed in the 1990s to brood stock for Wisconsin's Lake Michigan steelhead fishery. The facility is not only a hatchery, but also a research station that monitors the health of the migratory fishery in Lake Michigan.

The Root runs muddy after a rain, but almost any rain from fall through the following spring has the potential to draw in good numbers of fish. Most of the techniques for the Root involve sinking the fly quickly since it runs bank to bank with a fairly swift current. Swinging a fly is possible in some water. Access the river through a couple of parks. The Root is a good example of making the most out of a given situation, and you can have a quality outing here under the right conditions.

About 80 miles north of Milwaukee, traveling on Interstate 43, you will encounter one of the premier steelhead rivers in the Badger State—at least from a Spey fishing standpoint. The Manitowoc River flows out of the farmlands of the northeastern part of the state and enters Lake Michigan at the city of Manitowoc. You can fish for steelhead in some 20 miles of river before the Clarks Mill Dam cuts off farther upstream migration.

Some of Wisconsin's tributaries have more intimate water. Here, an angler fights a steelhead on a crisp fall morning. NATE SIPPLE PHOTO

The Manitowoc is a sizable piece of water with rural sections of great fly water, especially for the wet-fly swing presentation.

As with other longer river systems in the Great Lakes region, steelhead have plenty of room to spread out on the Manitowoc, making it difficult to find concentrations and numbers of fish. But this is part of the river's charm, and it begs for Spey-fishing techniques that can efficiently cover the water. The Manitowoc is a relatively low-gradient river with flat, boulder-strewn runs and pools. Steelhead often sit in fairly shallow water, so you can use floating lines in place of sinking-tips. Even under the best of conditions, the river has a murky tinge. Unofficial access can be gained at several bridge crossings. Wading the Manitowoc can be a little tricky, so care in wading is essential, especially when the water is up and off-color.

If the Manitowoc is too high and stained to fish, you have other options nearby. The Pigeon River, Sauk River, and Sheboygan River all see solid runs of steelhead. The Sheboygan may offer the best opportunity of the three. It is a moderate-size river with a number of miles of steelhead water all the way up to Sheboygan Falls. There are stretches of both public and private water on the Sheboygan, and you can access much of the private water with a special permit. The river enters Lake Michigan at the town of Sheboygan.

North of the Manitowoc is one of the best-known and most consistent Wisconsin steelhead rivers. The Kewaunee River is located near the town of Kewaunee at the base of the Door Peninsula, 25 miles southeast of Green Bay. After fishing many of the rivers in the Great Lakes, I feel the Kewaunee is among the region's prettiest. Another attractive feature is that the Kewaunee runs unencumbered for approximately 22 miles, allowing steelhead access to its upper reaches, which creates some known natural reproduction.

Along with the Root River, the Kewaunee is the other Wisconsin river that the state uses to collect brood stock to maintain its Lake Michigan stocking program. Migrating steelhead are diverted by a cement weir to gathering points at the fish facility on the lower river. Some fish are taken away to the state hatchery, and others are allowed to continue their migration into the upper water.

From the fish facility down to the point where the river flows into the lake, there are several runs and pools that are ideal for swinging a fly on a light two-handed rod or switch rod. Both the lower water and a beautiful 6-mile section of river above the fish facility lie within the C. D. "Buzz" Besadny Fish and Wildlife Area, which provides public access to all the water via parking areas and trails. The upper water winds through hardwood forests and open meadows with soft runs and riffles. The Kewaunee receive steelhead runs beginning in the fall and peaking the following spring—April offers some of the best fishing of the year.

North of the Kewaunee, extending out on the Door Peninsula, are a few beautiful pieces of water known to produce wild steelhead. The two with the best potential are Silver Creek and Stony Creek.

The Door Peninsula forms Green Bay in the northwestern part of Lake Michigan. Flowing into the bay at the town of Oconto is the Oconto River. The lower river below the dam in Stiles is host to a consistent steelhead run. The Oconto is a broad river that runs tannic and clear. Wading is fairly easy, and the river has some easy-to-read riffles and pools in some areas and more subtle depressions and short runs in others. The Oconto can receive strong runs in both the fall and spring.

Access the water below the dam by following Highway 141 to Stiles or off of County Road J. Consistent releases from the dam are key to the river maintaining a fishable flow. North of the Oconto lies the Peshtigo River, which also receives a good run of steelhead. It is big water that matches well with a two-handed rod.

At the western end of the state, where Wisconsin touches the southwest tip of Lake Superior, lies the jewel of its steelhead fishery. The Brule River creates a scenic corridor as it passes through hardwood and cedar forests. The Brule has a long steelhead history, and accounts of anglers traveling to sample its fishing for migratory rainbows date back to the 1920s. The Brule is a modest-size river that is fairly easy to wade and consists of an array of riffles, runs, pools, and pockets requiring a range of techniques. It is a perfect candidate for a switch rod, and aggressive fish will take a swung fly with vigor.

One of the most impressive aspects of the Brule is its wild steelhead. The run is supported entirely by naturally reproduced fish, which adds significantly to the charm of the river. The runs had become depleted in the 1980s, mostly from overharvest. Dramatic measures were taken through restrictive size and daily limit changes as well as seasonal closures to fishing to protect nursery waters. These measures seem to have worked, as fish counts in recent years at the river's lamprey barrier indicate recovery and stabilization. However, as with any wild steelhead population, natural factors will cause wide fluctuations.

The Brule has good fall fishing from mid-September through November, depending on water flow. Fall rains draw fish into the system. Spring fishing picks up at the end of March and can last into May. There are about 12 miles of fishable water from the headwaters to Lake Superior as the river flows through the town of Brule, with good access off County Forest Road H. Stay at one of the beautiful campgrounds along the river for the full experience.

A wild steelhead caught on Wisconsin's Brule River.
JOHN FEHNEL PHOTO

Two other smaller waters along the Superior shoreline are Cranberry River and Flag River. These are good options if the Brule isn't fishable. Both produce wild steelhead.

Minnesota

The state of Minnesota borders Lake Superior for a portion of its north shore. Amazingly, approximately 60 tributaries flow into the lake along Minnesota's shoreline. Many of these rivers and streams have a very limited amount of water up to the first natural or man-made barrier to upstream migration. About 20 of these rivers or streams receive a fishable run of steelhead, and about half of these are large enough to use the wet-fly swing technique. Minnesota is the only Great Lakes state or province where I have not caught a steelhead. But in researching *Fly Fishing for Great Lakes Steelhead*, my brother Jerry spent a considerable amount of time steelhead fishing in Minnesota and was duly impressed with the sheer beauty of some of the water that he explored.

The north shore of Lake Superior is rugged country with a relatively short growing season. The rivers are in fishable condition for only a limited time. The extreme conditions limit the return of adult fish, and catch rates throughout the state are approximately one steelhead for eight hours of effort. The returning fish are a mix of naturally produced steelhead and stocked fish generated from wild brood stock.

Historically, Minnesota's section of north shore streams and rivers produced significant numbers of wild fish. Verbal and written accounts of steelhead fishing in the 1960s and '70s tell of high angler catch rates of naturalized steelhead. However, the prevalent catch-and-keep mentality in those days significantly reduced the runs.

Two other factors developed that also impacted smolt survival: Restoration of the native lake trout and introduction of Pacific salmon into Lake Superior led to high predation on steelhead smolts, and changes in land use negatively influenced the temperature regime and the general makeup of spawning water and nursery habitats. All of these factors working together have put stress on the ability of the system to produce wild fish.

While steps are being taken to restore and improve habitat, managers rely on hatchery fish to produce fishable runs of adult steelhead. But Minnesota still values naturally produced fish, and special regulations are in effect to protect wild adults. The fins are clipped on hatchery steelhead to make it easy to tell a naturally produced fish from a planted fish. Overall there is good reason to be hopeful about the future of the Minnesota steelhead fishery.

The most important river from a wild fish standpoint is the Knife River, which enters Superior at the town of the same name. With some improvements to the quality of the upper river, wild fish counts have increased in recent years. A fish trap below the Highway 61 bridge allows fisheries managers to count the returning adults and collect wild brood stock for planting in other Minnesota rivers. It also allows only wild fish to pass to the upper river spawning areas.

The Knife typically flows with a bit of a stain and can muddy significantly after a rain. It is a moderate-size piece of water averaging 50 to 60 feet wide, with small pools, quick runs, and pocketwater with room to swing flies in some areas. Above the fish trap, the Knife flows unencumbered for miles. The character of the river also changes in its upper reaches, splitting into several tributaries that provide prime spawning water.

The most picturesque of Minnesota's rivers may be the Baptism. It enters the lake approximately 60 miles east of Duluth. It flows for less than 2 miles before a falls prevents steelhead's upstream migration, but the steelhead water downstream of the falls is a dark flow with a combination of deep pools and pockets created by large, protruding boulders and rocks. The river runs through a small canyon, and variations in the water require a range of presentations and techniques.

A state park provides access near the main highway. The park also offers camping and access to a comfortable trail that leads to the falls. Since fishing the north shore of Superior often requires moving around among tributaries, the Baptism serves as a convenient base of operations for exploring a variety of other streams and rivers. The Baptism receives an annual stocking of steelhead that gives it a relatively consistent run.

Highway 61 provides access to a number of other rivers and streams that offer a good opportunity to catch a steelhead. To the west of the Baptism is the Split Rock River, which receives the largest stocking of the Minnesota waters. You can hike in to some inviting settings there. The Gooseberry River in Lake County, Lester River, and Silver Creek all receive annual plantings of steelhead. Streams and rivers in proximity to those that are stocked can receive runs of fish that stray from their waters of origin.

Minnesota steelhead tend to be more spring-run fish, with the runs often peaking in April. However, steelhead can commonly be found through May and into June, when many anglers have shifted their efforts toward other species. When proper water conditions exist, you can find somewhat inconsistent runs of fish from late September until the rivers ice over.

Ontario

The province of Ontario encompasses a vast area with shoreline along four of the five Great Lakes. Within its boundaries is tremendously diverse steelhead water: some large river systems cutting through miles of countryside, intimate creeks running through relatively unspoiled areas, and everything in between. There is even the opportunity for a near wilderness experience on some northern shore rivers.

The characteristics that clearly define the Ontario steelhead fishery, however, are its water quality and natural reproduction. Most of the runs on the province's rivers are entirely composed of wild steelhead. The wild fish have drawn me to these waters for years as the esthetic value of naturally produced steelhead is so significant. But with runs of wild fish you must temper your expectations. Catch rates will never compare to those in some rivers in the states that are laden with hatchery stocks. However, the beauty of a wild steelhead cannot be measured by numbers.

A wild steelhead I caught in Ontario.

Ontario puts forth a concerted effort to protect and expand its wild runs. Efforts to bypass dams and improve the carrying capacity of spawning tributaries are ongoing. Recent reductions of kill limits have helped restore the runs on some rivers where numbers had dwindled. And seasonal closures of rivers have historically protected Ontario's steelhead spawning.

Starting along the north shore of Lake Ontario, the first significant tributary enters the lake at Port Hope about 60 miles to the east of Toronto. The Ganaraska River is a smaller stream that flows through farmlands and new-growth forests. The Ganaraska supports a substantial run of wild steelhead. Historically, the total run has numbered between 10,000 and 15,000 fish, which is quite significant given the size of the watershed, but the run has decreased in recent years.

The Ganny is mainly a spring river. The water above the dam in town is considered sanctuary area and is closed to fishing from the late fall to Opening Day in late April. You can fish in the fall and winter in the water below the dam. Steelhead then bypass the dam through a fish ladder and lift system in the spring. Most fish successfully spawn before angling pressure disturbs the process.

The Ganaraska has a nice combination of riffles, runs, and small pools that make swinging a fly on a single-handed rod or switch rod a good way to fish the water. There is a mix of public and private water on the river. The most well-known public access is at the Sylvan Glen Conservation Area and has some excellent fly-fishing water.

When the season opens in late April, the Ganny commonly has both fresh and drop-back steelhead. Conditions dictate the duration of the fishing—a warm spring expedites the run, with fish dropping out quickly, but in cool, wet springs, steelhead linger well into May. The Ganny runs a considerable distance, so you have an opportunity to explore. Because of its relative proximity to the greater Toronto area, it can receive significant fishing pressure, but from my experience, when the run is strong, there are plenty of fish to go around.

Along the north shore are a few other smaller creeks that can provide a quality fishing experience with both their attractive nature and their runs of wild steelhead. Wilmot Creek receives a consistent run of naturally produced fish that have been genetically engineered for that drainage. Duffin's Creek is another of the smaller waters that can be quite surprising. These creeks fish best with dead-drift and pocketwater techniques.

The Humber River in Toronto provides the opportunity to fish for steelhead in an urban setting. To the west are the Credit River and Bronte Creek. Both receive considerable fishing pressure, but you can explore and find elbow room on the Credit. These rivers also receive runs of chinook salmon and lake-run browns.

Unlike the southern shore of Lake Erie, which has one river or stream after the next, the north shore in Ontario has a limited number. But what is missing in quantity is made up for in quality. The Grand River is the main Ontario tributary, and parts of it have great fishing for wild steelhead in a big river with a pleasant setting. The Grand's run of steelhead is entirely naturally reproduced and is living proof that wild steelhead can flourish in the Great Lakes region when given access to high-quality spawning and rearing water. The Grand's history as a quality steelhead river is quite short, beginning in the late 1980s, when the Lorne Dam deteriorated to the point that stray steelhead could pass. With access to a handful of spawning tributaries, the run has jumped by leaps and bounds even though the exact origin of the steelhead that established the run has remained a mystery.

Steelhead roam over 60 miles to a dam located in Paris. Steelhead have to clear another dam in the middle of the system in Caledonia to eventually make it to the preferred spawning water. This is a low-head dam that steelhead can move past by leaping and slithering up a sluiceway. When the run is on you can see fish regularly attempting to clear the dam. Since steelhead are more successful in clearing the dam when the water is warmer, the run is fairly early on the Grand, and you can find fish well up into the system by September.

The Grand is a classic Spey-fishing river. It is big and broad, and its steelhead are spread out over miles and miles. Covering a lot of water is the best approach to connect with a steelhead. The river is well over 200 feet wide in many places. The Grand hosts a well-attended Spey gathering, with the number of participants growing each year. Because of the river's short steelhead history, angling traditions are just being established on the Grand, and an ethic of pool rotation and traditional angling techniques are part of the culture that is being developed.

Grand River steelhead react very well to a swinging presentation and readily move up the water column to take a fly. Some anglers prefer to use a light tip or even a full floating line, and a few fish are caught on dry flies each year. There are two distinct sections to the steelhead water. The fly-fishing water below the dam in Caledonia extends a fair distance downriver,

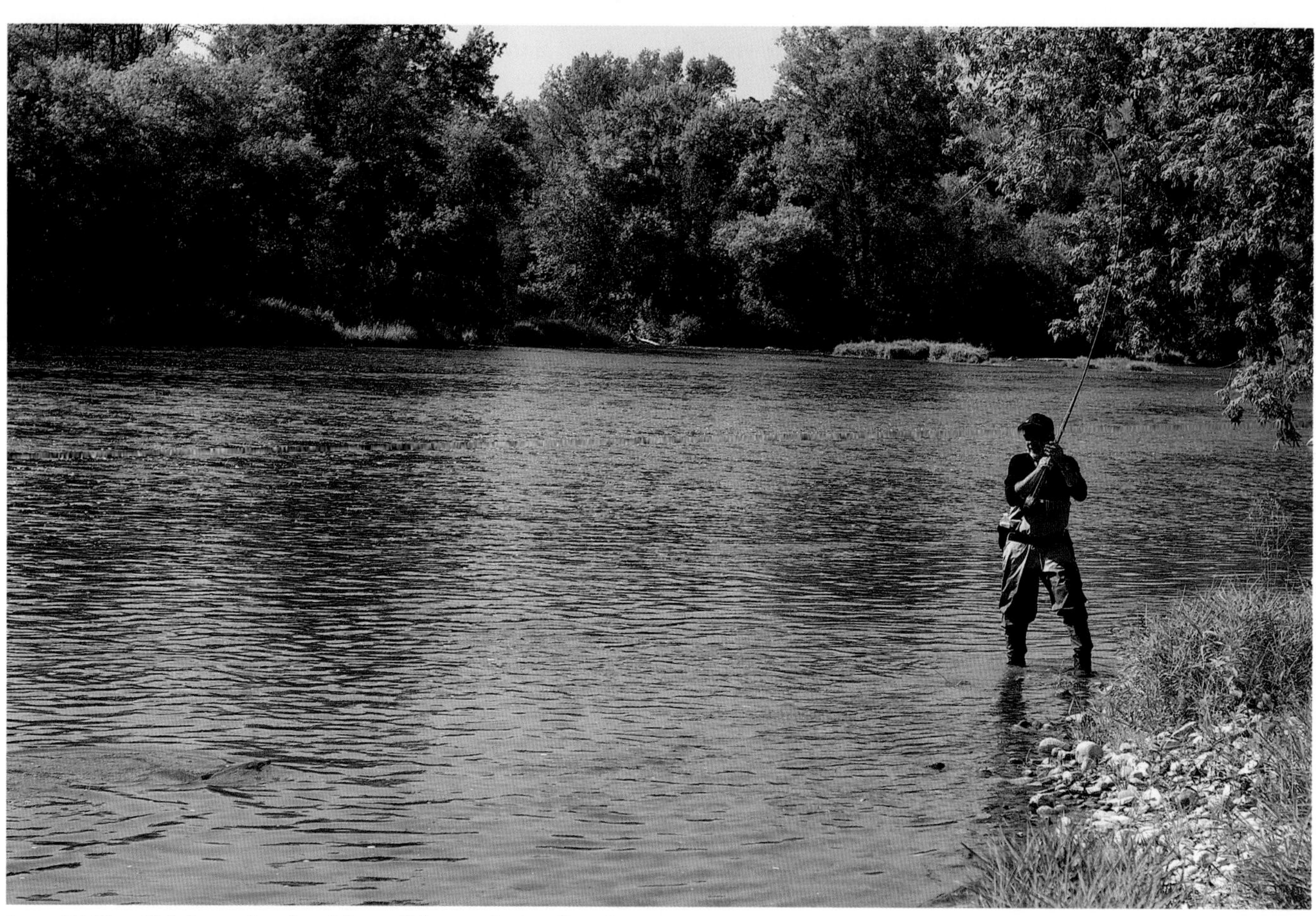

Larry Mellers finishes a battle with a wild Ontario steelhead. NICK PIONESSA PHOTO

Laying out a cast on the Grand.

well past the village of York. Below the dam the water runs with a tinge of green until it gets colder in late fall. Since there is a fair amount of bedrock on the river's floor in this section, the water can be a bit difficult to read and takes some time to learn. The bottom structure also creates some challenging wading.

The water upstream in the Brantford area is still big but has more distinct riffles and pools. The upper limit for steelhead fishing on the Grand is the dam in Paris. The Grand is also known for its trout fishery upriver near Fergus. There is good public access to the river in this section via a series of parks and trails. Some are widely recognized by anglers as the better options for Spey fishing, and usually a few anglers are found rotating through. But there are still miles of river to be explored here and new pools to be discovered. Special regulations in parts of this section include tackle restrictions to artificials only and mandatory release of steelhead and other gamefish.

Wild Grand River steelhead are beautiful fish that average 6 to 10 pounds, but a few truly large fish are caught on the fly each season. With a wild run spread out over 60 miles of water, catch rates are normally not high. One fish in a day is considered an accomplishment, but when conditions are favorable you can hook up more than once a day.

While the run continues to grow, its full wild steelhead potential has not yet been reached. Larry Halyk, a stewardship coordinator with the Ministry of Natural Resources, feels that water quality and habitat improvements could be made to other Grand River tributaries to further increase rearing capacity and create a stronger run in the river's upper section. The Nyth River enters the Grand at Paris, for example, and while the Nyth and its tributaries currently produce some wild fish, habitat improvements could make a huge difference. Larry feels that this is the next step in developing the Grand into a world-class steelhead fishery.

Another tributary along the north shore of Lake Erie is Big Creek, entering the lake at Long Point Bay. Big Creek flows out of the Norfolk Sand Plain, which provides a constant supply of groundwater to the base flow of the creek. It is a modest-size piece of water, comfortable for fishing a single-handed rod or a switch rod. The picturesque creek weaves and cuts through the landscape and collects deadfall in many of its turns and bends. Deep-cut runs provide good holding water for migrating steelhead. Despite its base flow, it needs rain in the fall to disperse steelhead throughout the system.

Big Creek's run of steelhead is composed entirely of wild fish. A fishway constructed in the mid-1990s allows fish to bypass a dam in Delhi, providing access to tributaries with high water quality. The fishing opportunities on Big Creek tend to pick up later in the fall with more consistent rainfall. Late November and December are good times to find steelhead spread throughout the creek. A long section of lower Big Creek is open to fishing year-round. The strong base flow keeps the upper part of this section ice-free through much of the winter. Young's Creek, which flows into Lake Erie near Big Creek and also supports a run of wild steelhead, has many of the same characteristics but is considerably smaller.

Some of Ontario's most notable rivers are those running into Lake Huron. Some have supported wild runs of steelhead for over 100 years and have developed a history of steelheading over the last 50 to 60 years. With the advances in fly equipment and technique, the approach to some of these rivers is changing. There is a lifetime of steelhead angling to be found in this area.

The Maitland River runs into Lake Huron along its eastern shore at the town of Goderich. The Maitland is big water, over 200 feet wide in its lower reaches, and is clearly one of the top Spey-fishing rivers in the entire Great Lakes region. It is a river of magnificent beauty with little development along much of its banks as it twists and turns through cedar and hardwood forests. The river is a continuum of riffles alternating with pools of various sizes and configurations. Many are long and spacious with plenty of room for numerous anglers to air out long Spey casts. Some of the pools take time to learn as bedrock ledges create sudden and distinct drop-offs where fish are likely to hold. The Maitland runs with a tannic flow, and its deeper holds are dark, almost black, and inviting for the fly.

The Maitland runs unencumbered for miles as its headwaters can be found some 50 to 60 miles from the lake. Steelhead can spread out into the river's tributaries and fertile headwaters. Maitland steelhead are wild, beautiful, sleek creatures that take a swung fly well. Local angling and steelhead groups who have rehabilitated and improved spawning habitat are responsible for at least a portion of the consistent runs of steelhead. Because of these efforts, the number of returning adults has grown over the years.

The Maitland has a fairly low base flow, so it requires fall rains to draw fish past the lower couple miles of river. Consistent flows are more likely in November and December—the prime months for fresh-run fish. The Maitland will muddy with

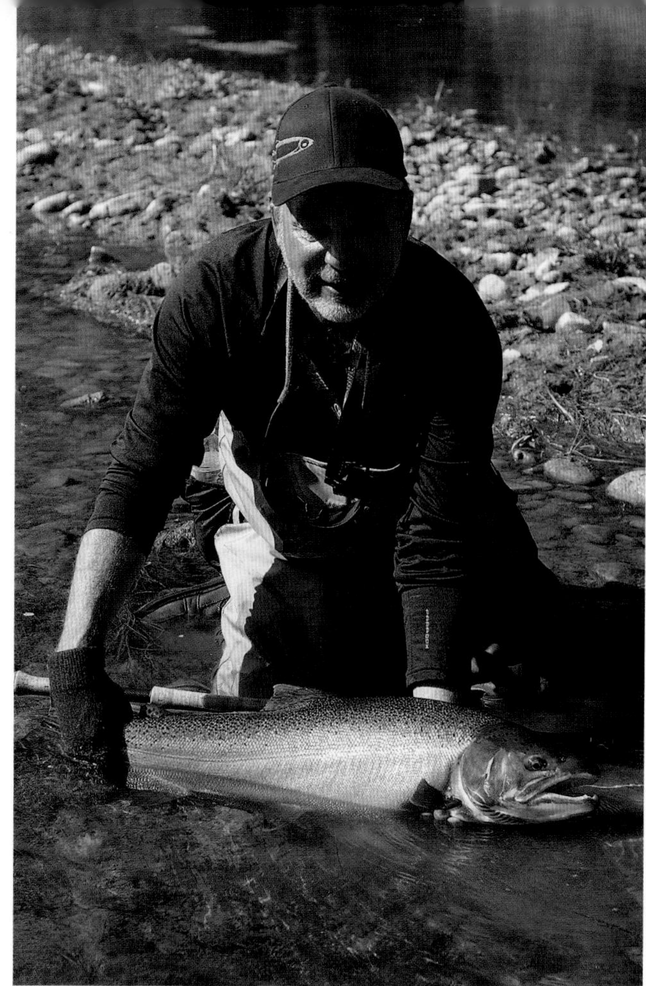

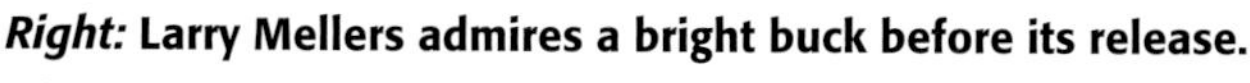

Right: **Larry Mellers admires a bright buck before its release.**
NICK PIONESSA PHOTO

A broad tailout on the Maitland River.

heavy rain but also drops and clears quickly, so trying to time the perfect conditions can be a little tricky.

You can find casual access points along the river if you have the time and inclination to explore. The pools near popular access points receive a fair amount of angling pressure, but with a little walking, you can find solitude.

Weather can play heavily into fishing the Maitland. Sunny days can turn to blustery snowstorms in an instant thanks to lake-effect snow. Water temperatures will normally remain in the 40s during most of November, and Maitland fish will still readily grab a fly even after temperatures have dropped into the 30s.

Most of the river is closed to fishing after December. The season begins again with the regular trout opener in April. In cooler years, you can find drop-back steelhead through May. The Maitland is a treat to fish and well deserving of any serious Spey fisher's efforts.

When the Maitland is unfishable because of high water, try one of the other, smaller rivers nearby. The Bayfield River is about 15 miles south of Goderich, and Nine Mile River is about the same distance to the north. Both the Bayfield and Nine Mile run dirty after a rain but tend to maintain their character and fishable size unless rainfall is extremely heavy. When flowing well, each is a nice size for fly fishing and can be covered with a single-handed rod or switch rod. Highway 21 crosses each river, providing access both upriver and down.

As you move north along the Lake Huron shoreline, the next significant river is the Saugeen, which dumps into the lake at Southampton. The Saugeen River is a gentle piece of water that winds though farmlands and small woodlots. The entire Saugeen system is quite remarkable and consists of some 120 miles of water including its branches. Its upper reaches are home to wild resident brown trout and native brookies. Other stretches host phenomenal fly fishing for warmwater species. But its steelhead bring a solid following of anglers to the river. Most of the river is of a substantial size so that Spey fishing is quite at home on the Saugeen.

Larry Halyk and Ontario guide Mike Verhoef pose with a wild steelhead before its release.

A fresh steelhead caught on the big water of the Saugeen River. MIKE VERHOEF PHOTO

The best opportunity to catch a steelhead, and consequently the highest fishing pressure, is found below Denny's Dam just outside of Southampton. From the dam downriver are a number of outstanding pools with easy access. The river is quite large at this point, impossible to cross but fairly easy to wade. Unfortunately, this section is short-lived and soon reaches estuary water. Although steelhead can migrate miles upstream of the dam, most are caught below the dam in this lower water, which is considered some of the most productive water in Ontario. And while this lower water offers excellent opportunities, it can be quite crowded at times. The Saugeen has a run of naturally produced fish but is also stocked, adding to the wild run to meet the demand of local anglers for higher catch rates.

The steelhead that do bypass the dam have access to the 50 or more miles of river up past the town of Walkerton. Over the years, a fishable run of steelhead has developed. Many feel that further improvements can be made to the bypass mechanism of the dam, which could draw more fish to the upper water and increase the run. But even under the dam's current operation, the wild run of fish allows anglers to spread out over a vast area.

To take advantage of this upper water, get to know the water. Access is limited, and there are often long stretches of flat, slow water between steelhead pools. Access from the bridges in the towns of Walkerton, Paisley, and Port Elgin offer some possibilities, and you can also ask local farmers for permission.

Floating may be the best option to get to the productive water above the dam. Hiring a knowledgeable guide is great way to see the water and ensure that you fish productive water. This is another piece of water where expectations need to be in line with reality. While big number days are possible on any steelhead water, a fish or two a day is considered good for this upper water.

As you continue north along Lake Huron, the expansive Georgian Bay breaks off to the east. This body of water is practically a lake on its own and has some quality steelhead water flowing into its beautiful blue waters. The Bighead River dumps into Georgian Bay at the town of Meaford to the east of Owen Sound. It is an enchanting small river that averages 60 to 80 feet in width and is characterized by a range of water from long pools and obvious runs to small, discreet pockets. It runs free for approximately 15 to 20 fishable miles. The water is generally not too deep and easily covered with a fly. Aggressive fish will readily take a swung fly when properly presented through a pool or run. But many experienced Bighead anglers prefer to work the pocketwater with a long leader and nymph patterns. While the Bighead can be covered readily with a single-handed rod, a switch rod is a perfect match for this water.

Timing may be more important on the Bighead than on most rivers in the Great Lakes region. Every freshet caused by rain in the fall seems to draw steelhead in from the bay. The river normally rises and colors with a moderate to heavy rain, but it drops and clears quickly. The Bighead is in prime condition when it is clearing and green. When the water is perfect, you can find fish in even the smallest pockets and runs. Many anglers are already clued in to the workings of the Bighead, and it has quite a following when conditions are good. Access is fairly good, and you can hike away from the main pools, which is your best bet for enjoying the overall experience of the river.

The Bighead's run is composed entirely of beautiful specimens of naturally reproduced steelhead. The current run is below historical levels, and fishing pressure has been blamed for the decline. While catch-and-release continues to grow in popularity in the Great Lakes region, it has been slow to catch on in some areas such as the Bighead. However, more restrictive limits have helped this situation to some degree.

The Beaver River, which enters Georgian Bay at Thornbury, is another intimate river similar in size to the Bighead. Unfortunately, the river is dammed less than a mile up from its mouth. The section between the dam and bay generally receives a large amount of angling pressure. A hydraulic lift takes steelhead above the dam, and that area has about 5 miles of good fly-fishing water. Access to this water is fairly limited, and this section of river is open to fishing only in the spring.

The next significant Georgian Bay river is the Nottawasaga, which enters at the town of Wasaga Beach. It is the right size for a light two-handed rod or switch rod, and many of the river's pools possess good characteristics for swinging a fly. The Notty is host to a wild run of fish that has been documented as early as 1903. The river drains a considerable area with more than a handful of tributaries that produce wild steelhead. The wild fish population has a rich genetic structure. A

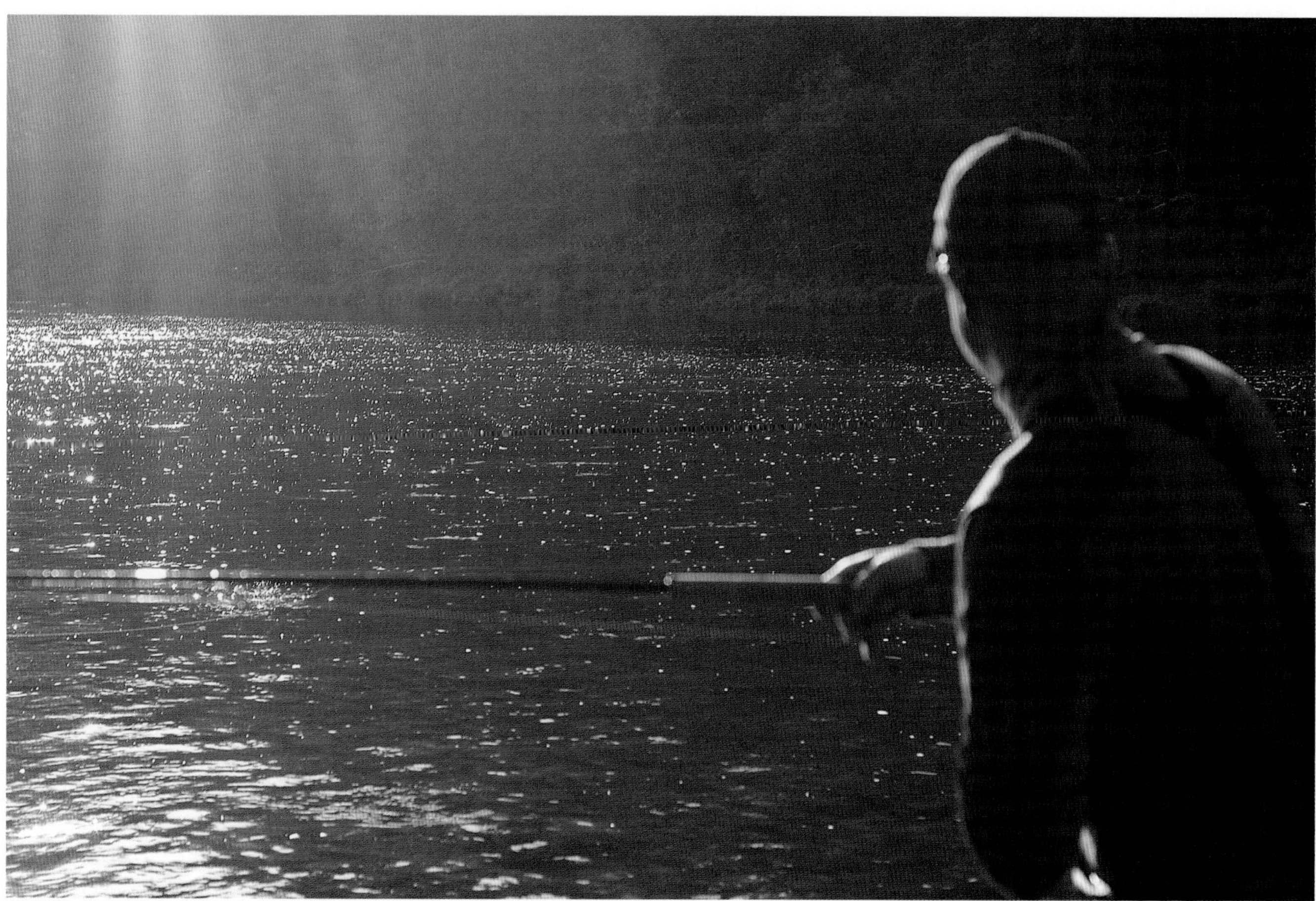

I use a low rod position to fight an Ontario steelhead. NICK PIONESSA PHOTO

Larry Halyk and I fish a perfect pool for the swung fly. A raft is good transportation for some of Ontario's longer rivers.
MIKE VERHOEF PHOTO

genetic study of the river system found 18 different strains, the highest of any Ontario river. The entire Nottawasaga system was shown to host fish that are genetically different from those in other Ontario rivers and have the highest variability recorded in the Great Lakes region. These features make the Notty a special river. The Nottawasaga River also boasts a unique and substantial naturalized run of chinook salmon. Chinooks can enter the Notty as early as July, and there is even a small run of salmon in the spring.

The Nottawasaga consists of two distinct sections. The lower river up from Highway 26 in town comprises about 3 miles of pools and runs that can be easily accessed by a road running parallel to the river. But each pool in this area is a puzzle and takes some time to learn. Above the town stretch, the river moves through a long swamp with no fly-fishing water. However, approximately 12 miles of water from the town of Alliston down to the swamp area runs with a similar character to the lower river.

A fresh Ontario steelhead that fell for a marabou Spey.

Access to the upper water is more limited than to the lower river, and it receives less fishing pressure. The upper water is more intimate but has the right speed and depth for a swung fly. Aggressive Notty fish will readily take a fly fished in this manner. The upper water may be best fished with a switch rod, although a light two-handed rod may provide more flexibility when heavier tips are required. Either way, the Nottawasaga is a quality Spey-fishing river. Steelhead begin to show up in September, with the fishing peaking through October and November. Historically, the river has produced some very big steelhead as well.

Around the north shore of Georgian Bay are a handful of smaller creeks that see returns of wild steelhead, including some on and around Manitoulin Island. These intimate creeks and rivers are best fished with a single-handed rod. Two of the most notable are on the south shore of the island: The Manitou River flows out of Lake Manitou and typically receives a significant run of steelhead in the fall. The Mindemoya River also hosts a good run that peaks in the spring. The water on each is approximately 30 to 50 feet wide, and while there is room to swing a fly in some areas, a dead-drift approach will work best in tight, confined runs and pockets.

The other significant piece of the Ontario steelhead fishery is the north shore of Lake Superior. Like the north-shore rivers in Minnesota, many of the Ontario rivers run rather short distances before hitting the first natural impassable barrier. But others have some length where steelhead can stretch back into near-wilderness surroundings. The north shore of Superior is marked by breathtaking coastline views and plentiful cascading steelhead rivers that make it a wonderful place to visit.

Almost all of these rivers support wild runs of fish. These are the hardiest of all Great Lakes steelhead, living in waters with the shortest growing season and the lowest average water temperature of any place where steelhead exist. Consequently, these steelhead are of a smaller average size, which they make up for in spirit. Steelhead runs in these rivers declined through the 1990s, and it was largely proven that fishing pressure and high kill limits were the causes. More restrictive regulations have clearly helped in reenergizing the runs.

As you move northwest along the Trans-Canada Highway from Sault Ste. Marie, one of the first significant tributaries along the north shore is the Pancake River, which is a tight, intimate river 40 to 60 feet wide. The Pancake's flow travels briskly over sand and gravel with runs and depressions carved into the bottom at curves in the riverbed or along logjams and root balls. The river requires careful analysis to identify potential holding water. Rains will freshen the water and draw fish into the river. Prime time in the spring runs from early to mid-May through early June. In the fall, late September through October is the prime period. A gravel road provides access to the river, and you can camp at the Pancake Bay Provincial Park near the river's mouth.

Two bigger rivers in the Pancake Bay offer great opportunities for a swung fly and Spey fishing—the Chippewa River and the Batchawana River. The Chippewa is short, with a handful of nice pools below a falls that prohibits farther upriver movement. Its tea-stained appearance adds to its northern charm. A decent number of steelhead enter this short section of water in both spring and fall. The Batchawana is slightly bigger and longer with approximately 5 miles of river before its natural impassable barrier. Access is limited and hiking can provide you with plenty of solitude.

Farther north toward the town of Wawa, the Old Woman River enters the lake at Old Woman Bay. It is an inviting river named after a nearby rock formation. It's mainly a spring steelhead river, and timing can be everything as fish use spring rains to quickly move through the lower river to reach the prime upper spawning waters.

The Michipicoten River, also in the Wawa area, is a large piece of water ideal for swinging a fly and using a two-handed rod. Spring and fall runs are not what they historically were, but there are good steelhead opportunities in the fall and spring. The Michipicoten is also known for steelhead running the river in the summer, presenting possibilities for lighter tips and even dry flies.

Moving up toward Terrace Bay, you'll find one of the true gems of the vast inventory of north-shore Superior rivers. It is

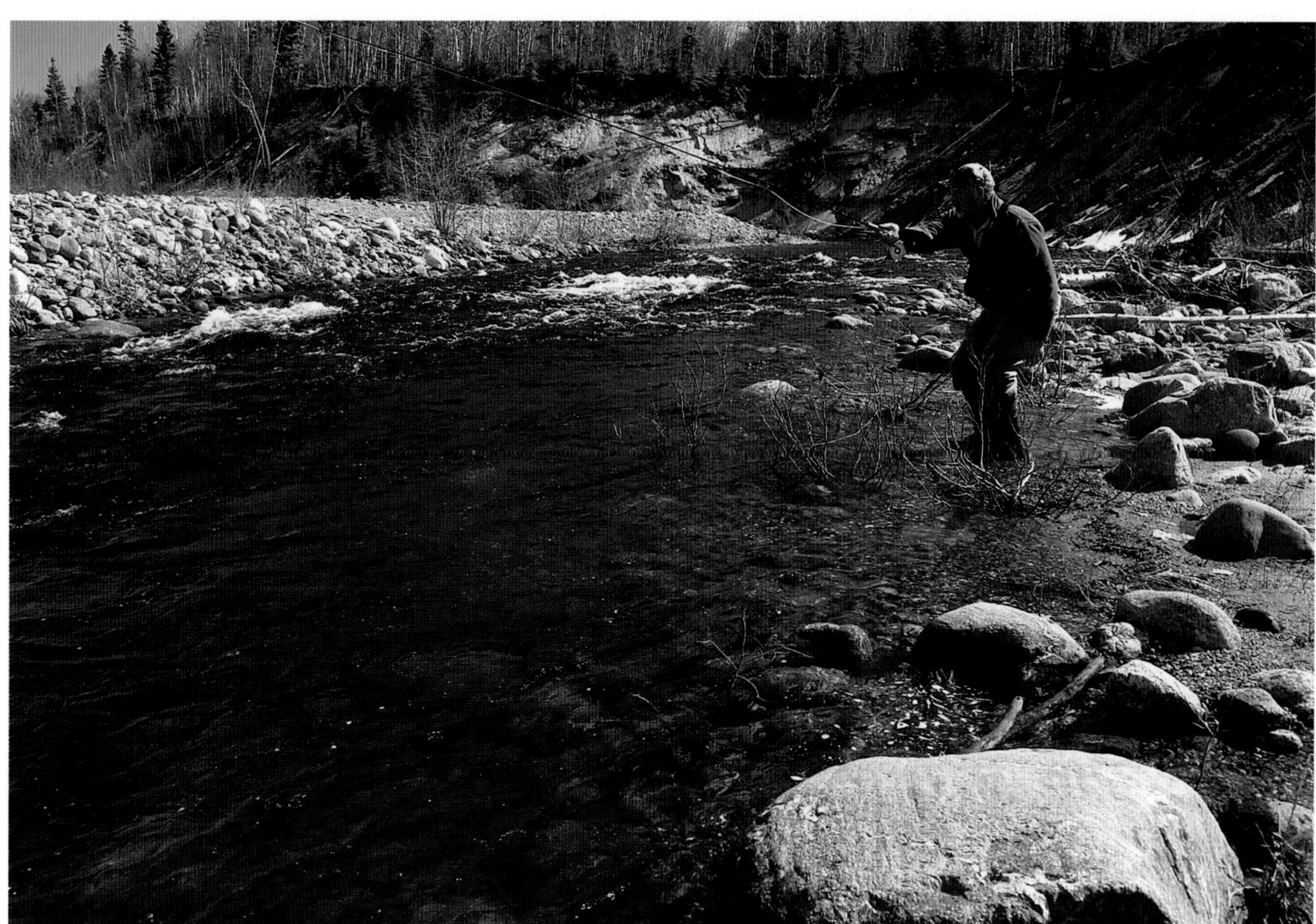

Fishing a fast run on the tea-colored Cypress River. SCOTT EARL SMITH PHOTO

A beautiful Lake Superior wild buck poses before its release.
SCOTT EARL SMITH PHOTO

a relatively large, impressive river that begs the use of a two-handed rod and a swung fly. Hiking up from the Trans-Canada Highway is the only way to access the 3 to 4 miles of water up to a natural falls that blocks farther migration. Good fall steelheading can be found through November, and the best spring fishing can last through June for aggressive fish that chase a fly and are also known to take on the surface.

To the northwest is a series of rivers and streams that host runs of steelhead. A notable duo are the Cypress River and the Jackpine River. The Cypress is a beautiful small river that flows with a reddish tinge because of its high iron content. It has an impressive combination of small pools, runs, and pocketwater and an impassable falls about 3 to 4 miles above the mouth. You need to use various techniques to cover it thoroughly. While you can find some steelhead in the fall, the Cypress is an exceptional spring river with a substantial wild run. The Cypress sees some lake-run brook trout or "coasters" in the late summer and early fall, which is something that happens on a number of the north-shore rivers.

The Jackpine is similar to the Cypress but is slightly smaller and swifter. You can access the Jackpine from the highway and hike upriver or down to get to its runs and pools. Like the Cypress, the Jackpine can see a significant run of wild fish and is mainly a spring river. Its higher gradient provides extra challenge and enjoyment when you're hooked up to one of its silver prizes.

Farther west are two larger river systems that are great for fishing with big streamers and a two-handed rod. The Nipigon River is most famous for its trophy brook trout—a fishery that still exists today. But its lower end also sees a run of steelhead, although some debate whether all the big rainbows caught in this lower section are truly migratory fish. The Nipigon makes me feel as if I am home on my own Niagara River. It is deep and requires a creative approach to presenting the fly.

The Black Sturgeon River, which flows into Black Bay, features both a fall and spring run of steelhead. Fall fish are known to be aggressive and take a swung fly very well. There is some room to spread out on the Black Sturgeon, and while catch rates may not be high, this river has the potential to provide a great north-country experience.

Also dumping into Black Bay is a beautiful intimate river called the Wolf, which has about 8 miles of river up to an impassable barrier to migration. The Wolf River is a nice size for a switch rod and requires a variety of techniques to cover all its water. It is somewhat unusual for a north-shore Superior river because it has a heavy spring-fed influence, and it has one of the better fall runs of steelhead in this part of the Great Lakes. Fish begin to show by late September.

Just outside of the city of Thunder Bay is another picturesque river—the McKenzie. It is a classic north-shore piece of water with plenty of pockets and short runs created by rocks and boulders that also line the river. The McKenzie is known for its fall steelhead as well as a spring run.

It would be remiss in covering the north shore of Lake Superior to leave out one of the most important and significant steelhead research projects in the Great Lakes region. Portage Creek historically had a significant run of steelhead. It also had a following of anglers with stories of consistent catch rates. Through the 1980s, catch rates declined and overharvesting was the suspected culprit. This came at a time when overall catch rates were diminishing on many north-shore rivers. In 1994, the creek was closed to public fishing, and steelhead biologist Jon George, along with a landowner, has used it ever since as a test lab for analyzing wild steelhead runs in the Great Lakes region. Research data is collected in the spring by traditional angling, and information is gathered from each fish. The results of the study over such a long period are fascinating.

After steelhead harvest was stopped on Portage Creek, numbers of returning adults increased sharply, rising from a run of about 400 fish to more than 2,000 in just over 10 years. Surprisingly, the number of returning adults fell off from 2004 to 2009. Less than 1,000 were estimated for 2009. The cause was most likely environmental. From 2002 through 2007, the area saw a series of hot, dry summers and extreme conditions in the winter, so fewer smolt survived. This data shows the significant impact of natural factors from year to year. The environmental variability accentuates the importance of repeat spawners in maintaining a healthy wild run of steelhead. Repeat spawners generally have superior genetics and can smooth out the effects of weaker year classes. Overharvest of these fish can strike at the core of a healthy wild steelhead population.

Migration data of Portage Creek and other Lake Superior steelhead indicated that steelhead that were carefully handled and released when caught had a very high survival rate. Mortality from angling was estimated at only 2 percent. This information was instrumental in changing regulations and kill limits throughout Ontario. Such scientific data also goes a long way toward changing angling attitudes. For all the results of the Portage Creek Steelhead Study, see www.northshoresteelhead.com.

CONCLUSION

The Great Lakes fishery continues to emerge and evolve. Over the years I have seen considerable changes and improvements that increase the opportunity for a high-quality experience. Certain trends have developed in recent years that should continue into the future. Of these trends the most important may be the effort to open up additional water to migrating fish through the removal or passage of dams. Removing a dam completely and restoring a river to its natural flow is always a boon from a steelheader's perspective. Cost and environmental factors commonly hinder full removal, but other options such as a fish ladder or a partial breach of the dam can be put into place. Not only does fish passage increase the amount of water for anglers to enjoy, but in many cases it opens up higher-quality water for wild fish production. Continuing to grow the base of naturally produced steelhead in the Great Lakes region is key for fisheries managers—from both an economic and esthetic standpoint.

The Great Lakes steelhead fishery has a bright future.
NICK PIONESSA PHOTO

Habitat rehabilitation is another key element in wild steelhead expansion. Anglers can help fuel dam removal and rehabilitation projects on a river. Getting involved can make a significant difference.

Angling techniques and stream etiquette also continue to change. Two-handed rods and tight-line techniques continue to grow in popularity among Great Lakes anglers. Advancements in equipment technology allow a greater number of anglers to enjoy a wider variety of techniques and approaches.

There certainly will be challenges to the fishery in the future as well. Public access issues and overall health and carrying capacities of the lakes will be constant concerns. Managers will have to balance steelhead with the overall mix in the lakes and maintain this balance in an environment of shrinking financial resources.

The Great Lakes steelhead fishery has grown and matured significantly in the last 30 years. Today the Great Lakes region is capable of providing an experience that is top-notch and on par with opportunities that exist in the steelhead's native range. This includes many beautiful rivers and places that embody and celebrate the spirit and essence of the steelhead in every way.

INDEX

For most subject entries additional information can be found under specific state's rivers and streams.
Names of specific flies are capitalized.